Municipal
Analysis Services, Inc.

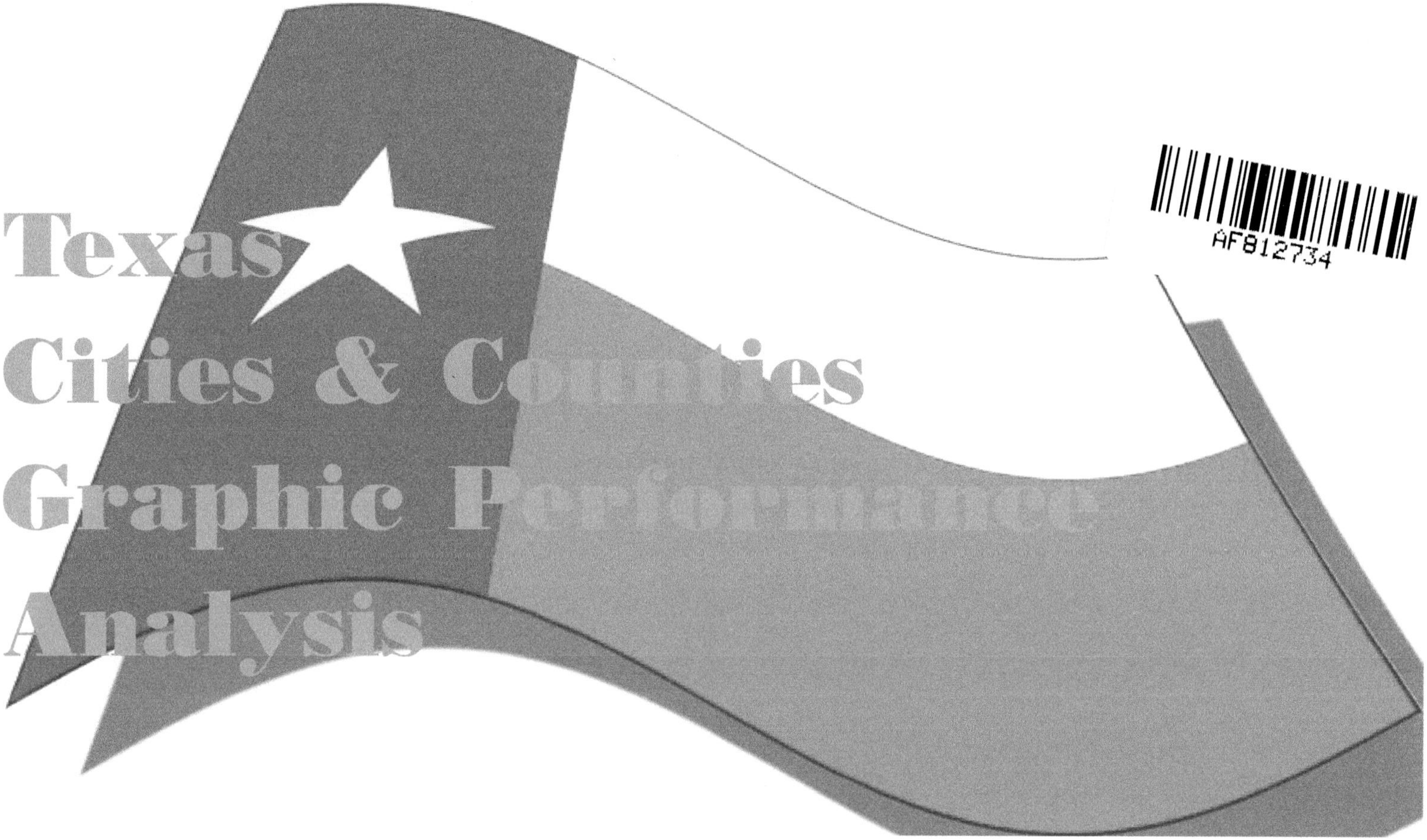

Texas Cities & Counties Graphic Performance Analysis

2009

Texas graph A1

Texas Cities & Counties
Graphic Performance Analysis 2009

Number 4 in this series
Years in this series to date: 2006, 2007, 2008, 2009

Published in 2009, by:
Municipal Analysis Services, Inc.
PO Box 13453, Capitol Station
Austin, Texas 78711

For All Inquiries. Please Call (512) 327-3328
Fax (413) 740-1294
Email: Munilysis@hotmail.com

Library of Congress ISSN: 1935-5440

ISBN: 978317826 6 2

EAN13 Code: pending

Retail Price $75.00 U.S.

For more detailed explanations, please visit: gregmichels.googlepages.com

Preface

This study is an experiment. I invite your comments. There are significant advantages to easily and quickly understanding the relative performance of governments, within their peer group. But can this be done economically?

In the past, we could only provide these graphs as a part of custom client reports, from our *Governments of Your State* data base, costing at least $10,000. But if we could deliver this universally to our clients, it may be more cost effective. So we started this experiment to find a universal set of graphic representations.

Our experiments have shown that government executives, policy experts, the press, and public interest groups are responding most readily and favorably to the relations that you now see in this study.

Then, from multiple permutations of each type of graphic presentation, the graphics you see here have been those most favorably reviewed. These charts have been found to be both functionally useful and most quickly understood by our said test groups. And now, because this study is universally available, we will offer it at an unusually low price to see if volume will be worth the effort.

However, this is still an experiment, so I welcome your comments and suggestons of what you would like to see. Please email me at munilysis@hotmail.com. Thank you.

Sincerely,

Greg Michels, President
Municipal Analysis Services, Inc.

Table of Contents

Introduction -- Management by Comparison & Exception

Overview -- Discussion of Charts used

Definitions & Explanations

Chart Sections:

Costs or expense charts

C1 Can Comparison of Your Expense Mix Save Your Budget?

C2 Are Common Expenses in line with Property Taxes?

C3 Which Departments are better funded than others?

Debt and related issues charts

D1 Are there Debt Issues in Your near Future?

Employees costs and productivity

E1 Can Your Employee Staffing Comparison Save Your Budget?

E2 Can Employee Productivity comparison Save You Money?

Revenues analysis charts

R1 Are You Getting Your Share of Revenues?

R2 Are You Getting Your Share of State and Federal Aid?

R3 Are User Charges in line with Operating Expenses?

County area charts

S1 Are You Getting Your Share of Debt and Taxes in Your County?

Introduction

Management by Comparison & Exception

Can you really manage a government by comparison? Of course, the answer is yes and no. Although there are large sections of management that are similar to other governments, the populace impresses onto the government its unique needs and priorities. Professional managers know that these priorities have effects within a government. Managers can get an understanding of the implied limits of priorities versus necessities by knowing what other governments have been able to do. This collective analysis gives implied ranges and their governments relative position within those ranges.

Assuming that this kind of analysis, within a similar group of governments, gives reasonable ranges of behavior, then comparison to one's peers will give the deviation from what is "reasonable".

It is then to the professional manager's advantage to communicate with the rest of the govenment and the public, what areas are unreasonable, within the context of his or her mandate.

Your State Cities & Counties Graphic Performance Analysis is designed to be the easiest way to 1. find implied ranges of behavior, to 2. determine your government's relation to "reasonable" and then to 3. communicate to the rest of government and the public.

All through pictures of these relationships. This Graphics Book contains charts covering 5 different areas of government management: revenues, expenses, employees, debt and community (county). The fact that we have included 3 ways to look at revenue, 3 ways to look at expenses, 2 ways to look at employees, and 1 way each to look at debt and county matters, is done to give you more angles to bolster your arguments and thus convince others.

Even so, after all that you will see here, these are just the basic templates that you can use to create your own key comparative points about any aspect of government. You can use the more detailed data. The data included in the following pages of charts, comes from the ***Governments of Your State*** series of books. This is a meticulously maintained set of annual publications for the past 20 years, and has over 600 data elements for each government per year.

Overview of Charts: R-Revenue Series

Are you getting your share of revenues?

Are there other sources or higher levels of revnue (per capita) that your peer group is finding? These are the principal questions that we start to answer with the 3 revenue charts. Conversely, if you are too dependent on a few sources of revenue, here is an opportunity to diversify and lighten the concentration on individual sources.

R 1

ARE YOU GETTING YOUR SHARE OF REVENUES?

Compare your government to similar governments to see additional revenue opportunities that they may be using

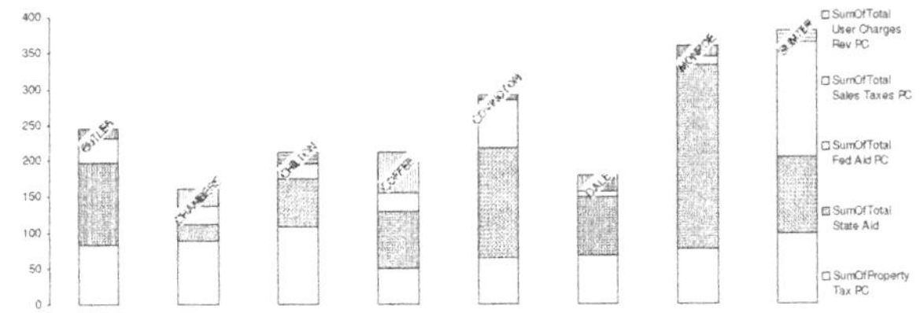

Group AL13

	Name	Population	Property Tax PC	Total State Aid	Total Fed Aid PC	Total Sales Taxes PC	Total User Charges Rev PC
AL	BUTLER	20911	82	115	0	35	13
AL	CHAMBERS	36251	89	23	0	25	24
AL	CHILTON	40516	108	86	1	21	17
AL	COFFEE	43878	50	79	0	27	56
AL	COVINGTON	36956	84	154	0	66	7
AL	DALE	49186	68	81	0	8	22
AL	MONROE	24043	76	256	0	13	14
AL	SUMTER	14378	98	107	0	158	17
		Average	79.4	110.1		44.0	21.2

For more information and detailed data, go to section Pricing Costs of Fee Based Services section Total Funds Flow

Revenue by major sources within your peer group. See who is getting more revenues (per capita) and where.

R 2

ARE YOU GETTING YOUR SHARE OF STATE AND FEDERAL AID? R2

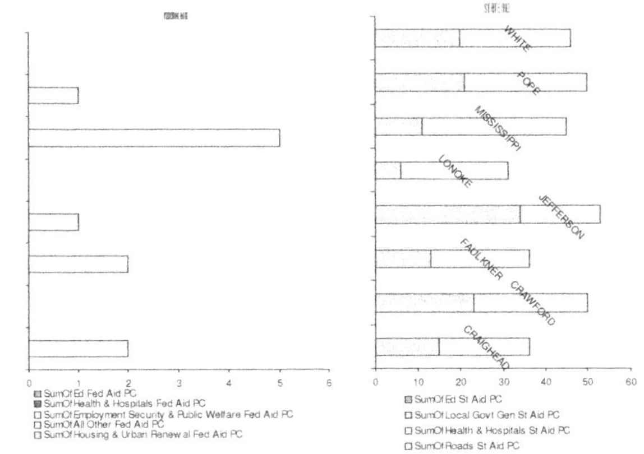

Group AR14

	Name	Population	Total Fed Aid PC	Total State Aid
AR	CRAIGHEAD	84074	2	36
AR	CRAWFORD	54973	1	50
AR	FAULKNER	89590	2	36
AR	JEFFERSON	83374	1	53
AR	LONOKE	55302	0	31
AR	MISSISSIPPI	50380	5	45
AR	POPE	55223	1	50
AR	WHITE	69354	0	46
		Averages	2	43

Federal and State Aid Revenue. Who is getting more aid and how much.

R 3

ARE USER CHARGES IN LINE WITH OPERATING EXPENSES? R3

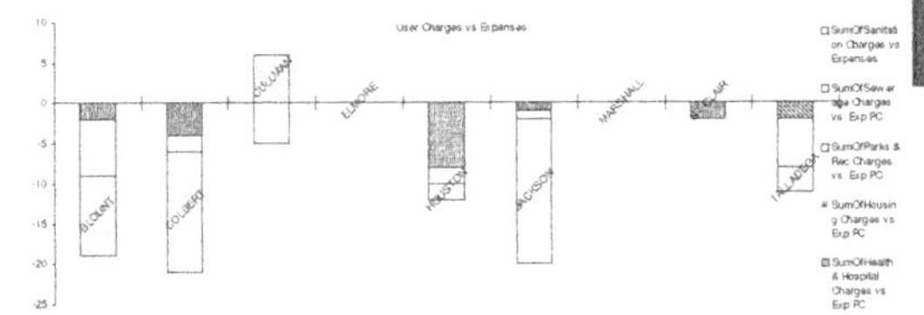

Group AL14

Name	Population	Health Hospital Charges vs Exp PC	Housing Charges vs Exp PC	Parks Rec Charges vs Exp PC	Sewerage Charges vs Exp PC	Sanitation Charges vs Expenses
BLOUNT	52968	-2	0	-7	0	10
COLBERT	54850	4	0	-2	0	15
CULLMAN	77973	0	0	-5	0	6
ELMORE	65771	0	0	0	0	0
HOUSTON	89966	8	0	-2	0	-2
JACKSON	54035	1	0	1	0	18
MARSHALL	83548	0	0	0	0	0
ST CLAIR	67215	2	0	0	0	0
TALLADEGA	80638	2	0	-6	0	3
Averages	66666	-2	0	-3	0	-5

User Charges vs. Expenses. Does anyone have a better balance of charges versus expenses in fee-based services and by how much?

Overview of Charts: C-Cost Series

Can comparison of your expense mix save you money?

If you compare per capita expense, by department, to your peer group, are there savings opportunities? These are the basic questions that we ask in this section of 3 charts. We present 3 different types of comparisons of expenses to give your many arguments with which to build your case.

Conversely, if your departments are "underfunded" or lower per capita costs than your peer group, then these charts give you reasons for additional funding.

C1

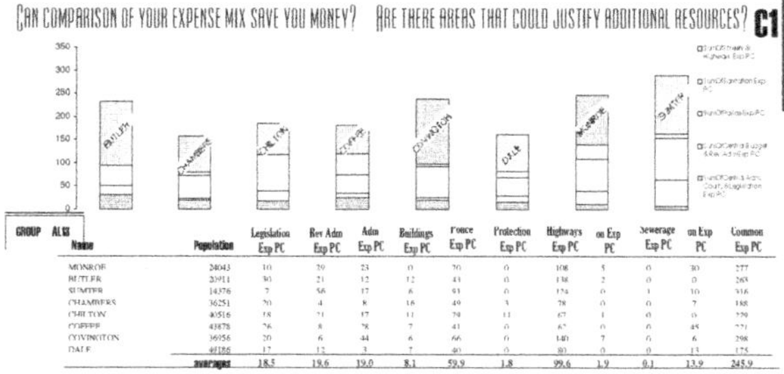

Name	Population	Legislation Exp PC	Rev Adm Exp PC	Adm Exp PC	Buildings Exp PC	Police Exp PC	Protection Exp PC	Highways Exp PC	on Exp PC	Sewerage Exp PC	on Exp PC	Common Exp PC
MONROE	24043	10	29	23	0	70	0	108	5	0	30	277
BUTLER	20911	30	21	12	12	43	0	138	2	0	0	263
SUMTER	14376	7	56	17	6	93	0	174	0	1	10	316
CHAMBERS	36251	20	4	8	16	49	3	78	0	0	7	188
CHILTON	40516	18	21	17	11	79	11	67	1	0	0	229
COFFEE	43878	26	8	28	7	41	0	67	0	0	45	221
COVINGTON	36956	20	6	44	6	66	0	140	7	0	6	298
DALE	49186	17	12	3	7	40	0	80	0	0	13	175
averages		18.5	19.6	19.0	8.1	59.9	1.8	99.6	1.9	0.1	13.9	245.9

C 2

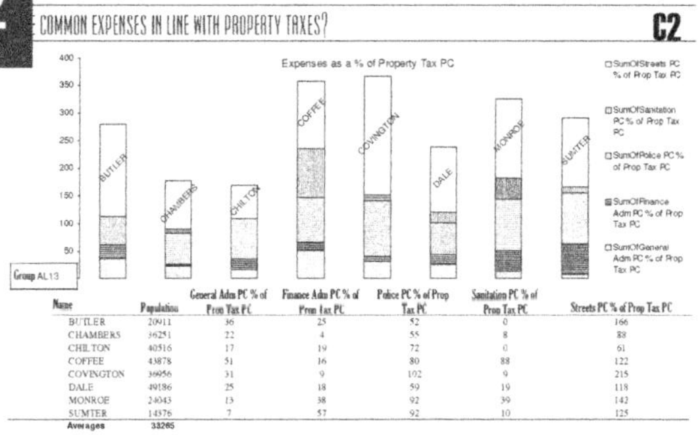

Name	Population	General Adm PC % of Prop Tax PC	Finance Adm PC % of Prop Tax PC	Police PC % of Prop Tax PC	Sanitation PC % of Prop Tax PC	Streets PC % of Prop Tax PC
BUTLER	20911	36	25	52	0	166
CHAMBERS	36251	22	4	55	8	88
CHILTON	40516	17	19	72	0	61
COFFEE	43878	51	16	80	88	122
COVINGTON	36956	31	9	102	9	215
DALE	49186	25	18	59	19	118
MONROE	24043	13	38	92	39	142
SUMTER	14376	7	57	92	10	125
Averages	33265					

Common Services as a % of property taxes collected per capita (a proxy for community wealth). So this is common expenses adjusted for community wealth.

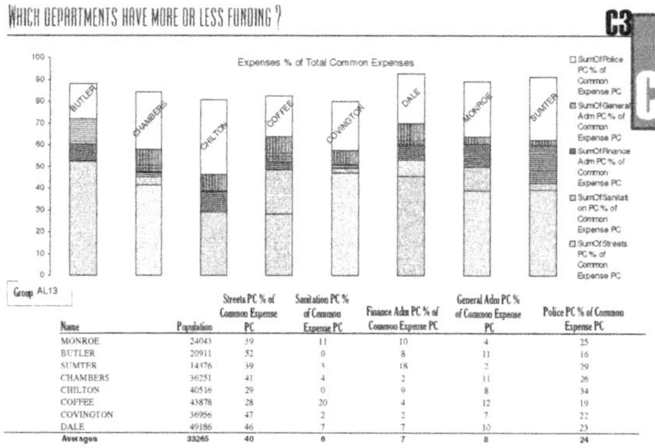

Name	Population	Streets PC % of Common Expense PC	Sanitation PC % of Common Expense PC	Finance Adm PC % of Common Expense PC	General Adm PC % of Common Expense PC	Police PC % of Common Expense PC
MONROE	24043	39	11	10	4	25
BUTLER	20911	52	0	8	11	16
SUMTER	14376	39	3	18	2	29
CHAMBERS	36251	41	4	2	11	26
CHILTON	40516	29	0	9	8	34
COFFEE	43878	28	20	4	12	19
COVINGTON	36956	47	2	2	7	22
DALE	49186	46	7	7	10	23
Averages	33265	40	6	7	8	24

C 3

Each common service as a % of total common expense, i.e. which services are taking more of your common budget than that of your peers.

Overview of Charts: E-Employee Series

Can your employee staffing comparison save you money?

Or, can comparisons to your peer group, justify additional staffing? These are the primary questions that we address with these 2 employee charts. E1 is simply employee staffing. E2 show 2 aspects of employee productivity.

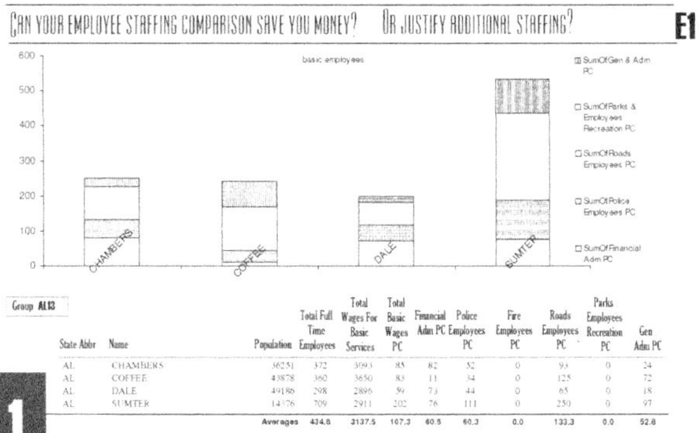

E1

E1 looks at staffing of common functions/departments. To compare, the staffing levels are normalized by population. That is # of employees in a department divided by (population divided by 10,000).

So a 10 score staff would be 10 employees per 10,000 population.

E2

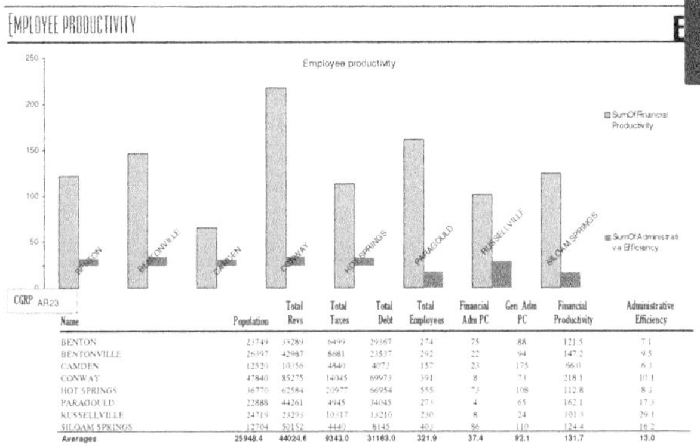

Employee Productivity measured in 2 ways:

1. G&A employees as a % of total common employees, and 2. Taxes collected divided by the # of Finance/Budget employees.

Overview of Charts: D-Debt, S-County Summary Series

Are there debt issues in the near future?

Are there areas that are much higher than other governments? Or is this an opportunity to justify the use of debt since others, in your peer group, have found it useful.

Interest expense per capita is added to debt outstanding per capita for you to see the range in your peer group.

D 1

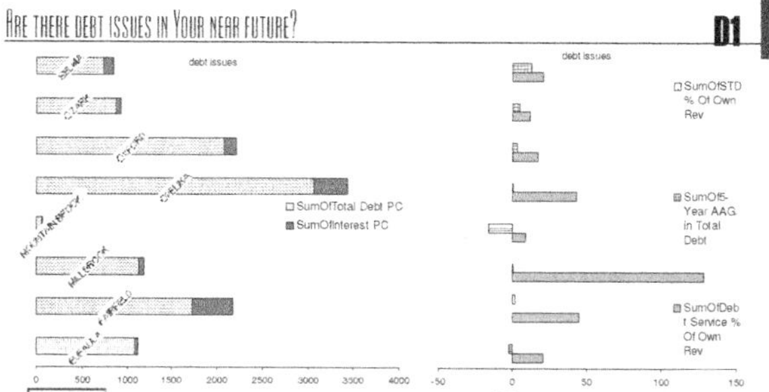

Name	State Abb	Population	Total Debt PC	Interest PC	Interest Rate	Debt Service % Of Own Rev	Gen Govt Debt Service	STD % Of Own Rev	5-Year AAG in Total Debt	5-Year AAG in GB Debt
MOUNTAIN BROOK	AL	19938	62	8	12.90%	9	2266	0	-16	0
OXFORD	AL	15212	2077	133	6.40%	17	3784	0	3	3
OPELIKA	AL	23608	3063	366	11.95%	43	15859	0	1	-2
OZARK	AL	14987	869	57	6.56%	12	1319	0	5	46
SELMA	AL	19630	730	106	14.52%	21	4771	0	13	8
FAIRFIELD	AL	11918	1727	451	26.11%	45	7829	2	0	-1
MILLBROOK	AL	11465	1130	61	5.40%	128	6033	0	1	0
EUFAULA	AL	13651	1080	44	4.07%	21	2137	0	-2	-4
		Average	1342.3	37.0					0.6	6.3

Getting your share of the debt & taxes in your county?

What is your share of debt versus your share of taxes in your county?

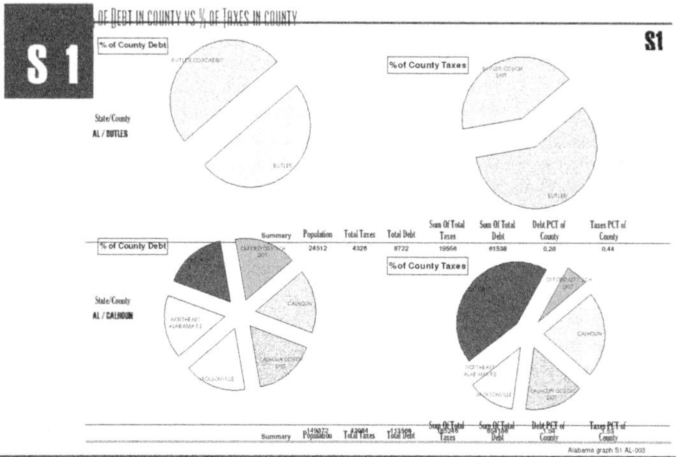

Of the governments included in the Governments of Your State this year, which ones are geeting a bigger share of your community's (county's) debt and taxes?
2 counties are displayed per page.

Definitions & Explanations

The data used in this *Graphic Performance Analysis* comes from the *Governments of Your State* series of books. These books are detailed, annually updated analysis of governments. There are 600 - 650 data elements for each government covered in their state book. This *Graphic Performance Analysis* is only a small fraction of the data available each year. The following is a general discussion of the definitions and explanations of the data contained in the *Governments of Your State* source:

Locating a Specific Local Government

Each city or county is found by finding its peer group. Groups are defined by their state/region, city or county, and their population size class. So, 'XX' for the state or region abbreviation. Then type: 1=counties, 2=cities, towns. Then population size class: 1=under 2,000 population, 2=2,000-10,000, 3=10,000-50,000, 4=50,000-100,000, 5=100,000-250,000, 6=over 250,000. For example, the group AL13 is Alabama='**AL**', counties='**1**', and size class of 10,000 to 50,000 population='**3**'. So this is displayed as: **'Group AL13'**.

Conversely, Denver, Colorado would be found in the Colorado book, in its peer group of state='CO' +cities= '2' + size greoup='6', that is, in each chart that is marked as 'CO26'.

There are ten sections in the State Graphics Book, 'CO26' will be one chart in each section.

Comparability

For comparability and simplicity, the many activities of a local government have been grouped into the following classifications:

Taxed-Based, Basic, or Common Functions

Those activities that most cities provide for the public good:

1 police protection
2 fire protection
3 general administration (including the judicial system, city inspection and regulations and the executive officials' staffs and offices)
4 general public buildings
5 roads and highways maintenance
6 sewerage
7 sanitation
8 parks and other public recreation

Fee-Based, or Non Common Functions

Include everything else (except for the four utility functions: water supply electric service, gas supply and transit system). Most typical noncommon services are:

1 education (including but not limited to local schools)
2 public welfare
3 hospitals
4 health services other than hospitals
5 airports

6 housing and urban renewal
7 libraries
8 parking facilities
9 water transportation services (coastal cities port facilities, etc.)

Enterprise or Utility Services

The *Governments of Your State* groups together the 4 most common utilities which are:

1 water supply
2 electric service
3 gas supply
4 transit service (bus, train, subway, etc.)

General Government

Functions include all functions of a local government except the four utility or enterprise activities.

Operating Surplus (deficit)

This is not the accounting equivalent of the general fund operating surplus. The *Governments of Your State* uses the operating surplus as simply the difference between the current revenues and the current expenses (that excludes sources of funds such as bond issues and uses of funds such as capital outlays and debt retirement).

Fiscal Year of Data

The data compiled for the **MAS** data base and presented in the *Governments of Your State* is for the fiscal year. The **MAS** data collection system updates 'late' fiscal years so that the publication will be for all data ending in the same calendar year.

Zero Data Fields

For the most part, the **MAS** data collection system has been able to identify and detail all major components of a local government's revenue and expenditure. However, if a revenue or expense item is zero in the *Governments of Your State* , it does not necessarily mean that the activity does not exist. Rather, there is a possibility that an activity's revenue or expense has been added, by the local government, into a common fund such as general or financial administration.

General Obligation, Enterprise, Utility, and Revenue Debt

In presenting the debt picture, the emphasis is on the whole government and its debt service management and not on individual agency debt issues.

General Obligation Debt is that which is guaranteed by the local government and is usually funded by general government revenues such as property taxes, etc.

Utility Debt is the water supply, electrical service, gas supply and transit system debt.

Definitions & Explanations

Enterprise and Revenue Debt includes utility debt and all other specific purpose debt that is funded by that specific activity and may also be guaranteed by the local government. This heading will not include industrial development or mortgage bonds that are issued by or for a private commercial interest.

Accounting Basis and Comparability

The method of accounting for government funds used for the **MAS** data base and the *Governments of Your State* largely reduces the differences between governments due to differences in their accounting methods. Governmental revenues are compiled in terms of net amounts collected (net of refunds, agency collections, suspense funds, and interfund transactions). Government expenditure reflects actual disbursements and accrued or incurred expenses where there are corresponding revenues in the same period (e.g. revenues taken from suspense funds).

Data Classification

The detailed financial and employee statistics are classified strictly and uniformly for all local governments. For example, all revenues and expenses detailed for fire protection are defined and classified the same for all local governments.

Governments Included

The **MAS** data base includes all local governments, school districts and special taxing authorities in the United States.
Periodically, due to a lack of reported data, some of the smaller governments of over 10,000 population cannot be included in their state book for a given year. However, the vast majority of all city , town, village, and county government activity for each state is included in the annual *Governments of Your State* . There are approximately 87,000 local governments and taxing authorities in the country. For some of the smallest governments with very small populations or no debt activity, the **MAS** data base may not update all of their statistics annually.

Data Sources and Collection Methods

The development of each year's edition of this book starts with data collection. Data is collected about the fiscal operations of all taxing and governmental authorities in the United States. This data is placed into our MAS Data Base.

To the extent possible, the data is collected from standardized forms filed by government units and collected by many state agencies in each state. Also, when a government unit files reports with federal agencies, we collect as many of these documents as possible. Data is also collected through manual collection of data from printed documents.

Due do the inconsistences of government functions throughout the United States some of the agencies subordinate to their local governments are merged into their controlling government, normally they are not legally separate governments under their state law. Subordinate agencies are normally controlled by their city or county, however, they may have wide-ranging powers to tax and issue debt. Subordinate agencies are also characterized as created and effectively controlled by only one city or county or may be apportioned to their city and county if they are a joint agency only within one county. Agencies of more than one county or city are usually not considered subordinate for the purpose of merging them into their parent governments.

The effect of merging subordinate agencies into a government is that the revenues, expenses and debt of the agency are added to the appropiate functional category of the parent government, only, so that the other functional areas of the government remain the same and can be compared to similar governments. Sales and property taxes levied by subordinate agencies are also added to the the parent government in specific categories.

C1 Can Comparison of Your Expense Mix Save Your Budget?

This is one of 3 graphs to find cost saving opportunities. By comparing your government to other governments of similar size and type (we call 'peer groups'), you can see if others are able to perform similar functions for less per capita than your government.

In this example, the group is AL13, that is Alabama='**AL**', counties='**1**', and size class of 10,000 to 50,000 population='**3**'. So this is displayed as: **'Group AL13'.**

CAN COMPARISON OF YOUR EXPENSE MIX SAVE YOU MONEY? ARE THERE AREAS THAT COULD JUSTIFY ADDITIONAL RESOURCES? **C1**

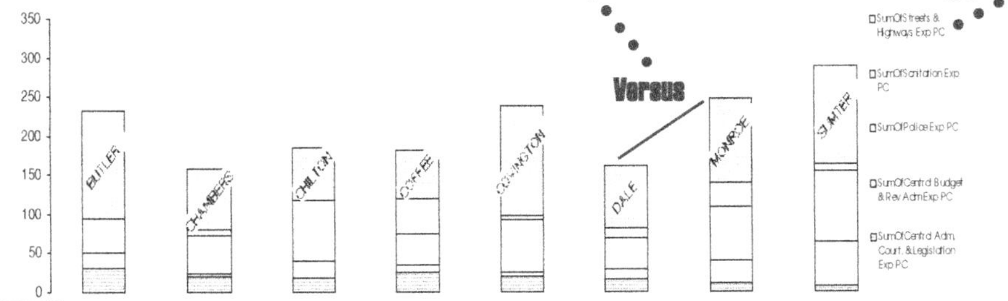

GROUP AL13

Name	Population	Central Adm, Court, Legislation Exp PC	Central Budget Rev Adm Exp PC	Other Adm Exp PC	Gen Public Buildings Exp PC	Police Exp PC	Fire Protection Exp PC	Streets Highways Exp PC	Parks Recreation Exp PC	Sewerage Exp PC	Sanitation Exp PC	Total Common Exp PC
MONROE	24043	10	29	23	0	70	0	108	5	0	30	277
BUTLER	20911	30	21	12	12	43	0	138	2	0	0	263
SUMTER	14376	7	56	17	6	91	0	124	0	1	10	316
CHAMBERS	36251	20	4	8	16	49	3	78	0	0	7	188
CHILTON	40516	18	21	17	11	79	11	67	1	0	0	229
COFFEE	43878	26	8	28	7	41	0	62	0	0	45	221
COVINGTON	36956	20	6	44	6	66	0	140	7	0	6	298
DALE	49186	17	12	3	7	40	0	80	0	0	13	175
	averages	18.5	19.6	19.0	8.1	59.9	1.8	99.6	1.9	0.1	13.9	245.9

Legend

C1

Listed in order of use on chart, top to bottom

- Street Maintenance Expense Per Capita
- Sanitation Expense Per Capita
- Police Expense Per Capita
- Financial Adm. Expense Per Capita
- General Adm., Courts Expense Per Capita

(Ignore the prefix "sumof" or "sumoftotal" in the legend, the system inserts this automatically.)

Finding Your City or County

Each government is found & compared within its peer group. Peer groups are defined by their state/region, their type of government, and their size class. So, 'XX' for the state or region abbreviation. Then type: 1=counties, 2=cities, towns. Then population size class: 1=under 2,000 population, 2=2,000-10,000, 3=10,000-50,000, 4=50,000-100,000, 5=100,000-250,000, 6=over 250,000.

This graph also includes data from various sections in the ***Governments of Your State*** book: Total Funds Flow, among other sections. For the greater detail, see these sections, in your state's book.

Texas graph C1 TX-000

Can comparison of your expense mix save your budget?

Are there areas that could justify additional resources ?

C1 $_2$

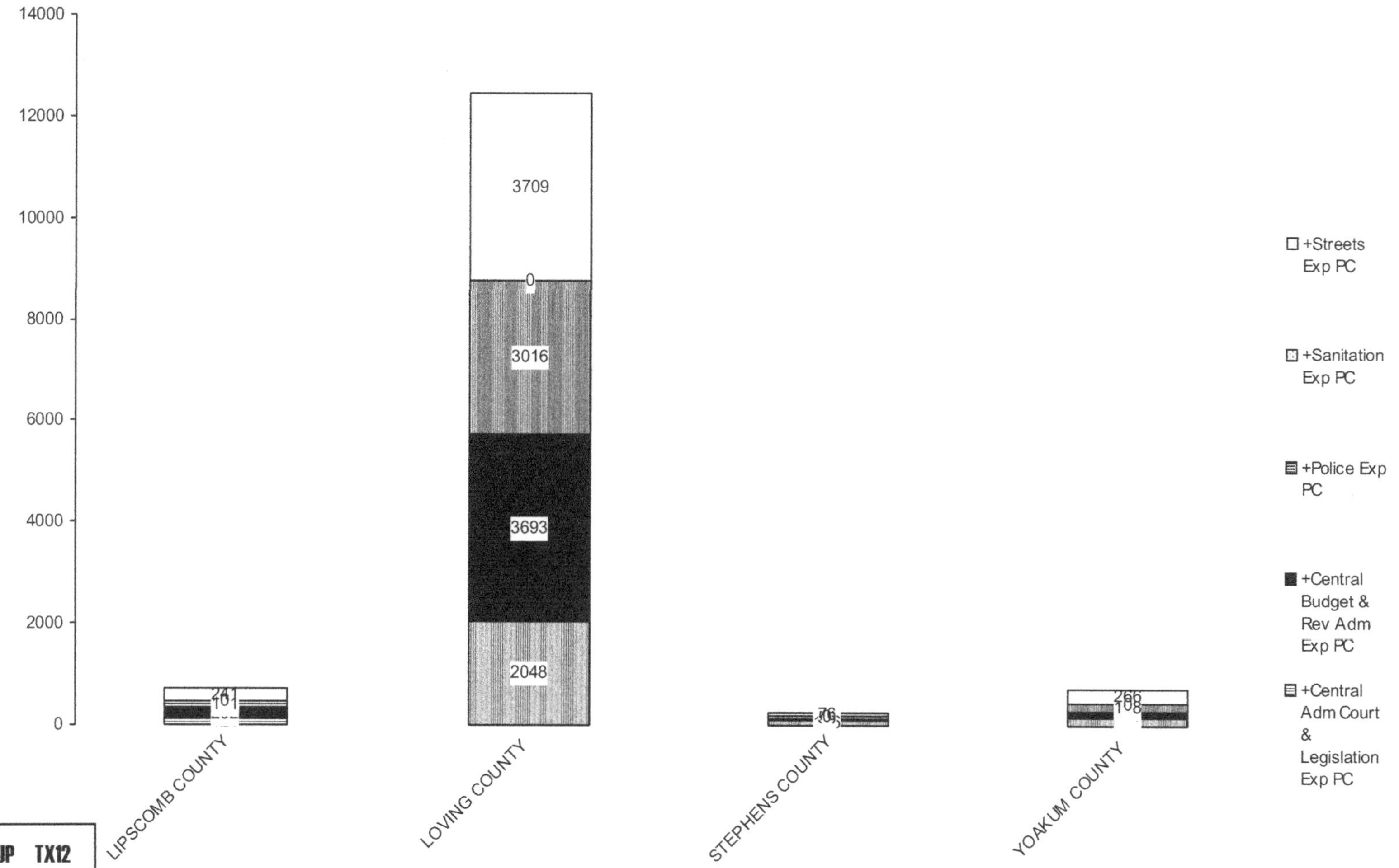

GROUP TX12

	Population	Central Adm, Court, Legislation Exp PC	Central Budget Rev Adm Exp PC	Other Adm Exp PC	Gen Public Buildings Exp PC	Police Exp PC	Fire Protection Exp PC	Streets Highways Exp PC	Parks Recreati on Exp PC	Sewerage Exp PC	Sanitati on Exp PC	Total Common Exp PC
averages	5,033	607.0	1,009.3	1,037.8	289.5	852.8	108.0	1,073.0	24.8	0.0	0.0	5,005.0

Can comparison of your expense mix save your budget?

Are there areas that could justify additional resources ?

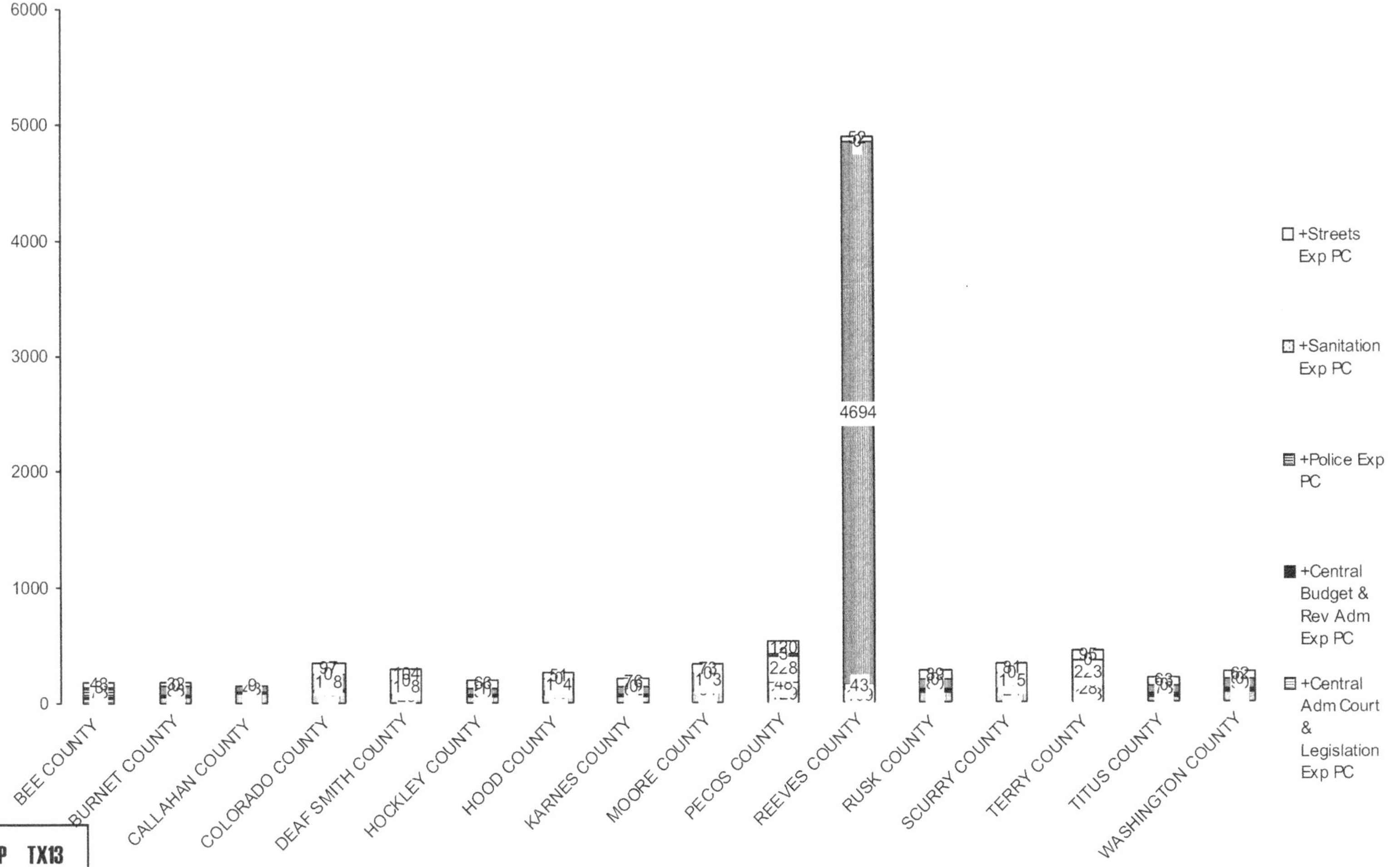

GROUP TX13

	Population	Central Adm, Court, Legislation Exp PC	Central Budget Rev Adm Exp PC	Other Adm Exp PC	Gen Public Buildings Exp PC	Police Exp PC	Fire Protection Exp PC	Streets Highways Exp PC	Parks Recreati on Exp PC	Sewerage Exp PC	Sanitati on Exp PC	Total Common Exp PC
averages	24,927	77.3	23.9	55.8	16.7	397.0	4.4	69.6	14.2	0.5	0.4	663.4

Can comparison of your expense mix save your budget?

Are there areas that could justify additional resources ?

C1 2

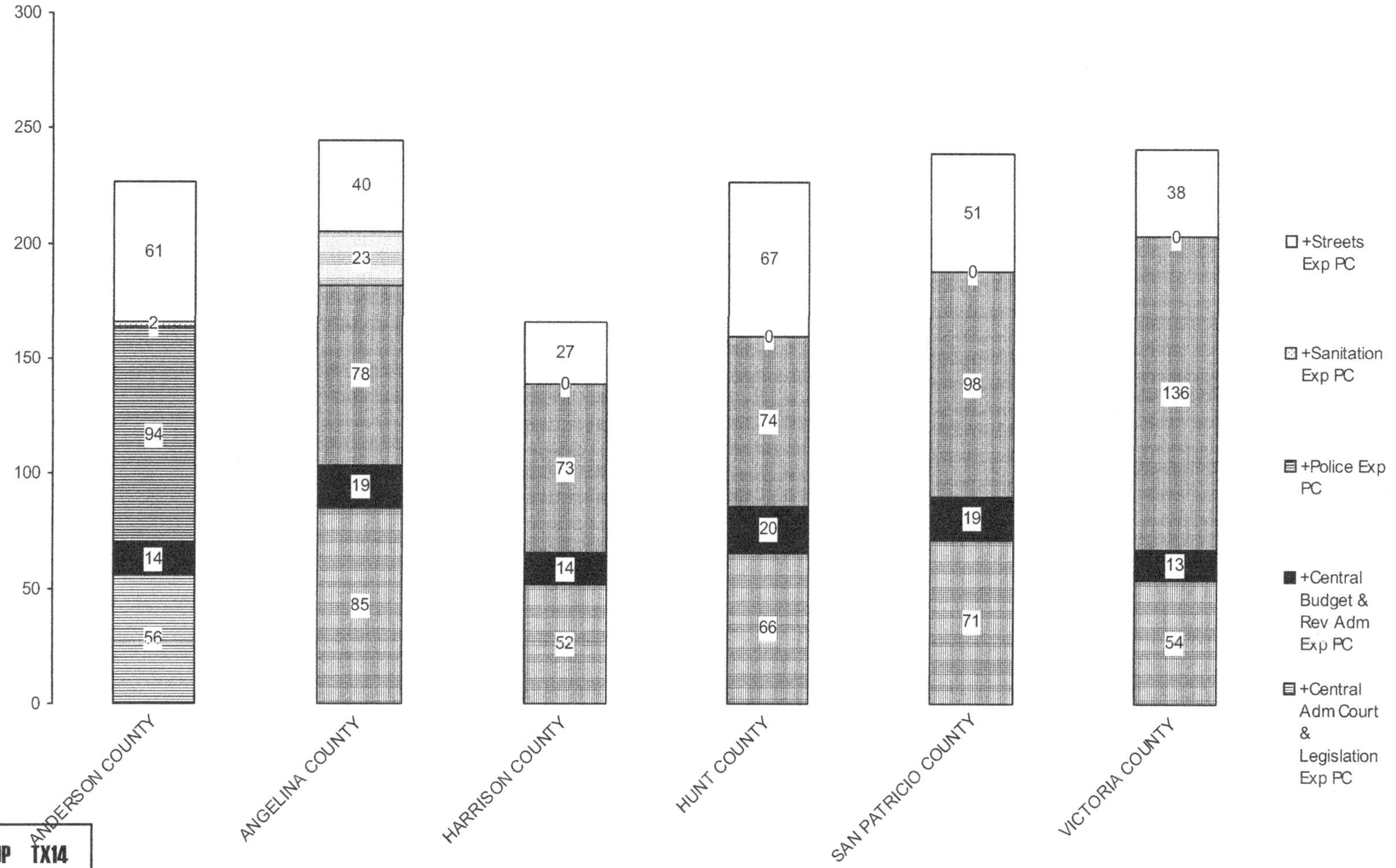

GROUP TX14

	Population	Central Adm, Court, Legislation Exp PC	Central Budget Rev Adm Exp PC	Other Adm Exp PC	Gen Public Buildings Exp PC	Police Exp PC	Fire Protection Exp PC	Streets Highways Exp PC	Parks Recreati on Exp PC	Sewerage Exp PC	Sanitati on Exp PC	Total Common Exp PC
averages	73,137	64.0	16.5	30.7	10.8	92.2	1.3	47.3	0.3	0.0	4.2	271.0

Can comparison of your expense mix save your budget?

Are there areas that could justify additional resources ?

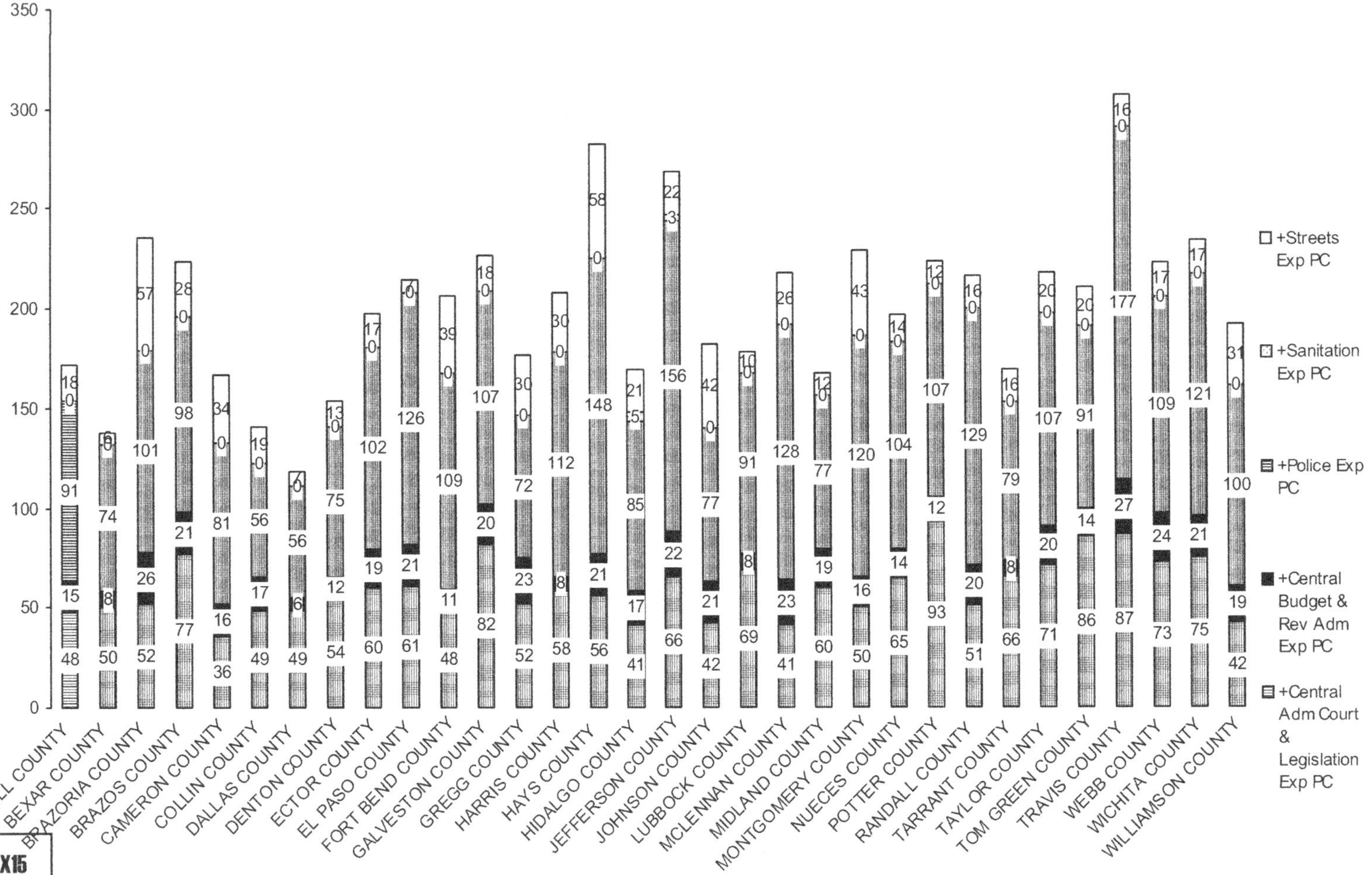

GROUP TX15

	Population	Central Adm, Court, Legislation Exp PC	Central Budget Rev Adm Exp PC	Other Adm Exp PC	Gen Public Buildings Exp PC	Police Exp PC	Fire Protection Exp PC	Streets Highways Exp PC	Parks Recreati on Exp PC	Sewerage Exp PC	Sanitati on Exp PC	Total Common Exp PC
averages	551,497	59.7	17.2	19.4	8.6	102.1	0.9	23.0	3.6	0.0	0.3	237.8

Can comparison of your expense mix save your budget?

Are there areas that could justify additional resources ?

C1 2

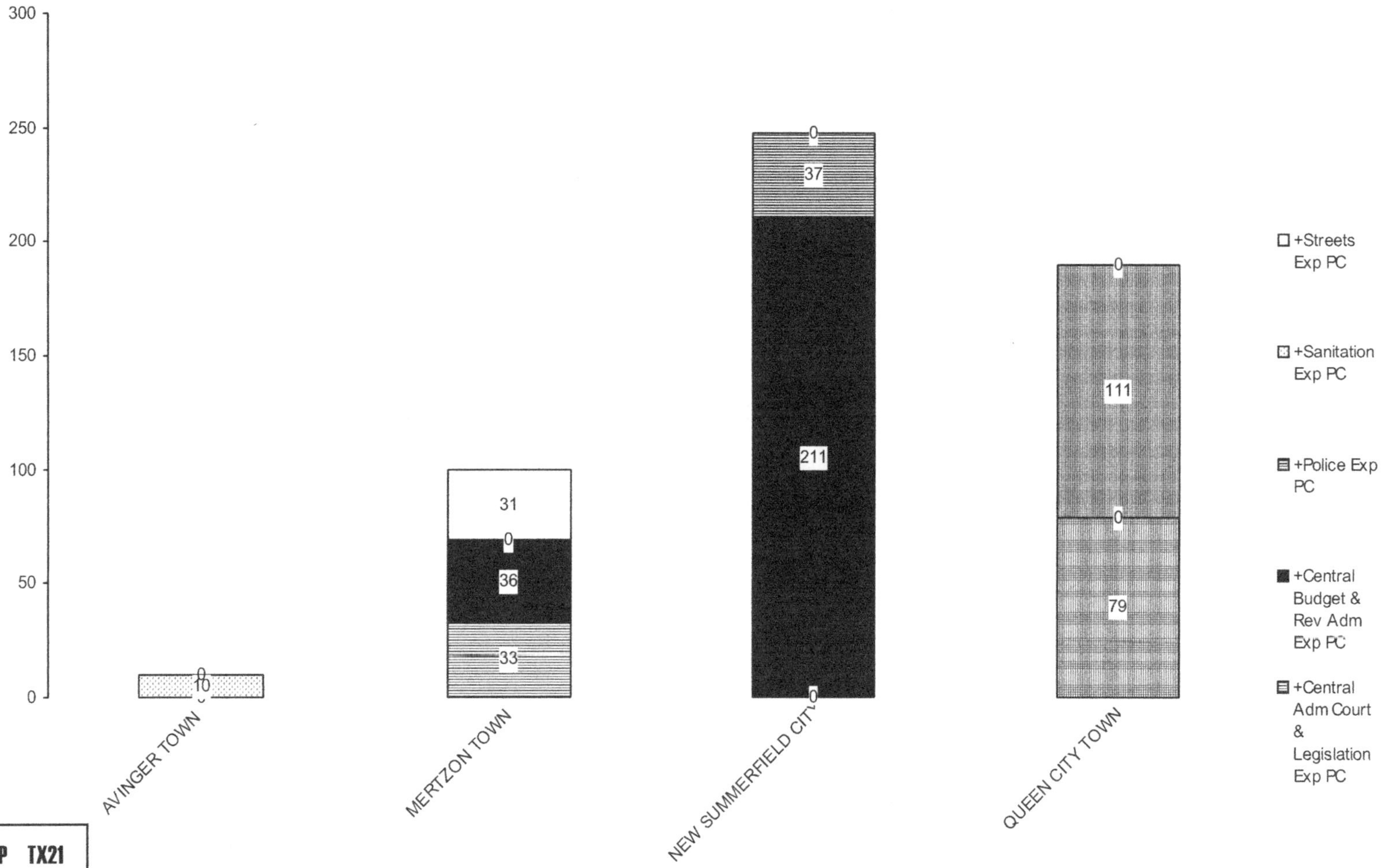

GROUP TX21

	Population	Central Adm, Court, Legislation Exp PC	Central Budget Rev Adm Exp PC	Other Adm Exp PC	Gen Public Buildings Exp PC	Police Exp PC	Fire Protection Exp PC	Streets Highways Exp PC	Parks Recreati on Exp PC	Sewerage Exp PC	Sanitati on Exp PC	Total Common Exp PC
averages	979	28.0	61.8	18.3	3.8	37.0	0.0	7.8	0.3	40.0	2.5	200.8

Can comparison of your expense mix save your budget?

Are there areas that could justify additional resources ?

C1 2

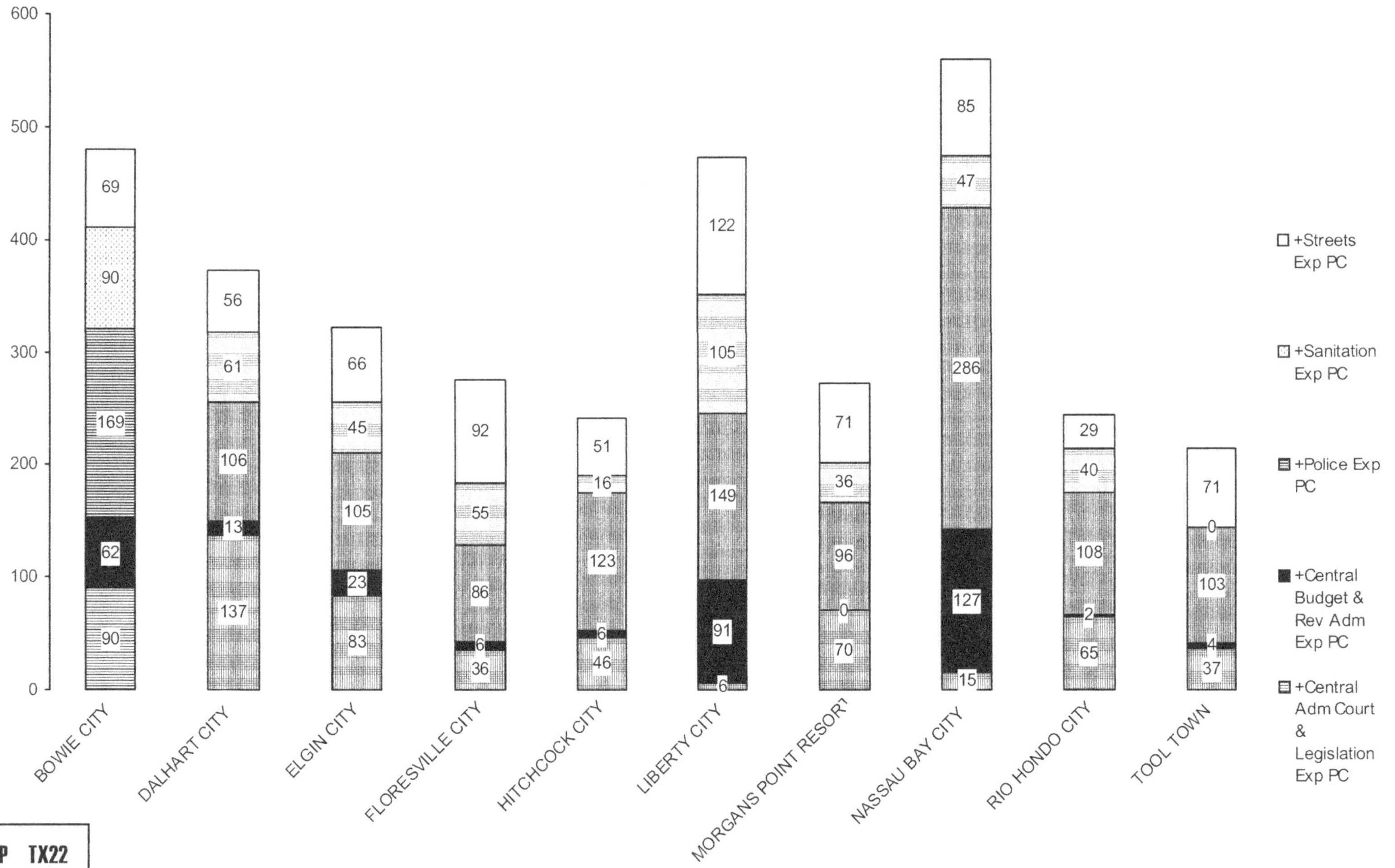

GROUP TX22

	Population	Central Adm, Court, Legislation Exp PC	Central Budget Rev Adm Exp PC	Other Adm Exp PC	Gen Public Buildings Exp PC	Police Exp PC	Fire Protection Exp PC	Streets Highways Exp PC	Parks Recreati on Exp PC	Sewerage Exp PC	Sanitati on Exp PC	Total Common Exp PC
averages	5,668	58.5	33.4	55.0	5.2	133.1	42.6	71.2	33.9	72.8	49.5	559.1

Can comparison of your expense mix save your budget?

Are there areas that could justify additional resources ?

C1 2

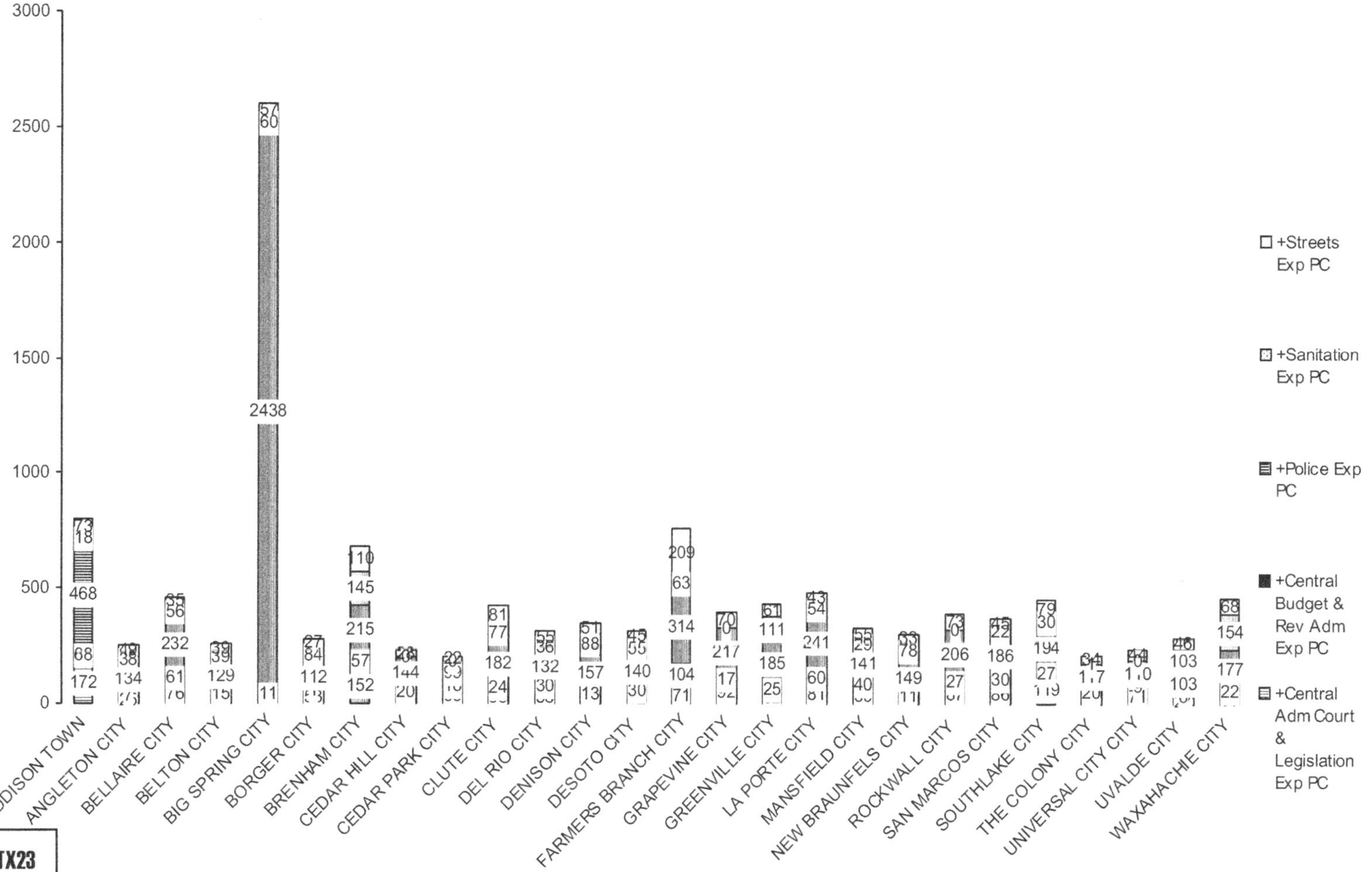

GROUP TX23

	Population	Central Adm, Court, Legislation Exp PC	Central Budget Rev Adm Exp PC	Other Adm Exp PC	Gen Public Buildings Exp PC	Police Exp PC	Fire Protection Exp PC	Streets Highways Exp PC	Parks Recreation Exp PC	Sewerage Exp PC	Sanitation Exp PC	Total Common Exp PC
averages	28,323	65.3	28.9	94.9	11.4	266.2	105.2	58.9	85.7	84.7	51.6	857.2

Can comparison of your expense mix save your budget?

Are there areas that could justify additional resources ?

C1 2

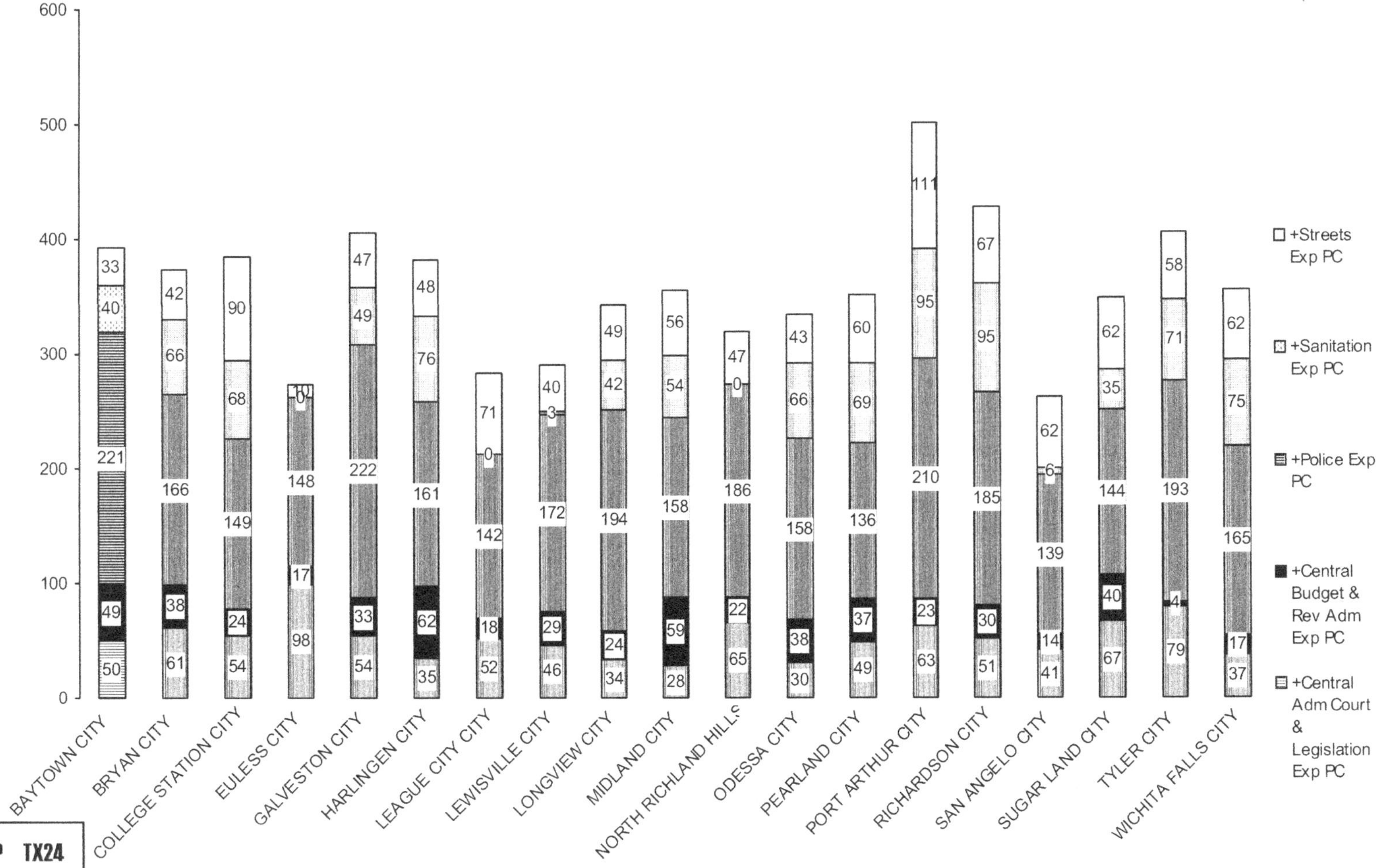

GROUP TX24

	Population	Central Adm, Court, Legislation Exp PC	Central Budget Rev Adm Exp PC	Other Adm Exp PC	Gen Public Buildings Exp PC	Police Exp PC	Fire Protection Exp PC	Streets Highways Exp PC	Parks Recreati on Exp PC	Sewerage Exp PC	Sanitati on Exp PC	Total Common Exp PC
averages	75,138	52.3	30.4	86.2	17.6	171.0	106.7	55.7	71.4	64.7	47.9	707.9

Can comparison of your expense mix save your budget?

Are there areas that could justify additional resources ?

C1 2

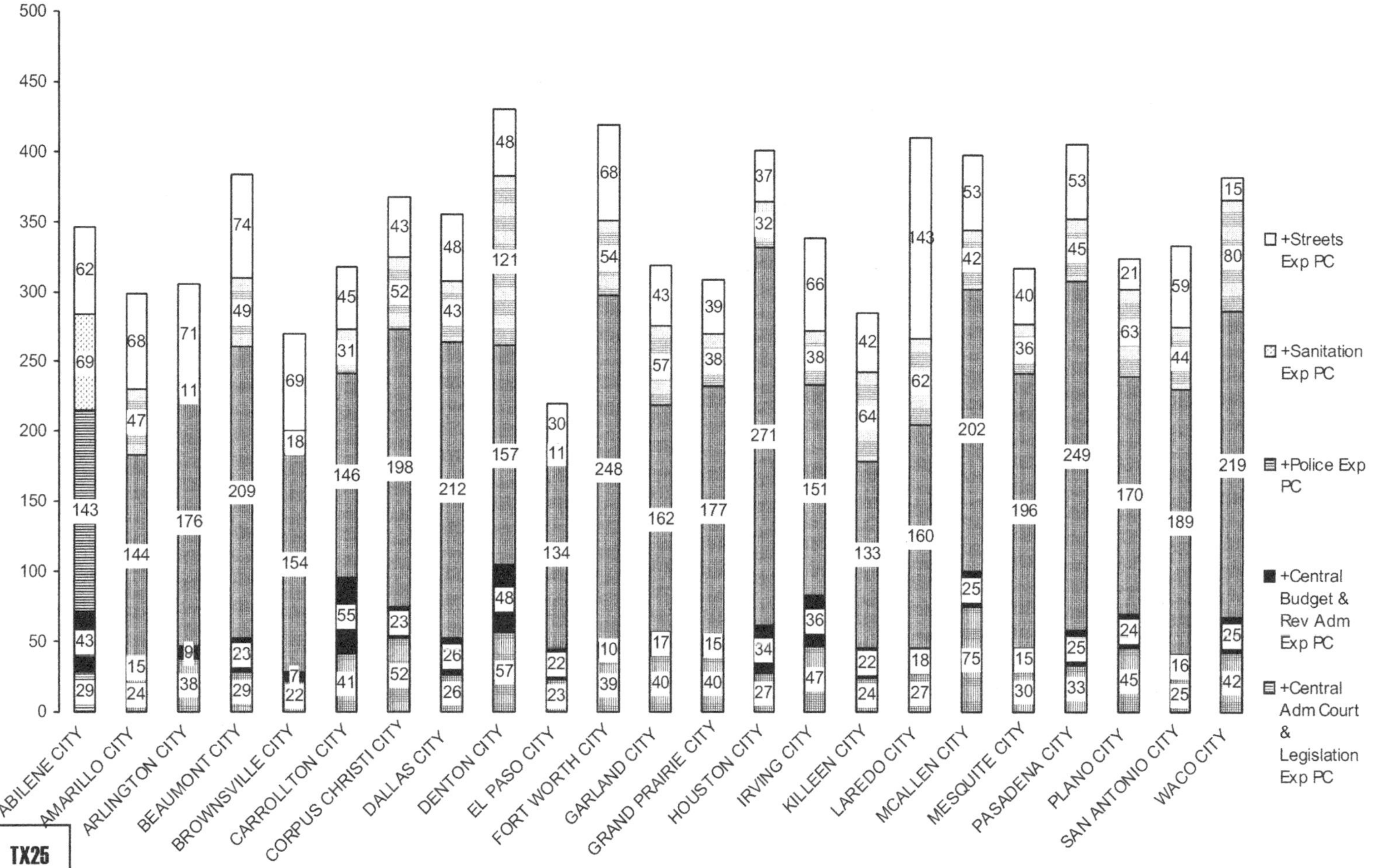

GROUP TX25

	Population	Central Adm, Court, Legislation Exp PC	Central Budget Rev Adm Exp PC	Other Adm Exp PC	Gen Public Buildings Exp PC	Police Exp PC	Fire Protection Exp PC	Streets Highways Exp PC	Parks Recreati on Exp PC	Sewerage Exp PC	Sanitati on Exp PC	Total Common Exp PC
averages	382,052	36.3	24.0	63.6	14.4	182.6	112.3	53.8	65.5	63.3	48.1	668.5

C2 Are Common Expenses In-line with Property Taxes?

This is one of 3 graphs to find cost saving strategies. By comparing your government to other governments of similar size and type (we call 'peer groups'), you can see if others are able to perform the same functions for less of a percent of property taxes per capita than your government.

In this example, the group is AL13, that is Alabama='**AL**', counties='**1**', and size class of 10,000 to 50,000 population='**3**'. So this is displayed as: **'Group AL13'**.

ARE COMMON EXPENSES IN LINE WITH PROPERTY TAXES? **C2**

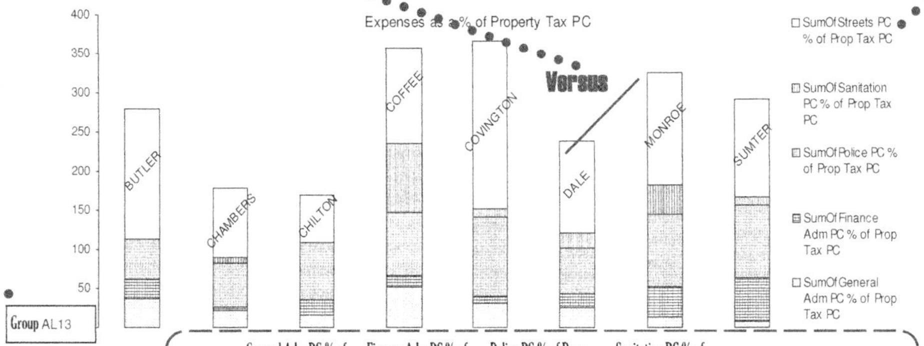

Name	Population	General Adm PC % of Prop Tax PC	Finance Adm PC % of Prop Tax PC	Police PC % of Prop Tax PC	Sanitation PC % of Prop Tax PC	Streets PC % of Prop Tax PC
BUTLER	20911	36	25	52	0	166
CHAMBERS	36251	22	4	55	8	88
CHILTON	40516	17	19	72	0	61
COFFEE	43878	51	16	80	88	122
COVINGTON	36956	31	9	102	9	215
DALE	49186	25	18	59	19	118
MONROE	24043	13	38	92	39	142
SUMTER	14376	7	57	92	10	125
Averages	33265					

Legend

Listed in order of use on chart, top to bottom

- Street Maint.Expense % of Property Taxes
- Sanitation Expense % of Property Taxes
- Police Expense % of Property Taxes
- Finance Adm. Expense % of Property Taxes
- General Adm., Courts % of Property Taxes

(Ignore the prefix "sumof" or "sumoftotal" in the legend, the system inserts this automatically.)

This graph also includes data from various sections in the ***Governments of Your State*** book: Total Funds Flow, among other sections. For the greater detail, see these sections, in your state's book.

Finding Your City or County

Each government is found & compared within its peer group. Groups are defined by their state/region, their type of government, and their size class. So, 'XX' for the state or region abbreviation. Then type: 1=counties, 2=cities, towns. Then population size class: 1=under 2,000 population, 2=2,000-10,000, 3=10,000-50,000, 4=50,000-100,000, 5=100,000-250,000, 6=over 250,000.

Texas graph C2 TX-000

Are common expenses in-line with property taxes?

C2 2

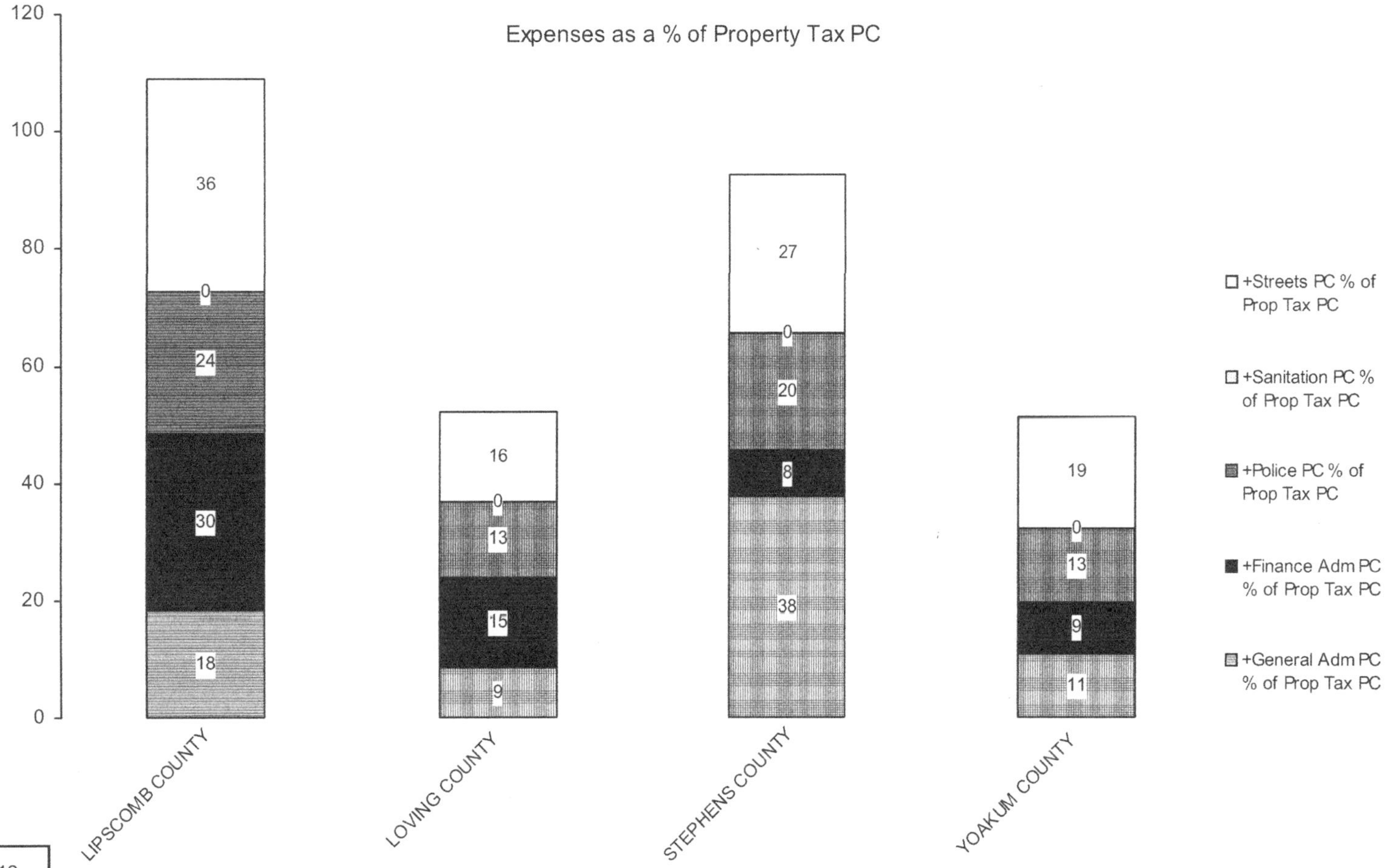

Group TX12

Name	Population	General Adm PC % of Prop Tax PC	Finance Adm PC % of Prop Tax PC	Police PC % of Prop Tax PC	Sanitation PC % of Prop Tax PC	Streets PC % of Prop Tax PC
Averages	5033	19	16	17	0	24

Are common expenses in-line with property taxes? C2 [2]

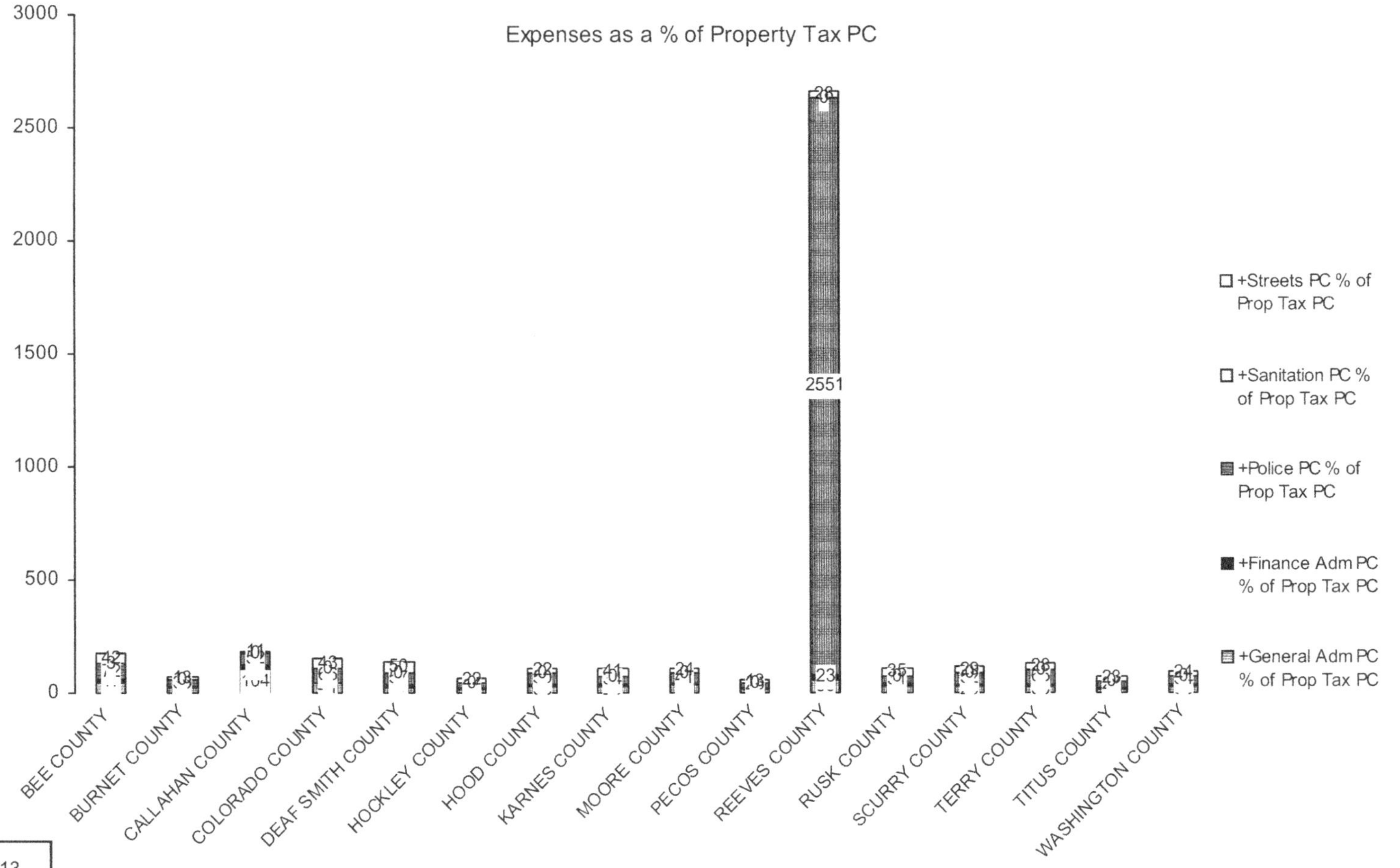

Group TX13

Name	Population	General Adm PC % of Prop Tax PC	Finance Adm PC % of Prop Tax PC	Police PC % of Prop Tax PC	Sanitation PC % of Prop Tax PC	Streets PC % of Prop Tax PC
Averages	24927	35	10	200	0	28

Are common expenses in-line with property taxes?

C2 2

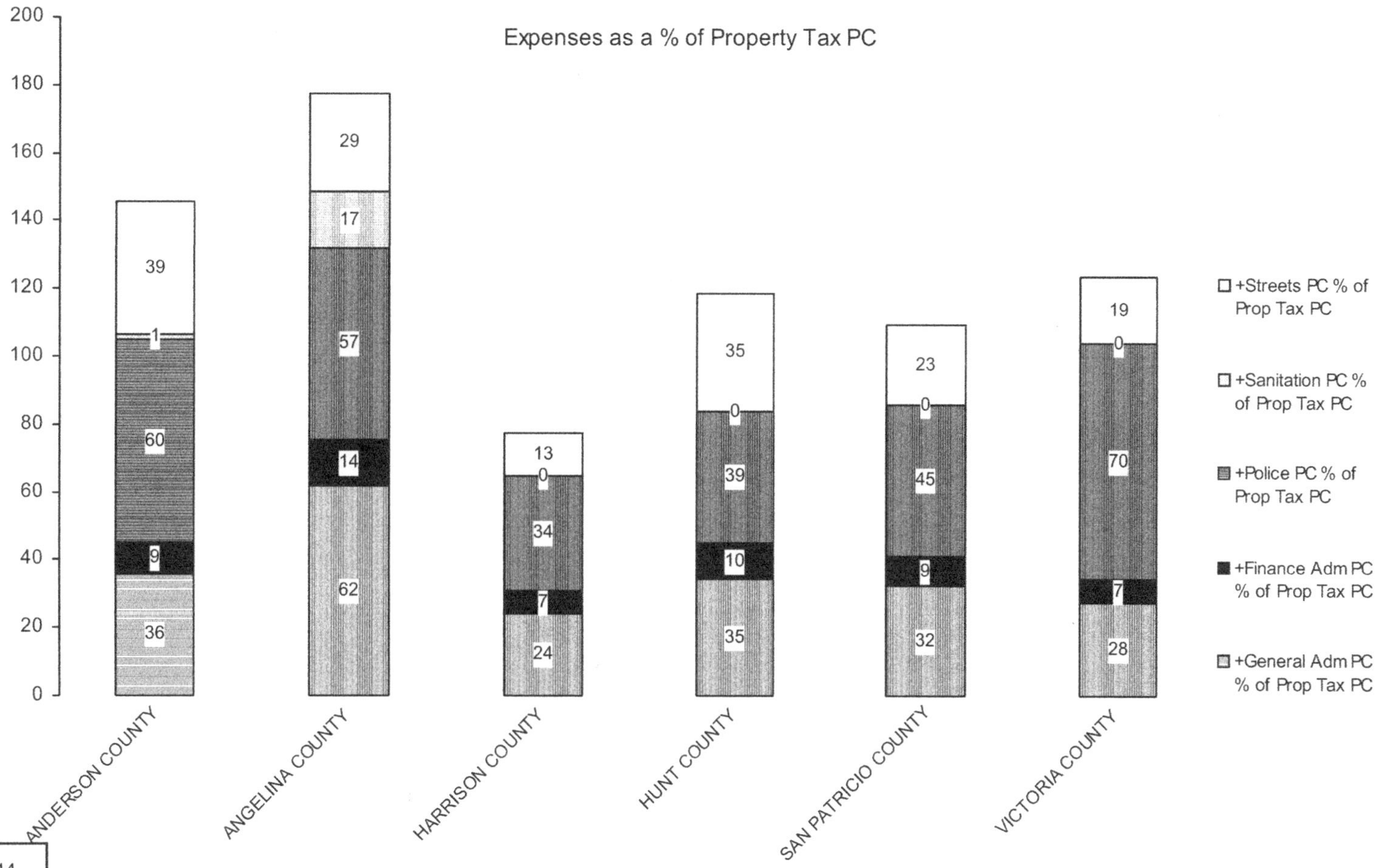

Group TX14

Name	Population	General Adm PC % of Prop Tax PC	Finance Adm PC % of Prop Tax PC	Police PC % of Prop Tax PC	Sanitation PC % of Prop Tax PC	Streets PC % of Prop Tax PC
Averages	73137	36	9	51	3	26

Are common expenses in-line with property taxes?

C2 2

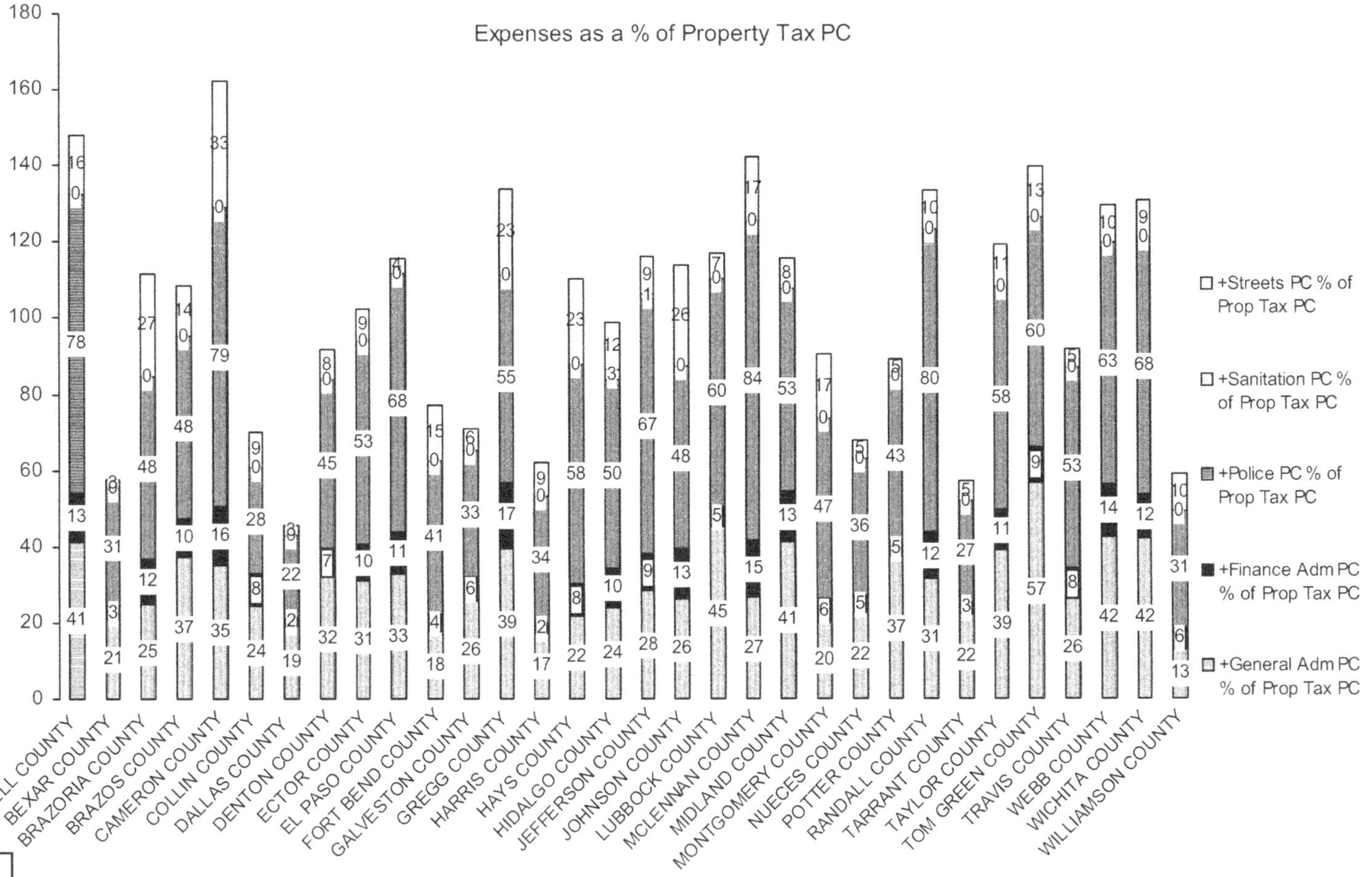

Group TX15

Name	Population	General Adm PC % of Prop Tax PC	Finance Adm PC % of Prop Tax PC	Police PC % of Prop Tax PC	Sanitation PC % of Prop Tax PC	Streets PC % of Prop Tax PC
Averages	551497	30	9	51	0	12

Are common expenses in-line with property taxes?

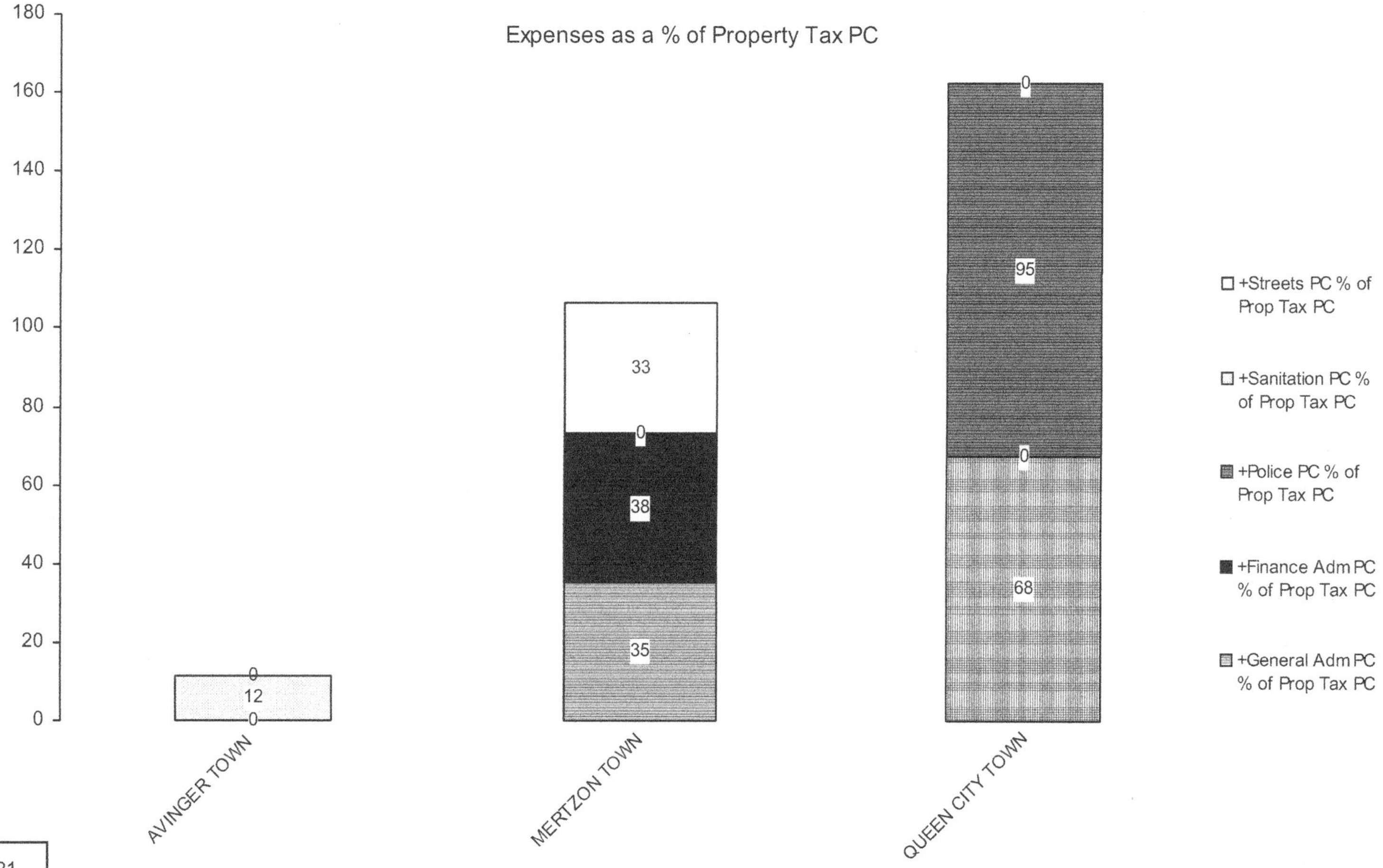

Group TX21

Name	Population	General Adm PC % of Prop Tax PC	Finance Adm PC % of Prop Tax PC	Police PC % of Prop Tax PC	Sanitation PC % of Prop Tax PC	Streets PC % of Prop Tax PC
Averages	960	34	13	32	4	11

Are common expenses in-line with property taxes?

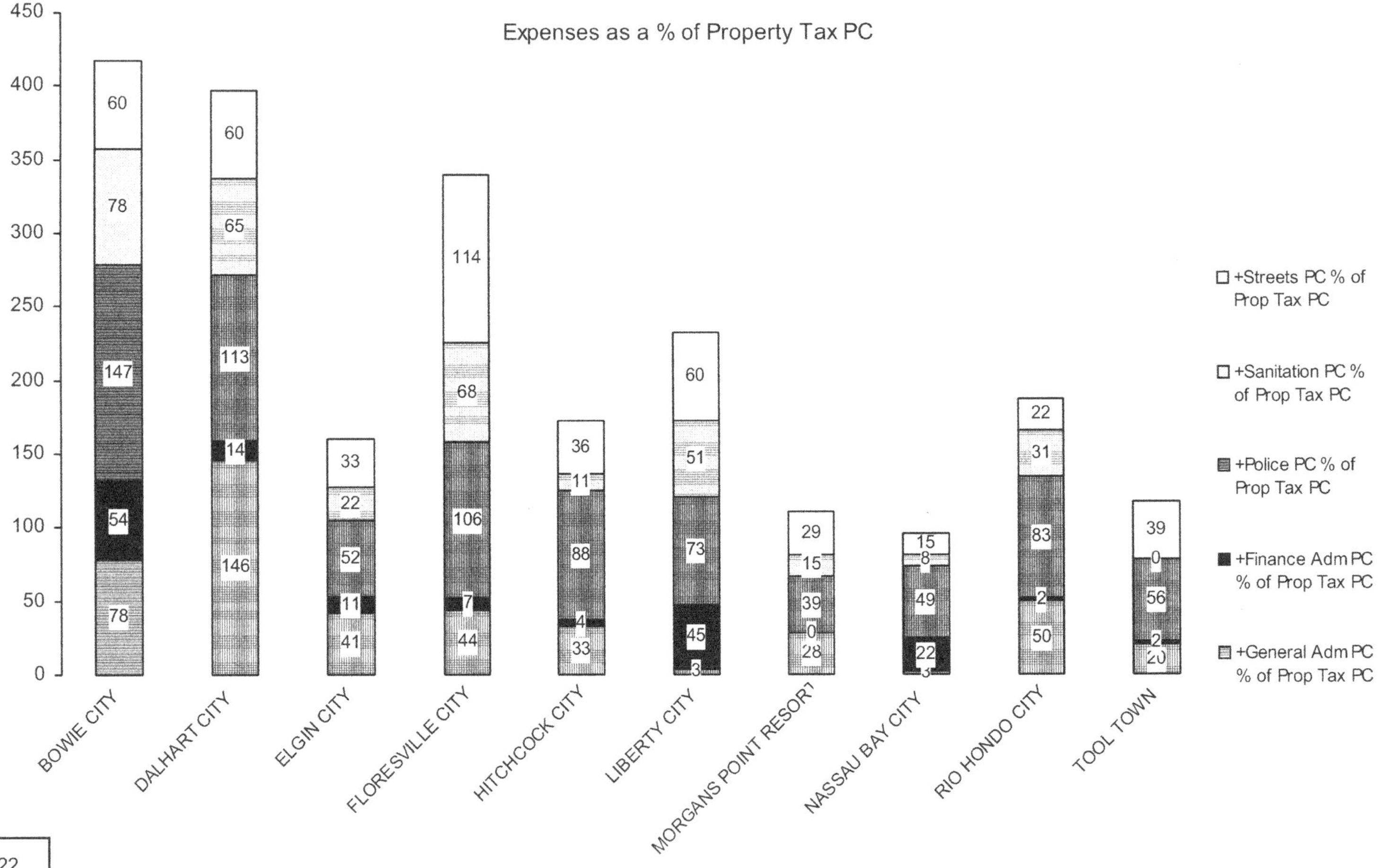

Group TX22

Name	Population	General Adm PC % of Prop Tax PC	Finance Adm PC % of Prop Tax PC	Police PC % of Prop Tax PC	Sanitation PC % of Prop Tax PC	Streets PC % of Prop Tax PC
Averages	5668	45	16	81	35	47

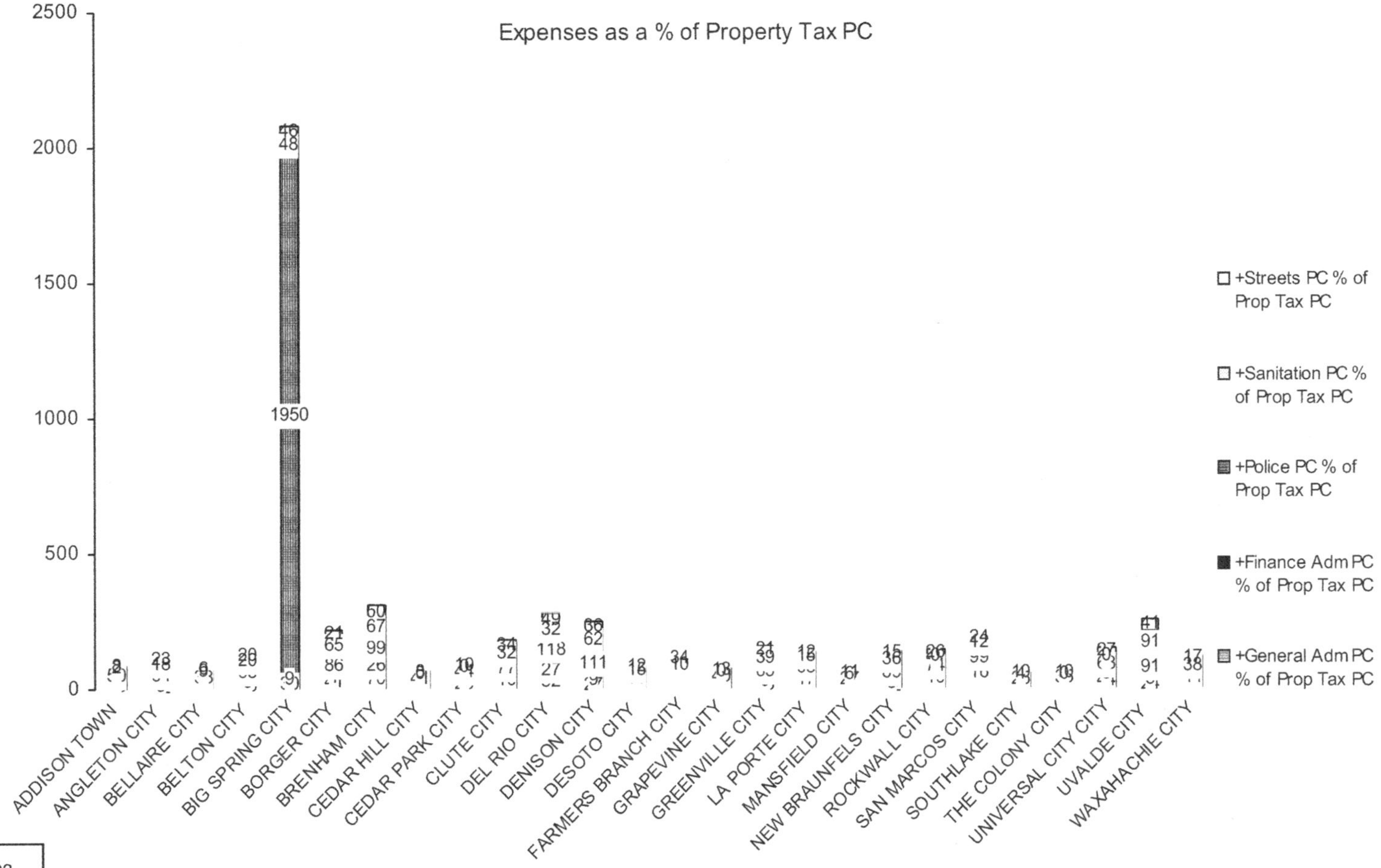

Group TX23

Name	Population	General Adm PC % of Prop Tax PC	Finance Adm PC % of Prop Tax PC	Police PC % of Prop Tax PC	Sanitation PC % of Prop Tax PC	Streets PC % of Prop Tax PC
Averages	28323	24	9	136	24	22

Are common expenses in-line with property taxes? C2 2

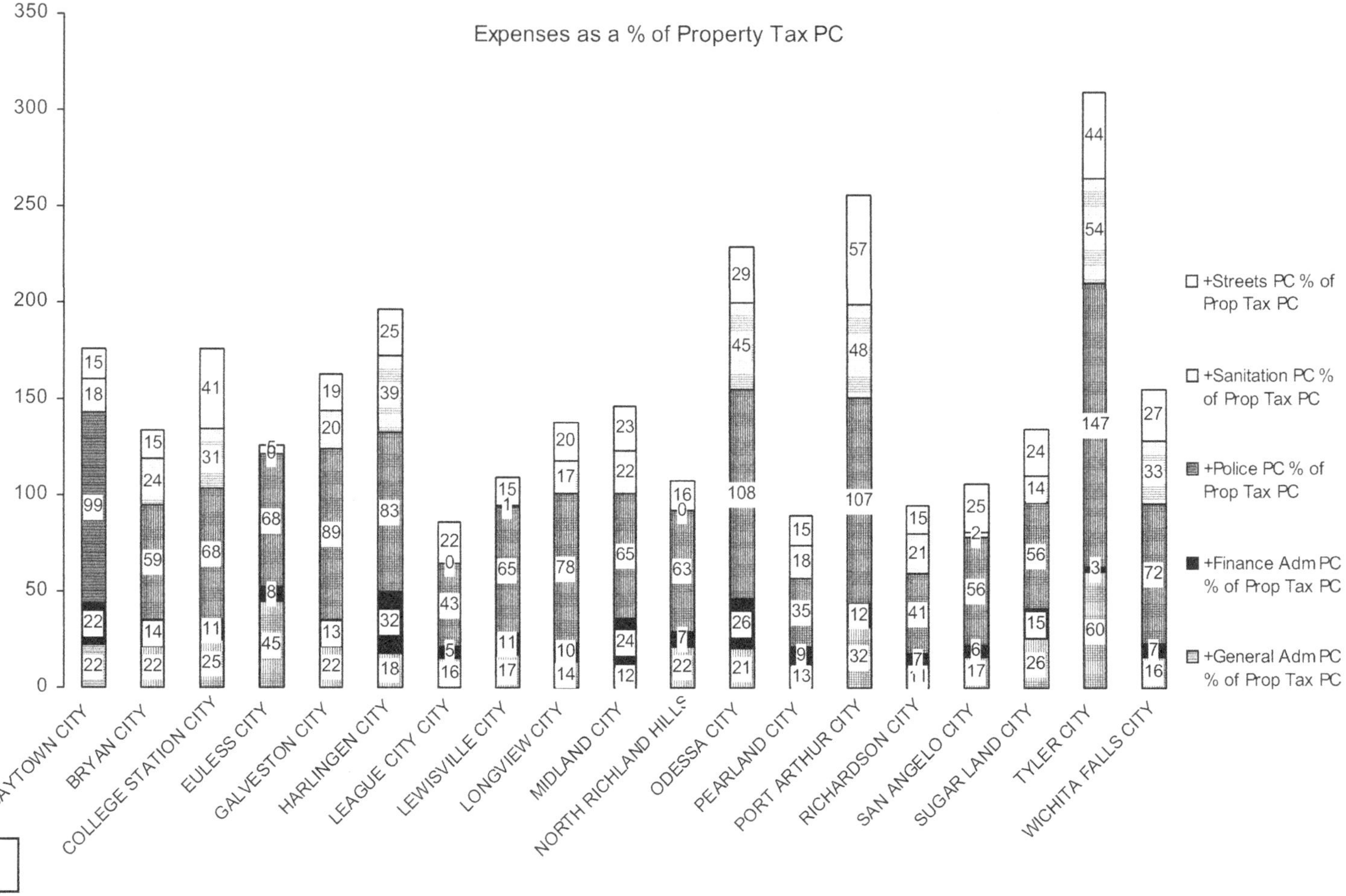

Name	Population	General Adm PC % of Prop Tax PC	Finance Adm PC % of Prop Tax PC	Police PC % of Prop Tax PC	Sanitation PC % of Prop Tax PC	Streets PC % of Prop Tax PC
Averages	75138	23	13	74	21	24

Are common expenses in-line with property taxes?

C2 2

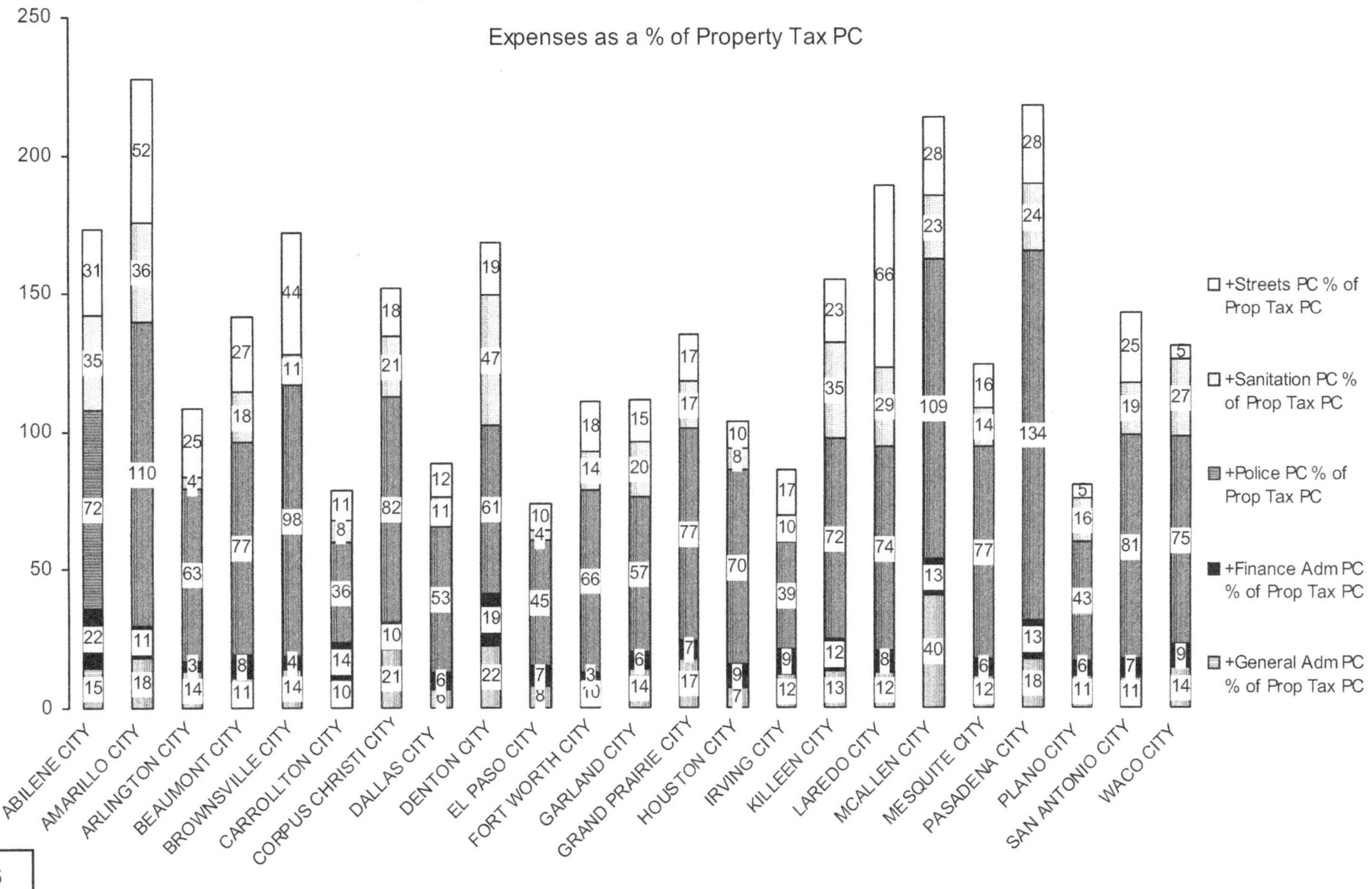

Group TX25

Name	Population	General Adm PC % of Prop Tax PC	Finance Adm PC % of Prop Tax PC	Police PC % of Prop Tax PC	Sanitation PC % of Prop Tax PC	Streets PC % of Prop Tax PC
Averages	382052	14	9	73	20	23

C3 Which Departments are Better Funded than Others?

This is one of 3 graphs to find cost saving strategies or addition funding justifications. By comparing your government to other governments of similar size and type (we call 'peer groups'), you can see if others are performing the same functions for more or less of a percent of the 'common' or 'basic' functions' budget.

In this example, the group is AL13, that is Alabama='**AL**', counties='**1**', and size class of 10,000 to 50,000 population='**3**'. So this is displayed as: **'Group AL13'**.

WHICH DEPARTMENTS HAVE MORE OR LESS FUNDING ? **C3**

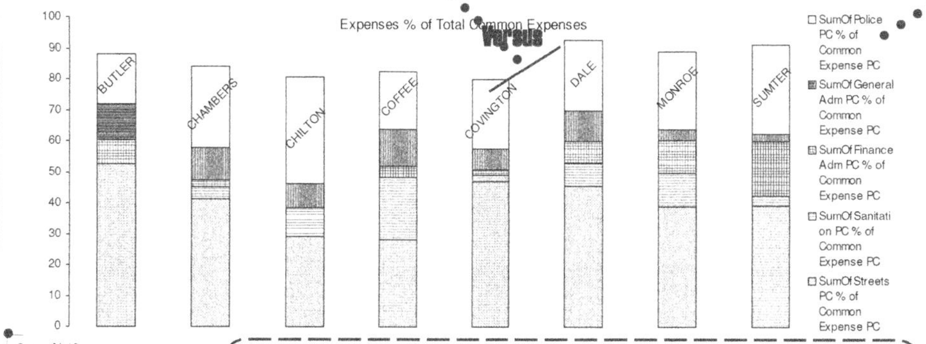

Name	Population	Streets PC % of Common Expense PC	Sanitation PC % of Common Expense PC	Finance Adm PC % of Common Expense PC	General Adm PC % of Common Expense PC	Police PC % of Common Expense PC
MONROE	24043	39	11	10	4	25
BUTLER	20911	52	0	8	11	16
SUMTER	14376	39	3	18	2	29
CHAMBERS	36251	41	4	2	11	26
CHILTON	40516	29	0	9	8	34
COFFEE	43878	28	20	4	12	19
COVINGTON	36956	47	2	2	7	22
DALE	49186	46	7	7	10	23
Averages	**33265**	**40**	**6**	**7**	**8**	**24**

Legend

C3 Listed in order of use on chart, top to bottom

- Police Expense % of Common Expense
- General Adm., Courts % of Common Expense
- Finance Adm. Expense % of Common Expense
- Sanitation Expense % of Common Expense
- Street Maint.Expense % of Property Taxes

(Ignore the prefix "sumof" or "sumoftotal" in the legend, the system inserts this automatically.)

This graph also includes data from various sections in the ***Governments of Your State*** book: Total Funds Flow, among other sections. For the greater detail, see these sections, in your state's book.

Finding Your City or County

Each government is found & compared within its peer group. Peer groups are defined by their state/region, their type of government, and their size class. So, 'XX' for the state or region abbreviation. Then type: 1=counties, 2=cities, towns. Then population size class: 1=under 2,000 population, 2=2,000-10,000, 3=10,000-50,000, 4=50,000-100,000, 5=100,000-250,000, 6=over 250,000.

Texas graph C3 TX-000

Which departments are better funded than others ? C3 2

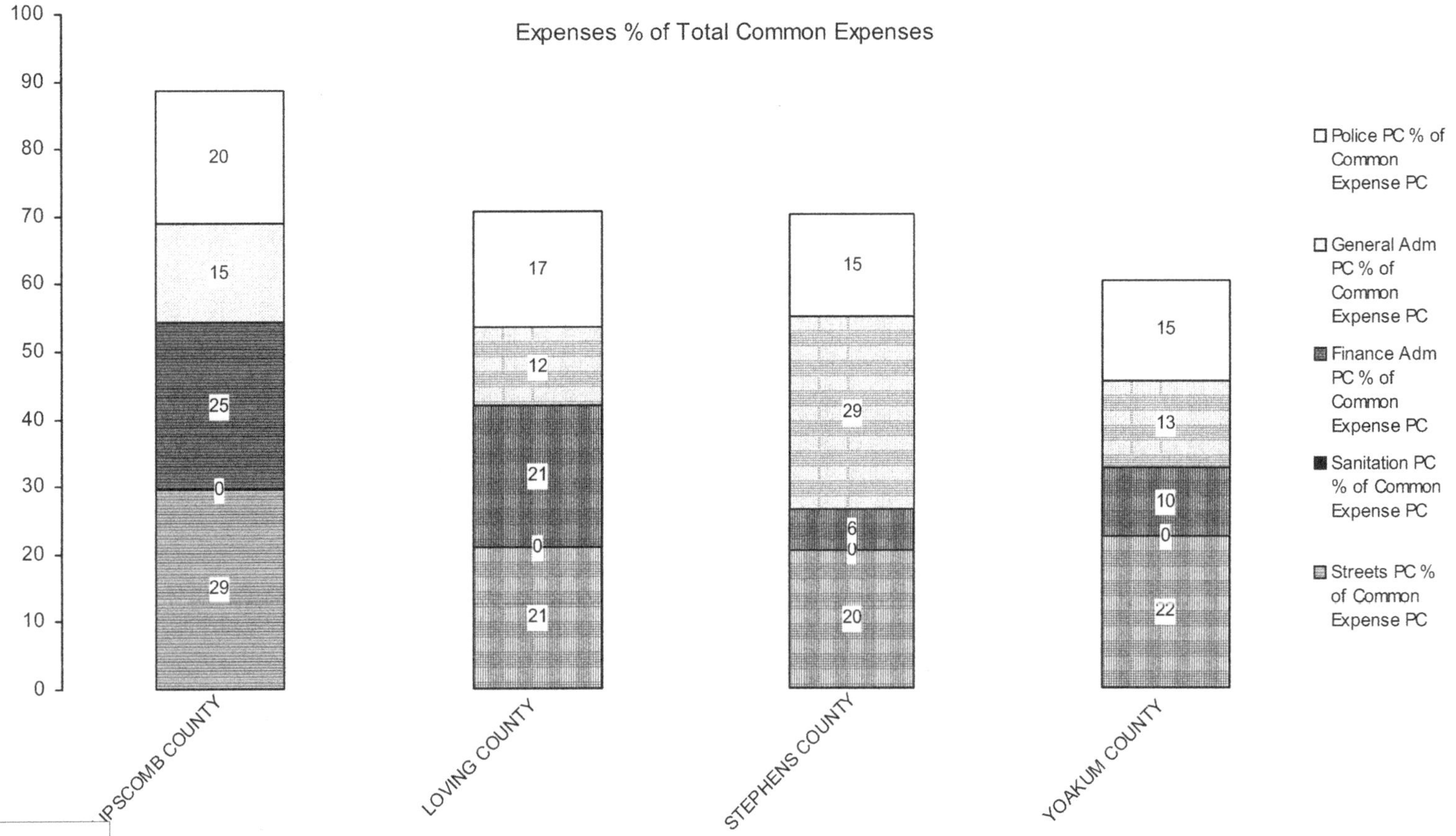

Group TX12

	Population	Streets PC % of Common Expense PC	Sanitation PC % of Common Expense PC	Finance Adm PC % of Common Expense PC	General Adm PC % of Common Expense PC	Police PC % of Common Expense PC
Averages	5033	23	0	15	17	17

Which departments are better funded than others ? C3 2

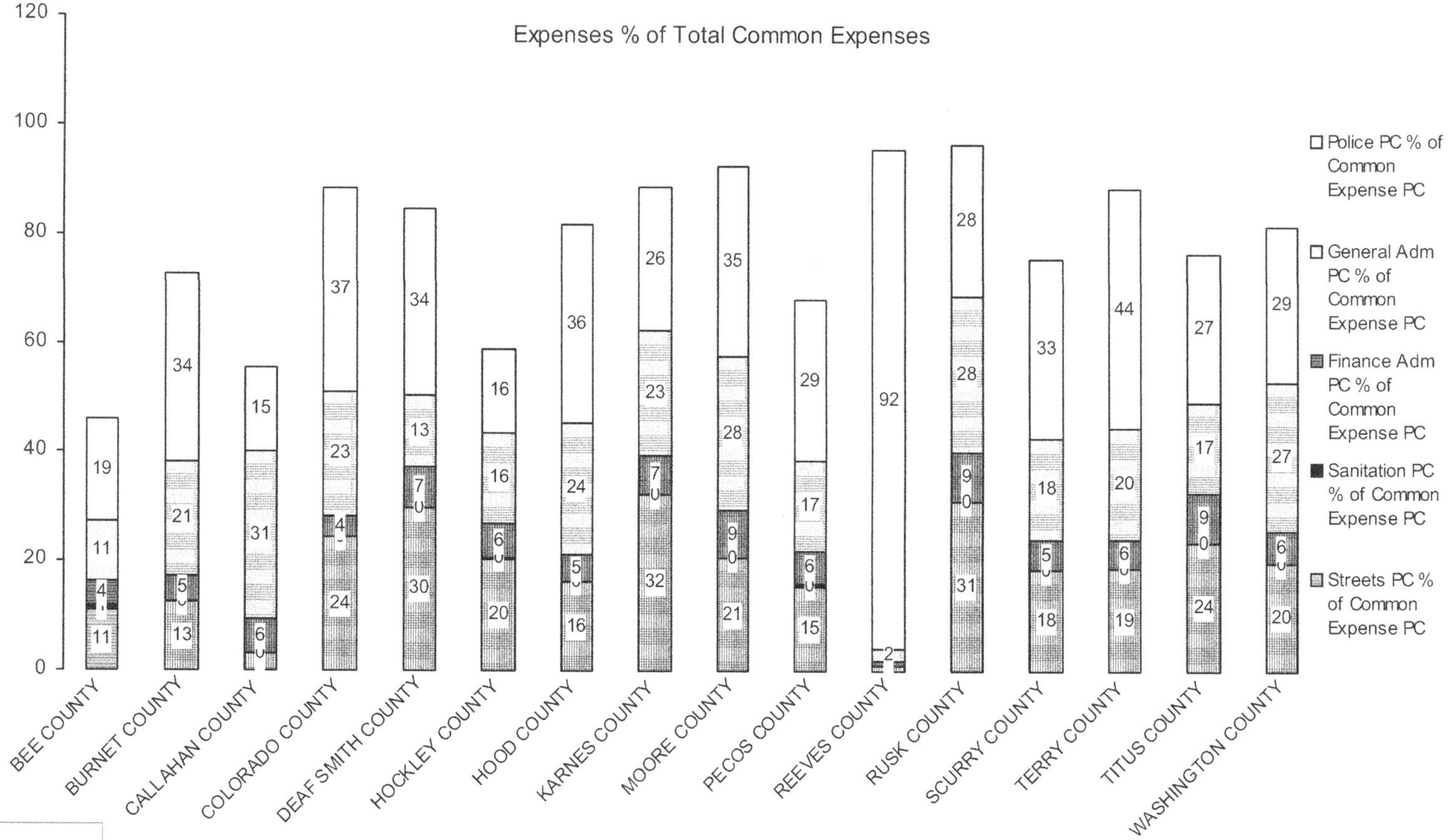

Group TX13

	Population	Streets PC % of Common Expense PC	Sanitation PC % of Common Expense PC	Finance Adm PC % of Common Expense PC	General Adm PC % of Common Expense PC	Police PC % of Common Expense PC
Averages	24927	19	0	6	20	33

Which departments are better funded than others ?

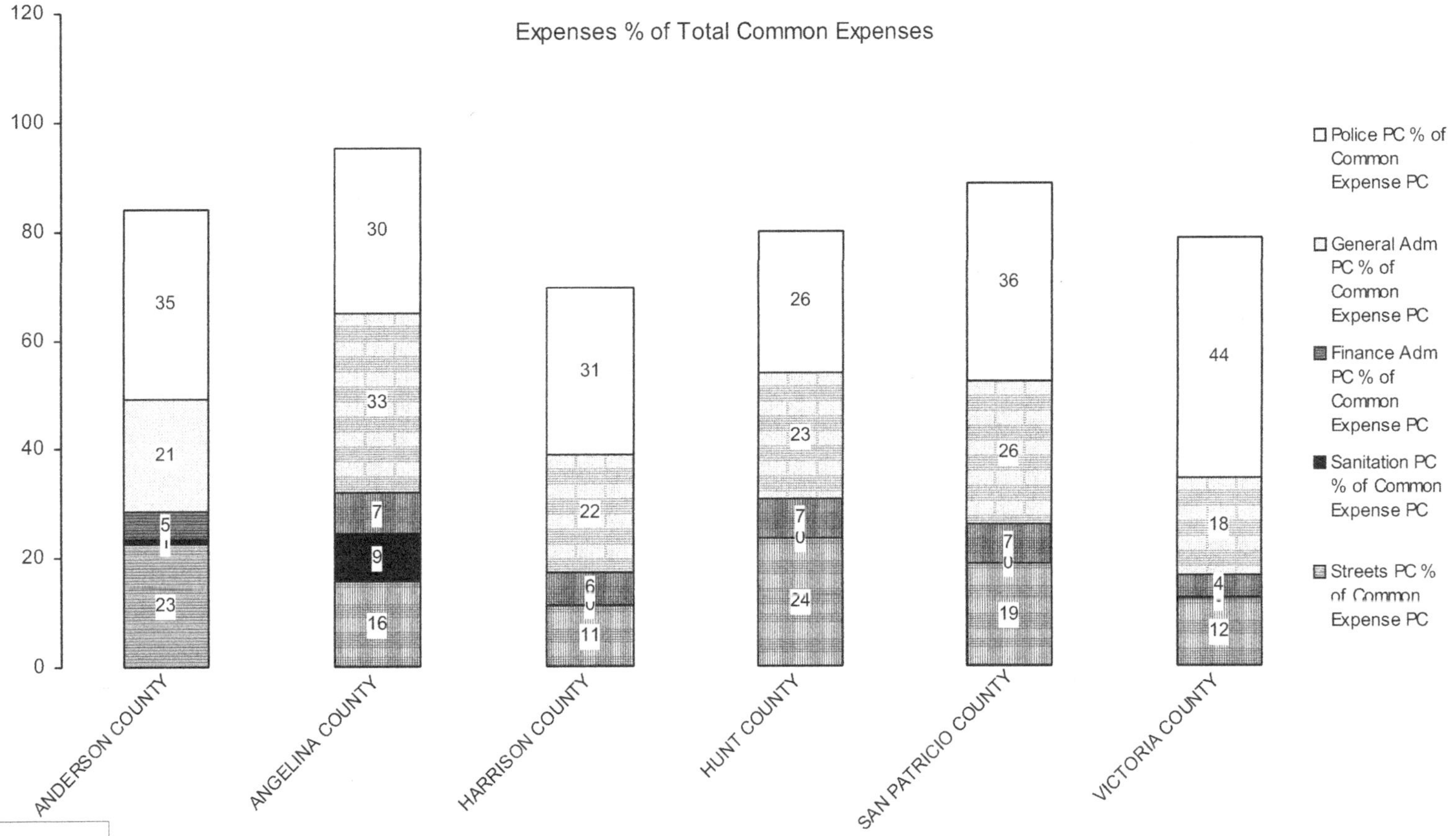

Group TX14

	Population	Streets PC % of Common Expense PC	Sanitation PC % of Common Expense PC	Finance Adm PC % of Common Expense PC	General Adm PC % of Common Expense PC	Police PC % of Common Expense PC
Averages	73137	17	2	6	24	34

Which departments are better funded than others ?

C3 2

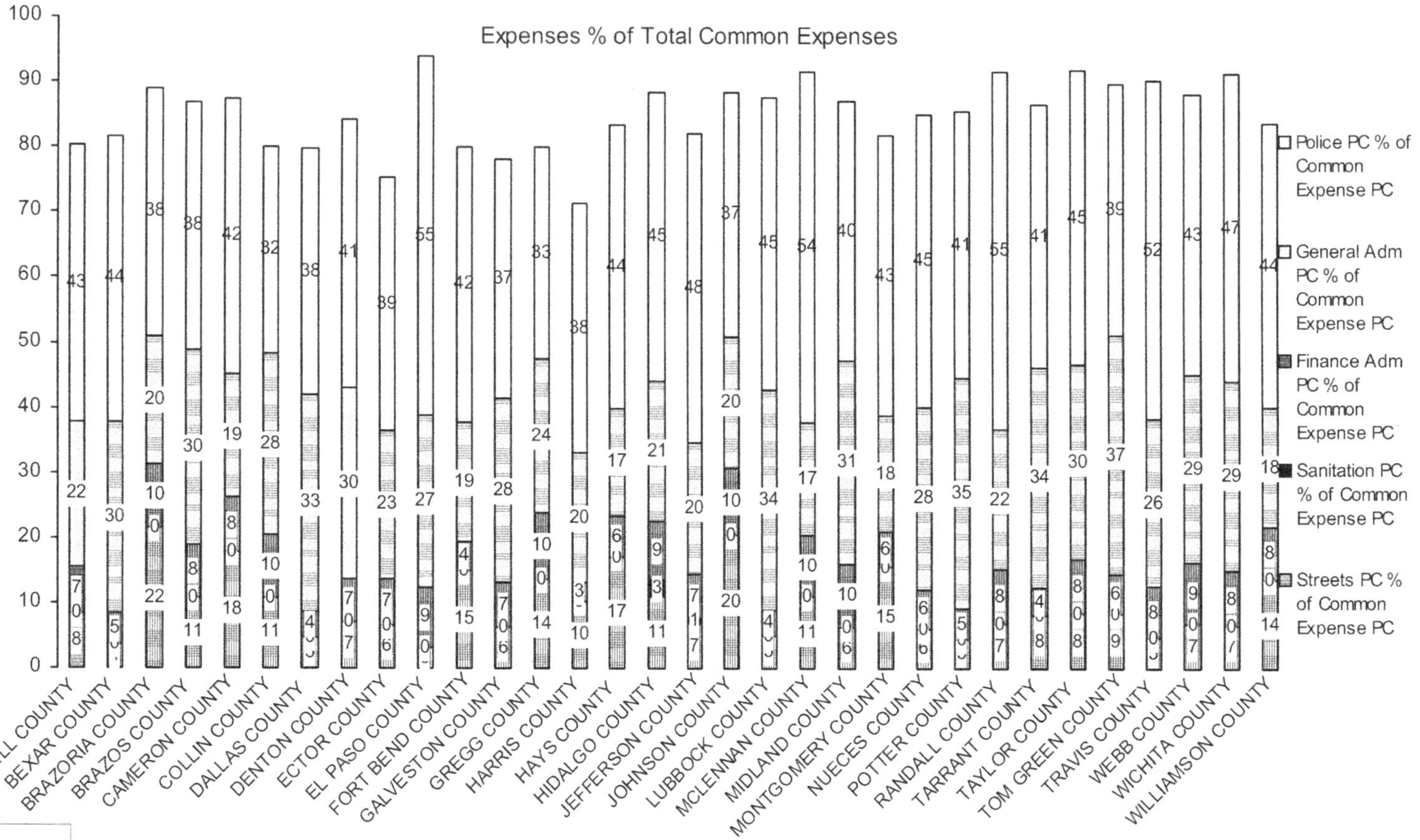

Group TX15

	Population	Streets PC % of Common Expense PC	Sanitation PC % of Common Expense PC	Finance Adm PC % of Common Expense PC	General Adm PC % of Common Expense PC	Police PC % of Common Expense PC
Averages	551500	10	0	7	26	43

Which departments are better funded than others ?

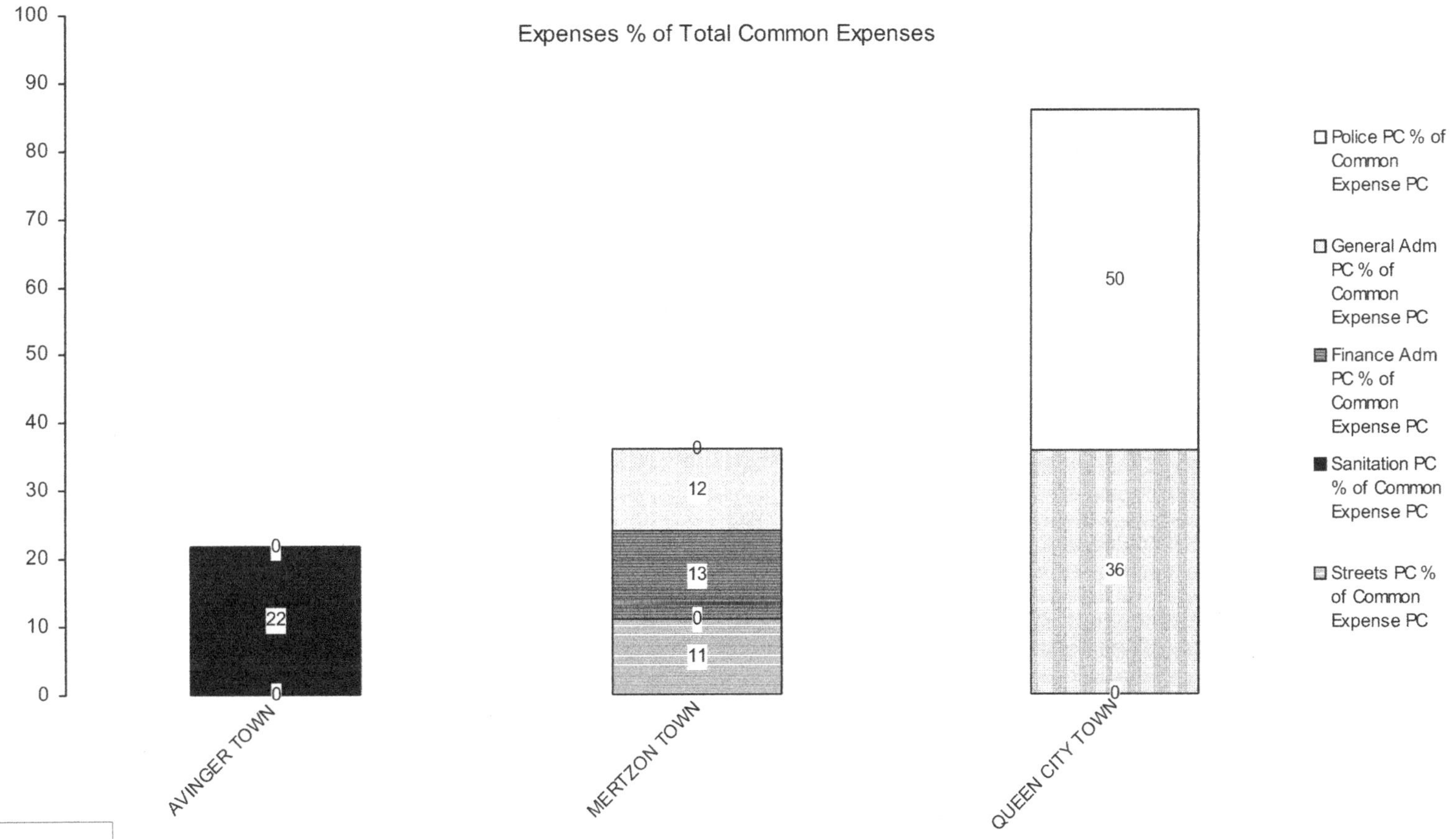

Group TX21

	Population	Streets PC % of Common Expense PC	Sanitation PC % of Common Expense PC	Finance Adm PC % of Common Expense PC	General Adm PC % of Common Expense PC	Police PC % of Common Expense PC
Averages	959.67	4	7	4	16	17

Which departments are better funded than others ? C3 2

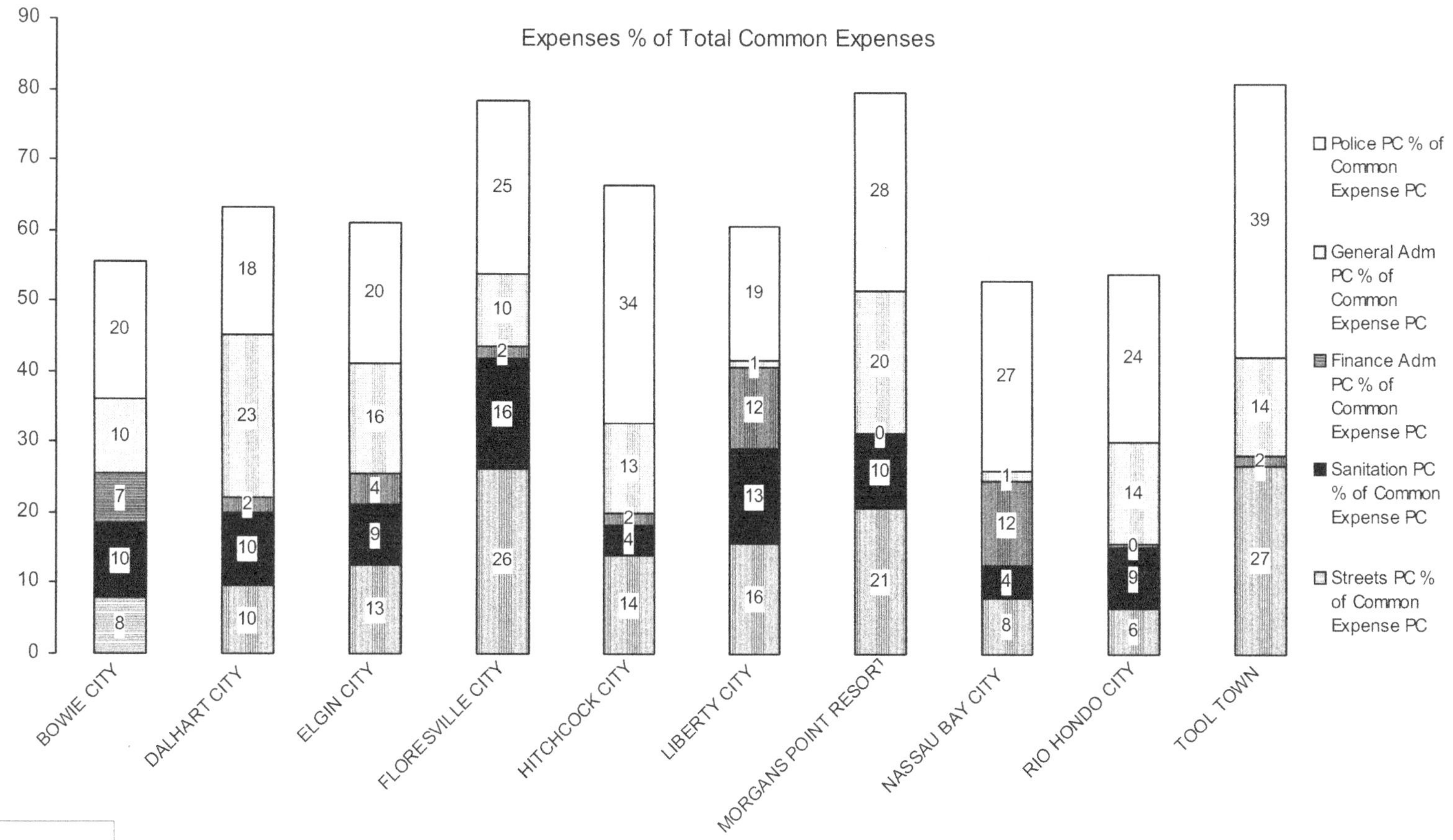

Group TX22

	Population	Streets PC % of Common Expense PC	Sanitation PC % of Common Expense PC	Finance Adm PC % of Common Expense PC	General Adm PC % of Common Expense PC	Police PC % of Common Expense PC
Averages	5667.9	15	9	4	12	25

Which departments are better funded than others ?

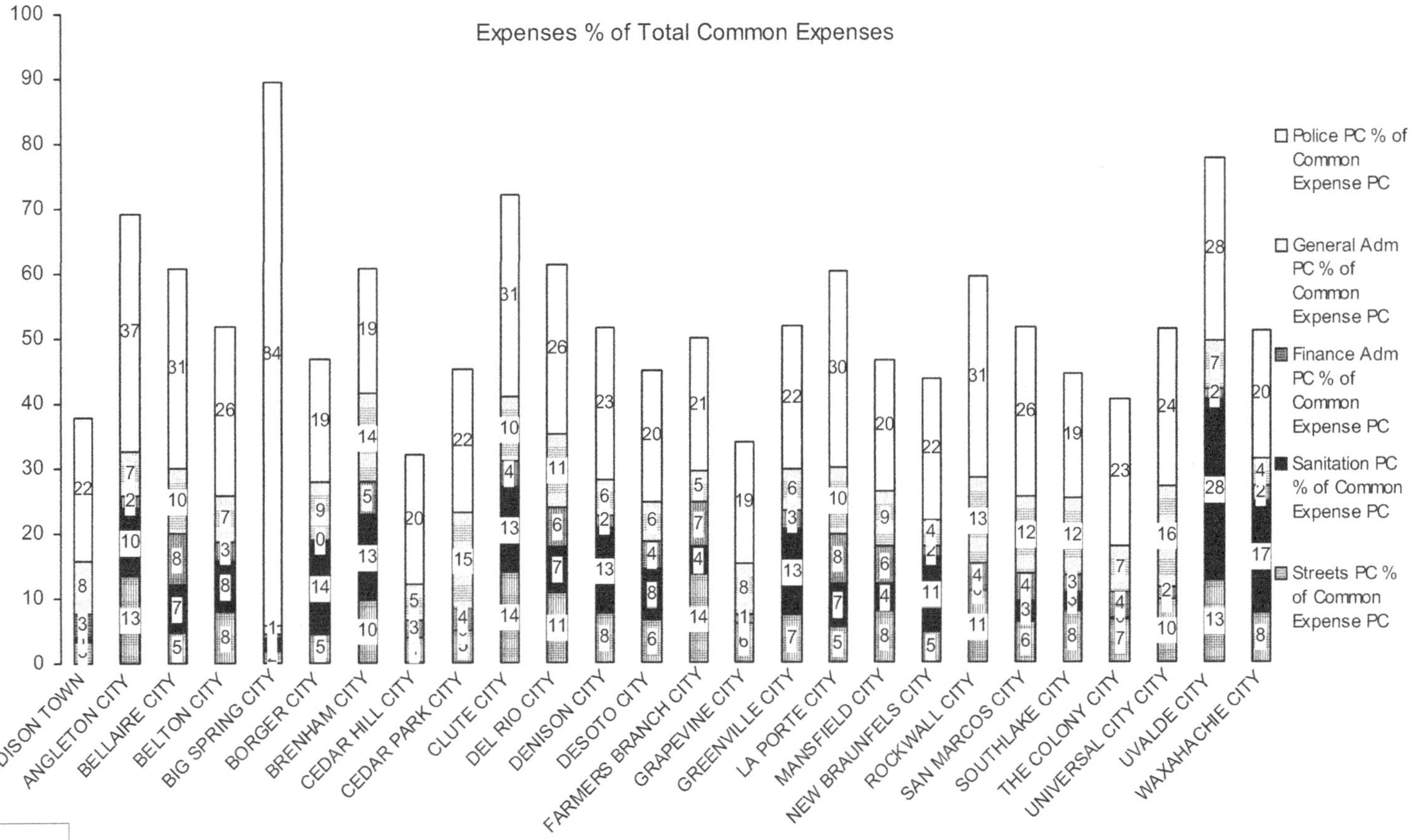

Group TX23

	Population	Streets PC % of Common Expense PC	Sanitation PC % of Common Expense PC	Finance Adm PC % of Common Expense PC	General Adm PC % of Common Expense PC	Police PC % of Common Expense PC
Averages	28323	8	7	4	9	26

Which departments are better funded than others ?

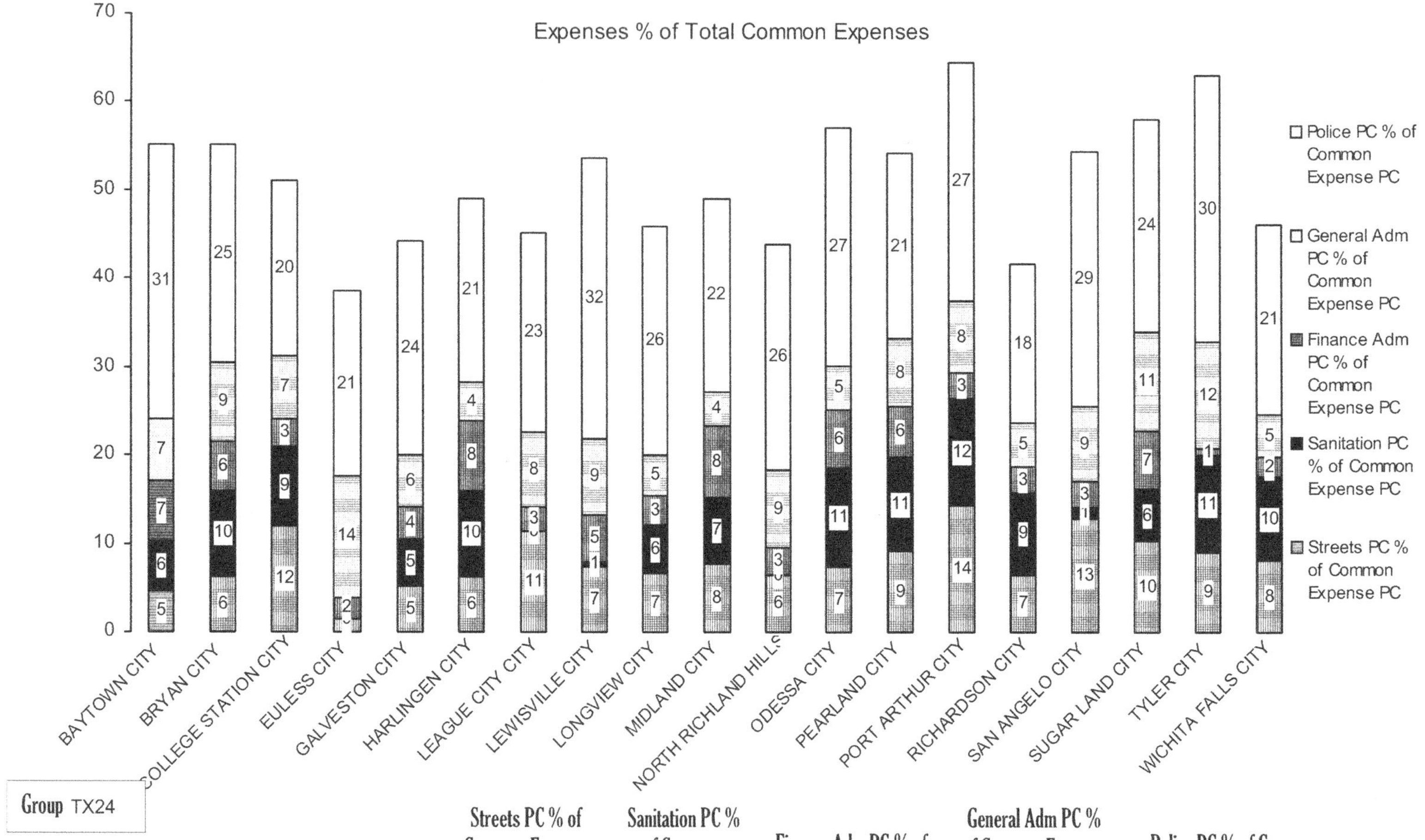

	Population	Streets PC % of Common Expense PC	Sanitation PC % of Common Expense PC	Finance Adm PC % of Common Expense PC	General Adm PC % of Common Expense PC	Police PC % of Common Expense PC
Averages	75138	8	7	4	8	25

Which departments are better funded than others ?

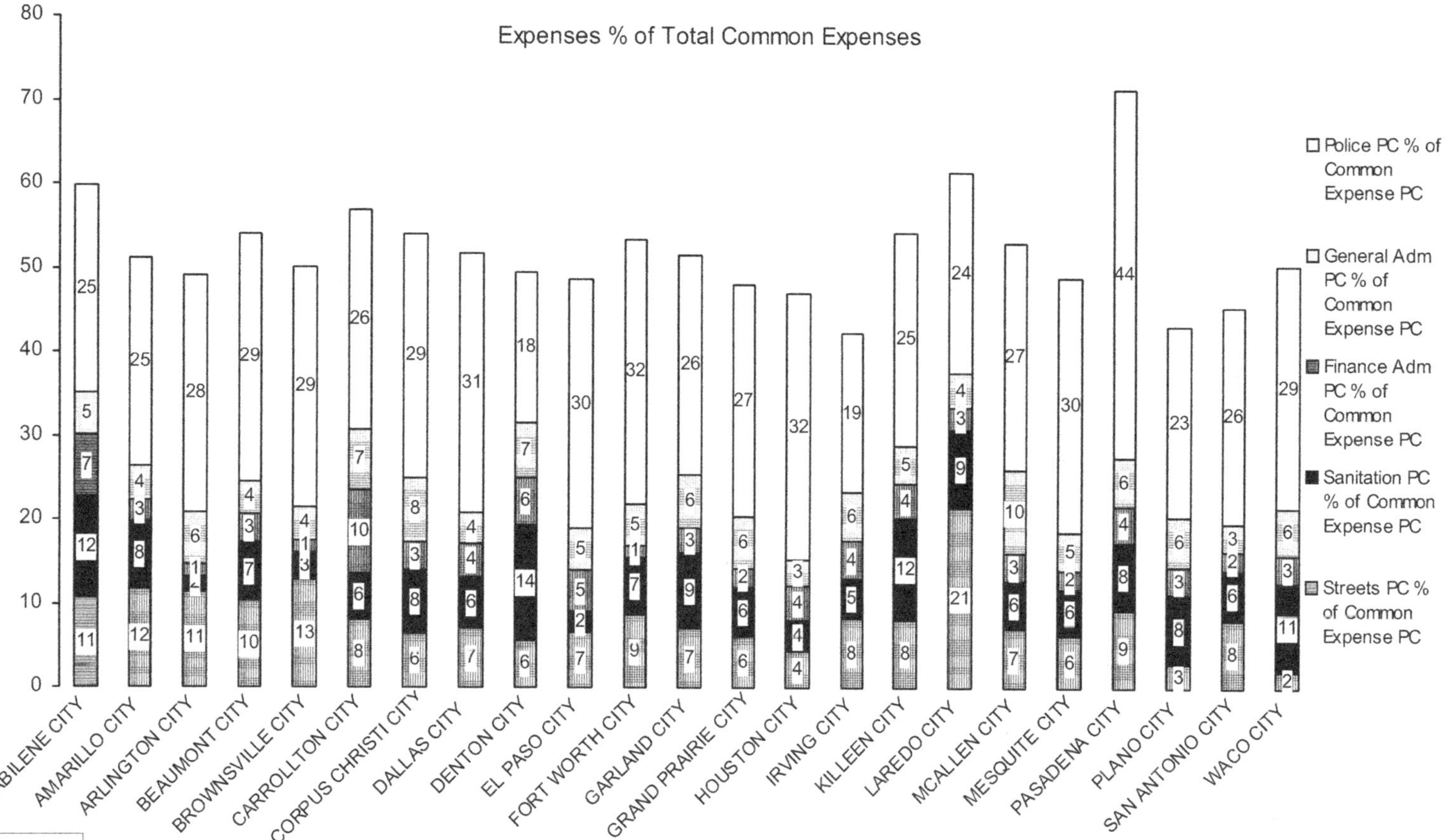

Group TX25

	Population	Streets PC % of Common Expense PC	Sanitation PC % of Common Expense PC	Finance Adm PC % of Common Expense PC	General Adm PC % of Common Expense PC	Police PC % of Common Expense PC
Averages	382050	8	7	4	5	28

D1 Are there Debt Issues in Your Near Future?

This is one graph to find if debt ratios are presenting any concern. By comparing your government to other governments of similar size and type (we call 'peer groups'), you can see if your government is in the normal range of debt burden per capita.

In this example, the group is AL23, that is Alabama='**AL**', cities='**2**', and size class of 10,000 to 50,000 population='**3**'. So this is displayed as: **'Group AL23'**.

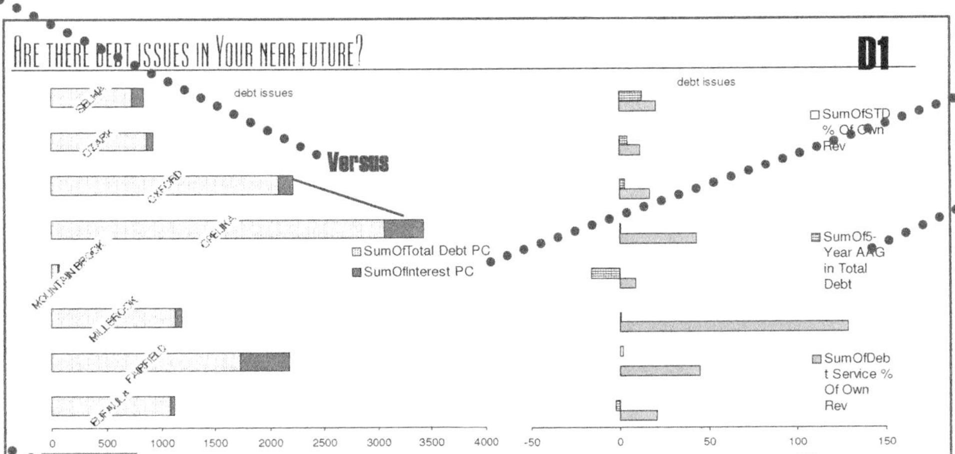

Group AL23

Name	State Abb	Population	Total Debt PC	Interest PC	Interest Rate	Debt Service % Of Own Rev	Gen Govt Debt Service	STD % Of Own Rev	5-Year AAG in Total Debt	5-Year AAG in GO Debt
MOUNTAIN BROOK	AL	19938	62	8	12.90%	9	2266	0	-16	0
OXFORD	AL	15212	2077	133	6.40%	17	3764	0	3	3
OPELIKA	AL	23608	3063	366	11.95%	43	15859	0	1	-2
OZARK	AL	14987	869	57	6.56%	12	1319	0	5	46
SELMA	AL	19630	730	106	14.52%	21	4771	0	13	8
FAIRFIELD	AL	11918	1727	451	26.11%	45	7829	2	0	-1
MILLBROOK	AL	11465	1130	61	5.40%	128	6033	0	1	0
EUFAULA	AL	13651	1080	44	4.07%	21	2137	0	-2	-4
		Average	1342.3	37.0					0.6	6.3

Legend

D1 — Listed in order of use on chart, top to bottom

- Total Debt Per Capita
- Total Interest Per Capita
- STD % of Own Revenue
- 5-year Avg Annual Growth in Total Debt
- Debt Service % of Own Revenue

(Ignore the prefix "sumof" or "sumoftotal" in the legend, the system inserts this automatically.)

Finding Your City or County

Each government is found & compared within its peer group. Peer groups are defined by their state/region, their type of government, and their size class. So, 'XX' for the state or region abbreviation. Then type: 1=counties, 2=cities, towns. Then population size class: 1=under 2,000 population, 2=2,000-10,000, 3=10,000-50,000, 4=50,000-100,000, 5=100,000-250,000, 6=over 250,000.

This graph also includes data from various sections in the ***Governments of Your State*** book: Total Funds Flow, among other sections. For the greater detail, see these sections, in your state's book.

Texas graph D1 TX-000

Are there debt concerns in Your near future?

D1

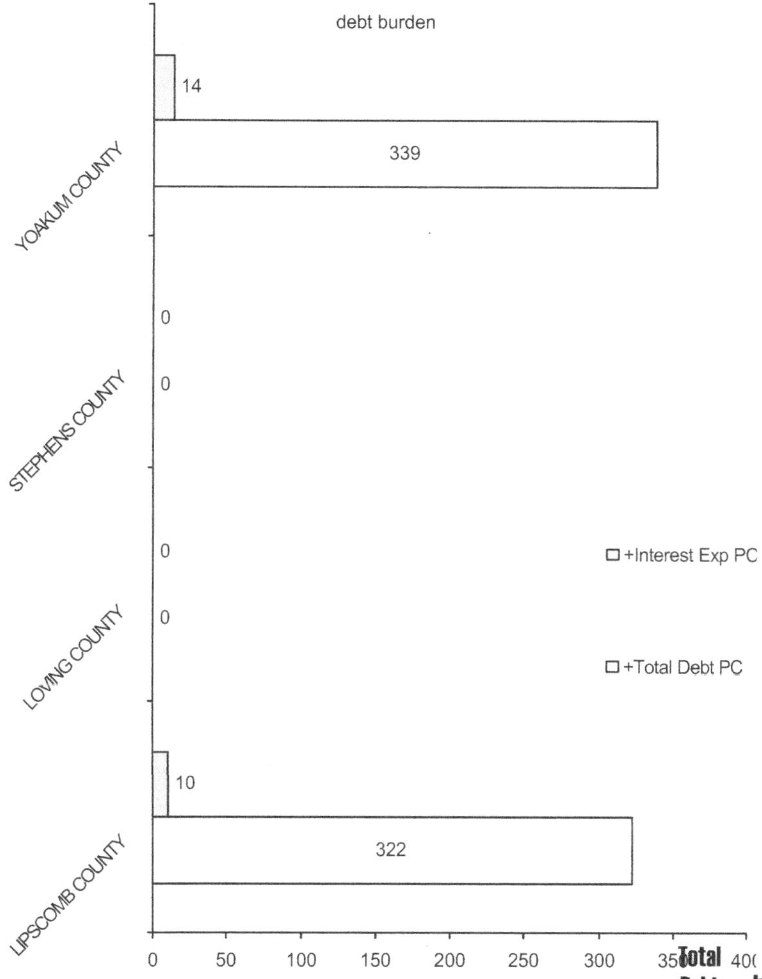

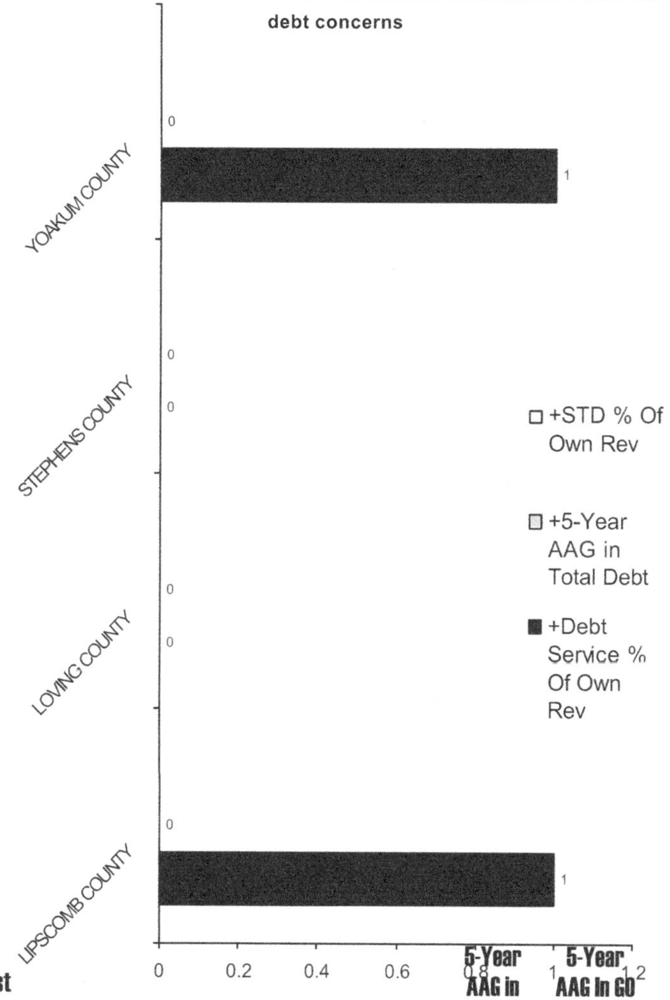

Population	Total Debt PC	Interest PC
Average	165.3	0.5

5-Year AAG in Total Debt	5-Year AAG In GO Debt
0.0	0.0

Group TX12

Are there debt concerns in Your near future? D1

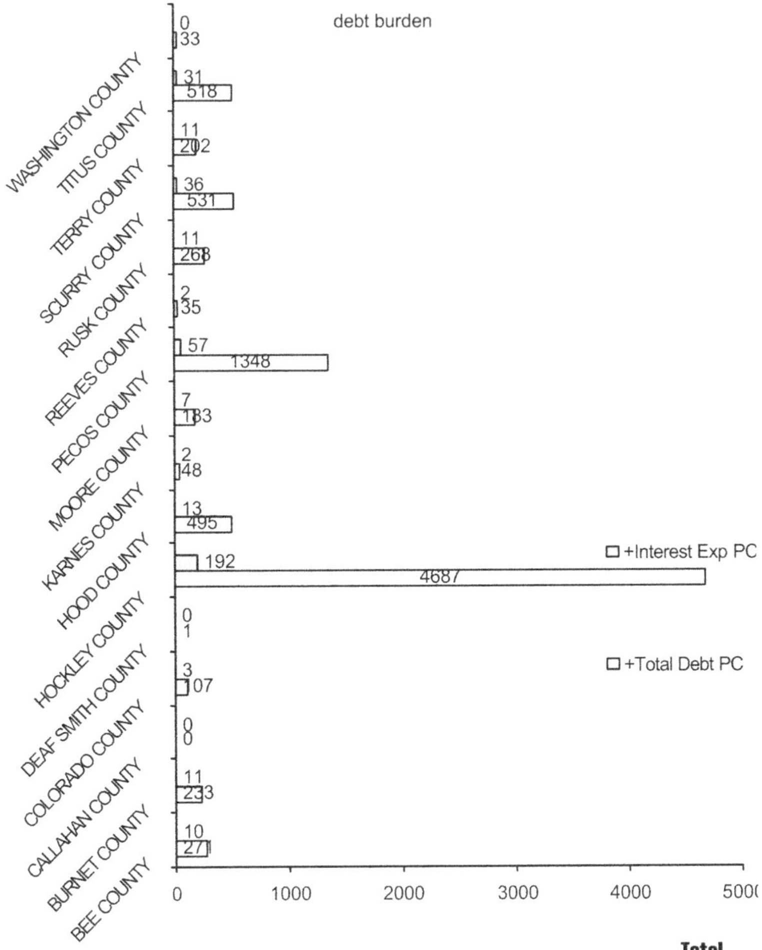

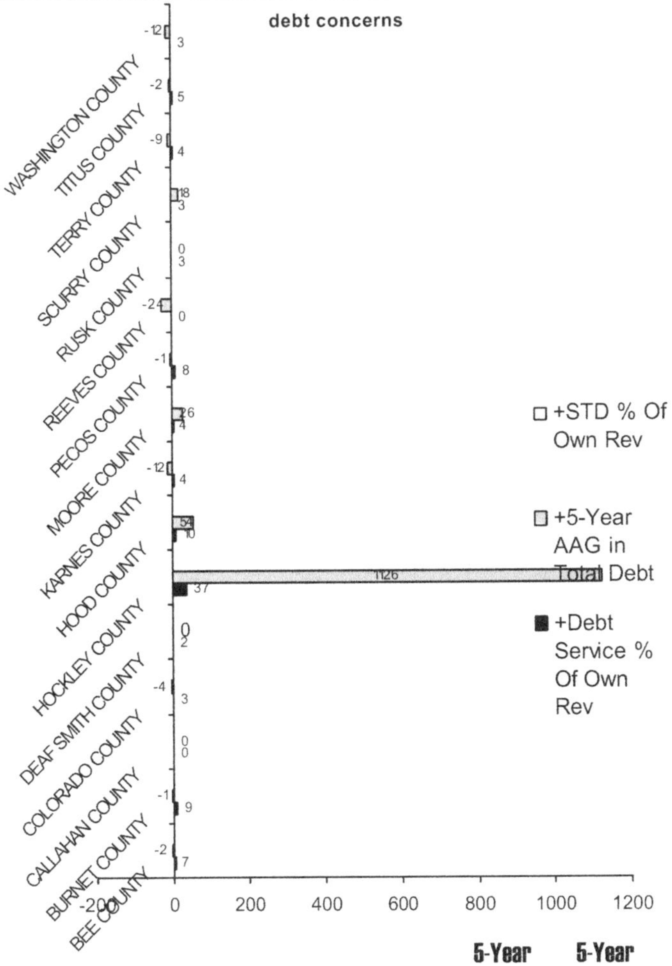

	Population	Total Debt PC	Interest PC	5-Year AAG in Total Debt	5-Year AAG In GO Debt
Group TX13	Average	560.0	6.4	72.3	6.3

Are there debt concerns in Your near future?

D1

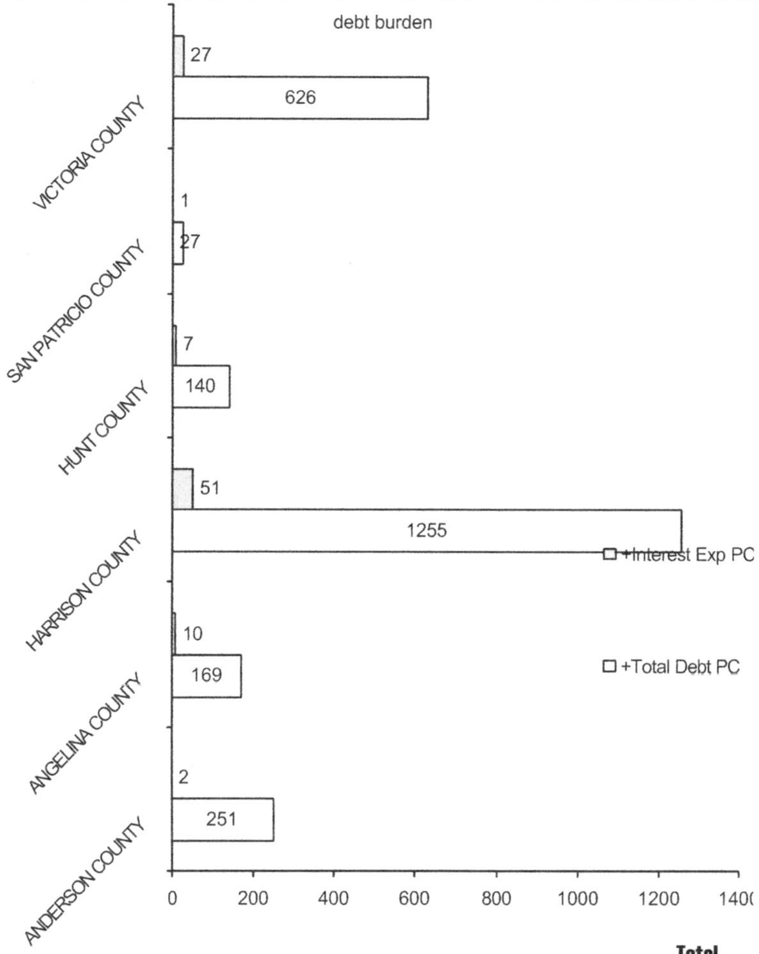

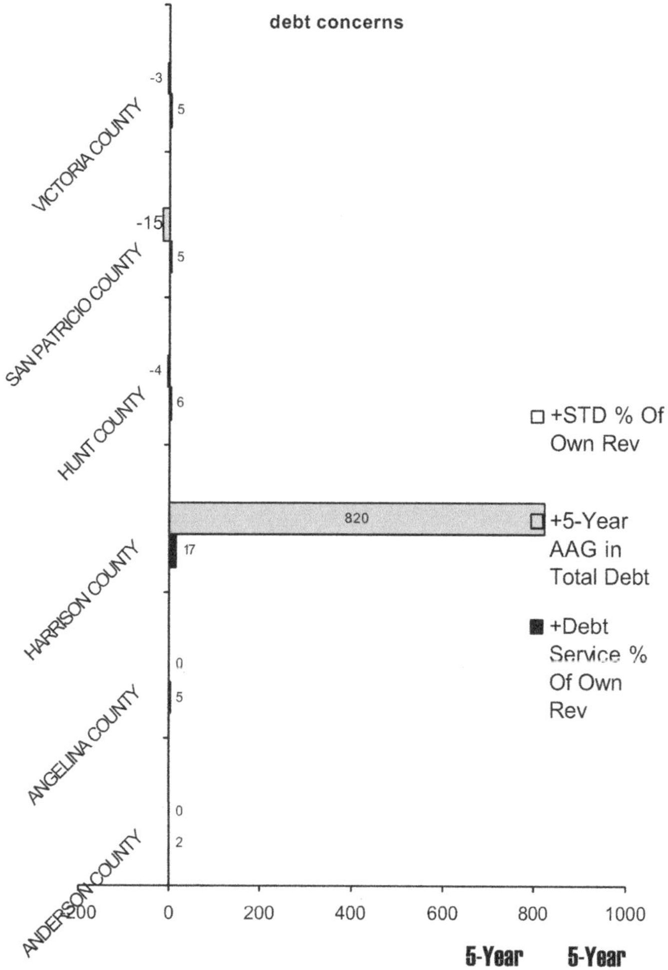

	Population	Total Debt PC	Interest PC	5-Year AAG in Total Debt	5-Year AAG in GO Debt
Group TX14	Average	411.3	6.7	133.0	7.3

Are there debt concerns in Your near future?

D1

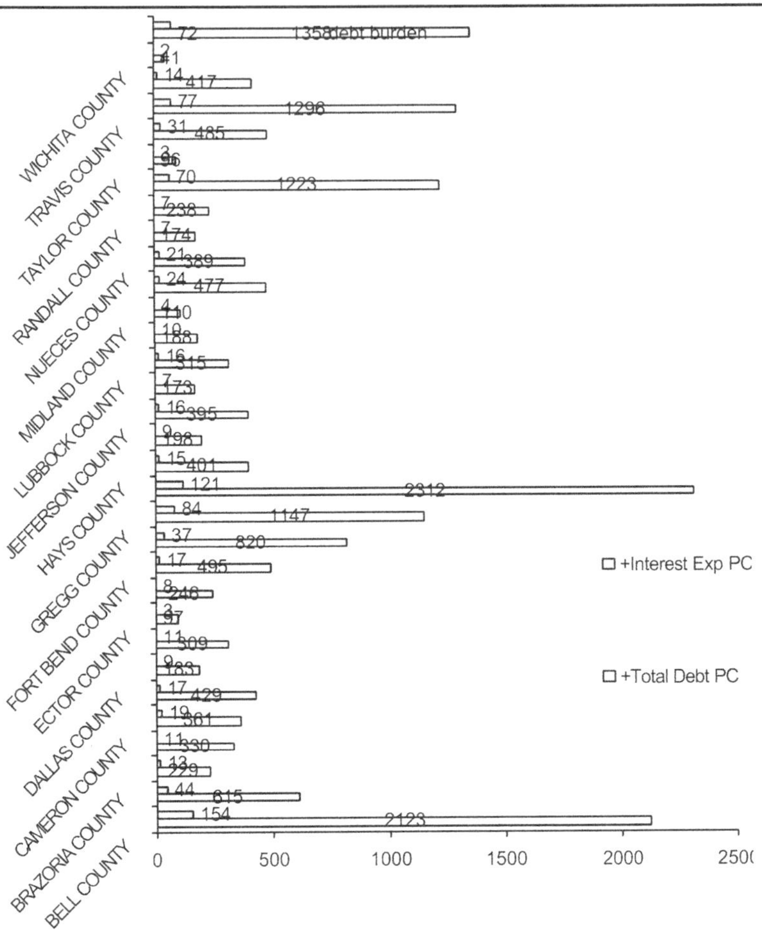

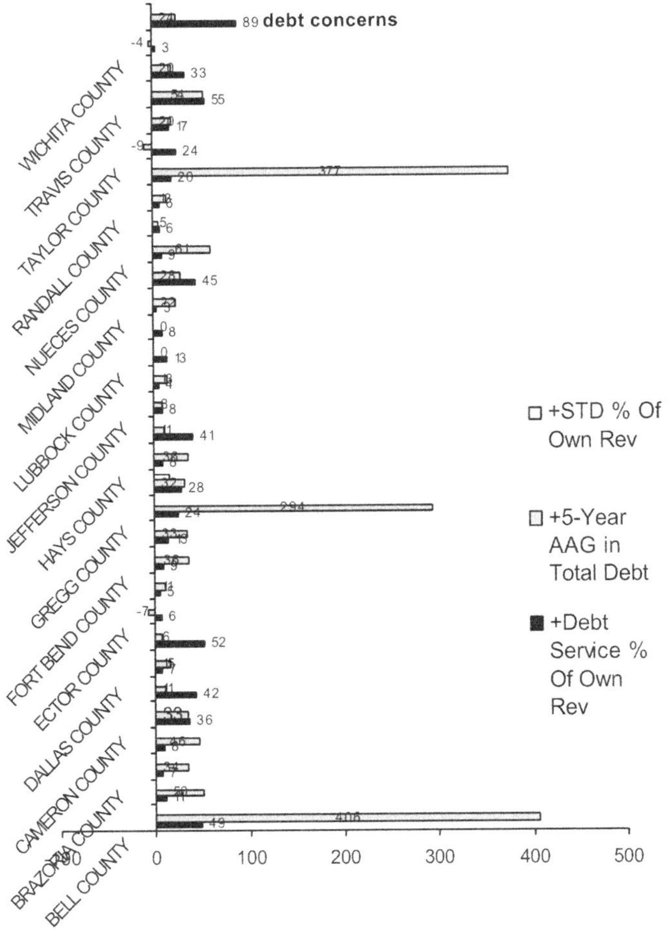

	Population	Total Debt PC	Interest PC	5-Year AAG in Total Debt	5-Year AAG In GO Debt
	Average	552.2	21.5	52.5	20.3

Group TX15

Are there debt concerns in Your near future?

D1

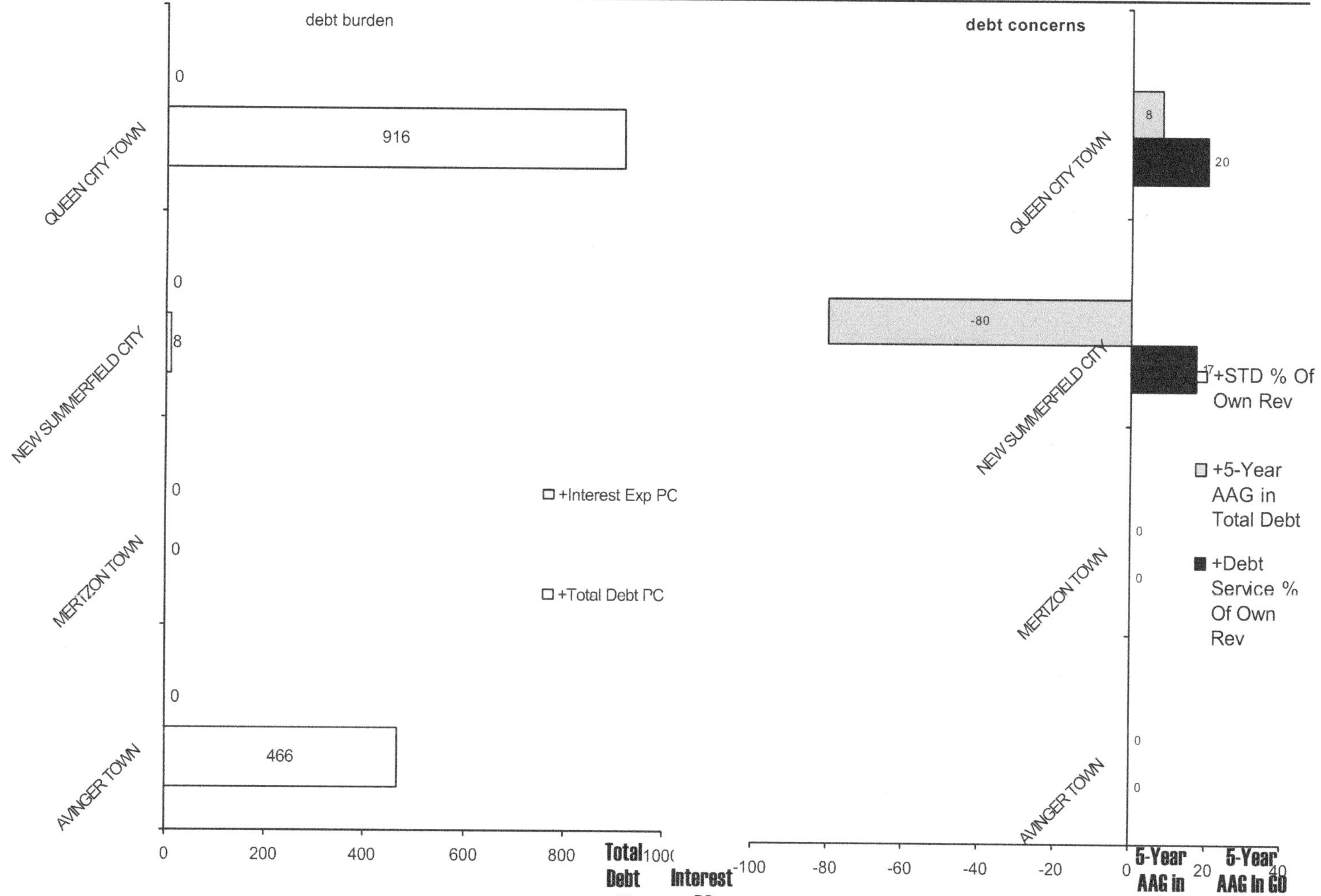

Population	Total Debt PC	Interest PC	5-Year AAG in Total Debt	5-Year AAG in GO Debt
Average	347.5	9.3	-18.0	-13.5

Group TX21

Are there debt concerns in Your near future? D1

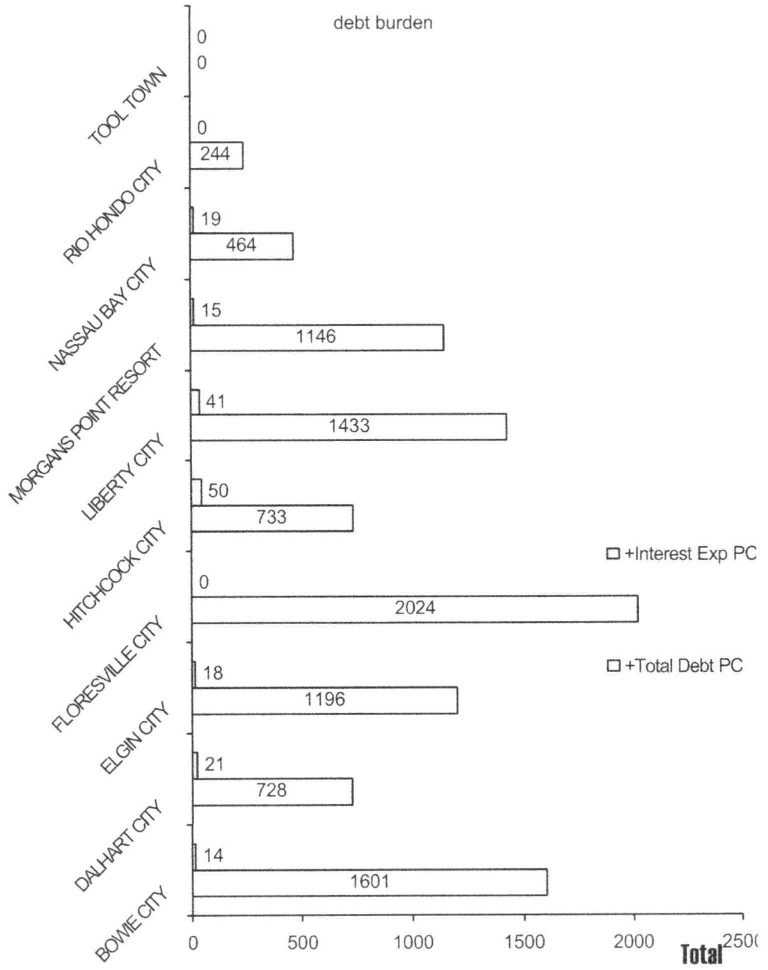

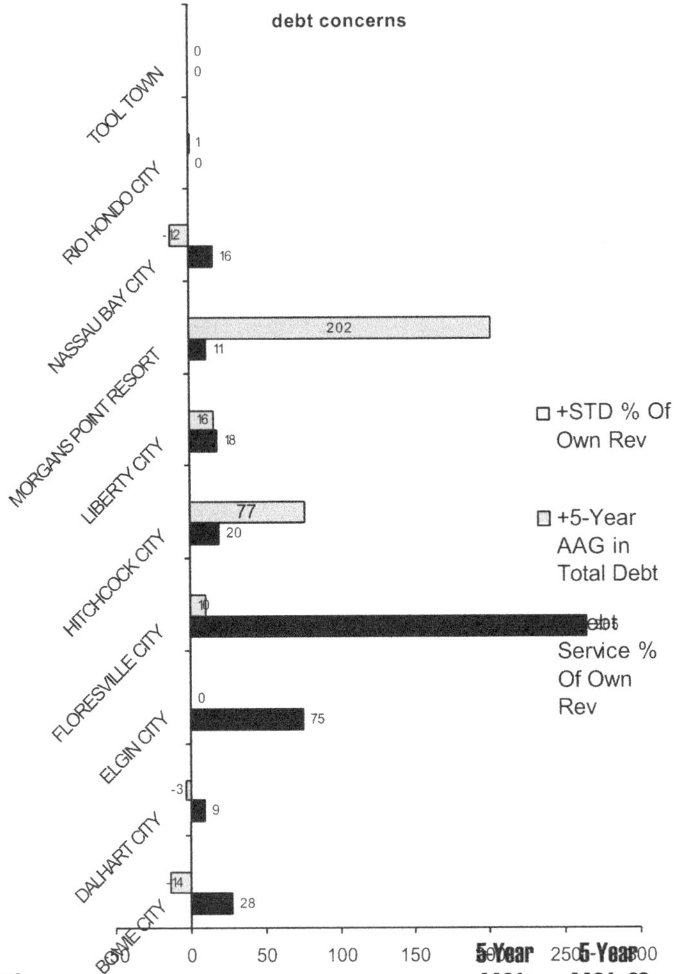

	Population	Total Debt PC	Interest PC	5-Year AAG in Total Debt	5-Year AAG in GO Debt
Average		956.9	44.2	27.7	174.7

Group TX22

Are there debt concerns in Your near future?

D1

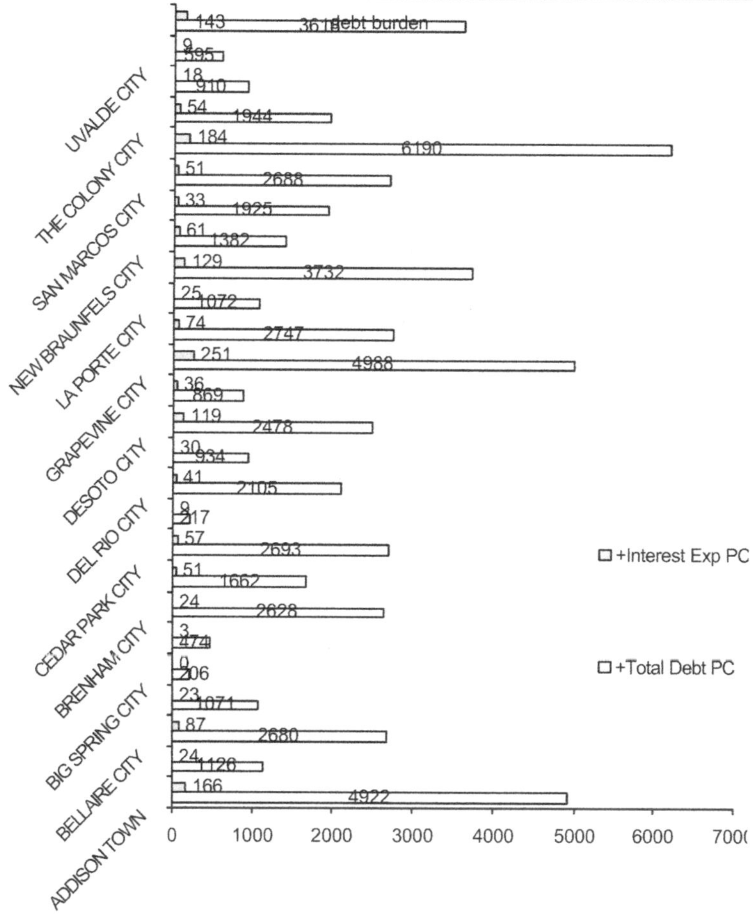

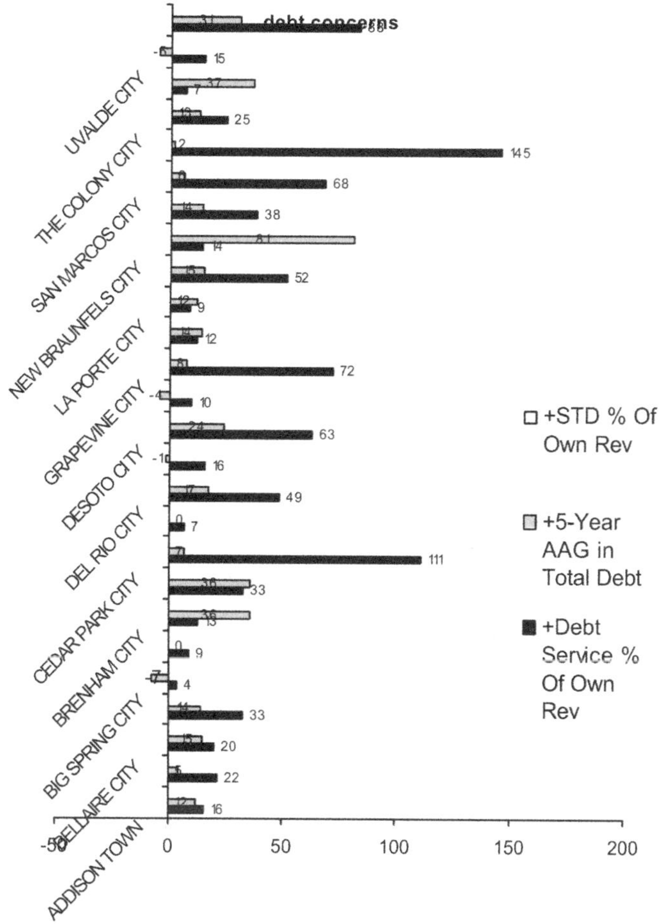

Group TX23	Population	Total Debt PC	Interest PC	5-Year AAG in Total Debt	5-Year AAG in GO Debt
	Average	2148.3	36.4	14.7	38.1

Are there debt concerns in Your near future?

D1

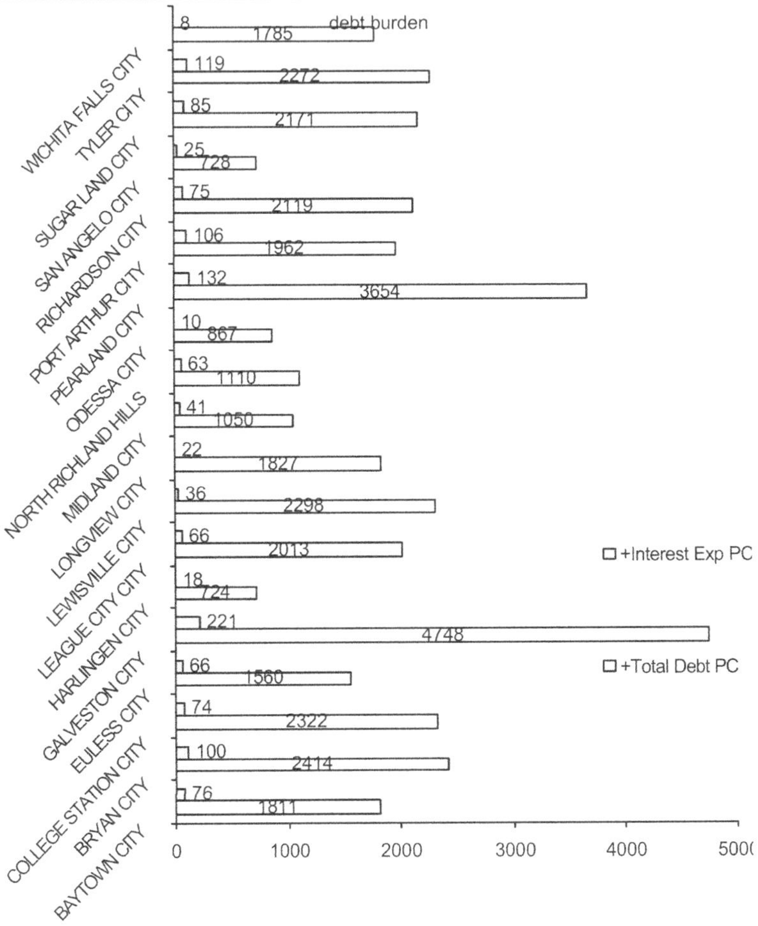

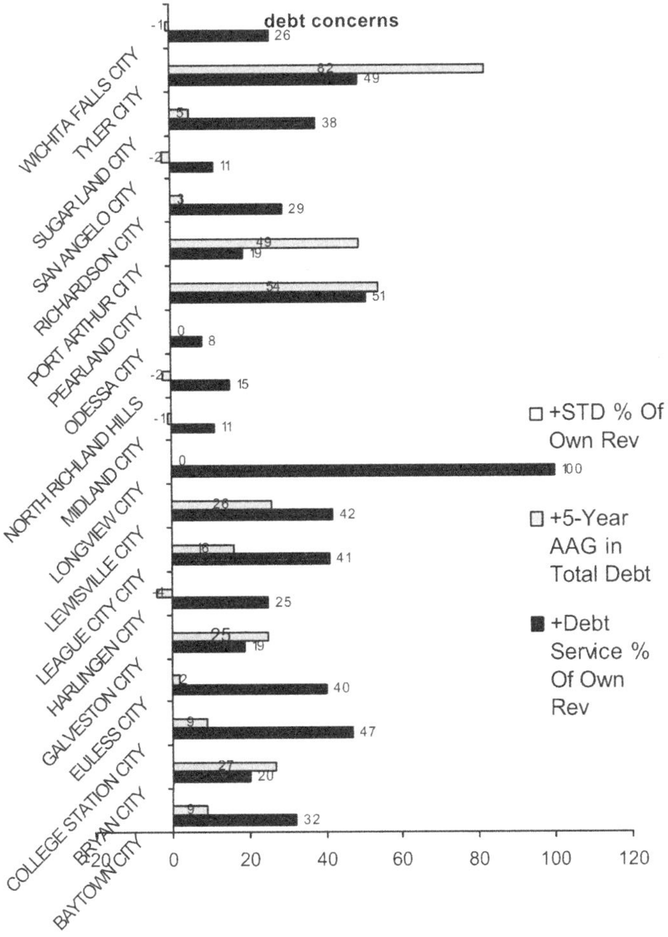

	Population	Total Debt PC	Interest PC	5-Year AAG in Total Debt	5-Year AAG In GO Debt
Group TX24	Average	1970.3	32.8	15.6	54.0

Are there debt concerns in Your near future?

D1

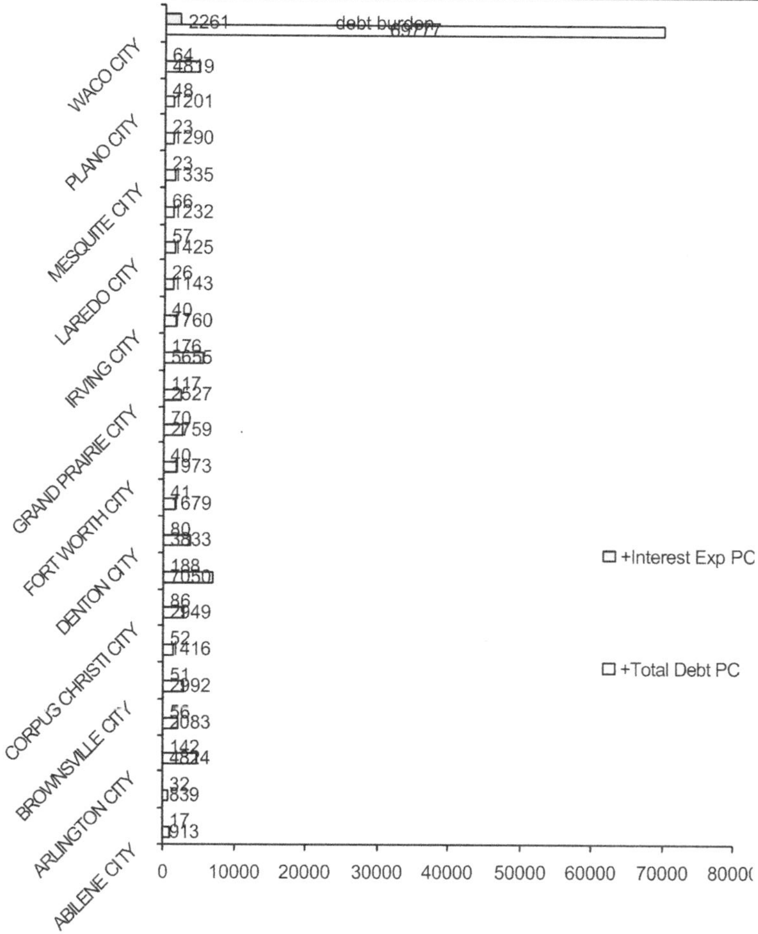

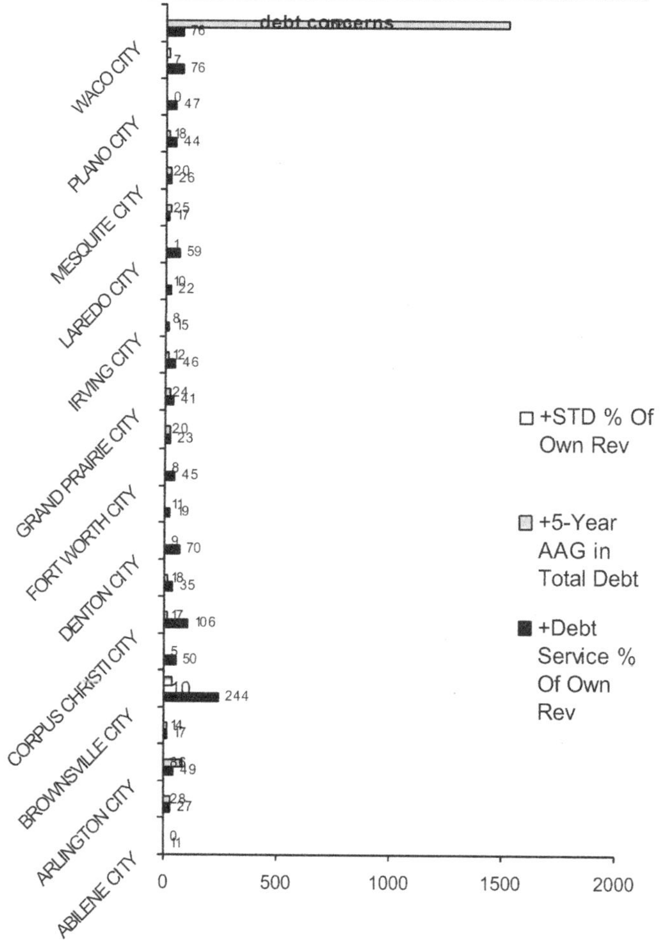

	Population	Total Debt PC	Interest PC	5-Year AAG in Total Debt	5-Year AAG In GO Debt
Group TX25	Average	5455.4	50.7	81.5	49.7

E1 Can Your Employee Staffing Comparison Save Your Budget?

This is one of 2 graphs to help with staffing level strategies. By comparing your government to other governments of similar size and type (we call 'peer groups'), you can see if others are performing similar functions with more or less employees than your government.

Legend

Listed in order of use on chart, top to bottom

- General Adm., Employee / 10K Capita
- Parks & Recreation Employee / 10K Capita
- Street Maint.Expense Employee / 10K Capita
- Police Expense Employee / 10K Capita
- Finance Adm. Expense Employee / 10K Capita

(Ignore the prefix "sumof" or "sumoftotal" in the legend, the system inserts this automatically.)

In this example, the group is AL13, that is Alabama='**AL**', counties='**1**', and size class of 10,000 to 50,000 population='**3**'. So this is displayed as: **'Group AL13'**.

CAN YOUR EMPLOYEE STAFFING COMPARISON SAVE YOU MONEY? OR JUSTIFY ADDITIONAL STAFFING? E1

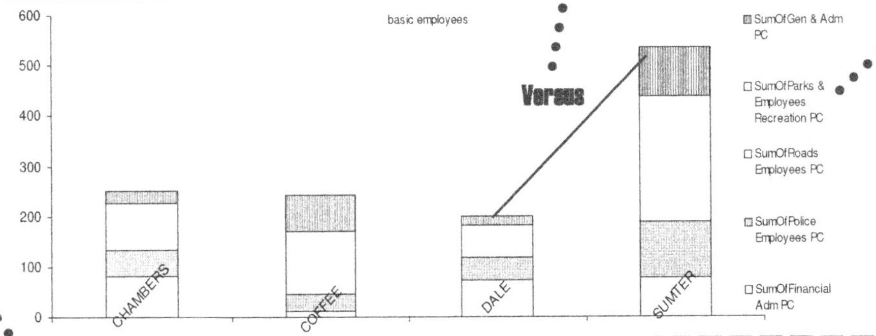

Group AL13

State Abbr	Name	Population	Total Full Time Employees	Total Wages For Basic Services	Total Basic Wages PC	Financial Adm PC	Police Employees PC	Fire Employees PC	Roads Employees PC	Parks Employees Recreation PC	Gen Adm PC
AL	CHAMBERS	36251	372	3093	85	82	52	0	93	0	24
AL	COFFEE	43878	360	3650	83	11	34	0	125	0	72
AL	DALE	49186	298	2896	59	73	44	0	65	0	18
AL	SUMTER	14376	709	2911	202	76	111	0	250	0	97
		Averages	434.8	3137.5	107.3	60.5	60.3	0.0	133.3	0.0	52.8

This graph also includes data from various sections in the ***Governments of Your State*** book: Total Funds Flow, among other sections. For the greater detail, see these sections, in your state's book.

Finding Your City or County

Each government is found & compared within its peer group. Groups are defined by their state/region, their type of government, and their size class. So, 'XX' for the state or region abbreviation. Then type: 1=counties, 2=cities, towns. Then population size class: 1=under 2,000 population, 2=2,000-10,000, 3=10,000-50,000, 4=50,000-100,000, 5=100,000-250,000, 6=over 250,000.

Texas graph E1 TX-000

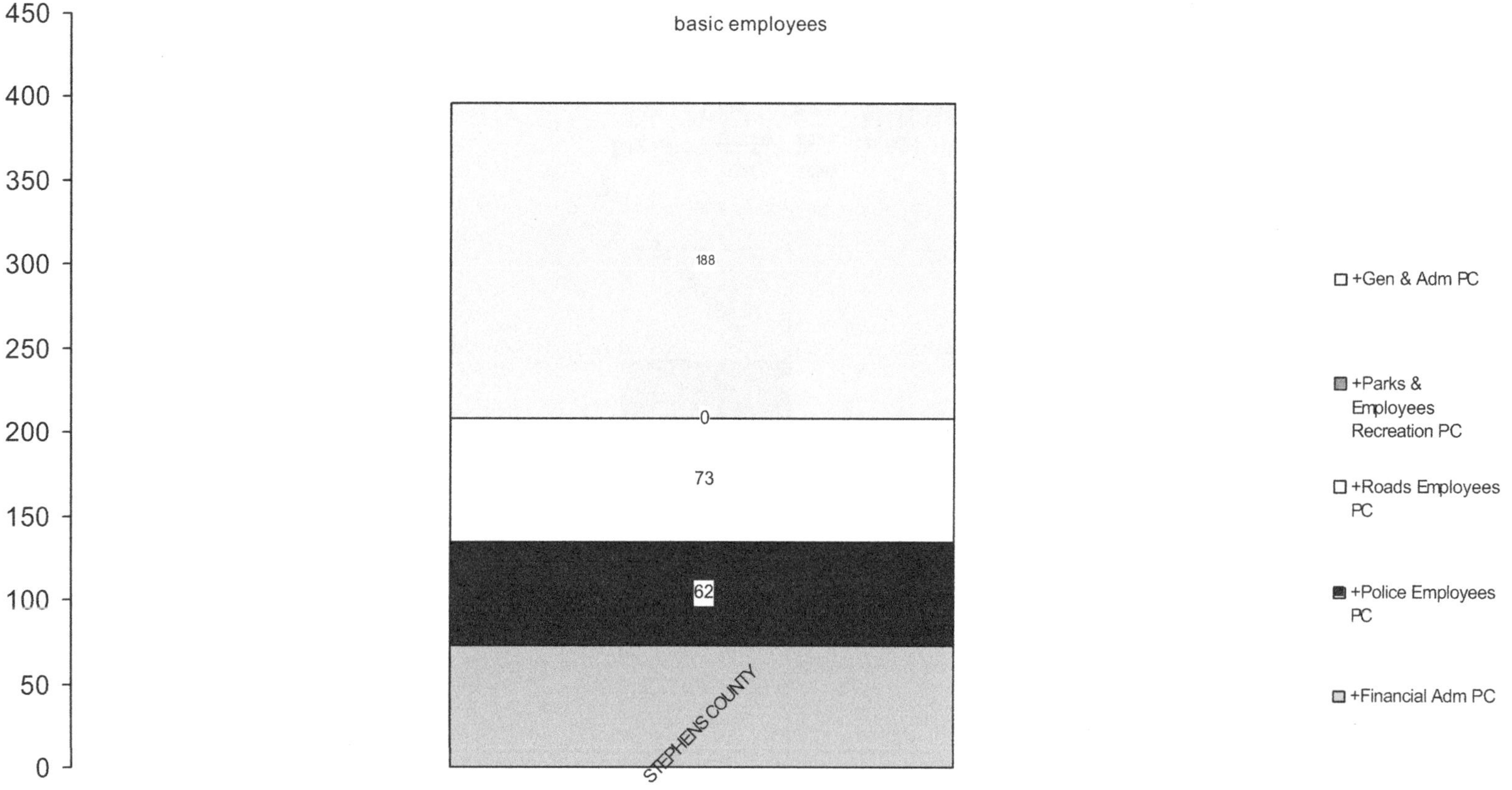

Group **TX12**

	Total Full Time Employees	Total Wages For Basic Services	Total Basic Wages PC	Financial Adm PC	Police Employees PC	Fire Employees PC	Roads Employees PC	Parks Employees Recreation PC	Gen Adm PC
Averages	1568.0	1365.0	143.0	22.0	62.0	0.0	73.0	0.0	188.0

Can your employee staffing comparison save your budget?

Or justify additional staffing?

E1 2

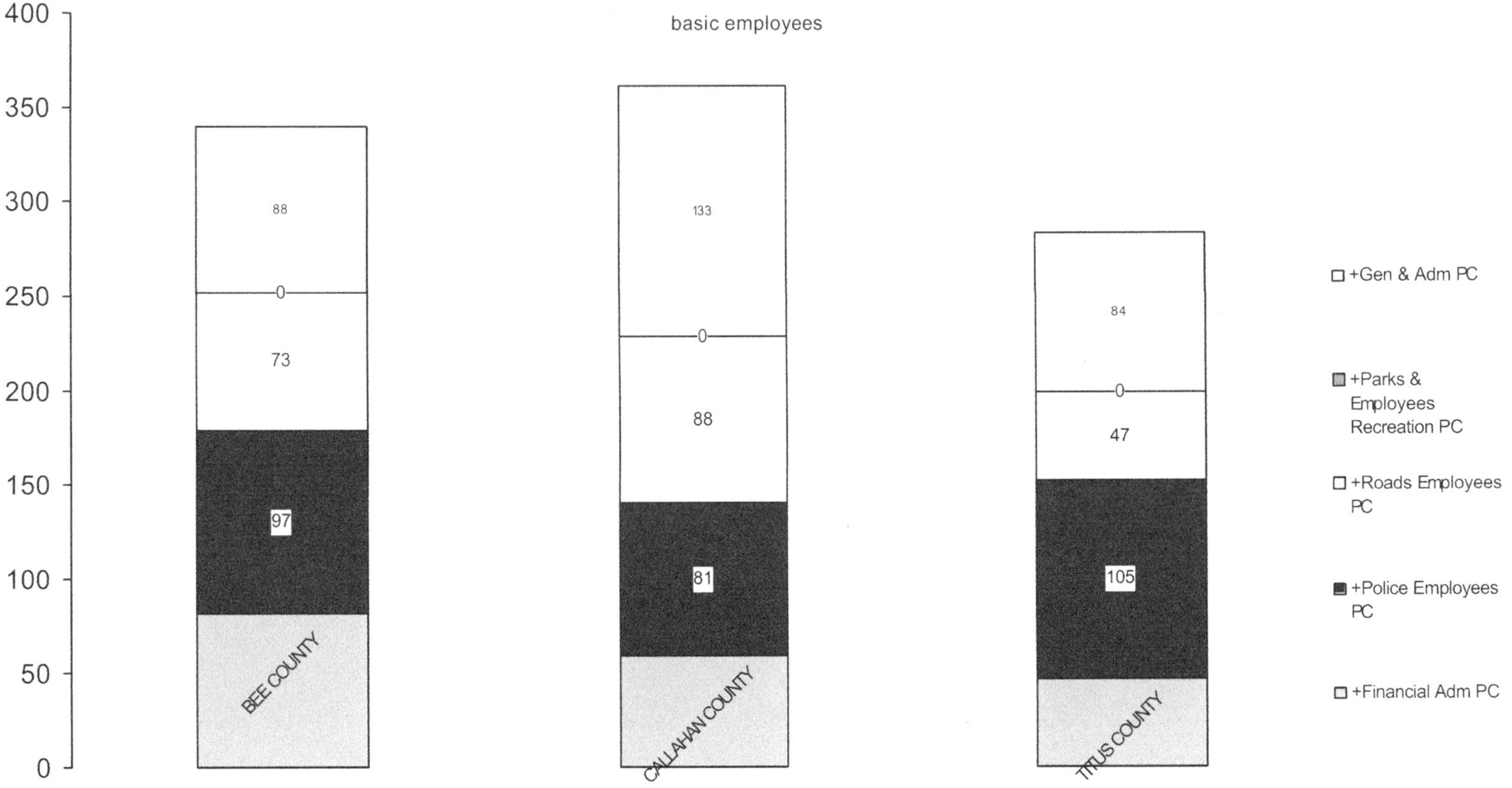

Group **TX13**

	Total Full Time Employees	Total Wages For Basic Services	Total Basic Wages PC	Financial Adm PC	Police Employees PC	Fire Employees PC	Roads Employees PC	Parks Employees Recreation PC	Gen Adm PC
Averages	1127.3	2656.3	101.7	19.3	94.3	0.0	69.3	0.0	101.7

Can your employee staffing comparison save your budget?

Or justify additional staffing?

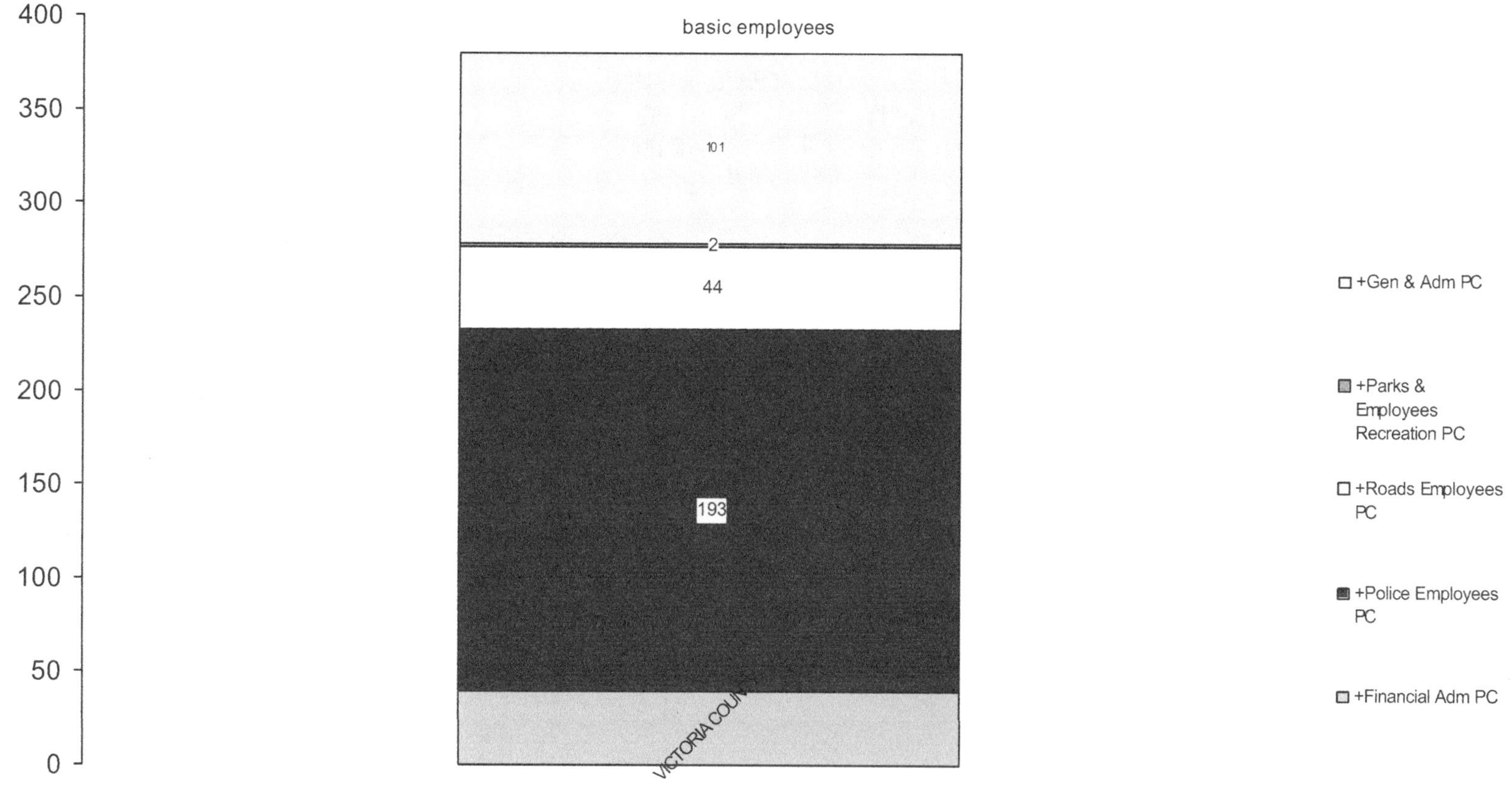

Group **TX14**

	Total Full Time Employees	Total Wages For Basic Services	Total Basic Wages PC	Financial Adm PC	Police Employees PC	Fire Employees PC	Roads Employees PC	Parks Employees Recreation PC	Gen Adm PC
Averages	1990.0	15956.0	186.0	13.0	193.0	4.0	44.0	2.0	101.0

Can your employee staffing comparison save your budget?

Or justify additional staffing?

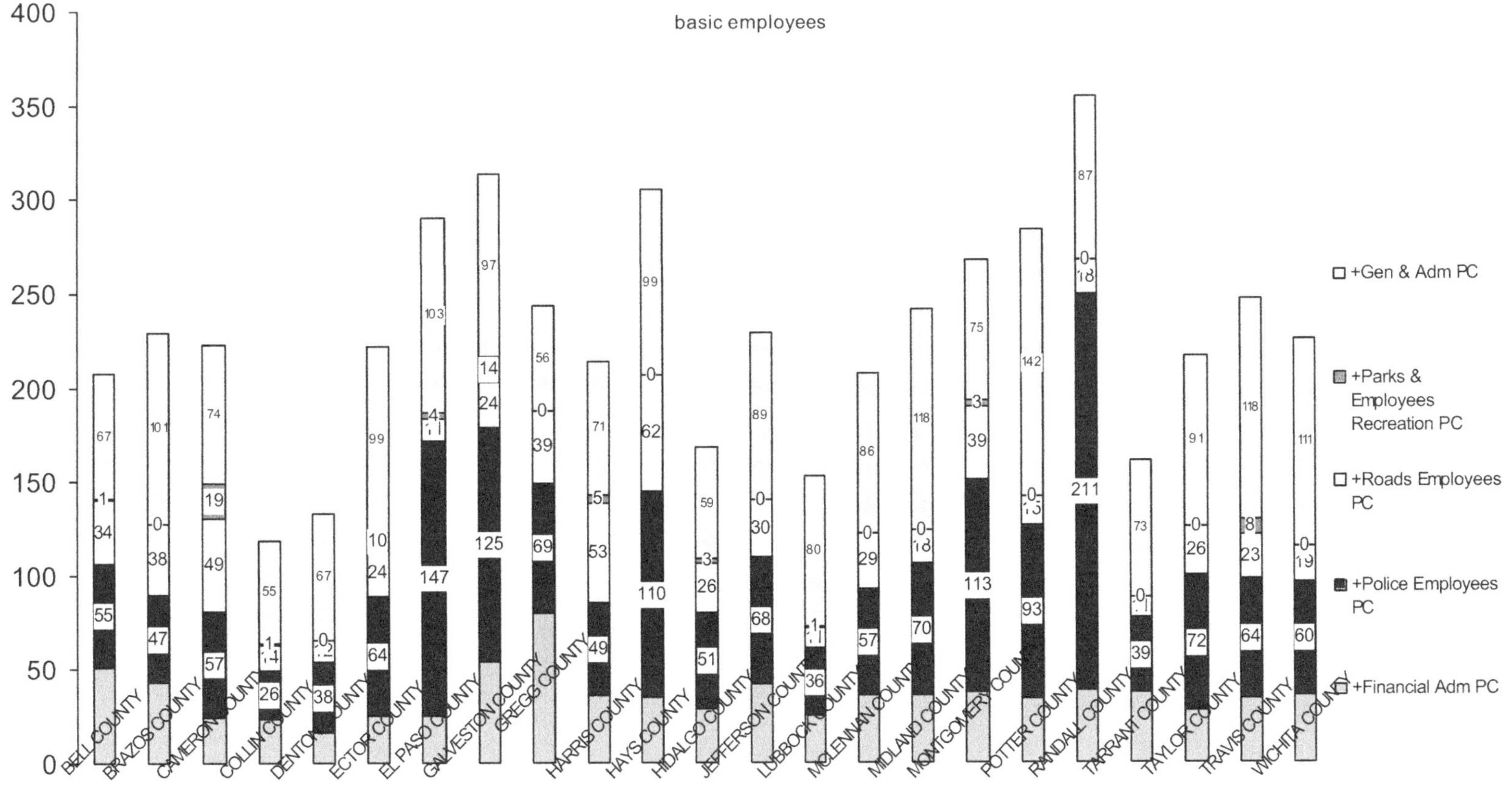

Group **TX15**

	Total Full Time Employees	Total Wages For Basic Services	Total Basic Wages PC	Financial Adm PC	Police Employees PC	Fire Employees PC	Roads Employees PC	Parks Employees Recreation PC	Gen Adm PC
Averages	482.4	67964.5	133.3	17.7	74.8	0.4	27.2	3.0	87.7

Can your employee staffing comparison save your budget? Or justify additional staffing?

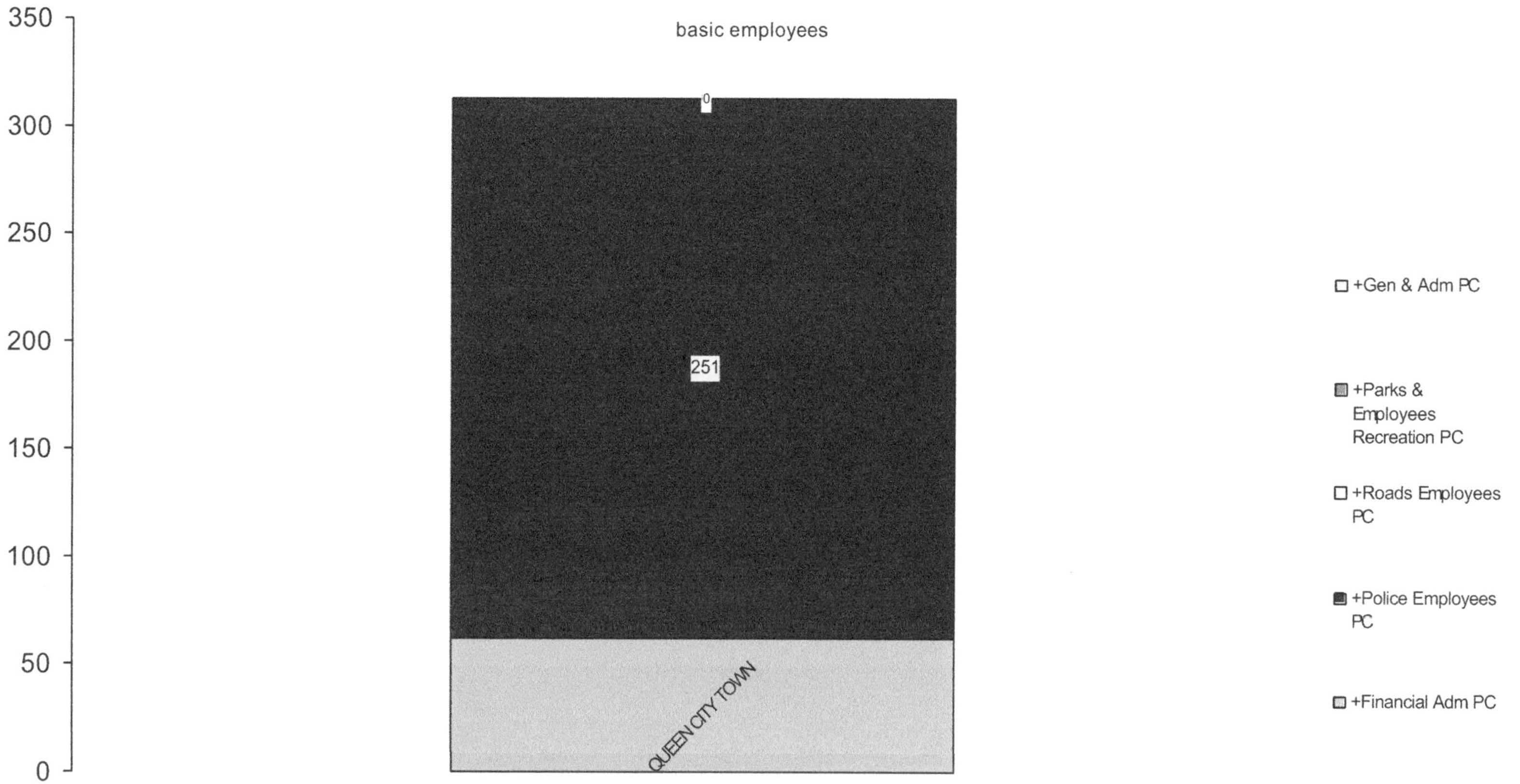

Group **TX21**

	Total Full Time Employees	Total Wages For Basic Services	Total Basic Wages PC	Financial Adm PC	Police Employees PC	Fire Employees PC	Roads Employees PC	Parks Employees Recreation PC	Gen Adm PC
Averages	628.0	175.0	110.0	0.0	251.0	0.0	0.0	0.0	0.0

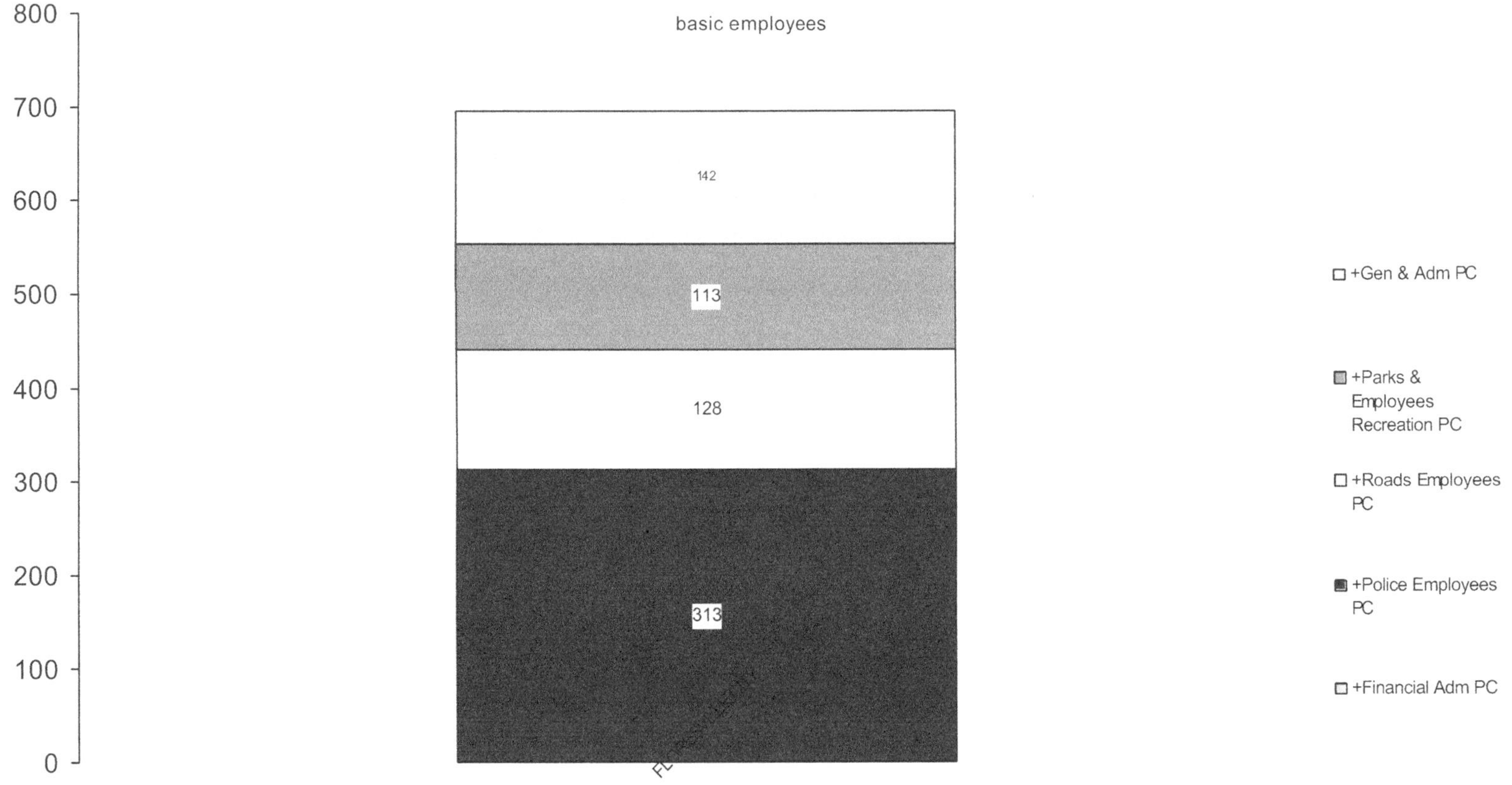

Group **TX22**

	Total Full Time Employees	Total Wages For Basic Services	Total Basic Wages PC	Financial Adm PC	Police Employees PC	Fire Employees PC	Roads Employees PC	Parks Employees Recreation PC	Gen Adm PC
Averages	1936.0	1603.0	228.0	6.0	313.0	0.0	128.0	113.0	142.0

Can your employee staffing comparison save your budget? Or justify additional staffing?

E1 2

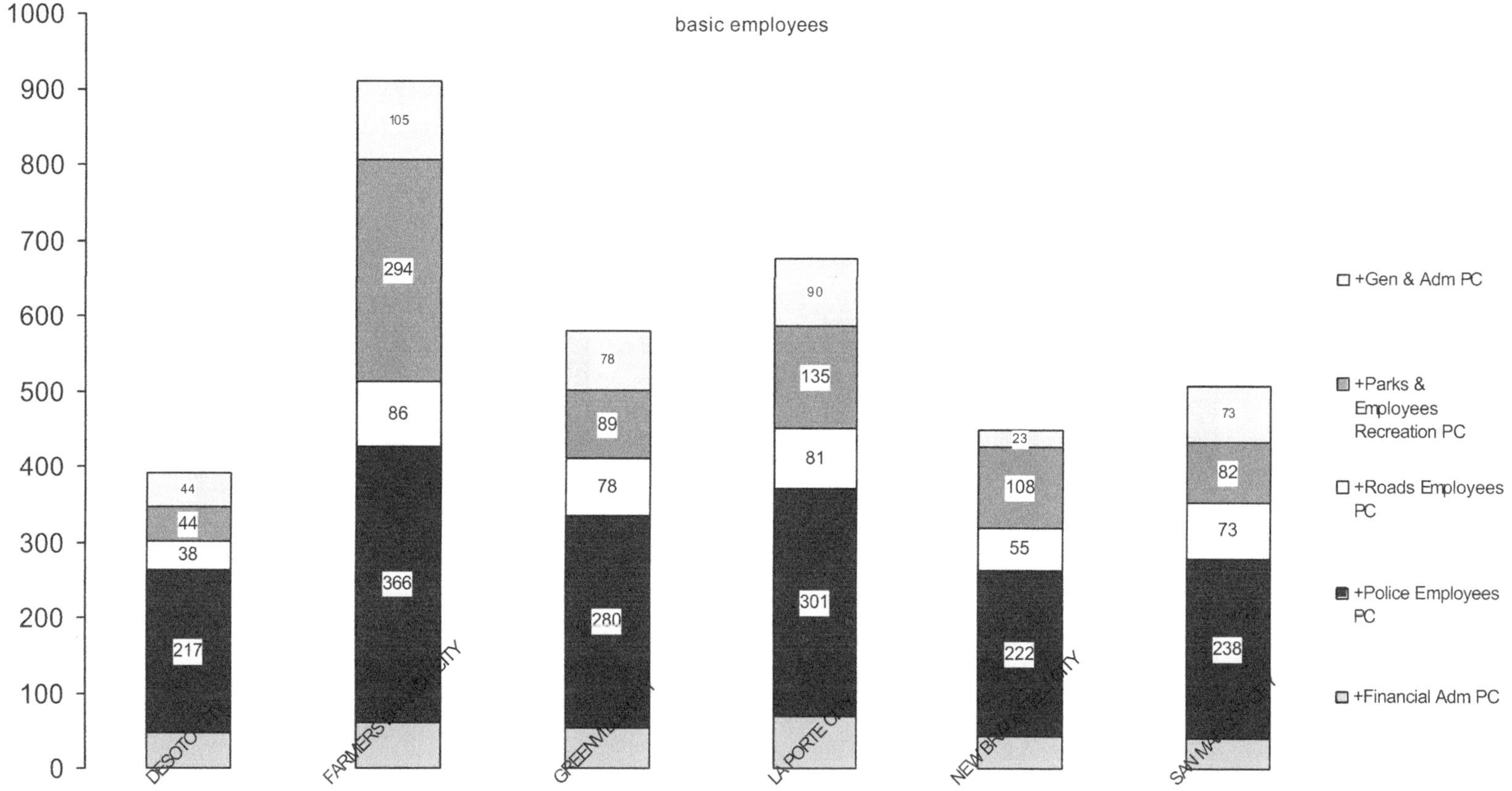

Group **TX23**

	Total Full Time Employees	Total Wages For Basic Services	Total Basic Wages PC	Financial Adm PC	Police Employees PC	Fire Employees PC	Roads Employees PC	Parks Employees Recreation PC	Gen Adm PC
Averages	1186.0	13847.7	393.0	43.3	270.7	158.5	68.5	125.3	68.8

Can your employee staffing comparison save your budget? Or justify additional staffing?

E1 2

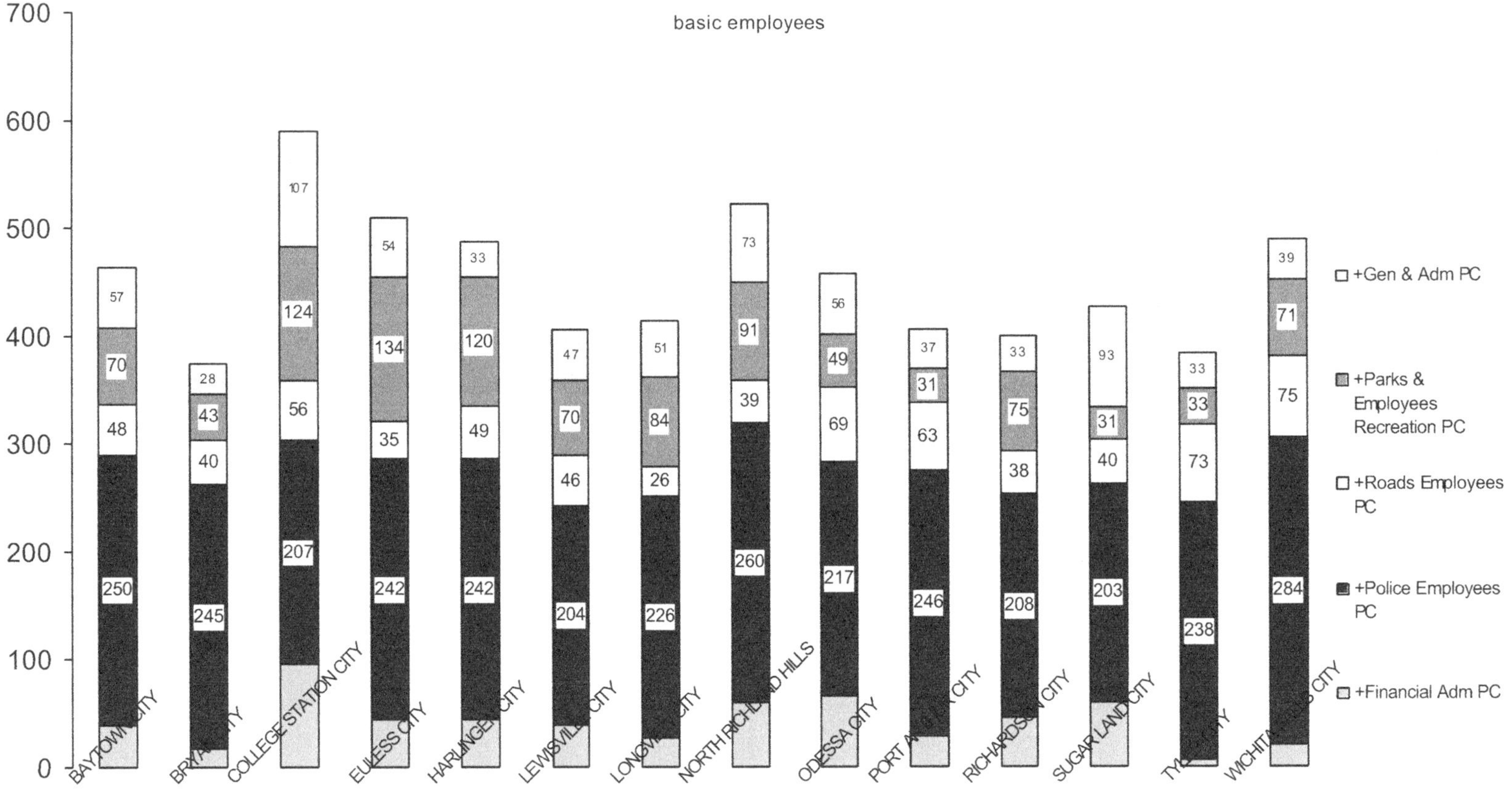

Group **TX24**

	Total Full Time Employees	Total Wages For Basic Services	Total Basic Wages PC	Financial Adm PC	Police Employees PC	Fire Employees PC	Roads Employees PC	Parks Employees Recreation PC	Gen Adm PC
Averages	933.4	23764.4	313.5	29.8	233.7	151.0	49.8	73.3	52.9

Can your employee staffing comparison save your budget?

Or justify additional staffing?

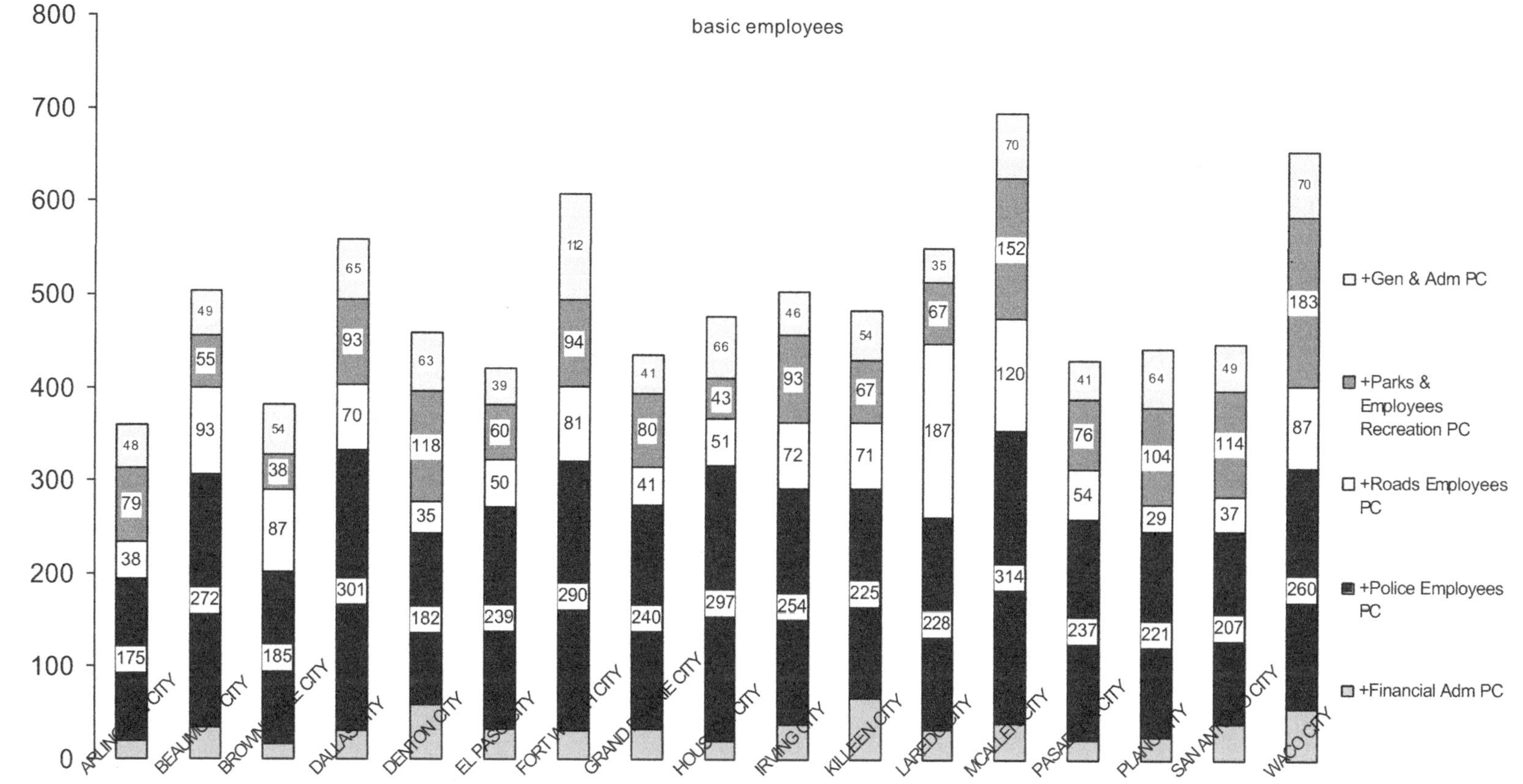

Group **TX25**

	Total Full Time Employees	Total Wages For Basic Services	Total Basic Wages PC	Financial Adm PC	Police Employees PC	Fire Employees PC	Roads Employees PC	Parks Employees Recreation PC	Gen Adm PC
Averages	990.3	158575.5	335.1	22.6	242.8	128.6	70.8	89.2	56.8

E2 Can Employee Productivity Comparison Save You Money?

This is one of 2 graphs to find staffing level adjustments. By comparing your government to other governments of similar size and type (we call 'peer groups'), you can see if others are collecting more taxes per employee or using less overhead than your government.

In this example, the group is AR23, that is Arkansas='**AR**', cities='**2**', and size class of 10,000 to 50,000 population='**3**'. So this is displayed as: **'Group AR23'**.

EMPLOYEE PRODUCTIVITY **E2**

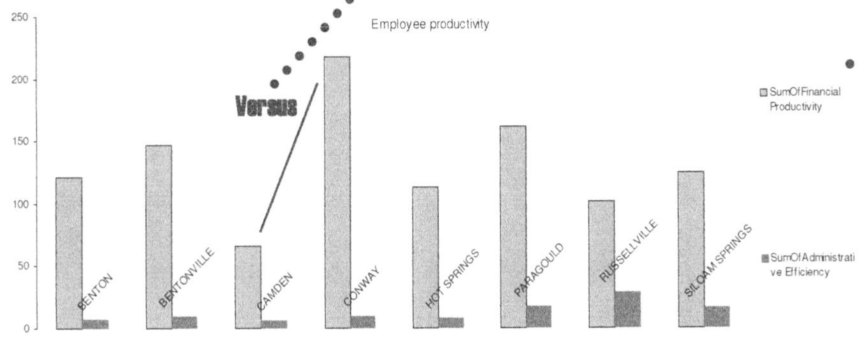

CGRP AR23

Name	Population	Total Revs	Total Taxes	Total Debt	Total Employees	Financial Adm PC	Gen Adm PC	Financial Productivity	Administrative Efficiency
BENTON	23749	33289	6499	29367	274	75	88	121.5	7.1
BENTONVILLE	26397	42987	8681	23537	292	22	94	147.2	9.5
CAMDEN	12520	10356	4840	4073	157	23	175	66.0	6.3
CONWAY	47840	85275	14045	69973	391	8	73	218.1	10.1
HOT SPRINGS	36770	62584	20977	66954	555	73	108	112.8	8.3
PARAGOULD	22888	44261	4945	34045	273	4	65	162.1	17.3
RUSSELLVILLE	24719	23293	10317	13210	230	8	24	101.3	29.1
SILOAM SPRINGS	12704	50152	4440	8145	403	86	110	124.4	16.2
Averages	**25948.4**	**44024.6**	**9343.0**	**31163.0**	**321.9**	**37.4**	**92.1**	**131.7**	**13.0**

Legend

E2 Listed in order of use on chart, top to bottom

- Finance Adm. Productivity (Tax collection per Finance Employee)
- General Administrative Efficiency (General Admin. % of Total Common Expense)

(Ignore the prefix "sumof" or "sumoftotal" in the legend, the system inserts this automatically.)

This graph also includes data from various sections in the ***Governments of Your State*** book: Total Funds Flow, among other sections. For the greater detail, see these sections, in your state's book.

Finding Your City or County

Each government is found & compared within its peer group. Peer groups are defined by their state/region, their type of government, and their size class. So, 'XX' for the state or region abbreviation. Then type: 1=counties, 2=cities, towns. Then population size class: 1=under 2,000 population, 2=2,000-10,000, 3=10,000-50,000, 4=50,000-100,000, 5=100,000-250,000, 6=over 250,000.

Texas graph E2 TX-000

Can Employee productivity comparisons save you money ?

E2 2

Employee productivity

a larger slice is more "productive", more revenue per employee

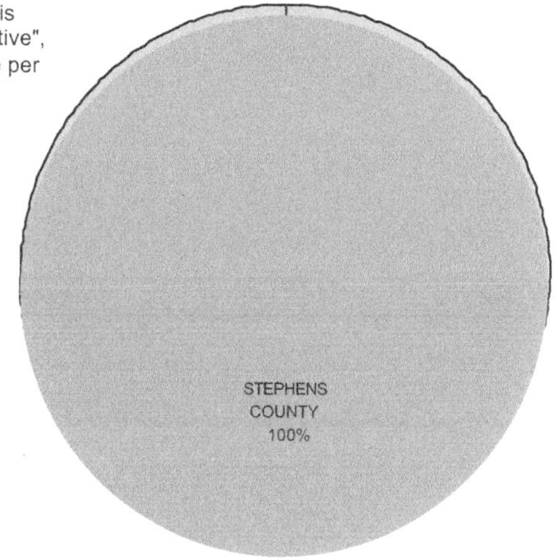

Administrative Efficiency

a larger slice is more "efficient", less overhead

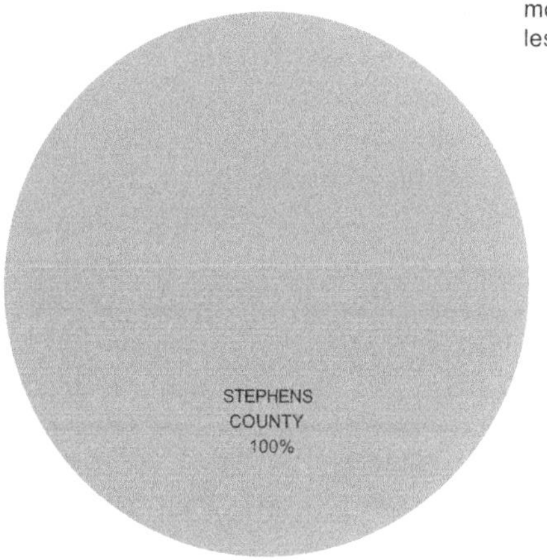

Group TX12

Name	Population	Total Revs	Total Taxes	Total Debt	Total Employees	Financial Adm PC	Gen Adm PC	Financial Productivity	Administrative Efficiency
STEPHENS COUNTY	9561	11119	3122	0	150	22	106	74.13	12.3
Averages	**9561.0**	**11119.0**	**3122.0**	**0.0**	**150.0**	**22.0**	**106.0**	**74.1**	**12.3**

Can Employee productivity comparisons save you money ?

E2 2

Employee productivity

a larger slice is more "productive", more revenue per employee

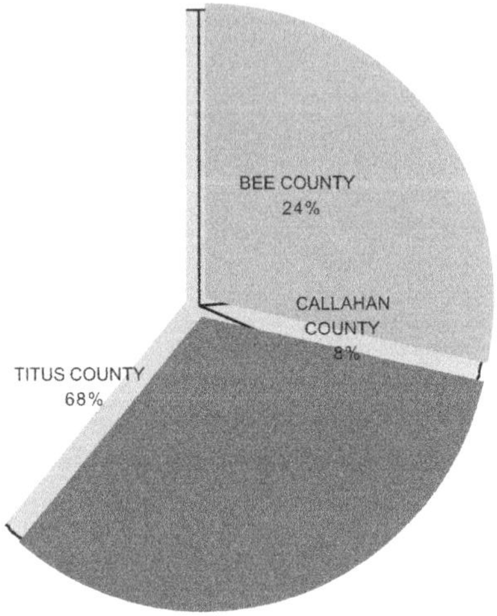

Administrative Efficiency

a larger slice is more "efficient", less overhead

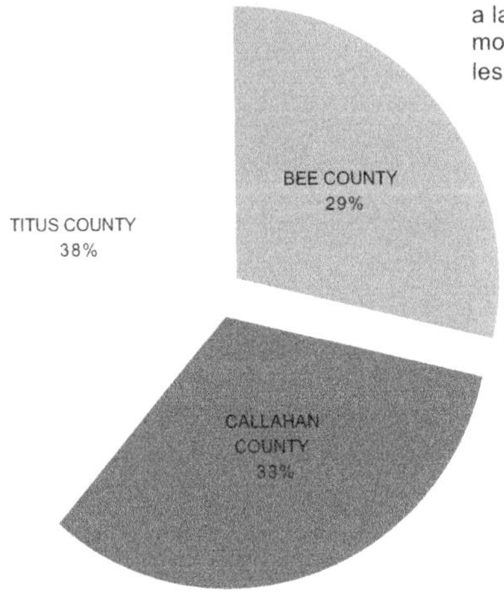

Group TX13

Name	Population	Total Revs	Total Taxes	Total Debt	Total Employees	Financial Adm PC	Gen Adm PC	Financial Productivity	Administrative Efficiency
BEE COUNTY	32873	15275	4792	8895	229	17	43	66.70	11.6
CALLAHAN COUNTY	13516	3932	2140	0	52	17	86	75.62	3.7
TITUS COUNTY	29445	61131	10906	15245	678	24	45	90.16	33.4
Averages	**25278.0**	**26779.3**	**5946.0**	**8046.7**	**319.7**	**19.3**	**58.0**	**77.5**	**16.2**

Can Employee productivity comparisons save you money ? E2

Employee productivity

a larger slice is more "productive", more revenue per employee

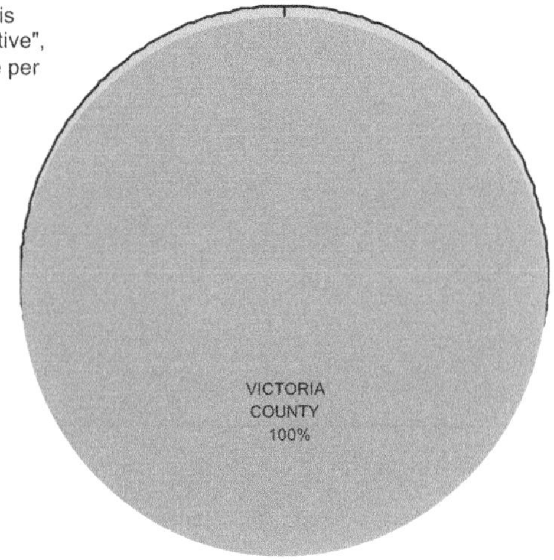

Administrative Efficiency

a larger slice is more "efficient", less overhead

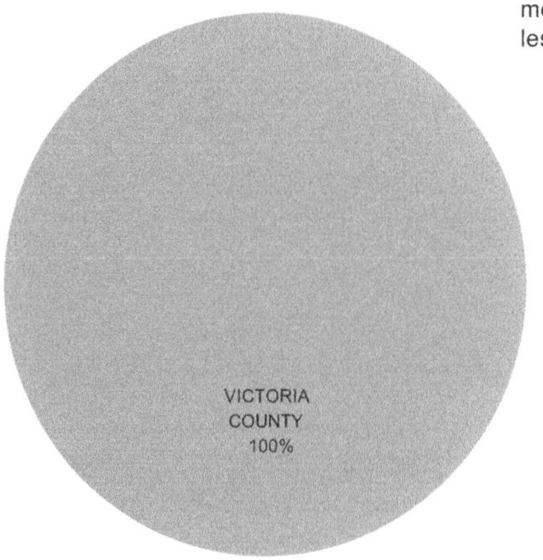

Group TX14

Name	Population	Total Revs	Total Taxes	Total Debt	Total Employees	Financial Adm PC	Gen Adm PC	Financial Productivity	Administrative Efficiency
VICTORIA COUNTY	85648	157442	24451	53605	1705	13	54	92.34	29.7
Averages	**85648.0**	**157442.0**	**24451.0**	**53605.0**	**1705.0**	**13.0**	**54.0**	**92.3**	**29.7**

Can Employee productivity comparisons save you money ? E2 2

Employee productivity

a larger slice is more "productive", more revenue per employee

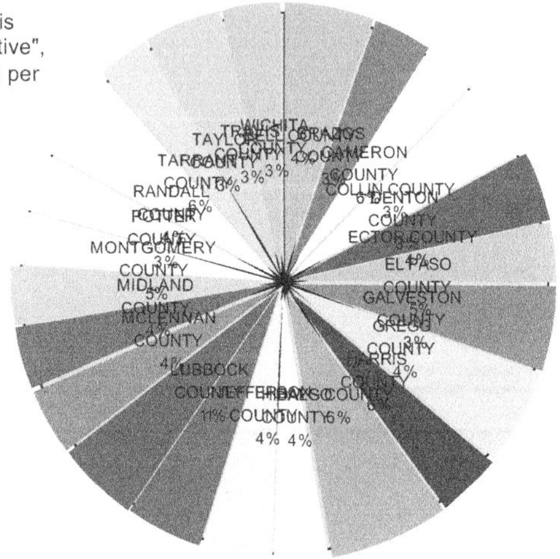

Administrative Efficiency

a larger slice is more "efficient", less overhead

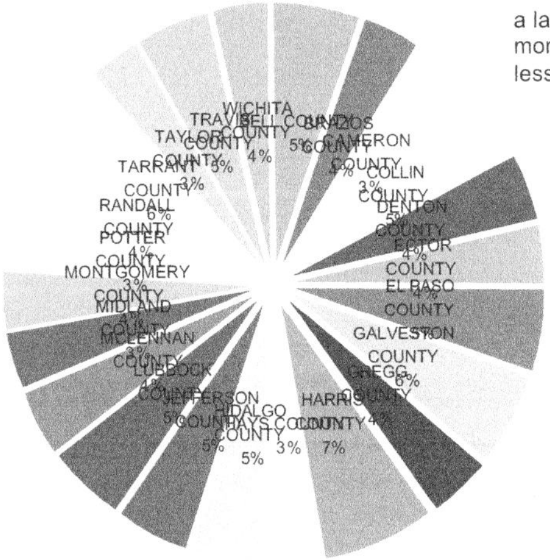

Group TX15

Name	Population	Total Revs	Total Taxes	Total Debt	Total Employees	Financial Adm PC	Gen Adm PC	Financial Productivity	Administrative Efficiency
BELL COUNTY	256057	108790	43133	53929	932	15	48	116.73	5.8
BRAZOS COUNTY	156305	56860	43545	51510	702	21	77	81.00	4.6
CAMERON COUNTY	378311	124933	41770	69425	1799	16	36	69.45	9.1
COLLIN COUNTY	659457	187766	143488	283235	1693	17	49	110.91	3.9
DENTON COUNTY	554642	150718	100277	171408	1673	12	54	90.09	4.6
ECTOR COUNTY	125339	41372	24519	12100	543	19	60	76.19	5.5
EL PASO COUNTY	721598	481624	173105	163015	4433	21	61	108.65	7.5
GALVESTON COUNTY	277563	141083	90899	197928	1146	20	82	123.11	4.0
GREGG COUNTY	115649	46732	28529	2575	539	23	52	86.70	6.2
HARRIS COUNTY	3693050	3164898	1318234	5579005	21005	8	58	150.67	8.6
HAYS COUNTY	124432	54819	41528	49935	767	21	56	71.47	8.0
HIDALGO COUNTY	678275	245217	119561	134292	2474	17	41	99.12	6.3
JEFFERSON COUNTY	247571	112800	73691	83430	1126	22	66	100.18	5.2
LUBBOCK COUNTY	252284	350802	55000	79381	3231	8	69	108.57	16.6
MCLENNAN COUNTY	224668	72248	46677	42216	843	23	41	85.70	5.9

MIDLAND COUNTY	121371	41303	30600	13410	566	19	60	72.97	5.9
MONTGOMERY COUNTY	378033	141962	103201	155043	1758	16	50	80.75	7.0
POTTER COUNTY	119852	39808	31930	20805	579	12	93	68.75	4.6
RANDALL COUNTY	110053	30690	20177	26229	398	20	51	77.11	5.1
TARRANT COUNTY	1620479	1150097	515322	207556	9682	8	66	118.79	8.1
TAYLOR COUNTY	125039	36187	26084	11970	496	20	71	72.96	4.4
TRAVIS COUNTY	888185	493255	314706	430317	4674	27	87	105.53	4.6
WICHITA COUNTY	125894	35683	24713	4325	474	21	75	75.28	3.9
Averages	**519743.8**	**317810.7**	**148290.8**	**341001.7**	**2675.3**	**17.7**	**61.0**	**93.5**	**6.3**

Can Employee productivity comparisons save you money ? E2 2

Employee productivity

a larger slice is
more "productive",
more revenue per
employee

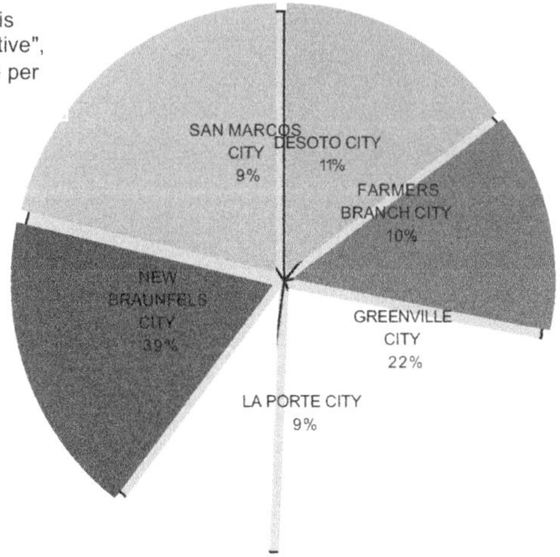

Administrative Efficiency

a larger slice is
more "efficient",
less overhead

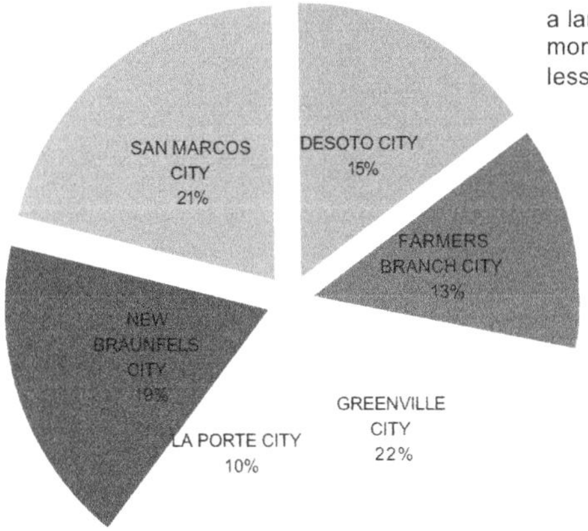

Group TX23

Name	Population	Total Revs	Total Taxes	Total Debt	Total Employees	Financial Adm PC	Gen Adm PC	Financial Productivity	Administrative Efficiency
DESOTO CITY	44653	52441	27240	78841	322	30	42	162.86	10.0
FARMERS BRANCH CITY	26487	58673	34193	23026	412	104	71	142.41	8.9
GREENVILLE CITY	25637	92980	15139	65453	384	25	52	242.14	19.5
LA PORTE CITY	33136	38623	17071	35520	369	60	81	104.67	7.9
NEW BRAUNFELS CITY	47168	120201	27950	65169	596	11	26	201.68	34.2
SAN MARCOS CITY	46111	102797	30792	123926	446	30	86	230.49	8.3
Averages	**37198.7**	**77619.2**	**25397.5**	**65322.5**	**421.5**	**43.3**	**59.7**	**180.7**	**14.8**

Can Employee productivity comparisons save you money ? E2 2

Employee productivity

a larger slice is more "productive", more revenue per employee

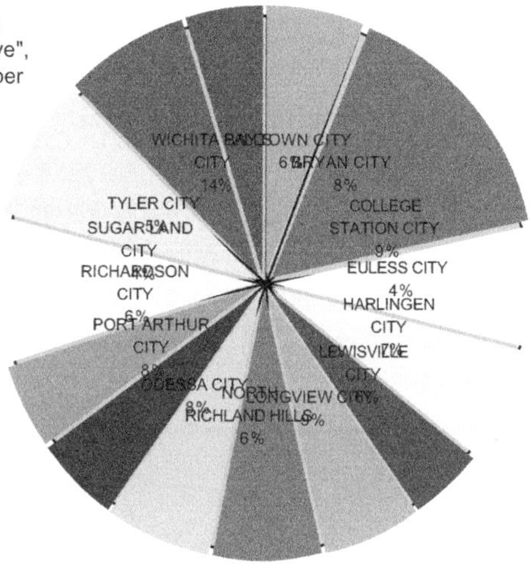

Administrative Efficiency

a larger slice is more "efficient", less overhead

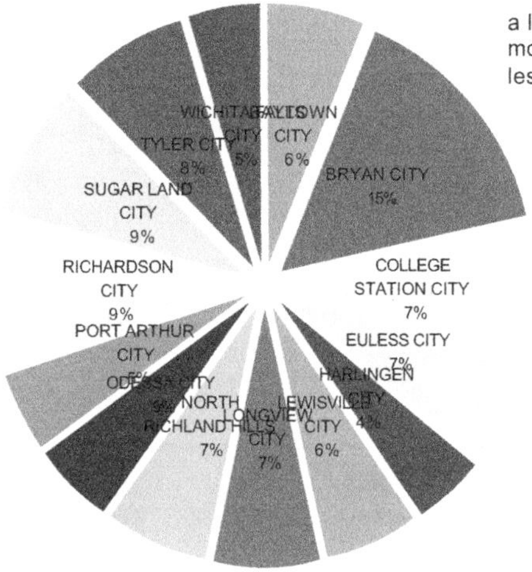

Group TX24

Name	Population	Total Rcvs	Total Taxes	Total Debt	Total Employees	Financial Adm PC	Gen Adm PC	Financial Productivity	Administrative Efficiency
BAYTOWN CITY	68371	88314	32276	121021	652	49	50	135.45	9.6
BRYAN CITY	66306	301305	36161	148250	850	38	61	354.48	12.9
COLLEGE STATION CITY	72388	125888	36644	168120	799	24	54	157.56	14.2
EULESS CITY	51226	63091	35680	72095	399	17	98	158.12	6.8
HARLINGEN CITY	62318	72107	33012	45095	715	62	35	100.85	11.8
LEWISVILLE CITY	90348	92426	54392	124018	661	29	46	139.83	9.8
LONGVIEW CITY	75609	94479	49135	134985	645	24	34	146.48	14.7
NORTH RICHLAND HILLS	61115	78284	39758	67851	519	22	65	150.84	9.8
ODESSA CITY	93546	101744	34136	60190	842	38	30	120.84	13.2
PORT ARTHUR CITY	56684	68761	23150	80465	611	23	63	112.54	12.5
RICHARDSON CITY	99187	152068	81411	210201	770	30	51	197.49	9.6
SUGAR LAND CITY	75754	101917	58284	164467	517	40	67	197.13	6.4
TYLER CITY	91936	117231	51796	63232	680	4	79	172.40	8.9
WICHITA FALLS CITY	99846	126760	55679	178267	1198	17	37	105.81	22.2
Averages	**76045.3**	**113169.6**	**44393.9**	**117018.4**	**704.1**	**29.8**	**55.0**	**160.7**	**11.6**

Can Employee productivity comparisons save you money ? **E2** 2

Employee productivity

a larger slice is more "productive", more revenue per employee

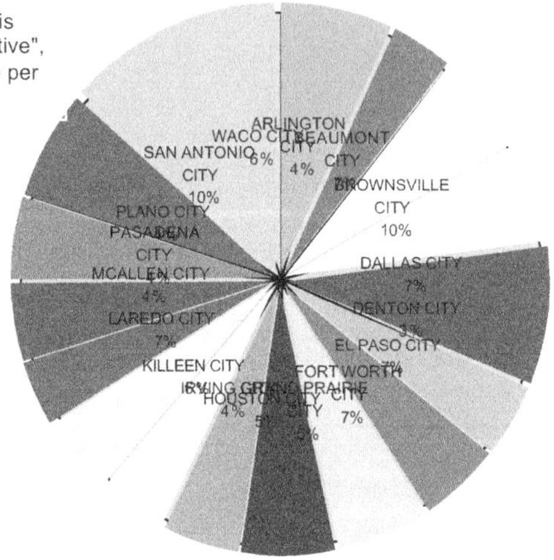

Administrative Efficiency

a larger slice is more "efficient", less overhead

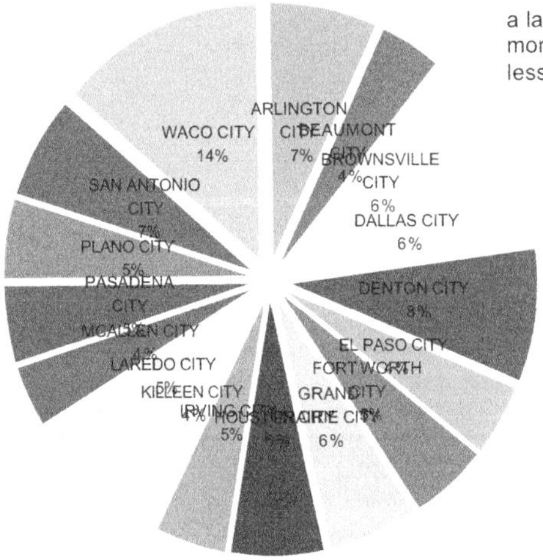

Group TX25

Name	Population	Total Revs	Total Taxes	Total Debt	Total Employees	Financial Adm PC	Gen Adm PC	Financial Productivity	Administrative Efficiency
ARLINGTON CITY	362805	426636	201069	662855	2201	9	38	193.84	12.9
BEAUMONT CITY	111799	140748	67176	206940	1200	23	29	117.29	20.6
BROWNSVILLE CITY	167493	264121	53577	501177	1534	7	22	172.18	31.6
DALLAS CITY	1213825	2483897	857334	7489035	14404	26	26	172.44	22.8
DENTON CITY	104153	275410	66779	394920	1166	48	57	236.20	10.7
EL PASO CITY	598590	707104	339294	854663	5729	22	23	123.43	21.3
FORT WORTH CITY	624067	895785	417248	1104888	6204	10	39	144.39	20.3
GRAND PRAIRIE CITY	144337	184594	80011	259112	1139	15	40	162.07	14.3
HOUSTON CITY	2016582	3459852	1492401	10086236	20944	34	27	165.20	17.0
IRVING CITY	193649	258378	146958	340735	1920	36	47	134.57	11.9
KILLEEN CITY	100233	105598	41601	114545	867	22	24	121.80	18.8
LAREDO CITY	208754	270413	91896	297551	2081	18	27	129.94	22.2
MCALLEN CITY	123622	173810	82394	47160	1553	25	75	111.92	12.6
PASADENA CITY	143852	133289	76067	185538	990	25	33	134.64	11.9
PLANO CITY	250096	315687	186196	300296	2186	24	45	144.41	12.7

SAN ANTONIO CITY	1256509	3041319	612268	6031219	16177	16	25	188.00	31.4
WACO CITY	120465	561052	74289	227936	1449	25	42	387.20	18.0
Averages	**455343.0**	**805746.6**	**287444.6**	**1712047.4**	**4808.5**	**22.6**	**36.4**	**167.0**	**18.3**

R1 Are You Getting Your Share of Revenues?

This is one of 3 graphs to find additional revenue opportunities. By comparing your government to other governments of similar size and type (we call 'peer groups'), you can see if others are acquiring more revenue per capita than your government. Only those governments covered this year are displayed.

Legend

R1

Listed in order of use on chart, top to bottom

- Total User Charges Per Capita
- Total Sales Taxes Per Capita
- Total Federal Aid Per Capita
- Total State Aid Per Capita
- Property Taxes Per Capita

(Ignore the prefix "sumof" or "sumoftotal" in the legend, the system inserts this automatically.)

ARE YOU GETTING YOUR SHARE OF REVENUES?

Compare your government to similar governments to see additonal revenue opportunities that they may be using.

R1

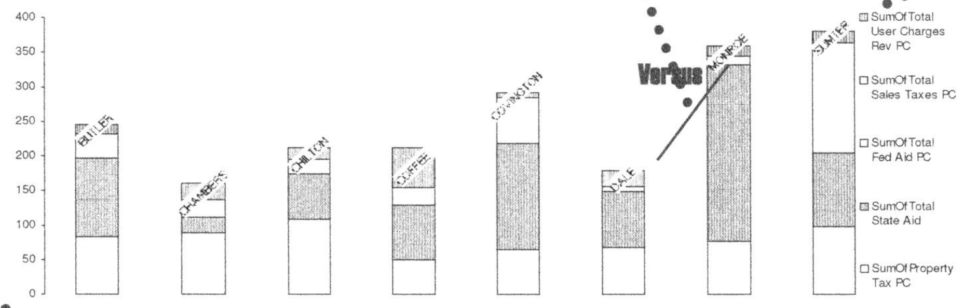

In this example, the group is AL13, that is Alabama='**AL**', counties='**1**', and size class of 10,000 to 50,000 population='**3**'. So this is displayed as: **'Group AL13'**.

Group AL13

	Name	Population	Property Tax PC	Total State Aid	Total Fed Aid PC	Total Sales Taxes PC	Total User Charges Rev PC
AL	BUTLER	20911	82	115	0	35	13
AL	CHAMBERS	36251	89	23	0	25	24
AL	CHILTON	40516	108	66	1	21	17
AL	COFFEE	43878	50	79	0	27	56
AL	COVINGTON	36956	64	154	0	66	7
AL	DALE	49186	68	81	0	8	22
AL	MONROE	24043	76	256	0	13	14
AL	SUMTER	14376	98	107	0	158	17
		Average	79.4	110.1		44.0	21.2

For more informaiton and detailed data, go to section: Pricing . Costs of Fee Based Services, section: Total Funds Flow

This graph also includes data from various sections in the ***Governments of Your State*** book: Total Funds Flow, among other sections. For the greater detail, see these sections, in your state's book.

Finding Your City or County

Each government is found & compared within its peer group. Groups are defined by their state/region, their type of government, and their size class. So, 'XX' for the state or region abbreviation. Then type: 1=counties, 2=cities, towns. Then population size class: 1=under 2,000 population, 2=2,000-10,000, 3=10,000-50,000, 4=50,000-100,000, 5=100,000-250,000, 6=over 250,000.

Texas graph R1 TX-000

Are you getting your share of revenues?

Compare your government to similar governments to see additonal revenue opportunities that they may be using.

R1 2

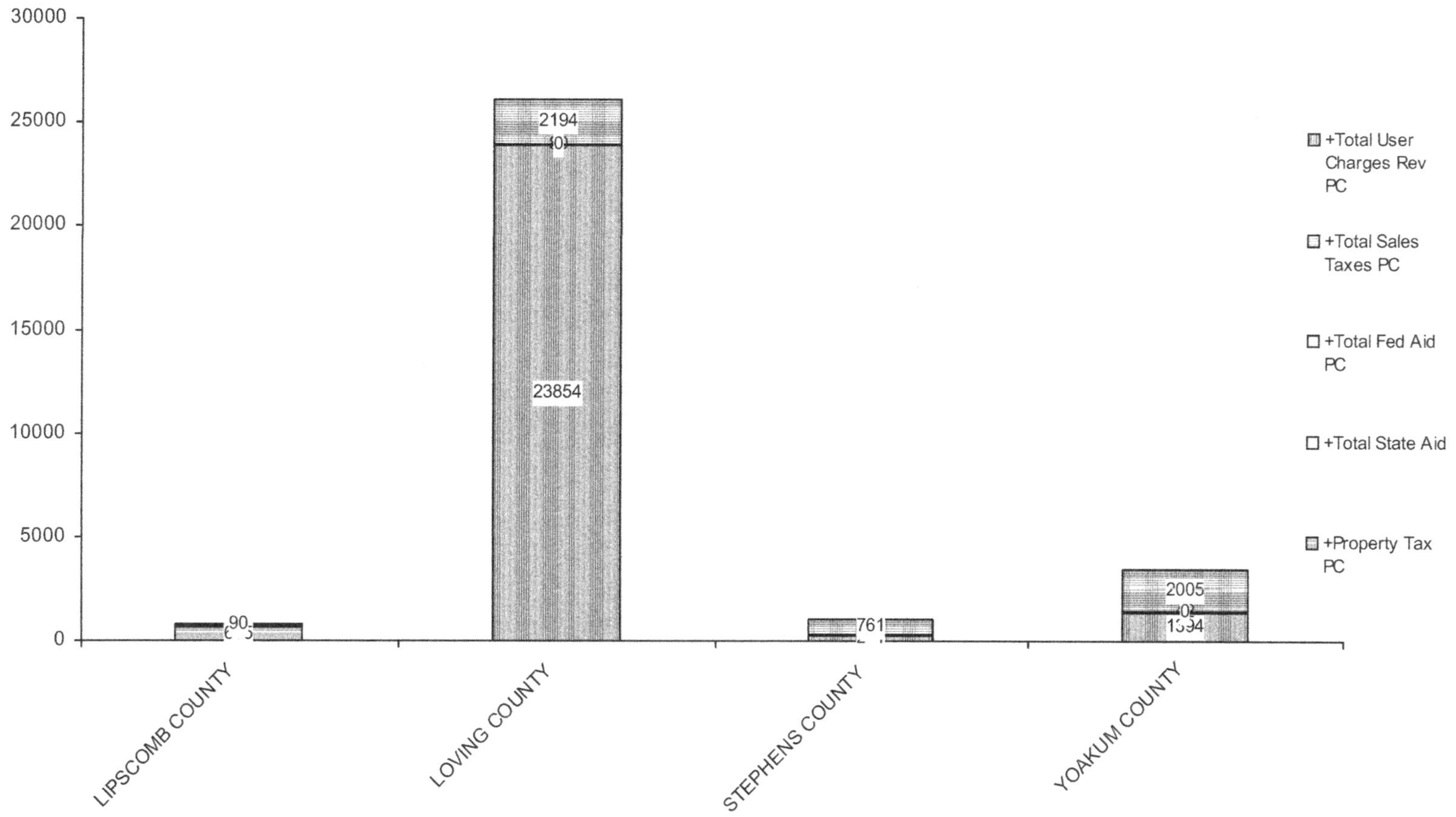

Group TX12

	Population	Property Tax PC	Total State Aid	Total Fed Aid PC	Total Sales Taxes PC	Total User Charges Rev PC
Average	5033.00	6548.50	38.00	0.00	0.26	1262.26

Are you getting your share of revenues?

Compare your government to similar governments to see additonal revenue opportunities that they may be using.

R1 2

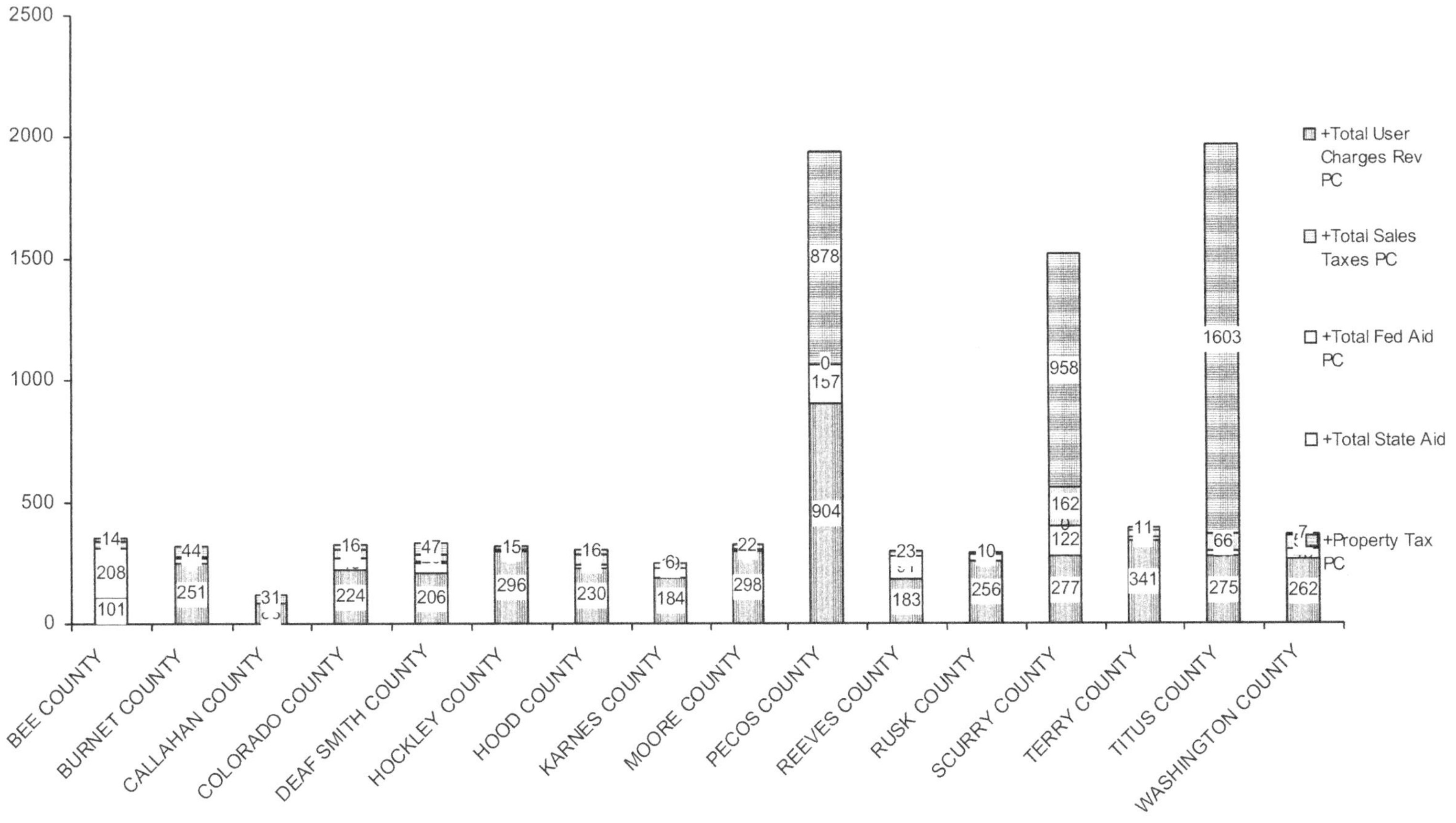

Group TX13

	Population	Property Tax PC	Total State Aid	Total Fed Aid PC	Total Sales Taxes PC	Total User Charges Rev PC
Average	24926.56	273.19	53.00	0.88	29.48	231.19

Are you getting your share of revenues?

Compare your government to similar governments to see additonal revenue opportunities that they may be using.

R1 2

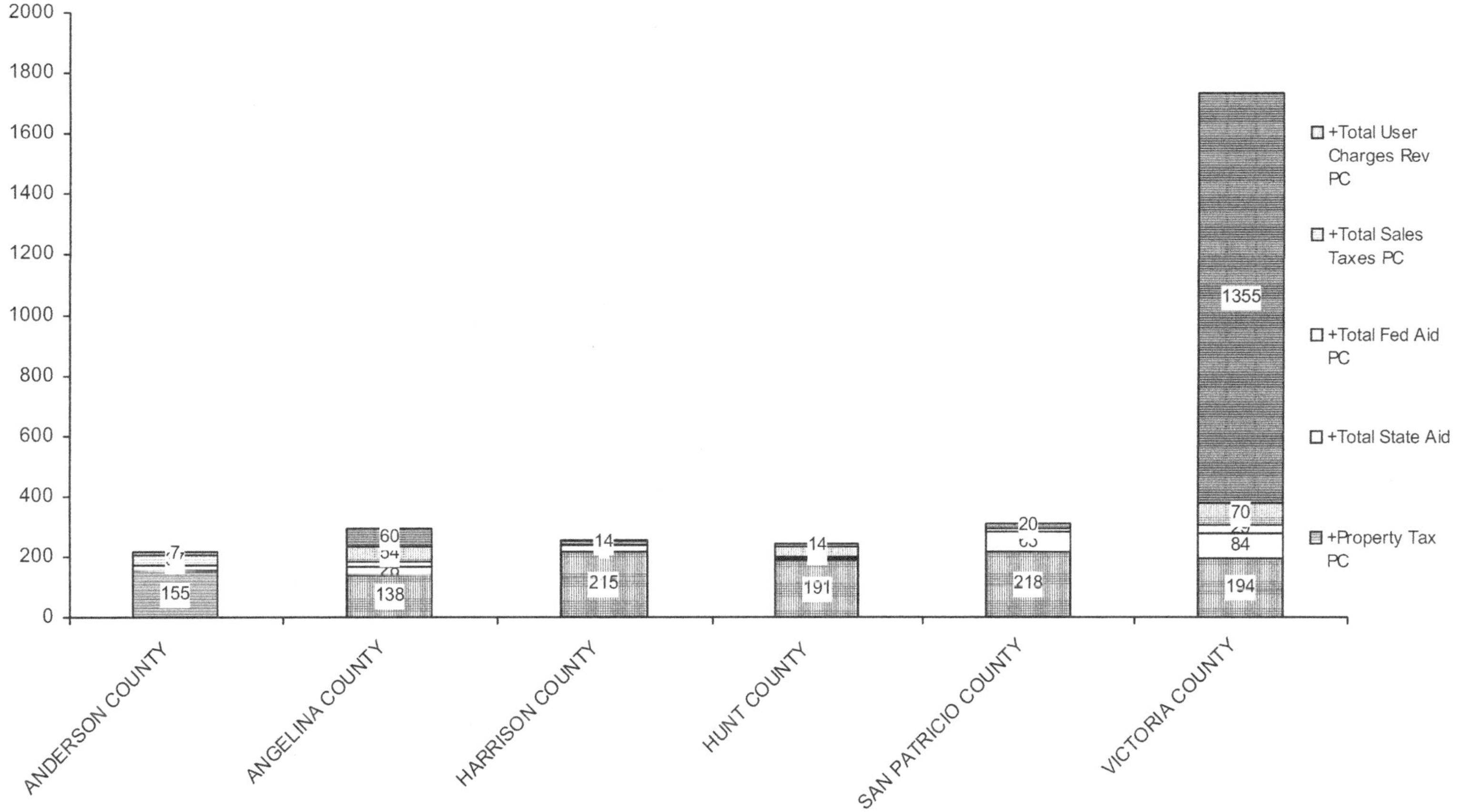

Group TX14

	Population	Property Tax PC	Total State Aid	Total Fed Aid PC	Total Sales Taxes PC	Total User Charges Rev PC
Average	73137.33	185.17	36.83	9.67	31.88	244.96

Are you getting your share of revenues?

Compare your government to similar governments to see additonal revenue opportunities that they may be using.

R1 2

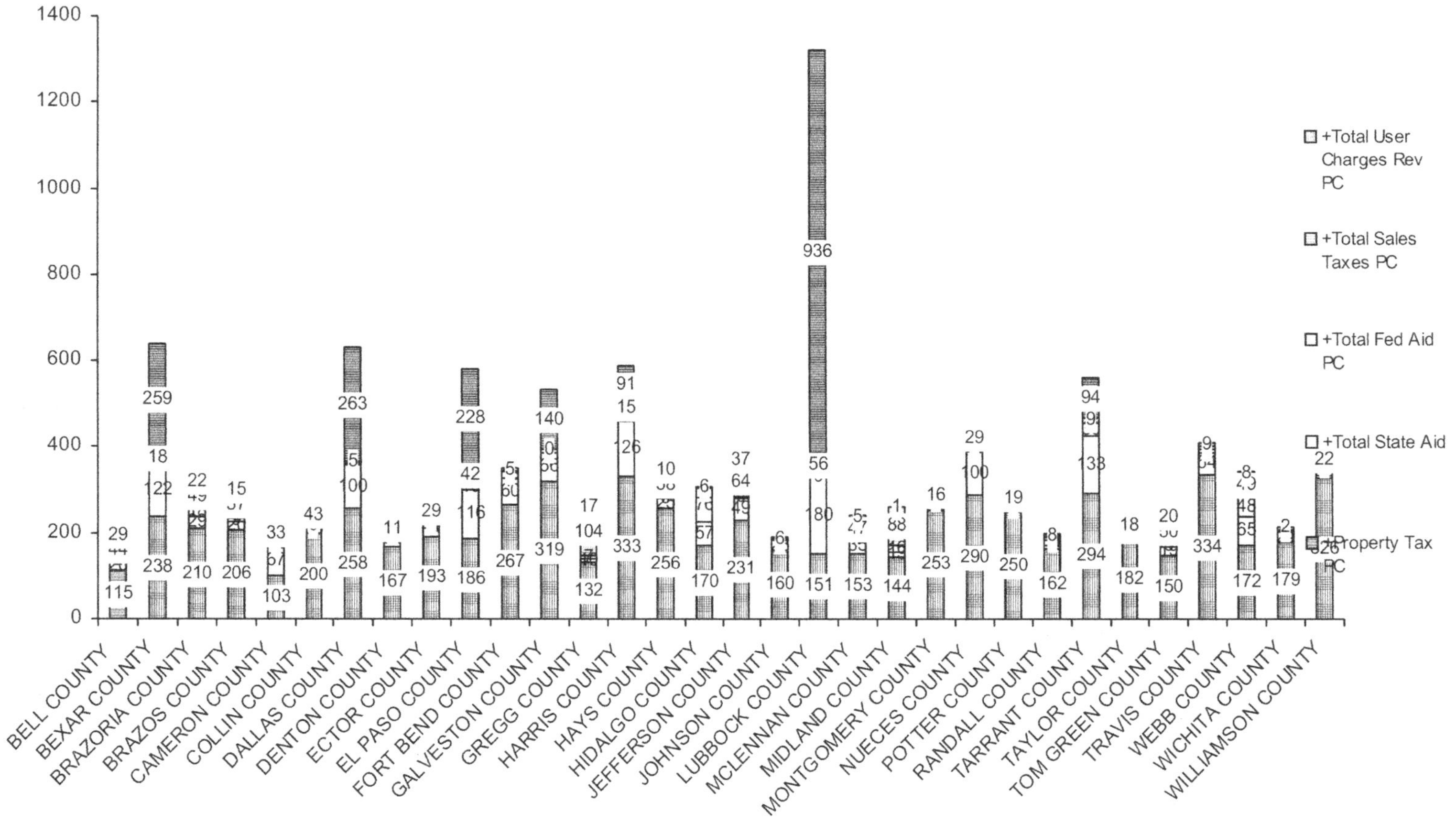

Group TX15

	Population	Property Tax PC	Total State Aid	Total Fed Aid PC	Total Sales Taxes PC	Total User Charges Rev PC
Average	551497.13	212.00	52.44	11.22	24.90	75.95

Are you getting your share of revenues?

Compare your government to similar governments to see additonal revenue opportunities that they may be using.

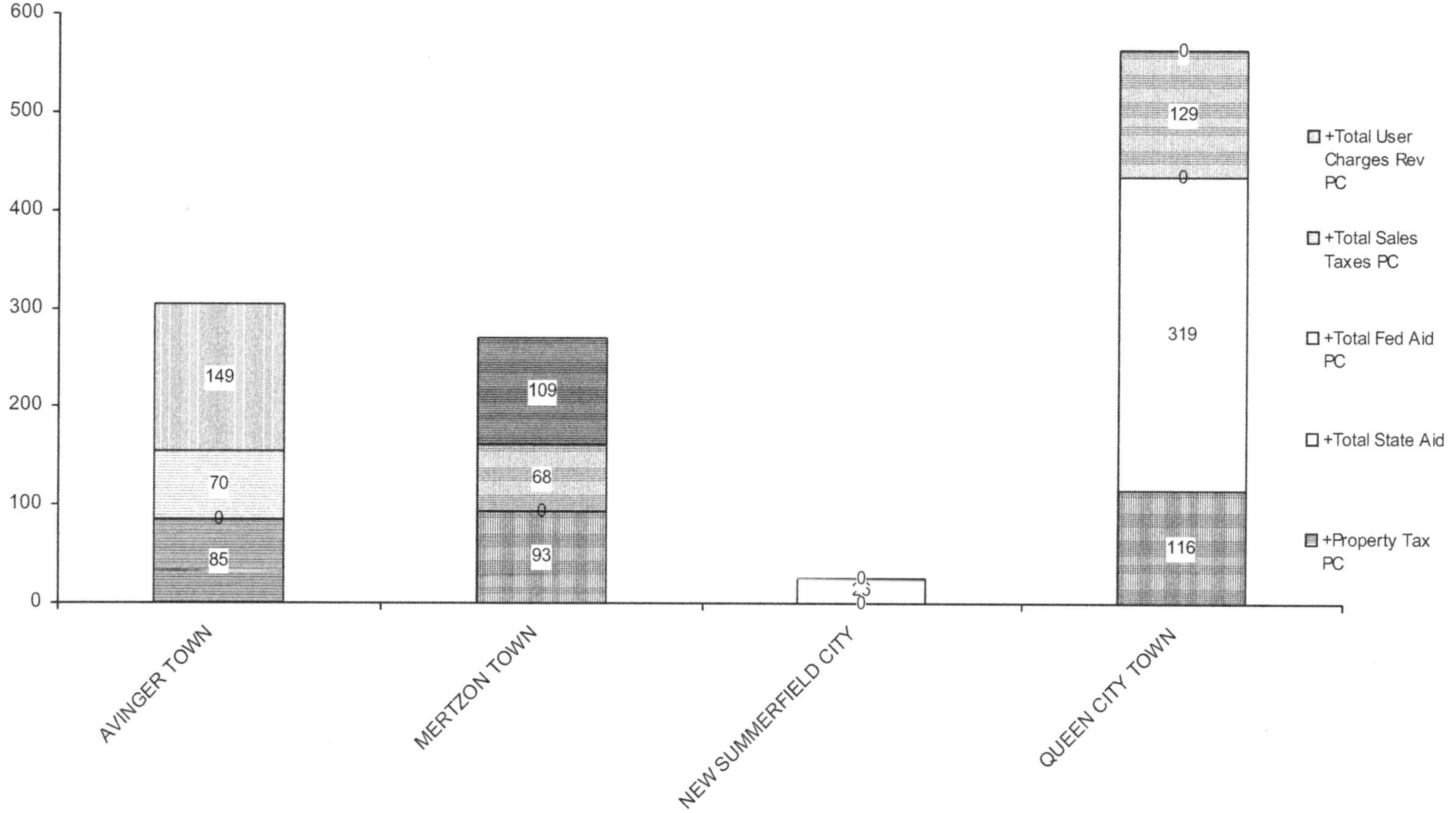

Group TX21

	Population	Property Tax PC	Total State Aid	Total Fed Aid PC	Total Sales Taxes PC	Total User Charges Rev PC
Average	979.00	73.50	86.25	0.00	66.90	64.67

Are you getting your share of revenues?

Compare your government to similar governments to see additonal revenue opportunities that they may be using.

R1 2

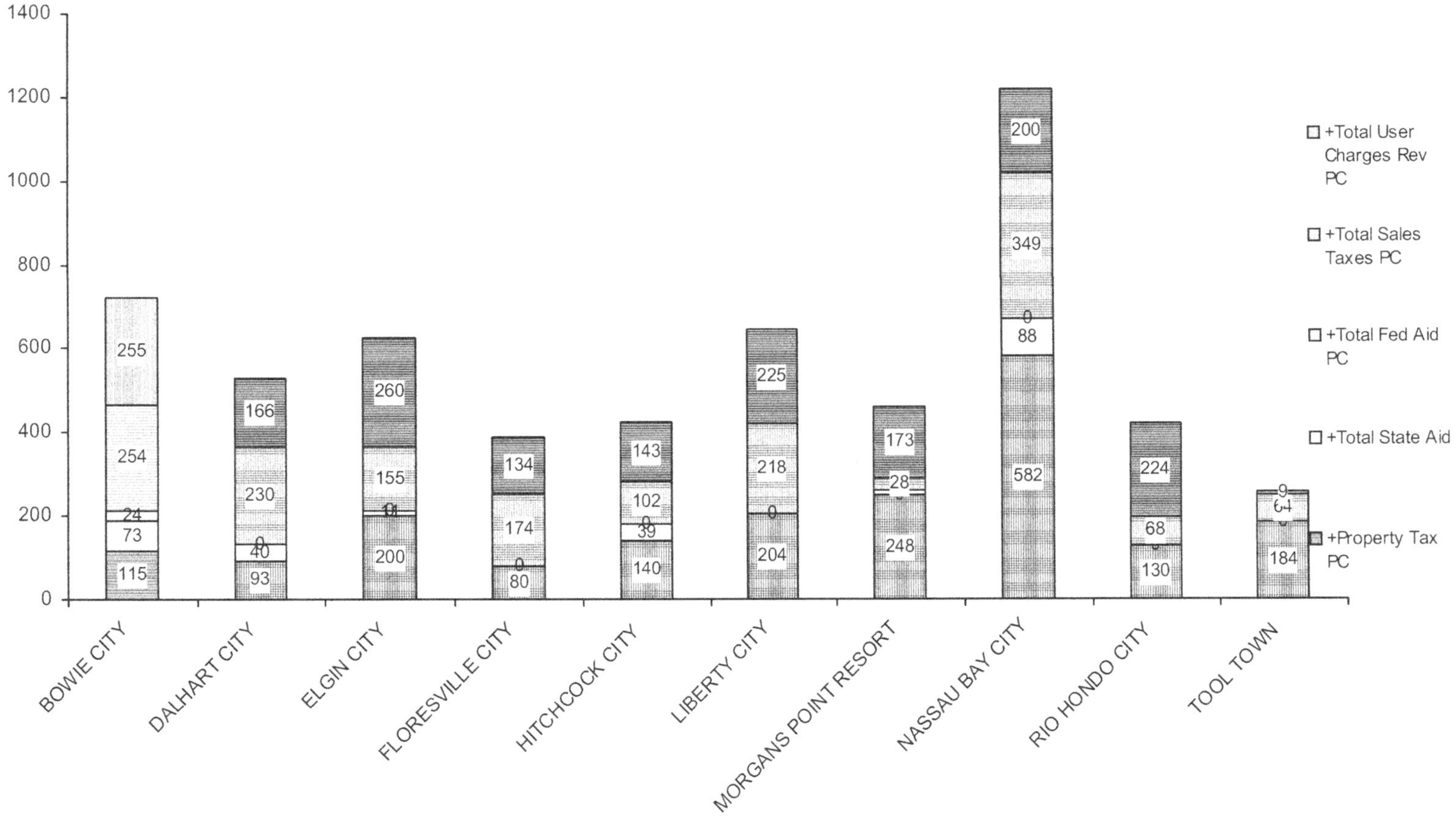

Group TX22

	Population	Property Tax PC	Total State Aid	Total Fed Aid PC	Total Sales Taxes PC	Total User Charges Rev PC
Average	5667.90	197.60	25.10	3.60	164.25	178.87

Are you getting your share of revenues?

Compare your government to similar governments to see additonal revenue opportunities that they may be using.

R1 2

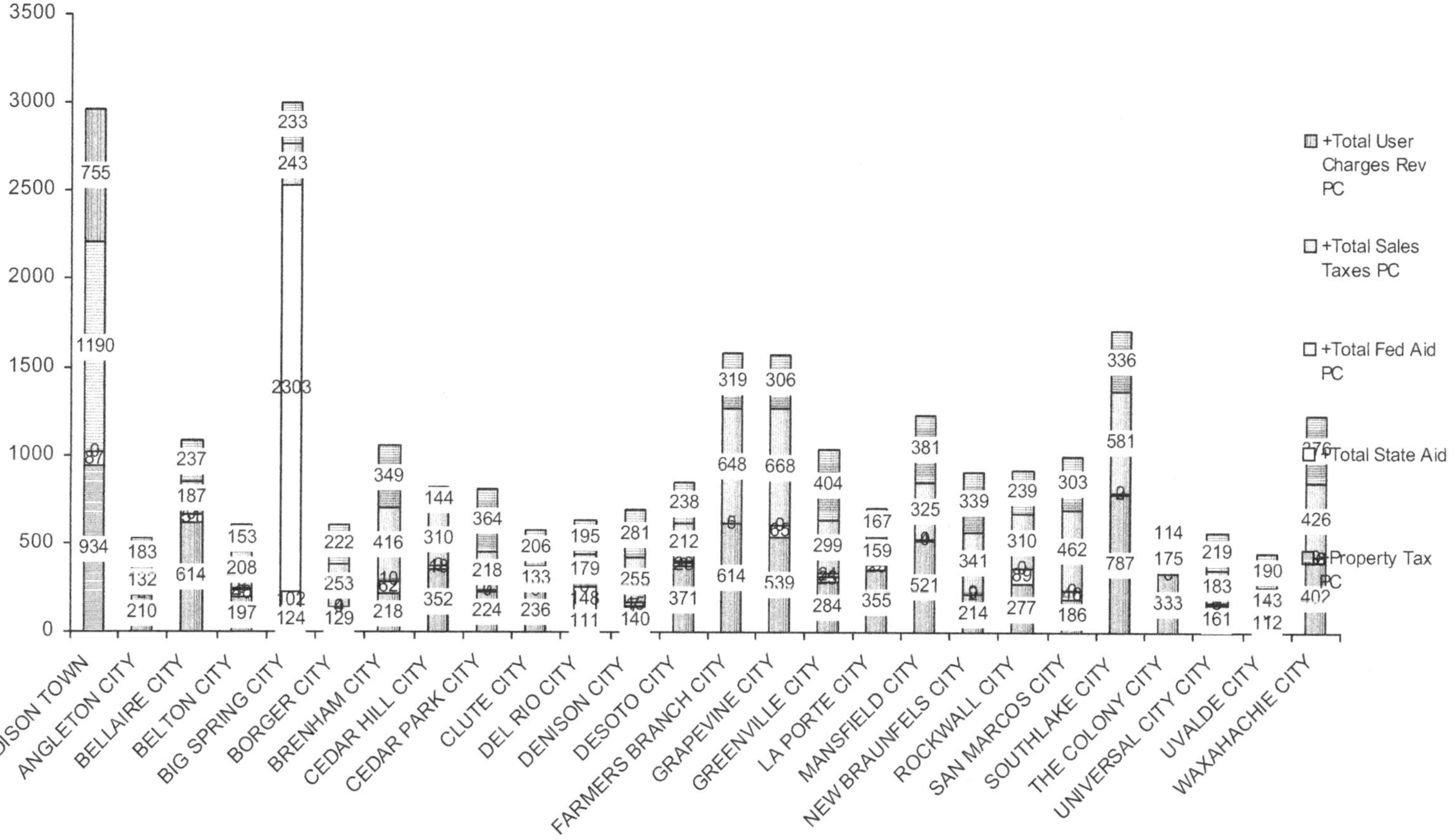

Group TX23

	Population	Property Tax PC	Total State Aid	Total Fed Aid PC	Total Sales Taxes PC	Total User Charges Rev PC
Average	28323.35	332.50	32.46	91.65	332.90	279.00

Are you getting your share of revenues?

Compare your government to similar governments to see additonal revenue opportunities that they may be using.

R1 2

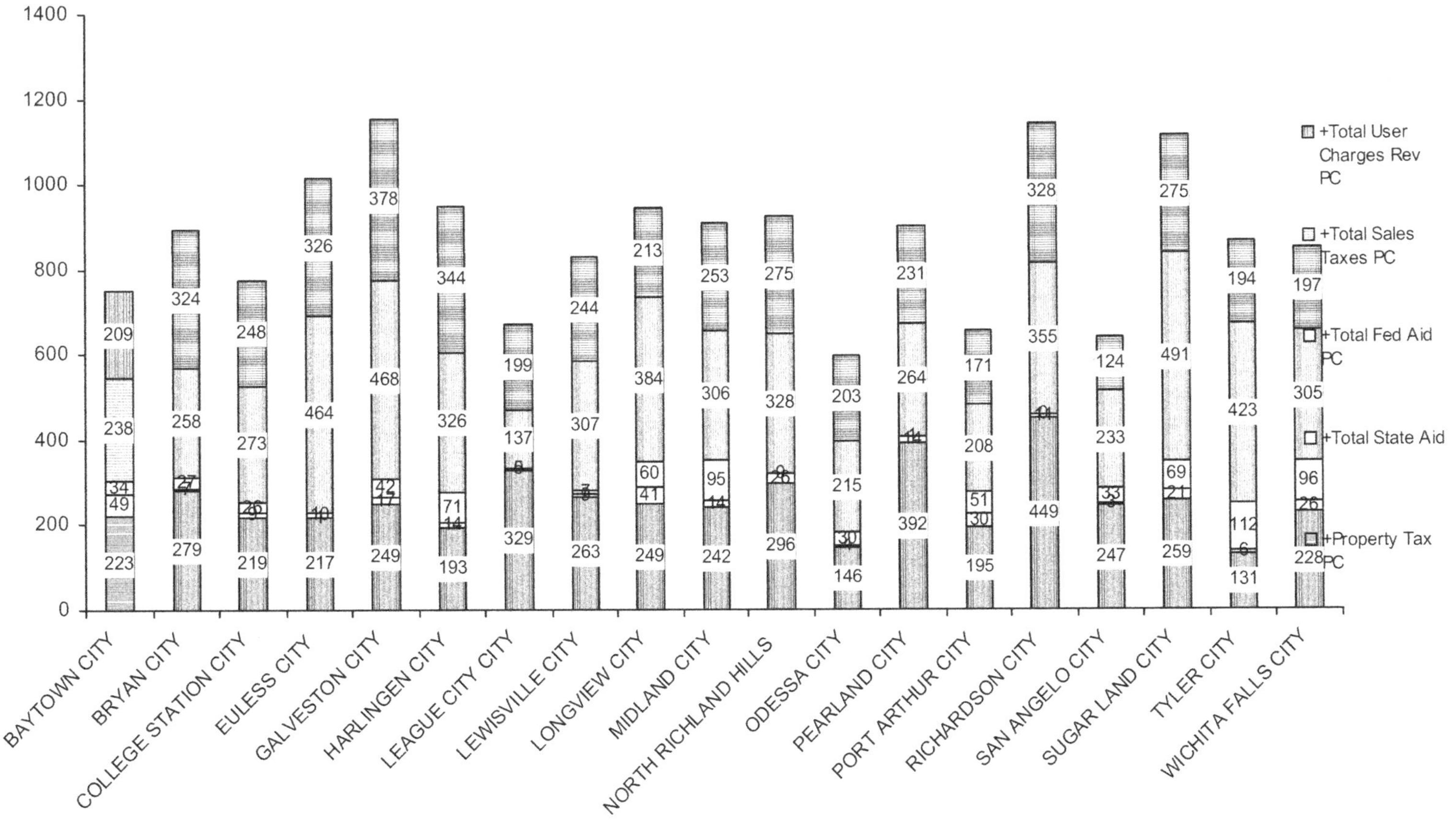

Group TX24

	Population	Property Tax PC	Total State Aid	Total Fed Aid PC	Total Sales Taxes PC	Total User Charges Rev PC
Average	75137.95	252.95	16.16	40.21	314.81	249.29

Are you getting your share of revenues?

Compare your government to similar governments to see additonal revenue opportunities that they may be using.

R1 2

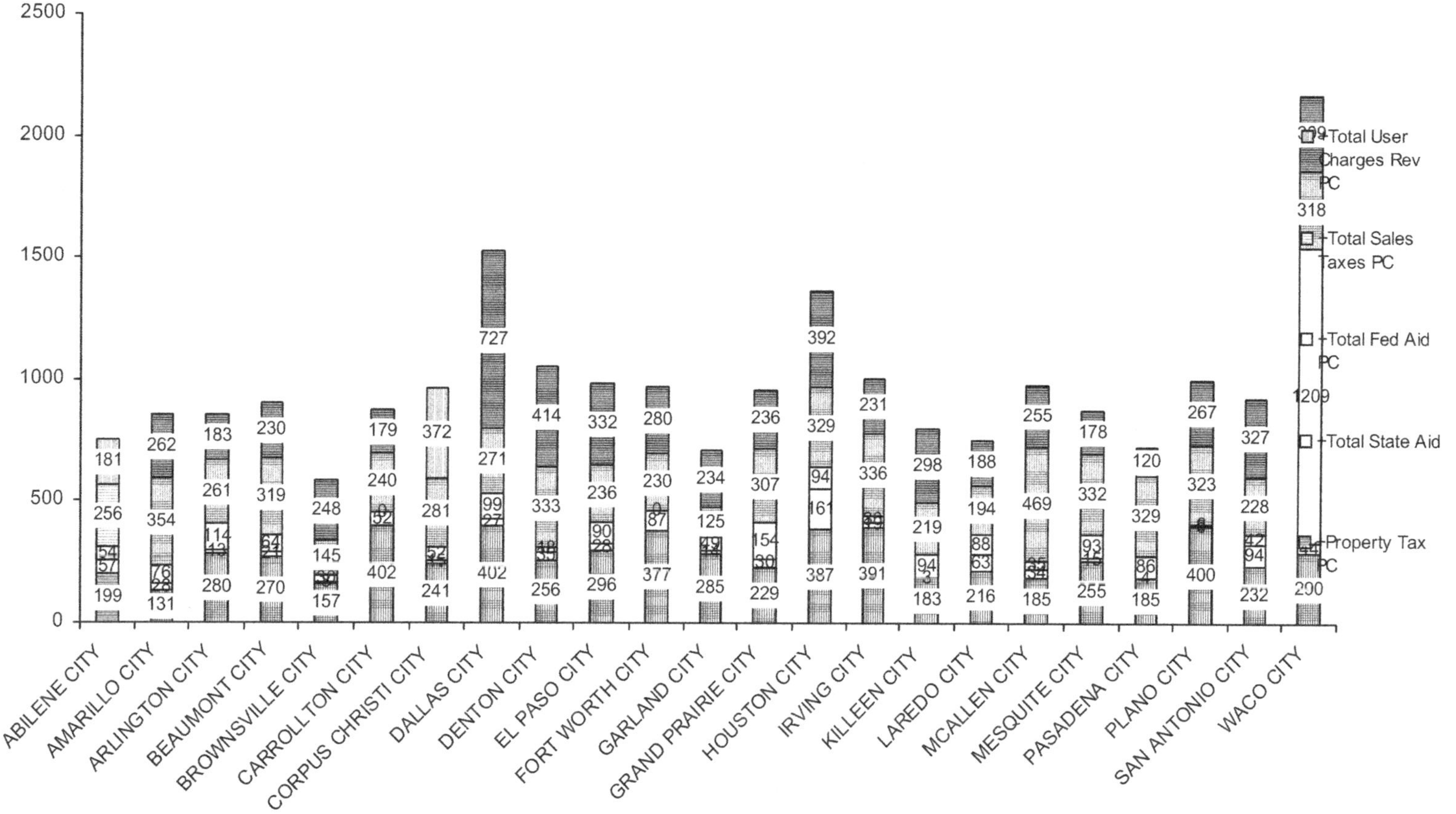

Group TX25

	Population	Property Tax PC	Total State Aid	Total Fed Aid PC	Total Sales Taxes PC	Total User Charges Rev PC
Average	382052.22	271.70	37.04	112.04	279.92	280.13

R2 Are You Getting Your Share of State and Federal Aid?

This is one of 3 graphs to find additional revenue opportunities. By comparing your government to other governments of similar size and type (we call 'peer groups'), you can see which others are acquiring more aid per capita than your government and in which areas.

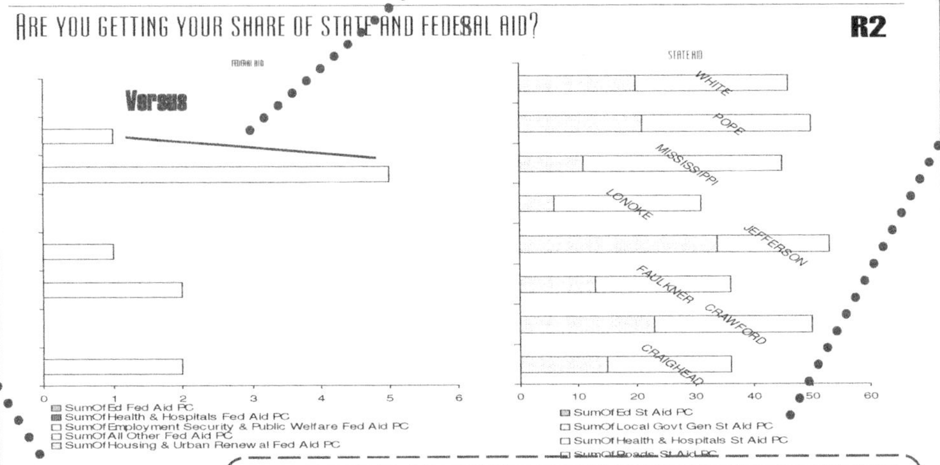

Group **AR14**

	Name	Population	Total Fed Aid PC	Total State Aid
AR	CRAIGHEAD	84074	2	36
AR	CRAWFORD	54973	1	50
AR	FAULKNER	89590	2	36
AR	JEFFERSON	83374	1	53
AR	LONOKE	55302	0	31
AR	MISSISSIPPI	50380	5	45
AR	POPE	55223	1	50
AR	WHITE	69354	0	46
		Averages	2	43

In this example, the group is AR14, that is Arkansas='**AR**', counties='**1**', and size class of 50,000 to 100,000 population='**4**'. So this is displayed as: **'Group AR14'**.

Legend

Listed in order of use on chart, top to bottom

- Education State Aid Per Capita
- Local Gov't General State Aid Per Capita
- Health and Hospitals State Aid Per Capita
- Roads State Aid Per Capita
- Housing & Urban State Aid Per Capita

(Ignore the prefix "sumof" or "sumoftotal" in the legend, the system inserts this automatically.)

This graph also includes data from various sections in the ***Governments of Your State*** book: Total Funds Flow, among other sections. For the greater detail, see these sections, in your state's book.

Finding Your City or County

Each government is found & compared within its peer group. Peer groups are defined by their state/region, their type of government, and their size class. So, 'XX' for the state or region abbreviation. Then type: 1=counties, 2=cities, towns. Then population size class: 1=under 2,000 population, 2=2,000-10,000, 3=10,000-50,000, 4=50,000-100,000, 5=100,000-250,000, 6=over 250,000.

Texas graph R2 TX-000

Are you getting your share of state and federal aid?

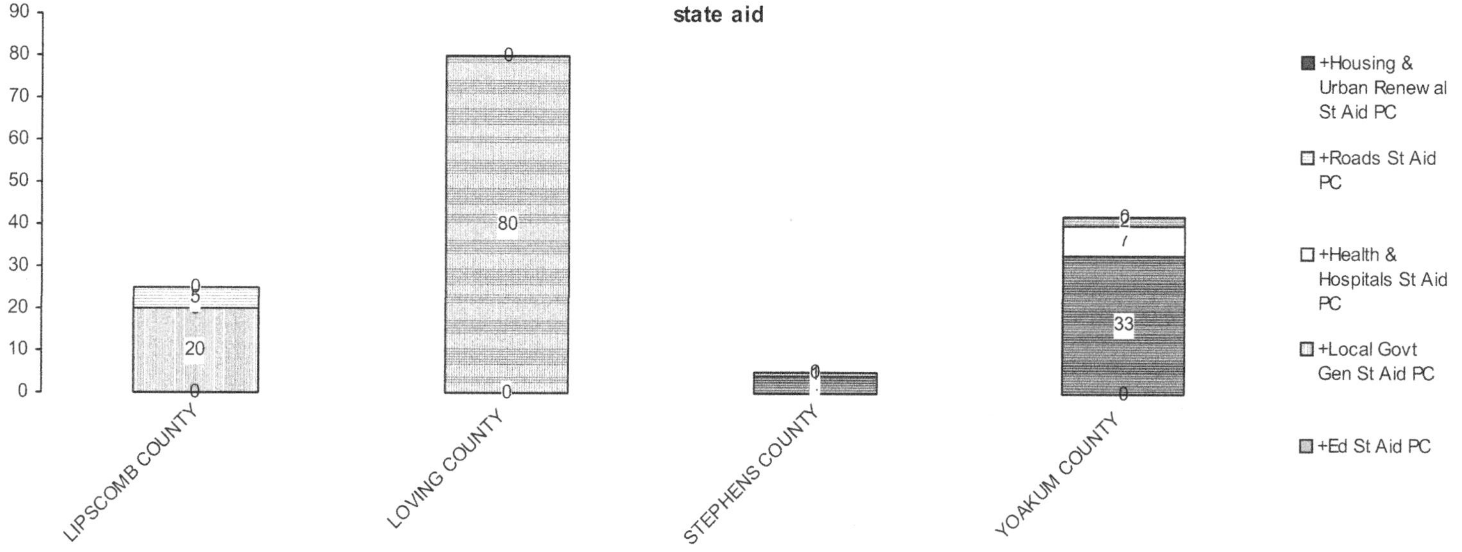

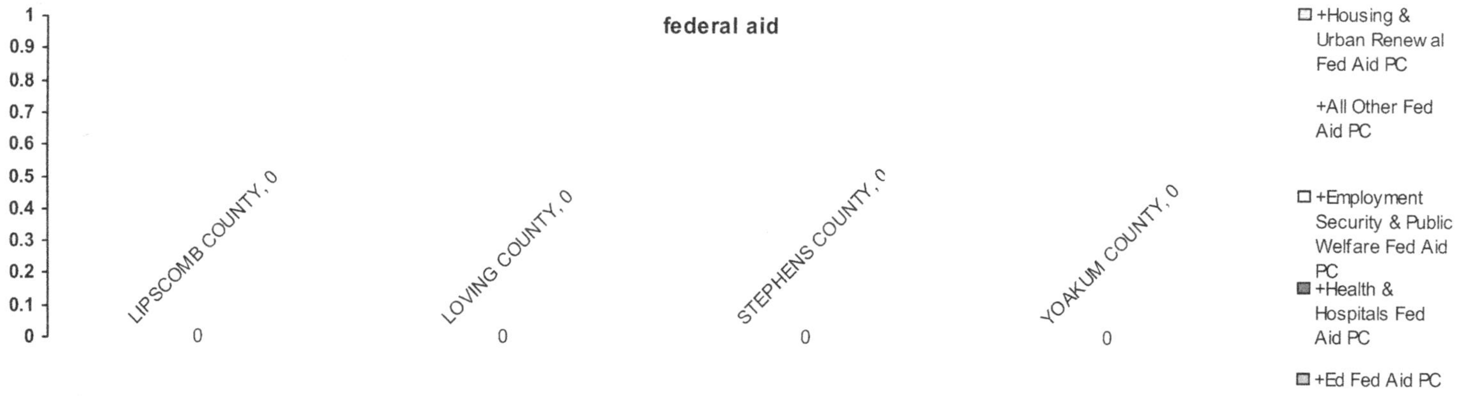

Group TX12

	Population	Total Fed Aid PC	Total State Aid
Averages	5033.00	0.00	38.00

Are you getting your share of state and federal aid?

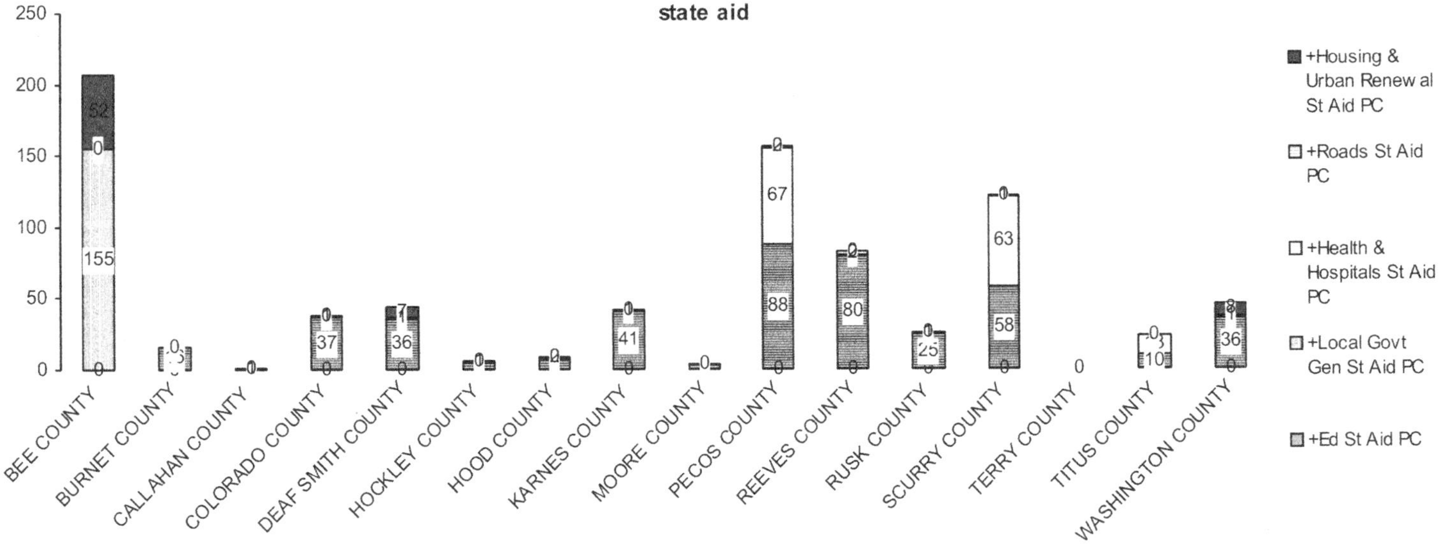

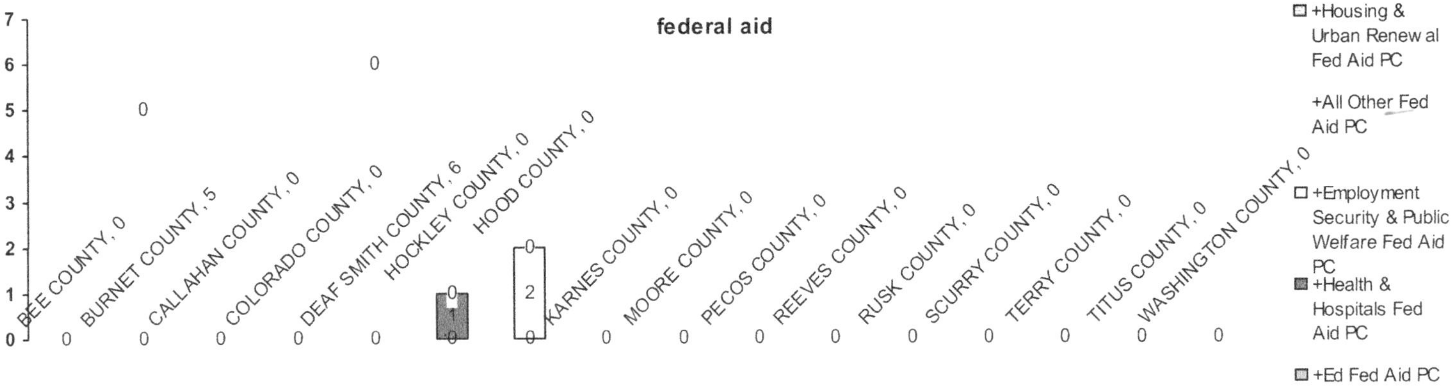

Group TX13

	Population	Total Fed Aid PC	Total State Aid
Averages	24926.56	0.88	53.00

Are you getting your share of state and federal aid?

R2 2

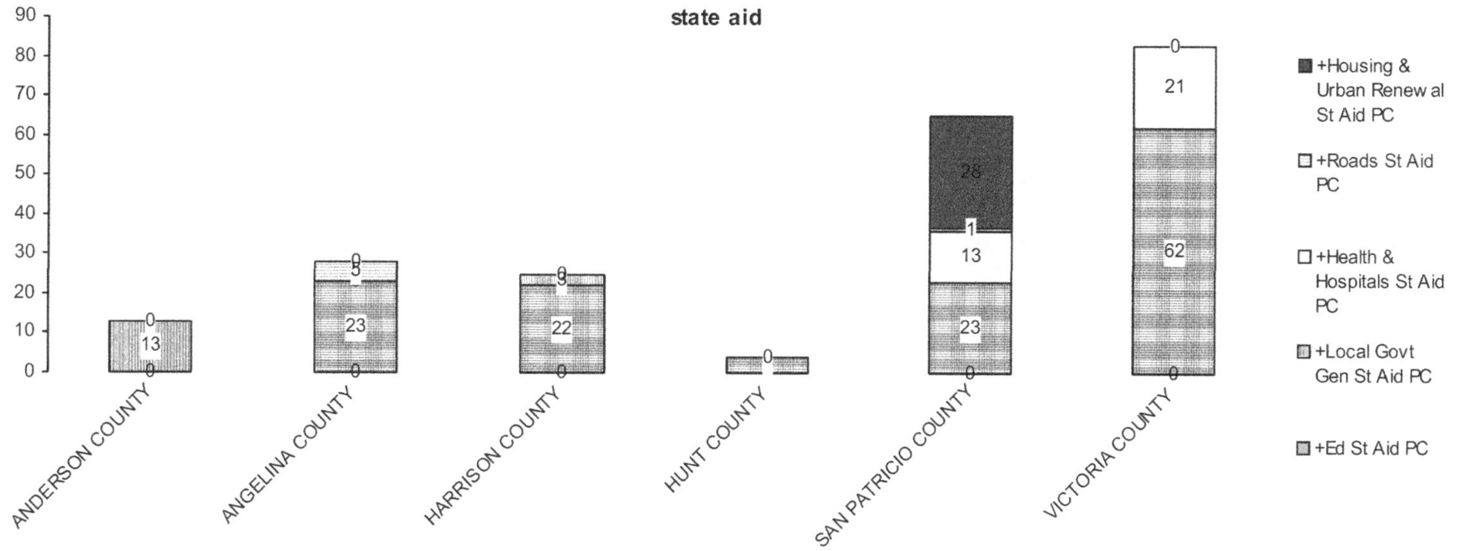

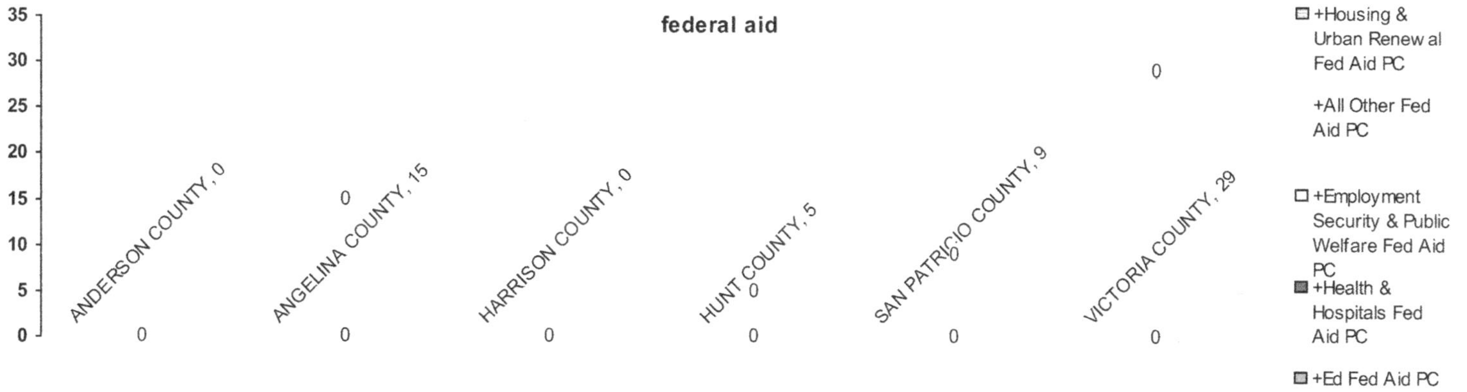

Group TX14

	Population	Total Fed Aid PC	Total State Aid
Averages	73137.33	9.67	36.83

Are you getting your share of state and federal aid?

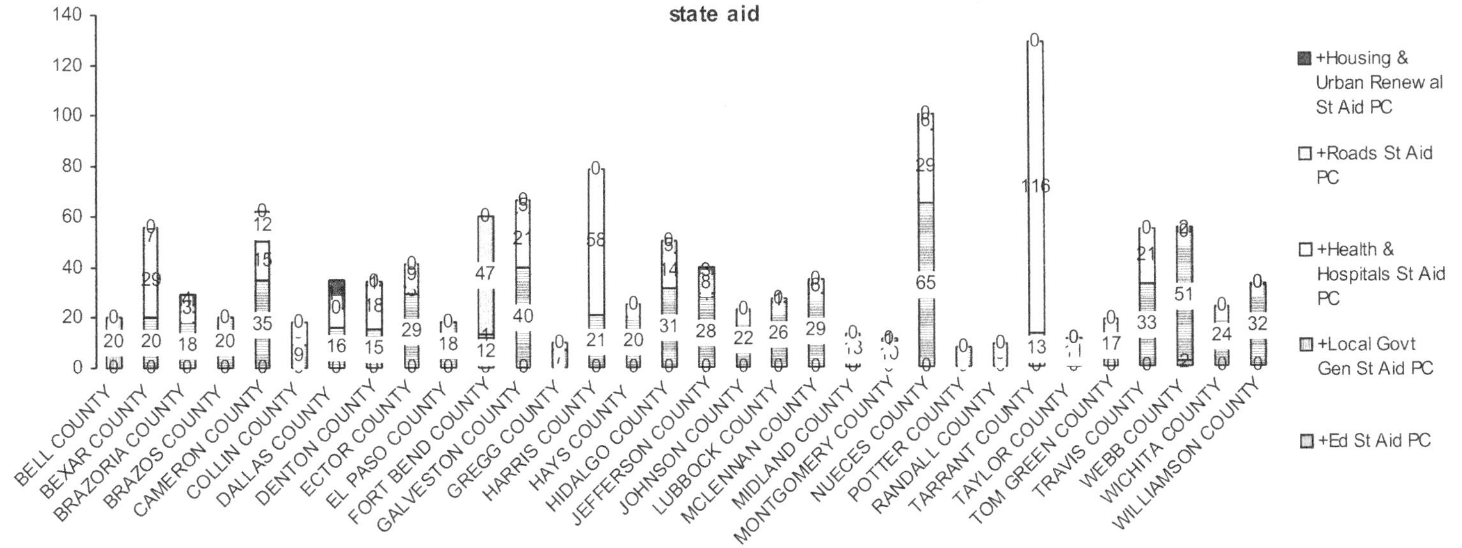

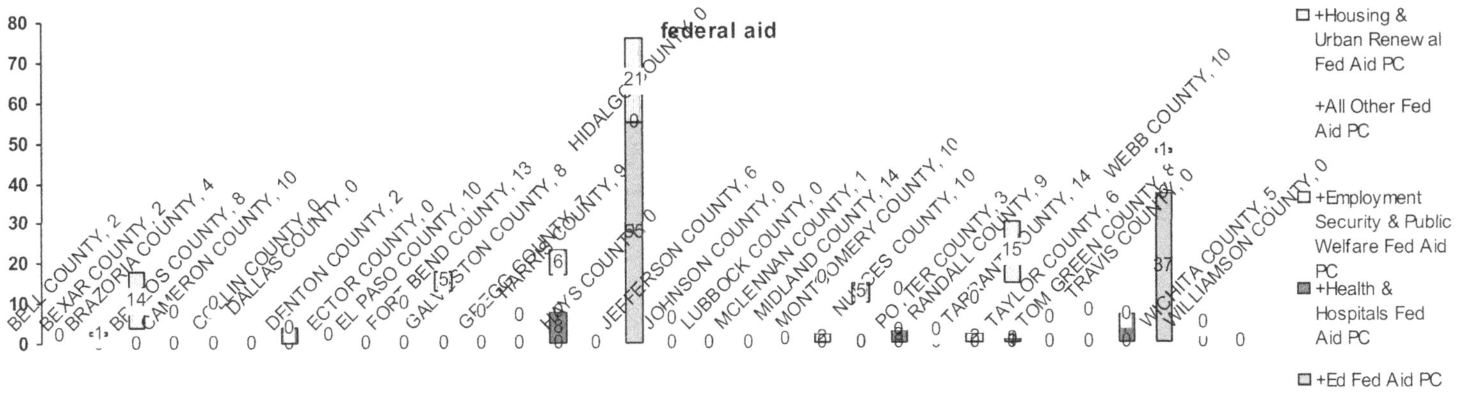

Group TX15

	Population	Total Fed Aid PC	Total State Aid
Averages	551497.13	11.22	52.44

Are you getting your share of state and federal aid?

R2 2

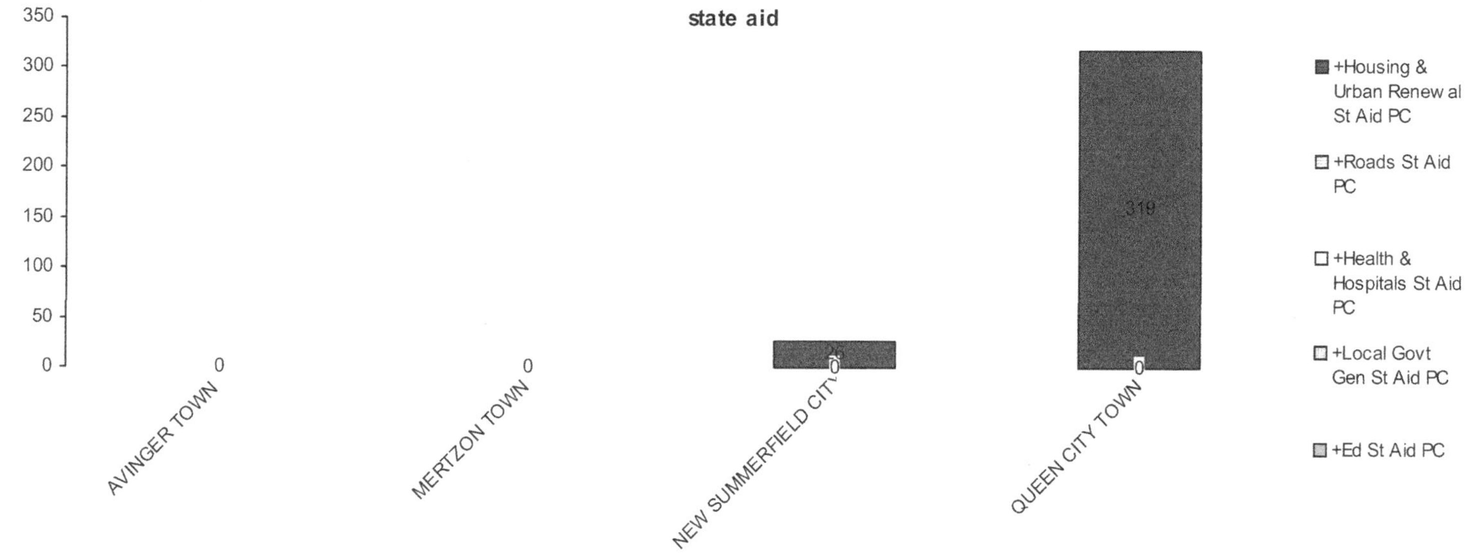

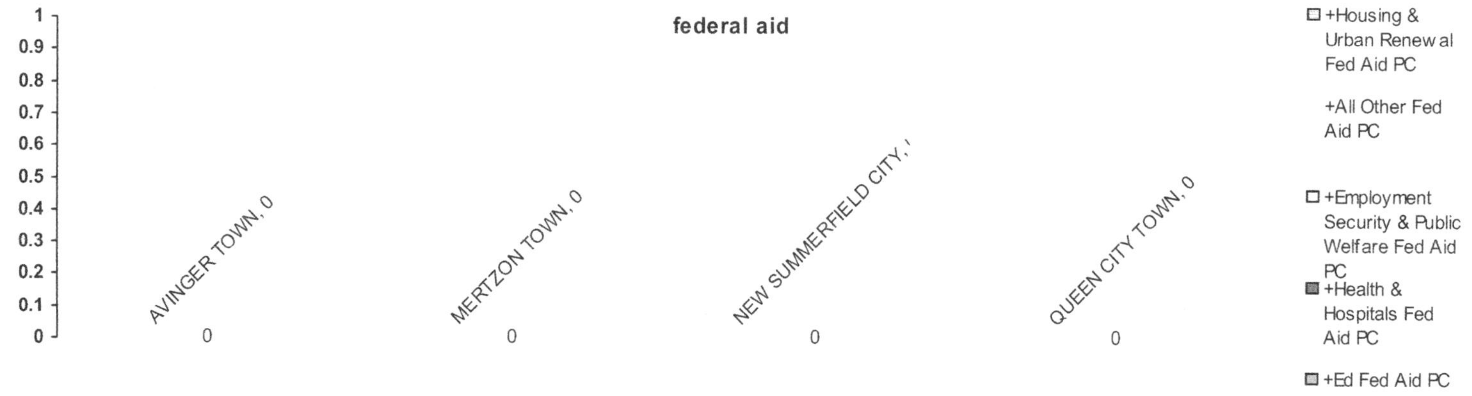

Group TX21

	Population	Total Fed Aid PC	Total State Aid
Averages	979.00	0.00	86.25

Are you getting your share of state and federal aid?

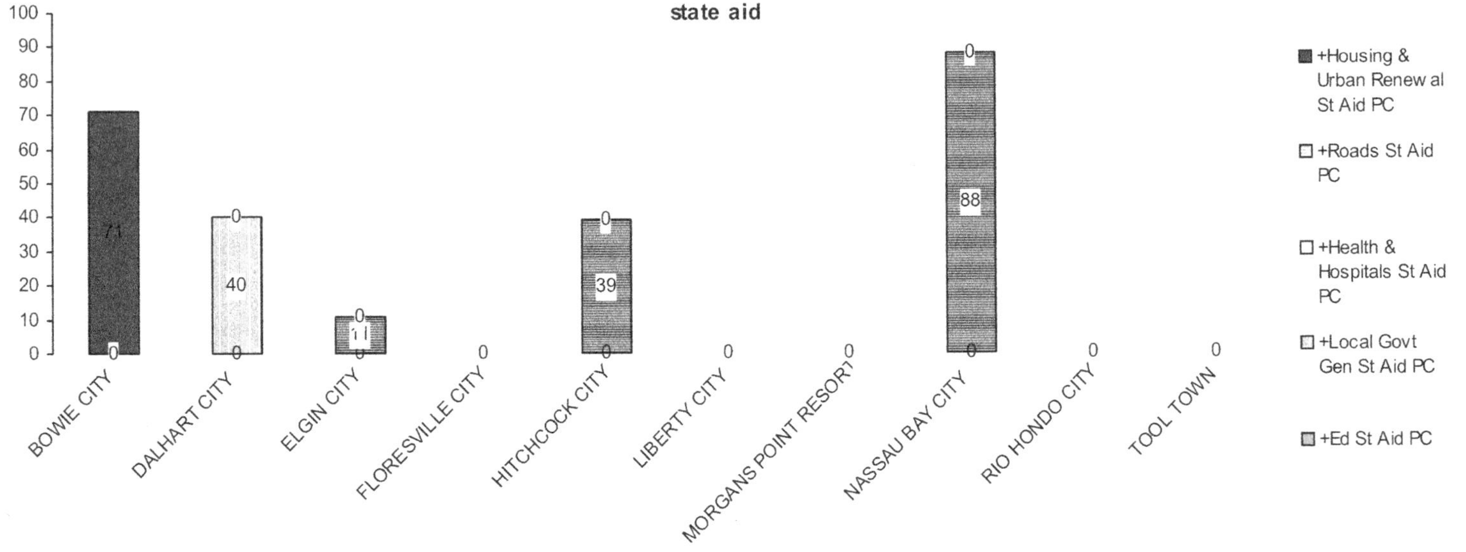

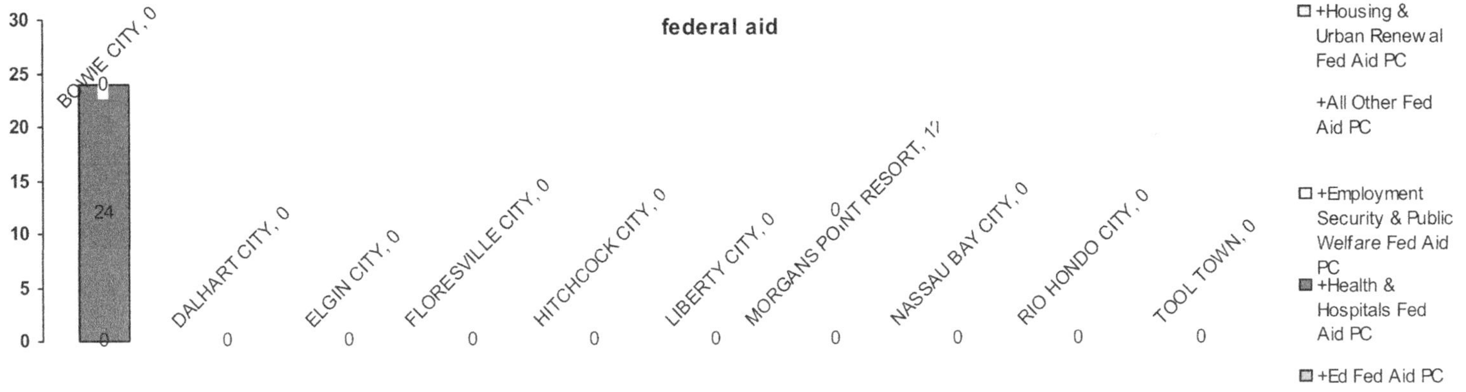

Group **TX22**

	Population	Total Fed Aid PC	Total State Aid
Averages	5667.90	**3.60**	**25.10**

Are you getting your share of state and federal aid?

R2

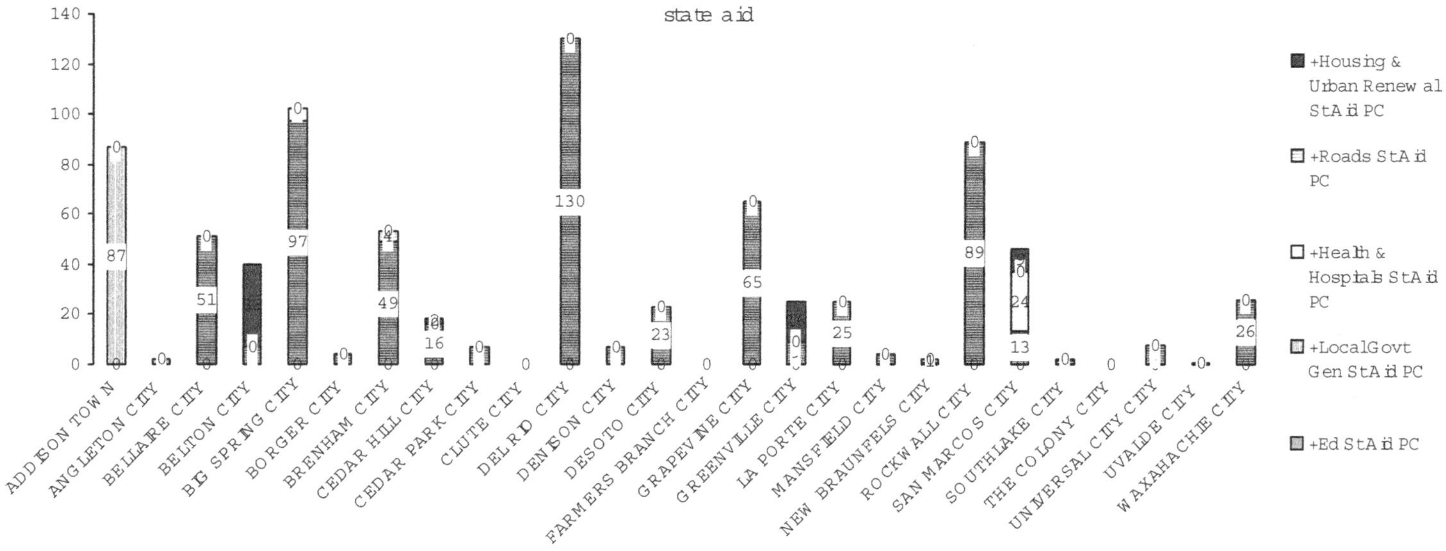

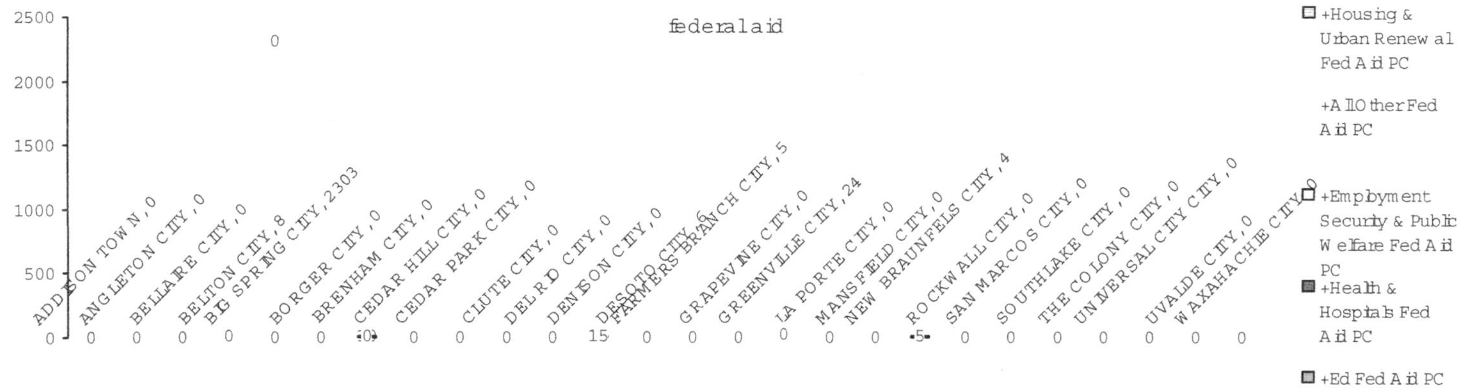

Group TX23

	Population	TotalFedAidPC	TotalStateAid
Averages	28323.35	91.65	32.46

Are you getting your share of state and federal aid?

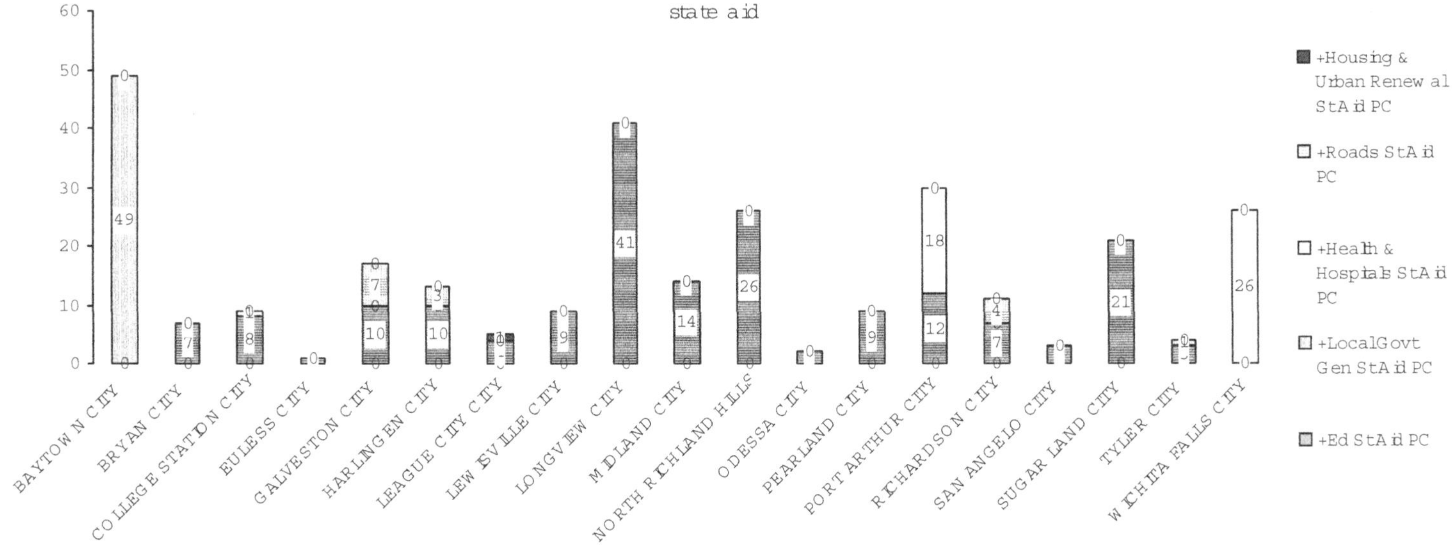

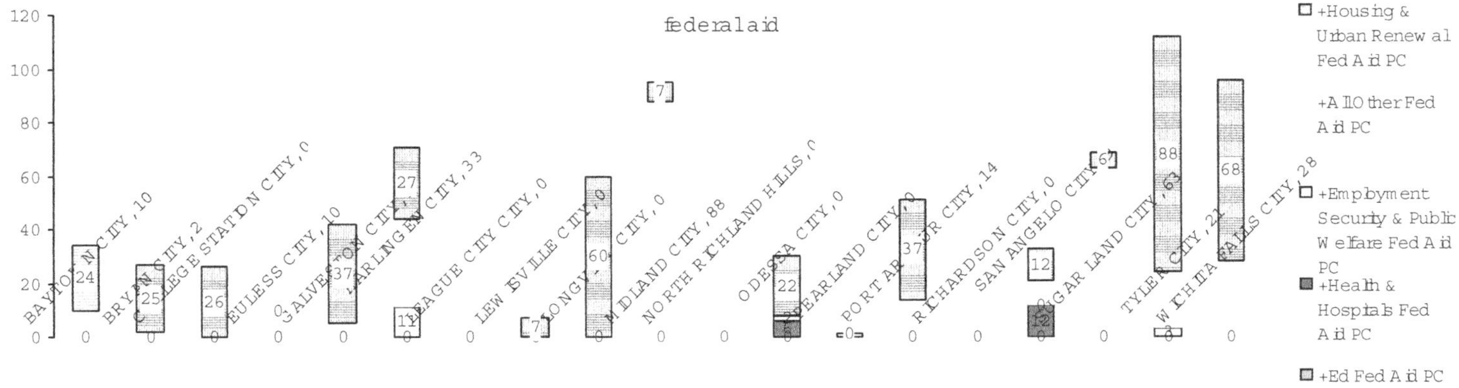

Group TX24

	Population	TotalFedAidPC	TotalStateAid
Averages	75137.95	40.21	16.16

Are you getting your share of state and federal aid?

R2₂

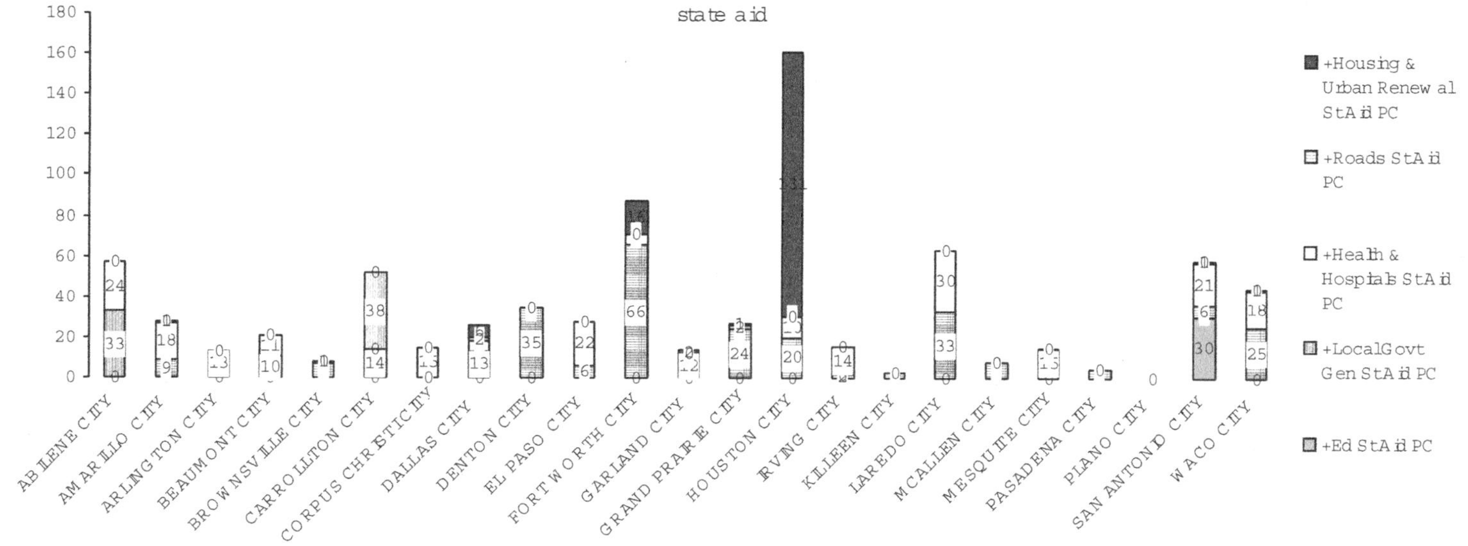

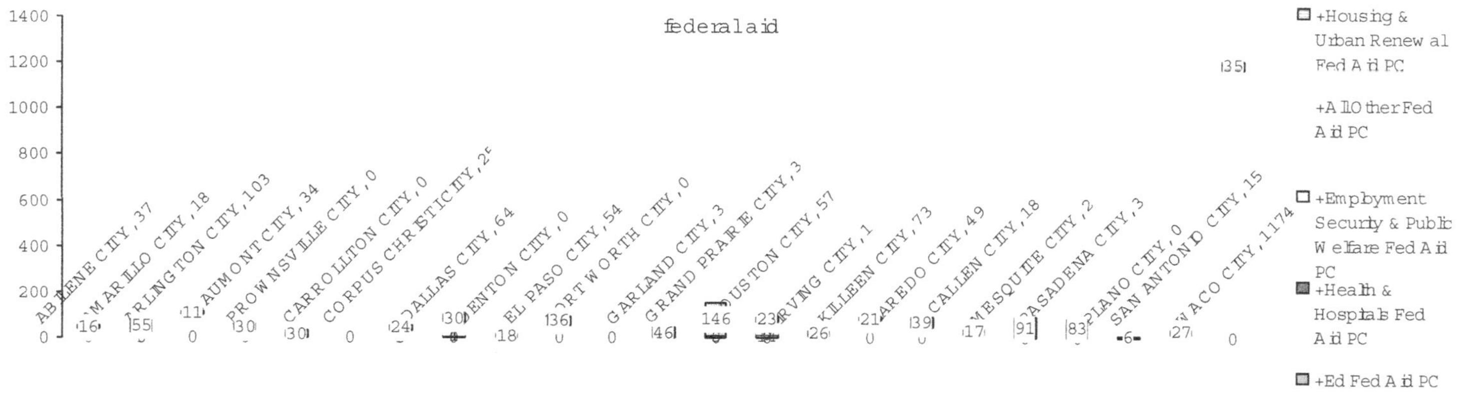

Group TX25

	Population	TotalFedAidPC	TotalStateAid
Averages	382052.22	112.04	37.04

R3 Are User Charges In-line with Operating Expenses?

This is one of 3 graphs to find additional revenue opportunities. By comparing your government to other governments of similar size and type (we call 'peer groups'), you can see if others are using more user charges (per capita) than your government and in which areas.

In this example, the group is AL14, that is Alabama='AL', counties='1', and size class of 50,000 to 100,000 population='4'. So this is displayed as: 'Group AL14'.

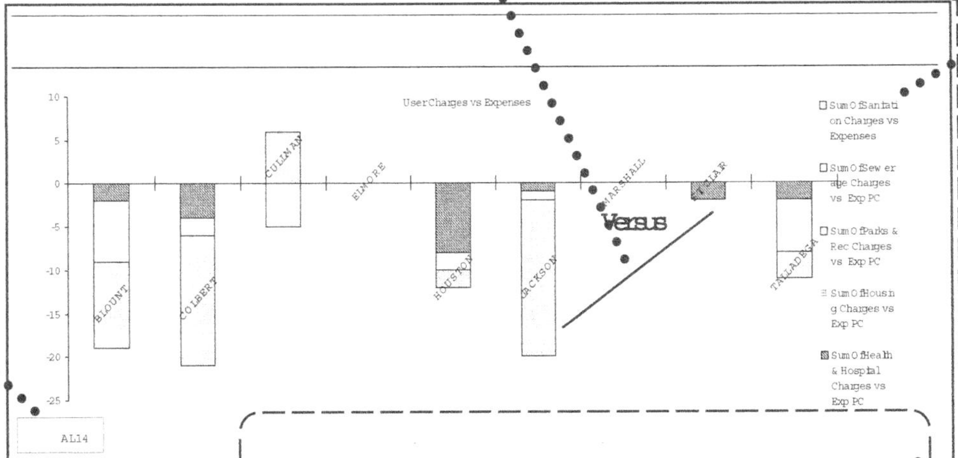

BLOUNT	52968	-2	0	-7	0	-10
COLBERT	54850	-4	0	-2	0	-15
CULLMAN	77973	0	0	-5	0	6
ELMORE	68771	0	0	0	0	0
HOUSTON	89966	-8	0	-2	0	-2
JACKSON	54035	-1	0	-1	0	-18
MARSHALL	83548	0	0	0	0	0
ST CLAIR	67215	-2	0	0	0	0
TALLADEGA	80638	-2	0	-6	0	-3
Averages	69996	-2	0	-3	0	-5

Legend

R3

Listed in order of use on chart, top to bottom

- Sanitation Charges - Expense Per Capita
- Sewerage Charges - Expense Per Capita
- Parks and Rec Charges - Expenses Per Capita
- Housing Charges - Expenses Per Capita
- Health & Hospital Charges - Expenses PC

(Ignore the prefix "sum of" or "sum of total" in the legend, the system inserts this automatically.)

This graph also includes data from various sections in the Governments of Your State book: Total Funds Flow, among other sections. For the greater detail, see these sections, in your state's book.

Finding Your City or County

Each government is found & compared within its peer group. Groups are defined by their state/region, their type of government, and their size class. So, 'XX' for the state or region abbreviation. Then type: 1=counties, 2=cities, towns. Then population size class: 1=under 2,000 population, 2=2,000-10,000, 3=10,000-50,000, 4=50,000-100,000, 5=100,000-250,000, 6=over 250,000.

Texas graph R3 TX-000

Are User Charges In-line with Operating Expenses?

R3

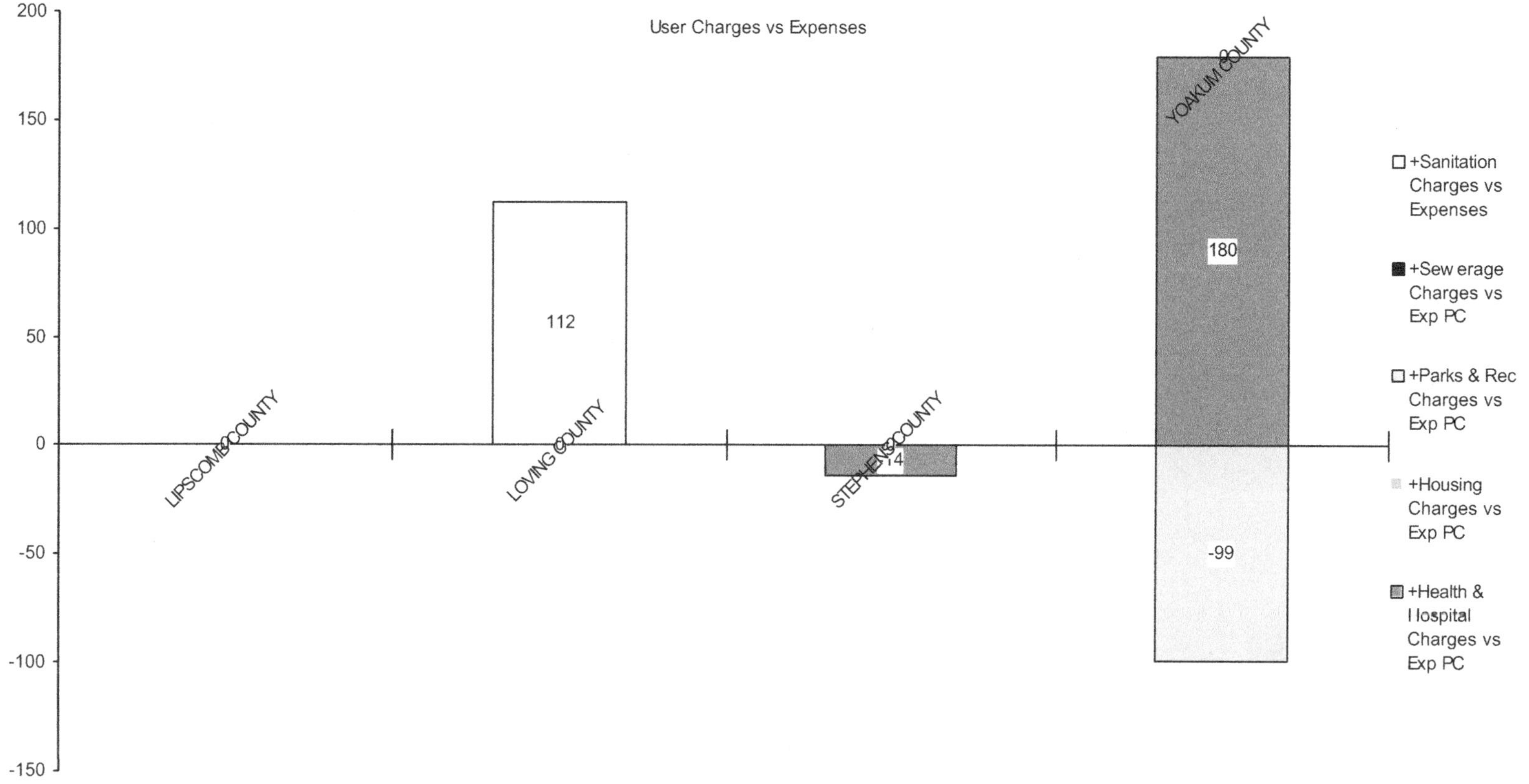

Group TX12 Name	Population	Health Hospital Charges vs Exp PC	Housing Charges vs Exp PC	Parks Rec Charges vs Exp PC	Sewerage Charges vs Exp PC	Sanitation Charges vs Expenses
Averages	**5033.00**	**41.50**	**0.00**	**-24.75**	**0.00**	**28.00**

Are User Charges In-line with Operating Expenses?

R3

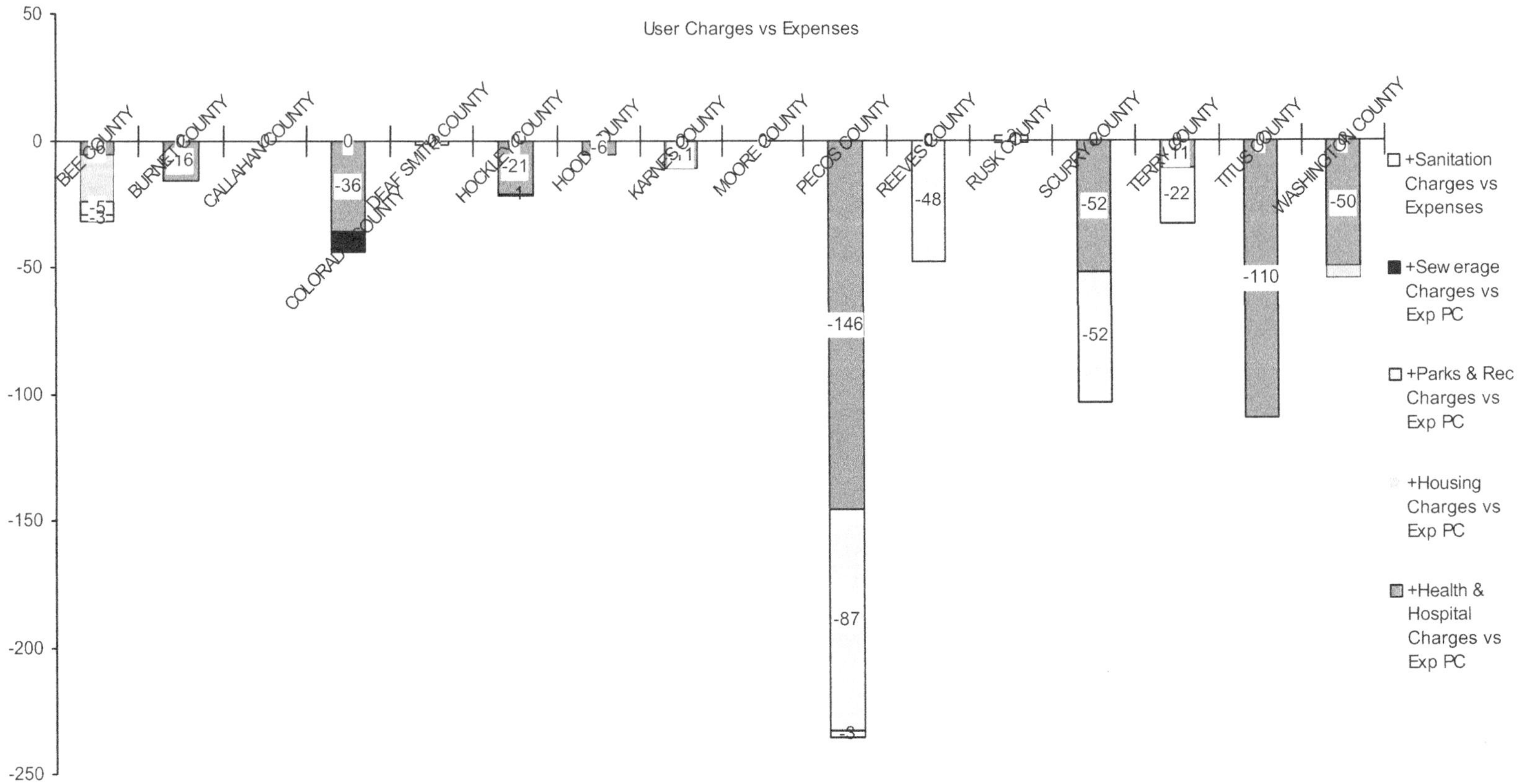

Group TX13 Name	Population	Health Hospital Charges vs Exp PC	Housing Charges vs Exp PC	Parks Rec Charges vs Exp PC	Sewerage Charges vs Exp PC	Sanitation Charges vs Expenses
Averages	24926.56	-29.06	-1.44	-13.56	-0.50	-0.31

Are User Charges In-line with Operating Expenses?

R3

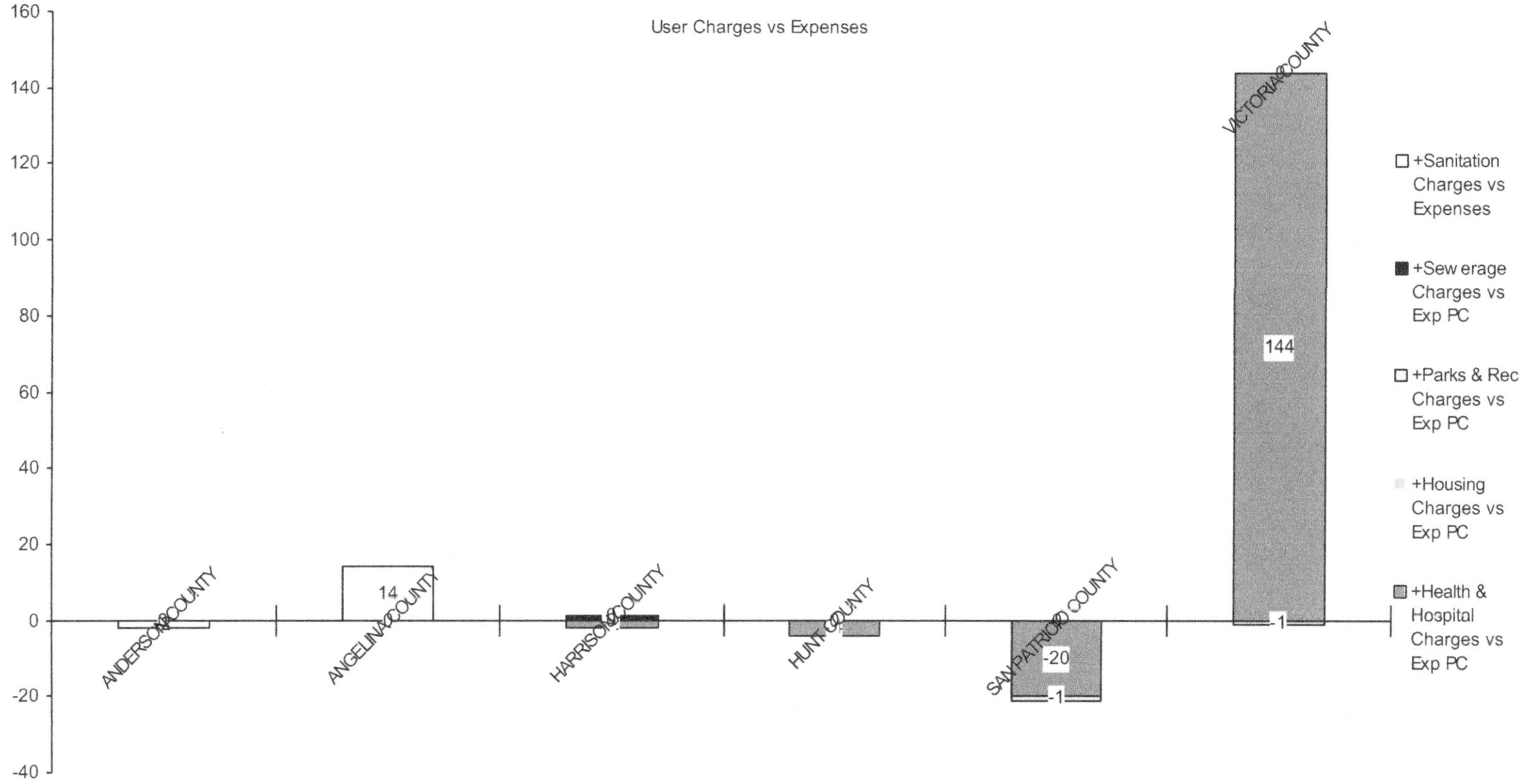

Group TX14 Name	Population	Health Hospital Charges vs Exp PC	Housing Charges vs Exp PC	Parks Rec Charges vs Exp PC	Sewerage Charges vs Exp PC	Sanitation Charges vs Expenses
Averages	**73137.33**	**19.67**	**0.00**	**-0.33**	**0.17**	**2.00**

Are User Charges In-line with Operating Expenses? R3

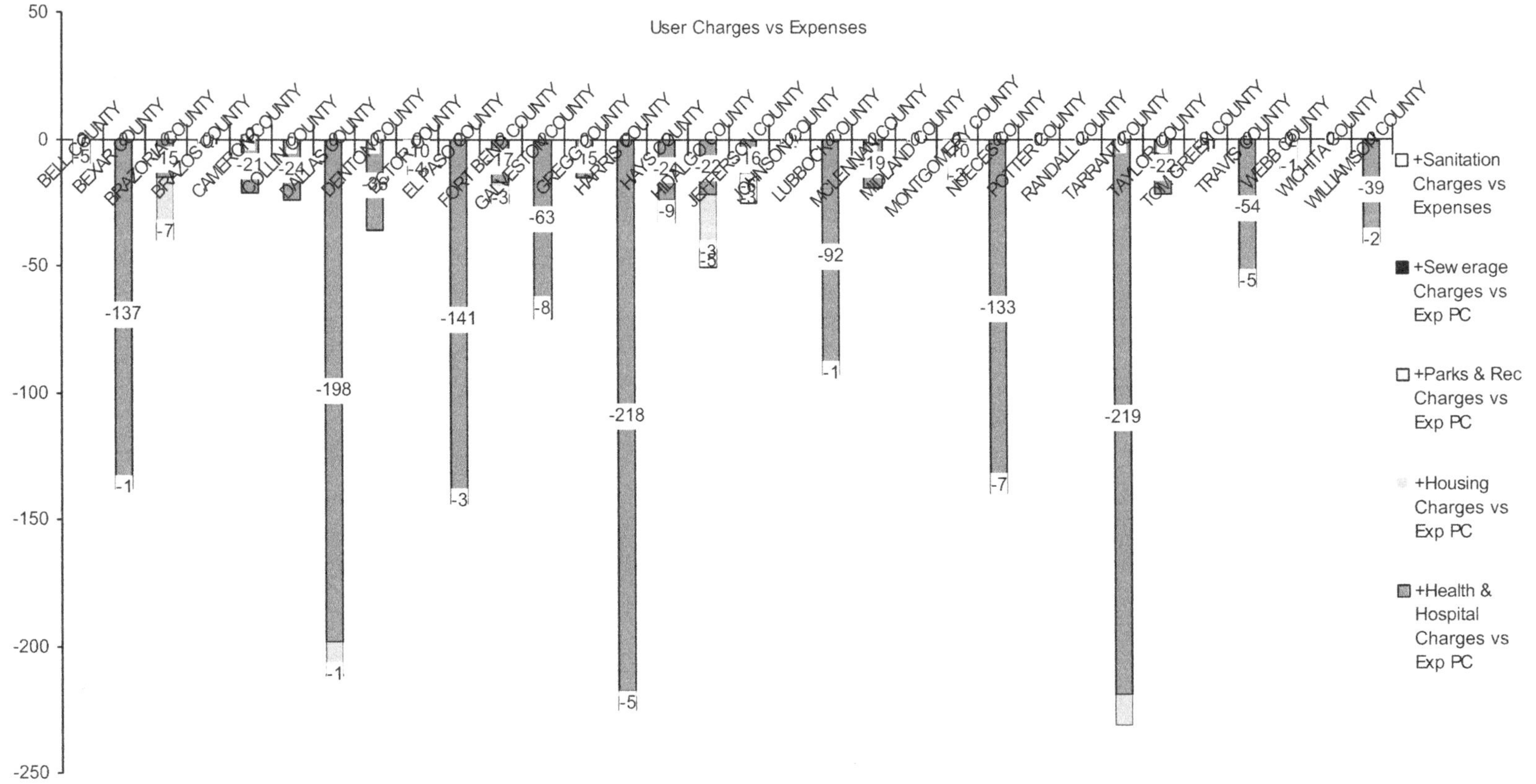

Group TX15 Name	Population	Health Hospital Charges vs Exp PC	Housing Charges vs Exp PC	Parks Rec Charges vs Exp PC	Sewerage Charges vs Exp PC	Sanitation Charges vs Expenses
Averages	551497.13	-48.75	-2.63	-2.25	0.00	-0.25

Are User Charges In-line with Operating Expenses? R3

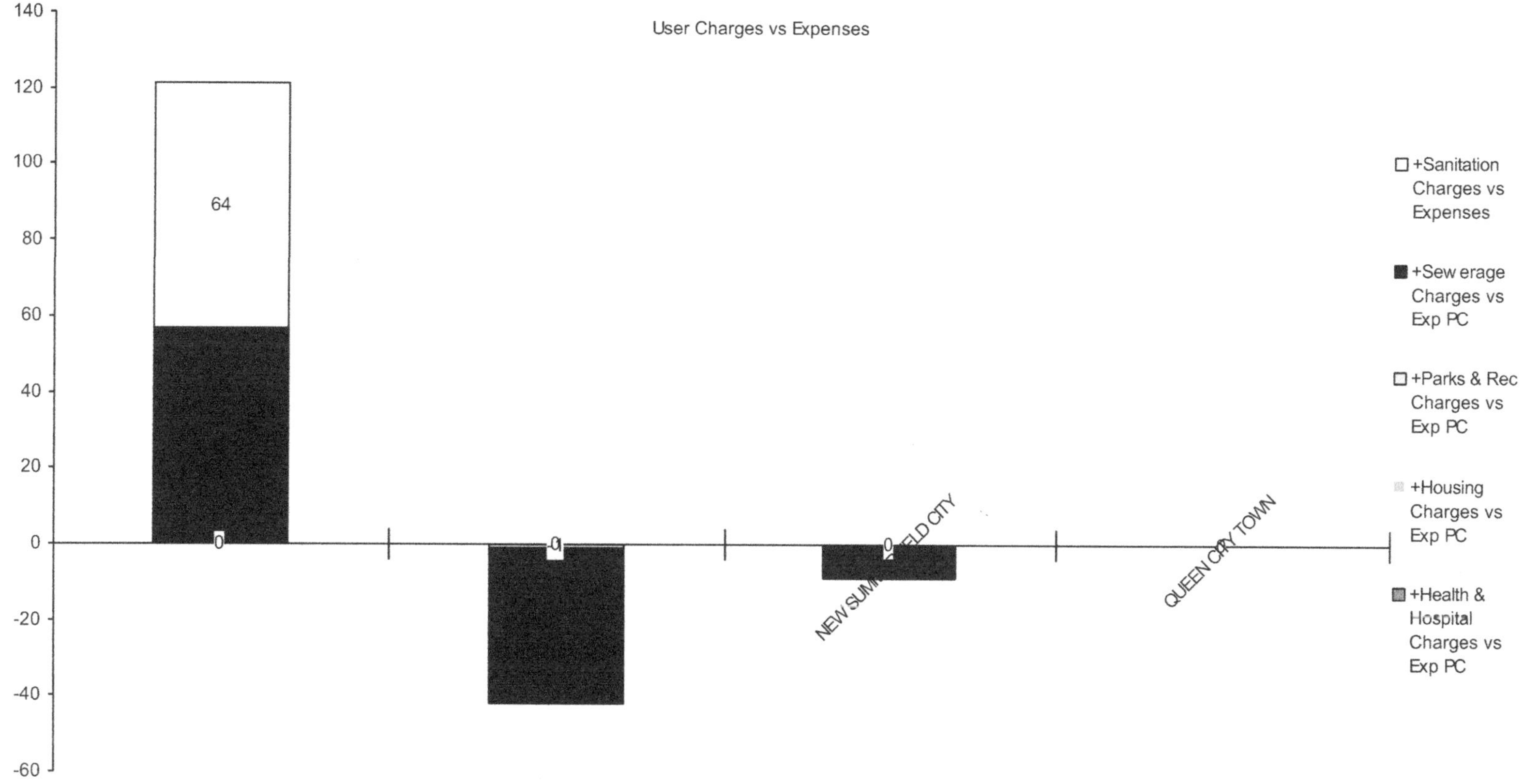

Group TX21 Name	Population	Health Hospital Charges vs Exp PC	Housing Charges vs Exp PC	Parks Rec Charges vs Exp PC	Sewerage Charges vs Exp PC	Sanitation Charges vs Expenses
Averages	979.00	0.00	0.00	-0.25	1.75	16.00

Are User Charges In-line with Operating Expenses? **R3**

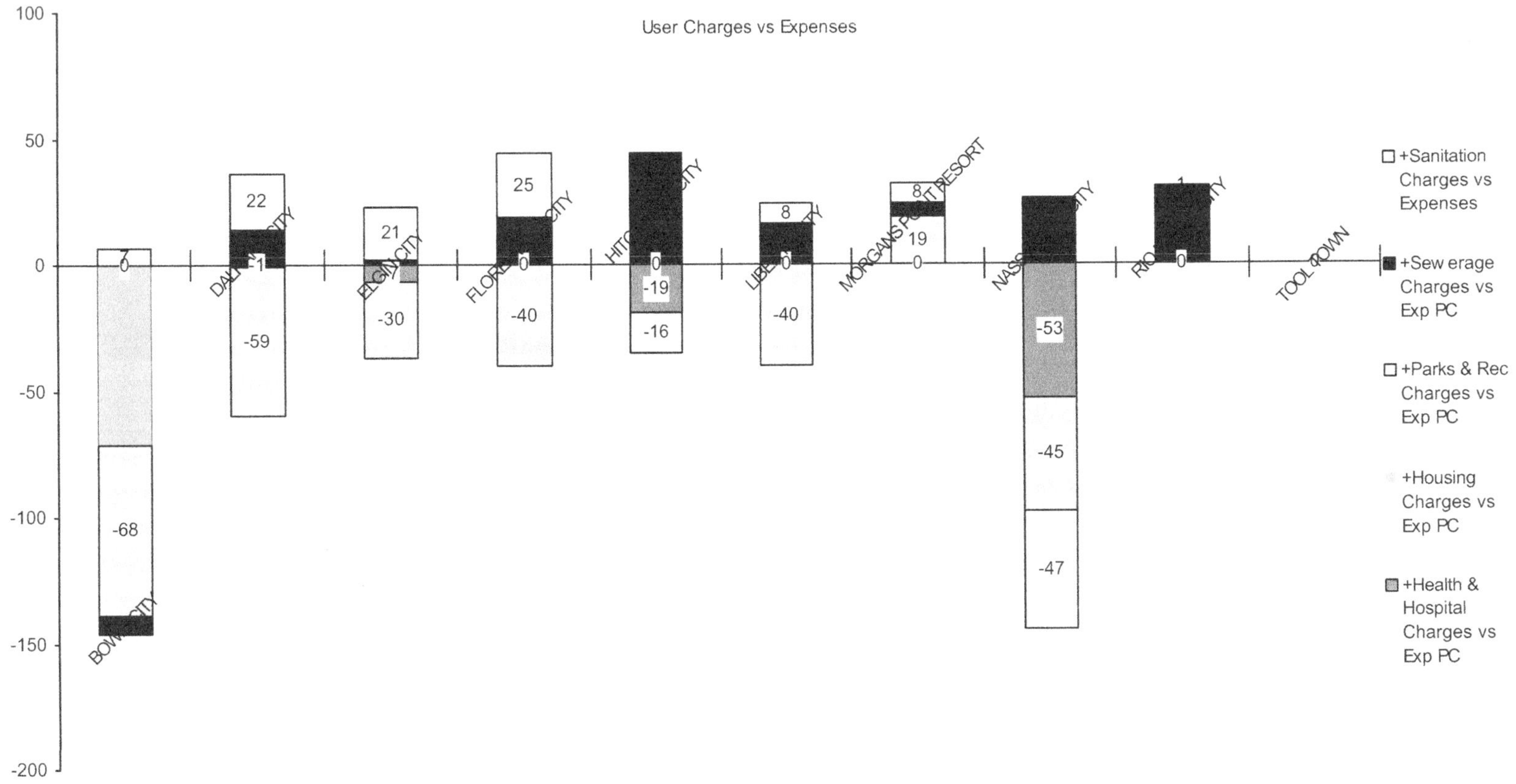

Group TX22 Name	Population	Health Hospital Charges vs Exp PC	Housing Charges vs Exp PC	Parks Rec Charges vs Exp PC	Sewerage Charges vs Exp PC	Sanitation Charges vs Expenses
Averages	5667.90	-8.00	-7.10	-26.30	14.90	2.90

Are User Charges In-line with Operating Expenses?

R3

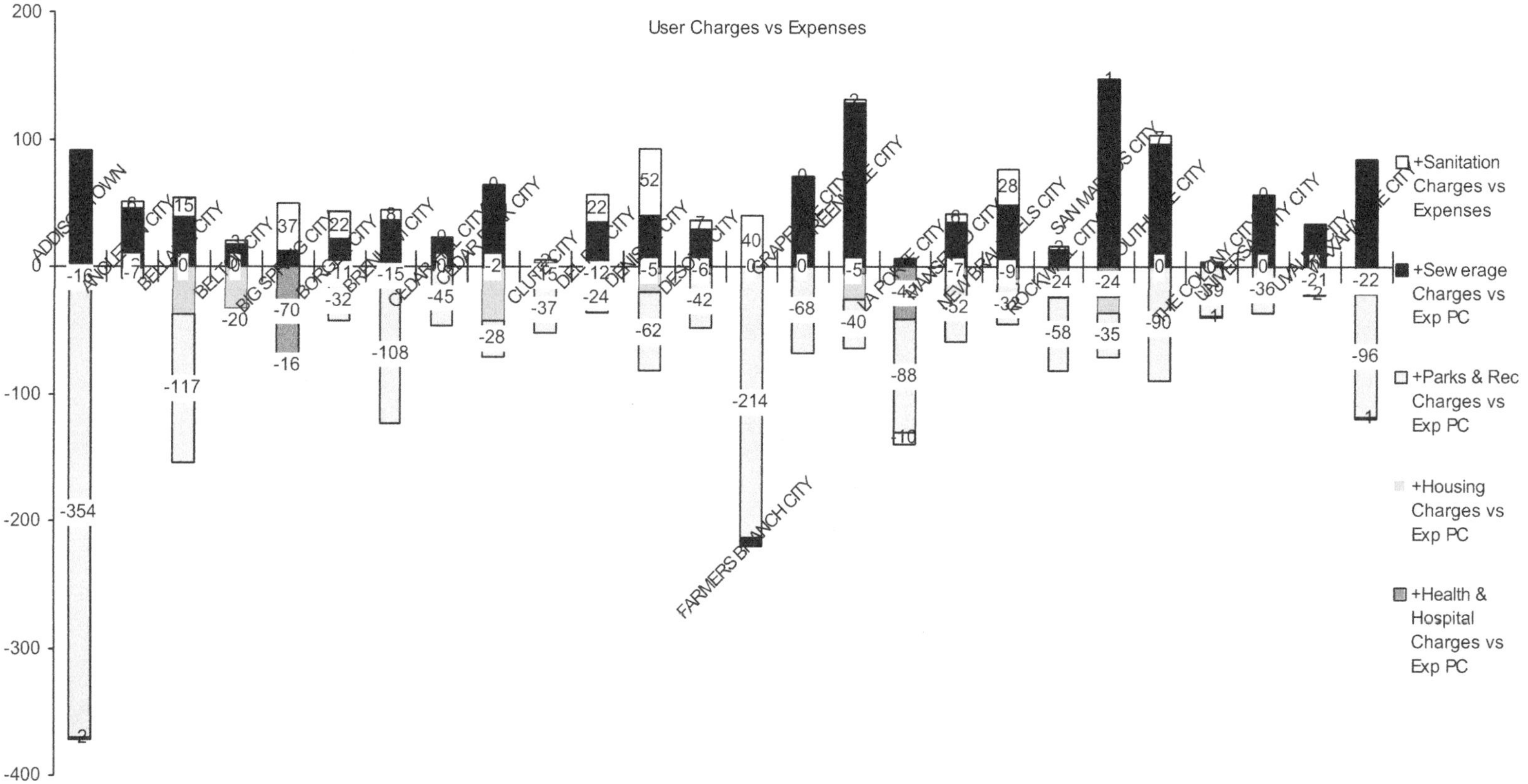

Group TX23 Name	Population	Health Hospital Charges vs Exp PC	Housing Charges vs Exp PC	Parks Rec Charges vs Exp PC	Sewerage Charges vs Exp PC	Sanitation Charges vs Expenses
Averages	**28323.35**	**-11.04**	**-6.38**	**-67.73**	**45.27**	**9.38**

Are User Charges In-line with Operating Expenses?

R3

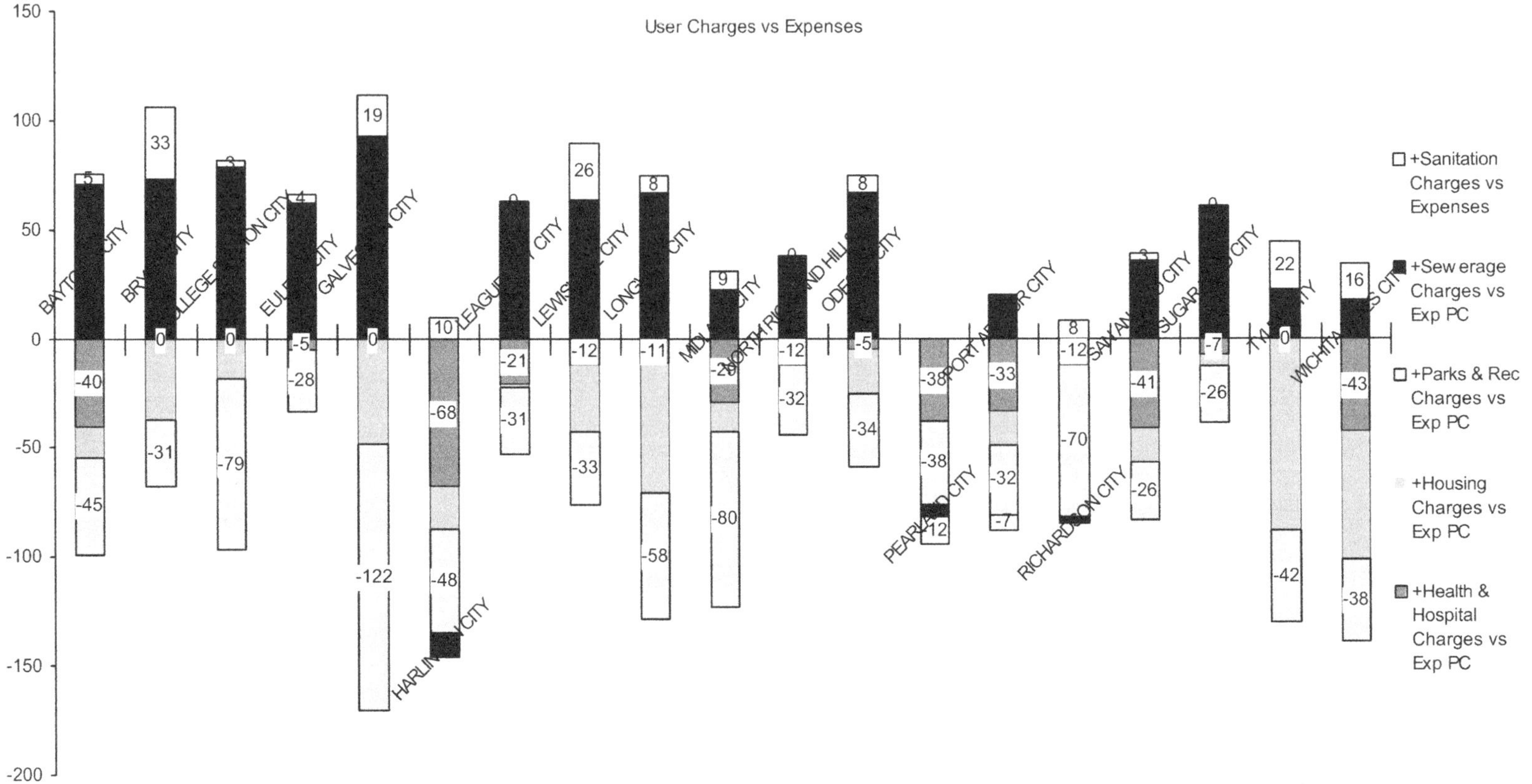

Group TX24 Name	Population	Health Hospital Charges vs Exp PC	Housing Charges vs Exp PC	Parks Rec Charges vs Exp PC	Sewerage Charges vs Exp PC	Sanitation Charges vs Expenses
Averages	75137.95	-19.84	-23.47	-47.00	44.00	8.16

Are User Charges In-line with Operating Expenses? R3

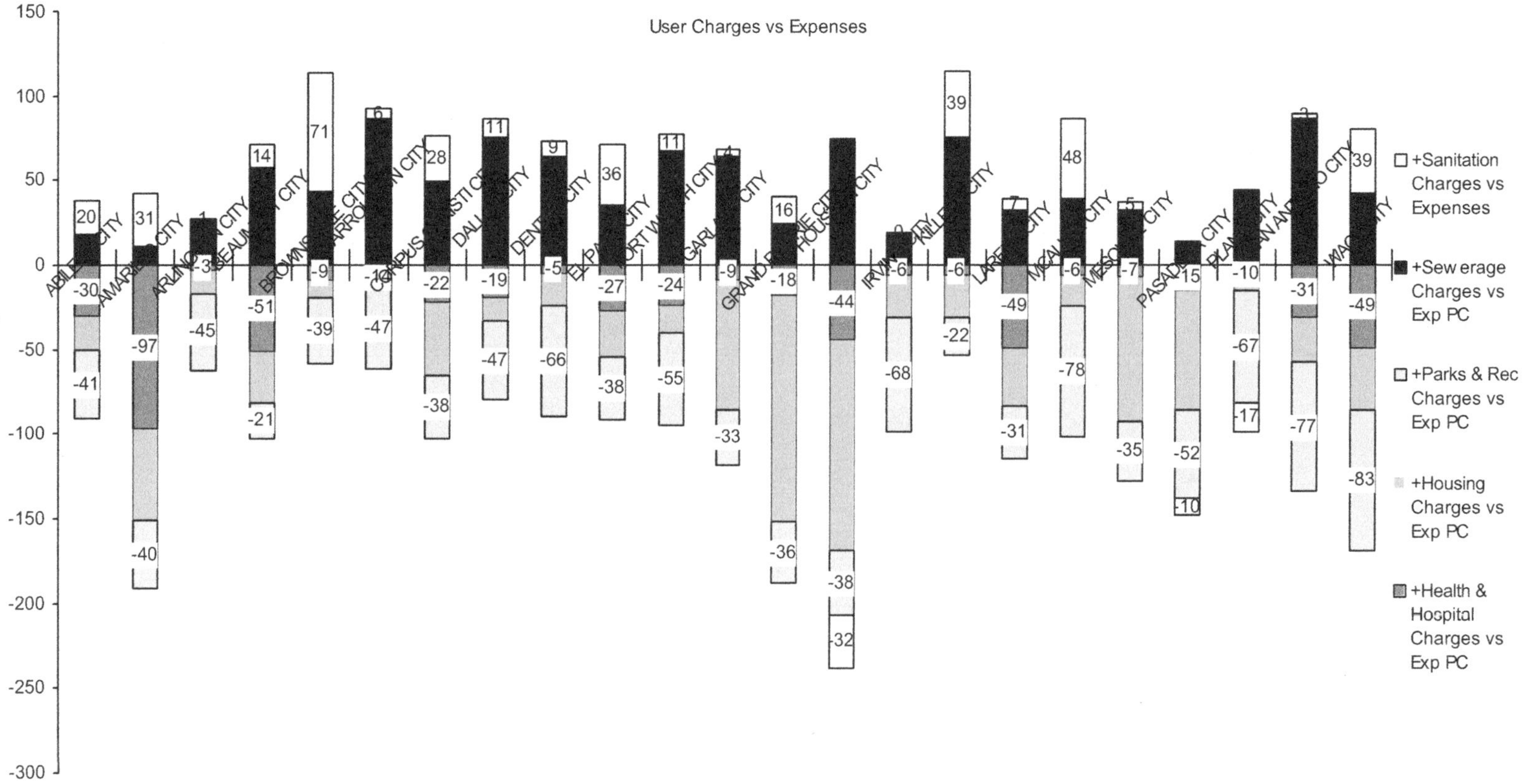

Group TX25 Name	Population	Health Hospital Charges vs Exp PC	Housing Charges vs Exp PC	Parks Rec Charges vs Exp PC	Sewerage Charges vs Exp PC	Sanitation Charges vs Expenses
Averages	**382052.22**	**-23.96**	**-39.65**	**-47.70**	**46.96**	**14.78**

S1 Are You Getting Your Share of Debt and Taxes in Your County?

This is one graph to find if your governments is getting a fair share of the debt and taxes used by governments in your county. Only those governments covered this year are displayed. Governments shown here must have at least 5% of either county debt or taxes.

Legend

S1 Listed in order of use on chart, top to bottom

Each government in the county is shaded slightly differently. Usually the shade is the same in the Debt and Taxes pie.

(Ignore the prefix "sum of" or "sum of total" in the legend, the system inserts this automatically.)

In this example, the groups are the governments that we covered in 2 Alabama counties. The group for Calhoun County is displayed as: 'State/County: AL/CALHOUN'.

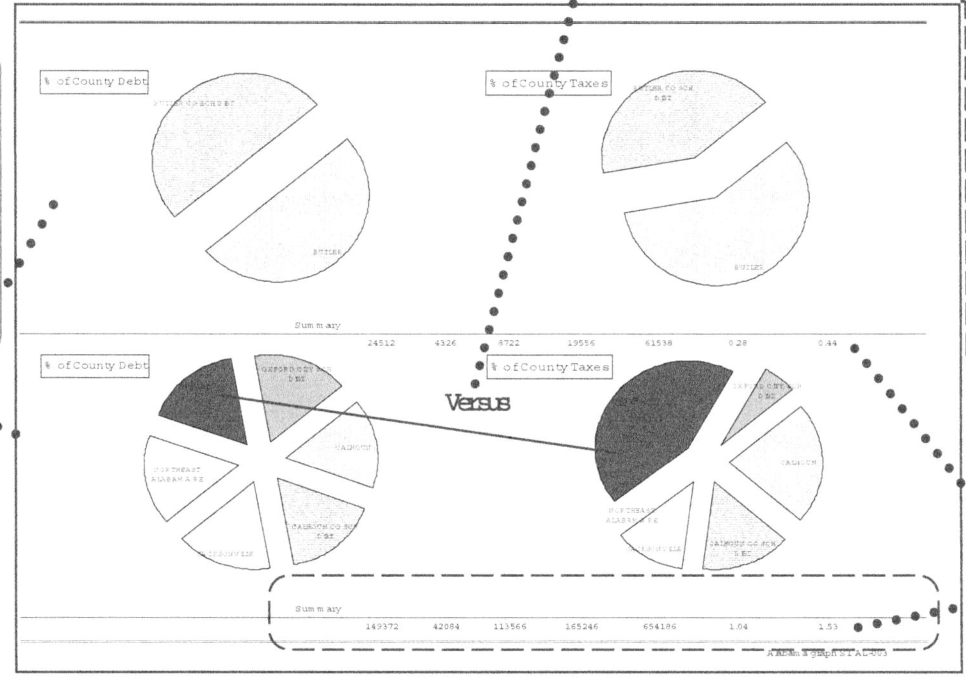

This graph also includes data from various sections in the Governments of Your State book: Total Funds Flow, among other sections. For the greater detail, see these sections, in your state's book.

Finding Your City or County

Texas graph S1 TX-000

Are you getting your share of debt and taxes in your county? S1

% of County Debt

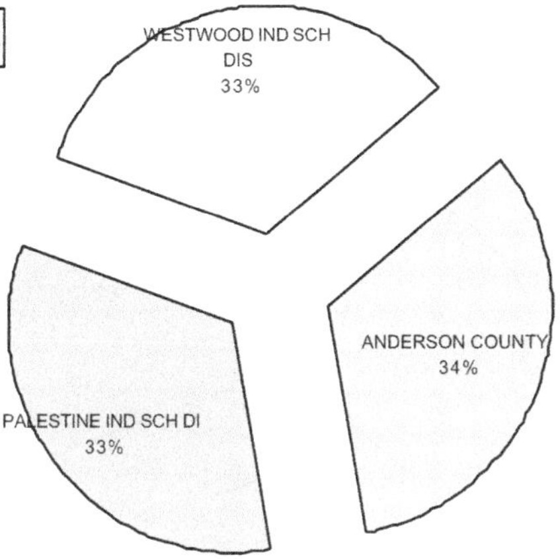

State/County

TX / ANDERSON

VERSUS

% of County Taxes

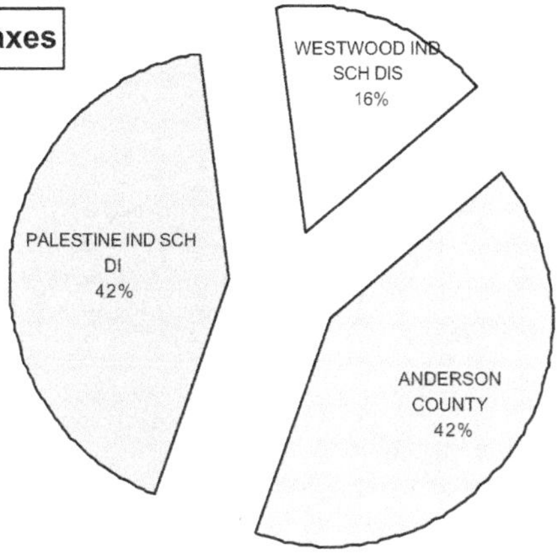

% of County Debt

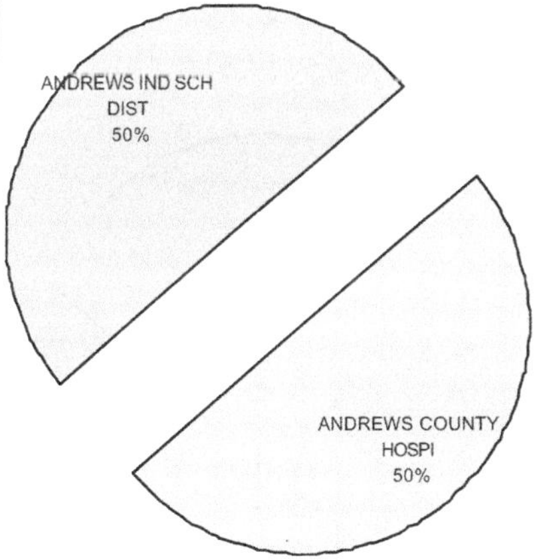

State/County

TX / ANDREWS

VERSUS

% of County Taxes

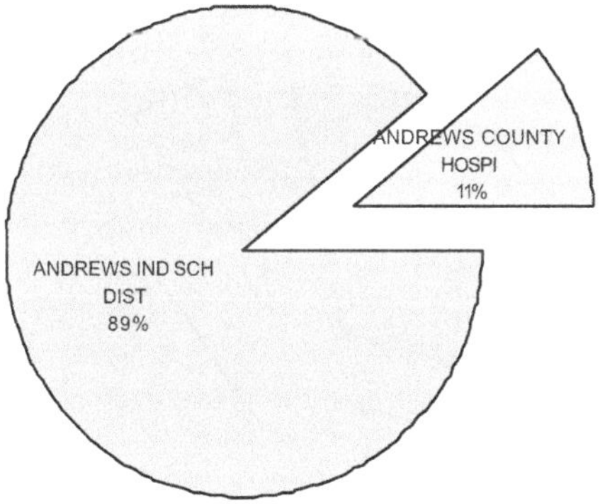

Are you getting your share of debt and taxes in your county?

S1

State/County

TX / ANGELINA

% of County Debt

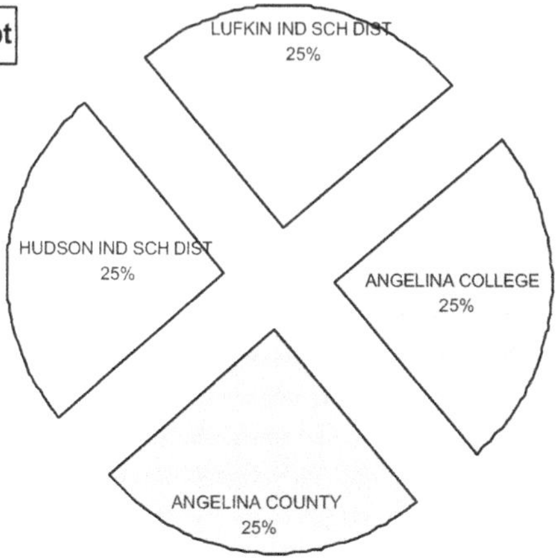

VERSUS

% of County Taxes

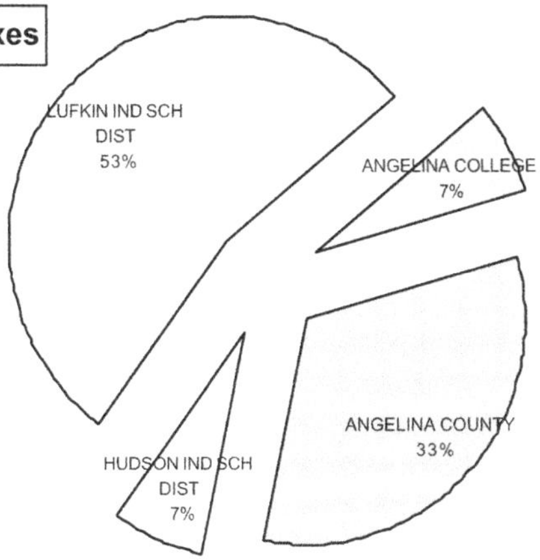

State/County

TX / ARCHER

% of County Debt

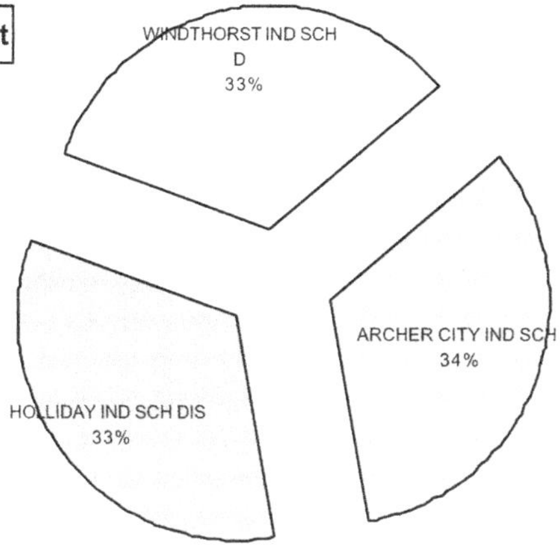

VERSUS

% of County Taxes

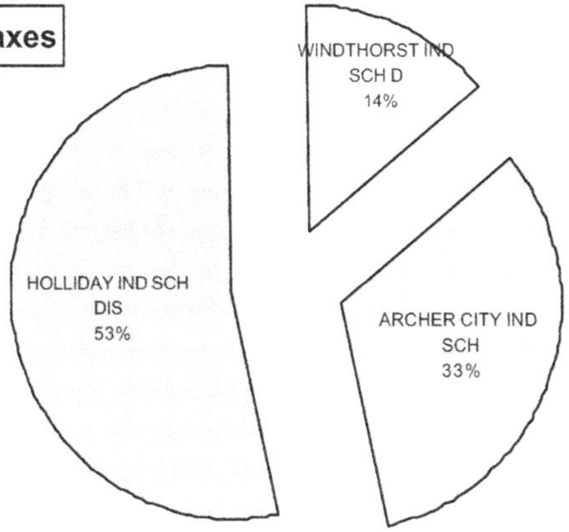

Are you getting your share of debt and taxes in your county? S1

State/County
TX / ATASCOSA

% of County Debt

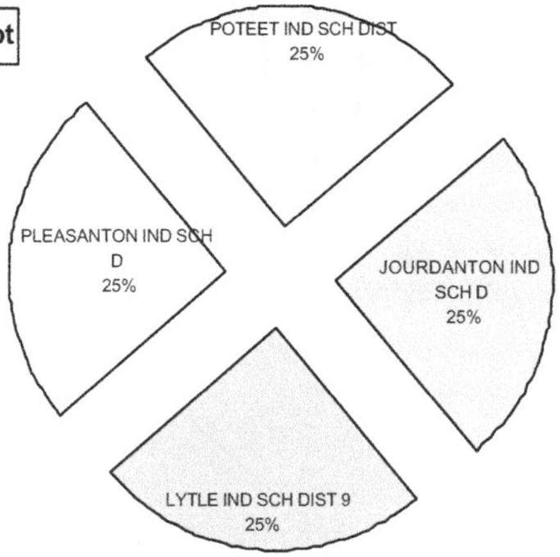

VERSUS

% of County Taxes

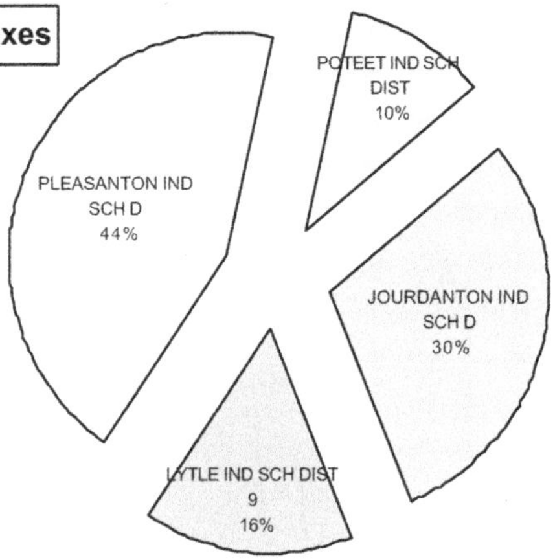

State/County
TX / AUSTIN

% of County Debt

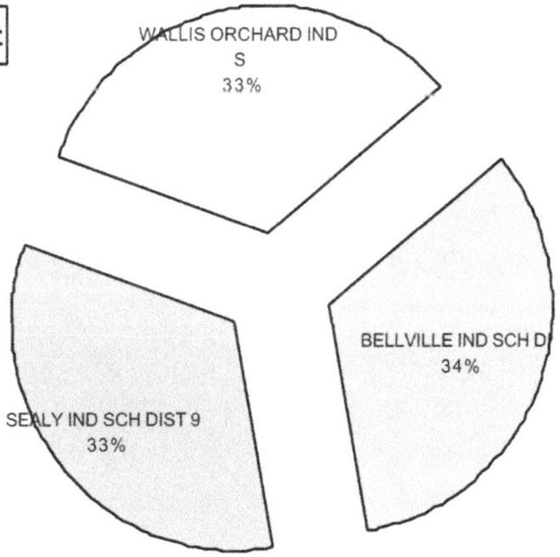

VERSUS

% of County Taxes

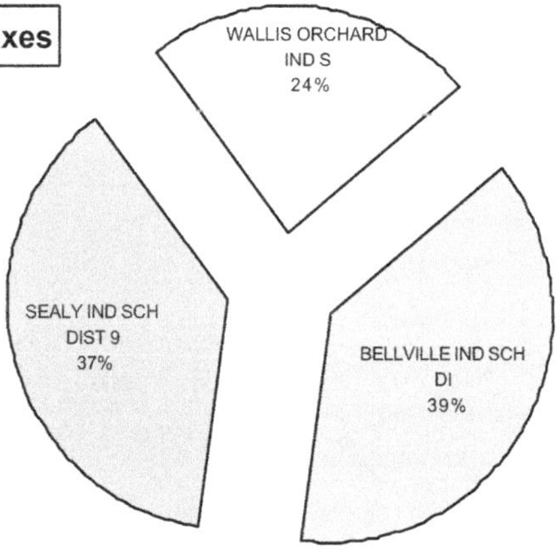

Are you getting your share of debt and taxes in your county?

S1

% of County Debt

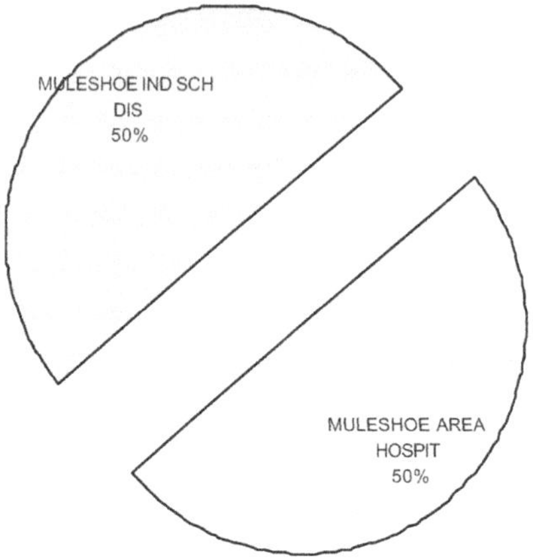

State/County

TX / BAILEY

VERSUS

% of County Taxes

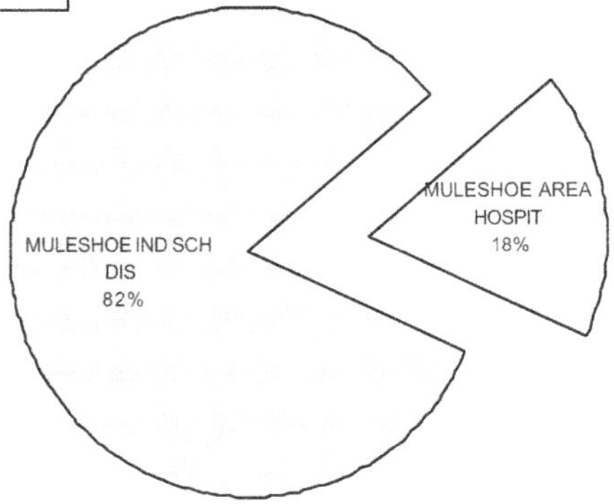

% of County Debt

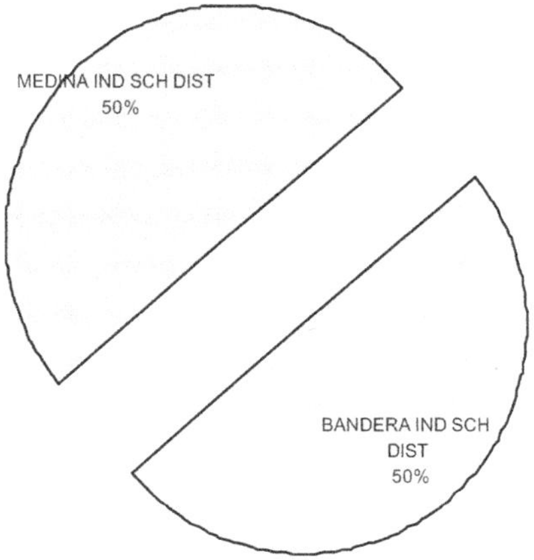

State/County

TX / BANDERA

VERSUS

% of County Taxes

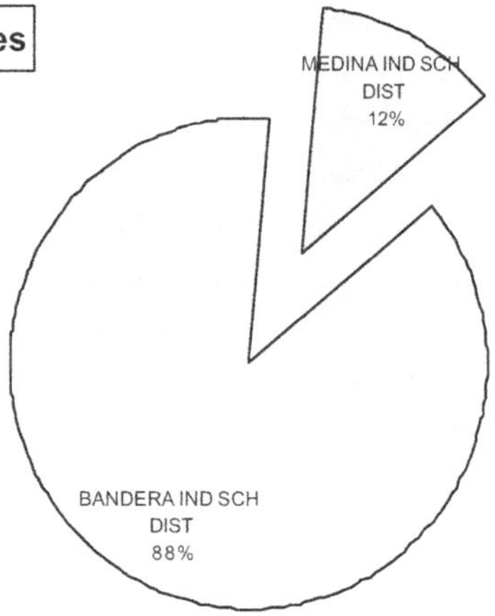

Are you getting your share of debt and taxes in your county? S1

% of County Debt

State/County

TX / BASTROP

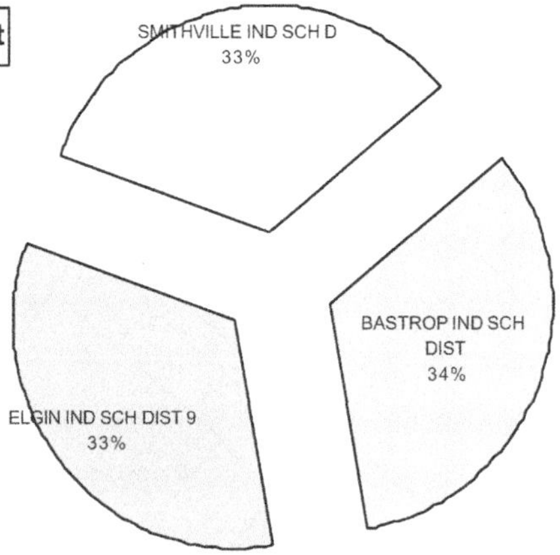

VERSUS

% of County Taxes

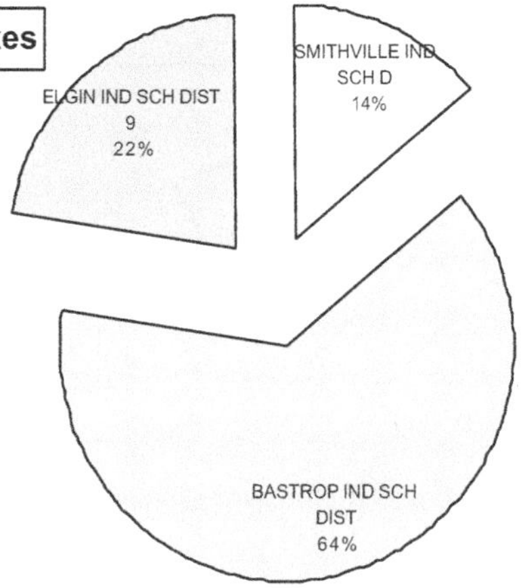

% of County Debt

State/County

TX / BEE

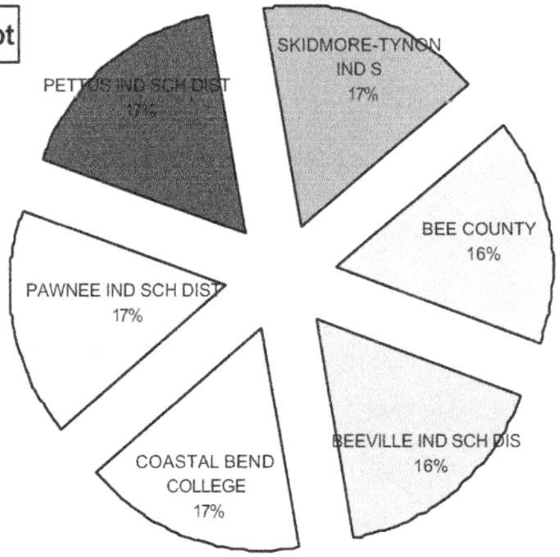

VERSUS

% of County Taxes

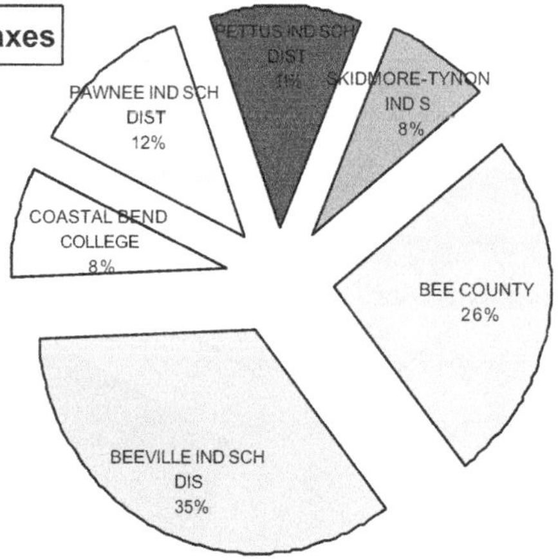

Are you getting your share of debt and taxes in your county? **S1**

State/County
TX / BELL

% of County Debt

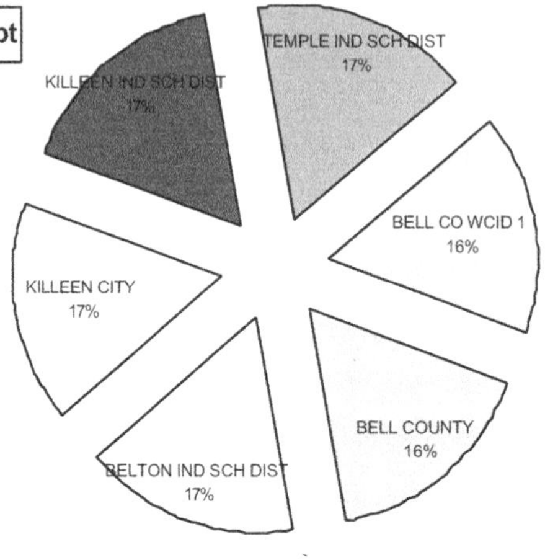

VERSUS

% of County Taxes

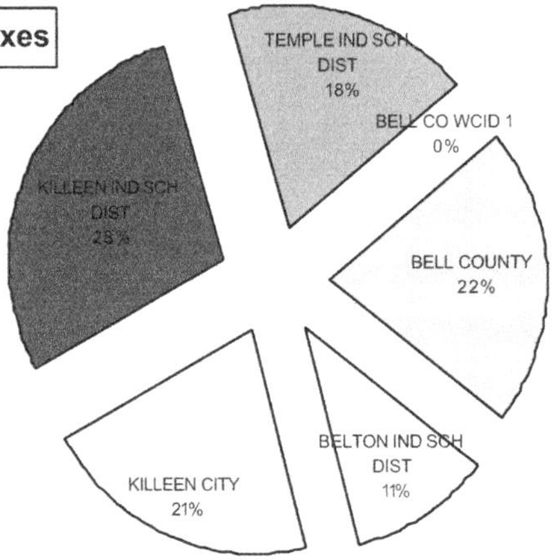

State/County
TX / BEXAR

% of County Debt

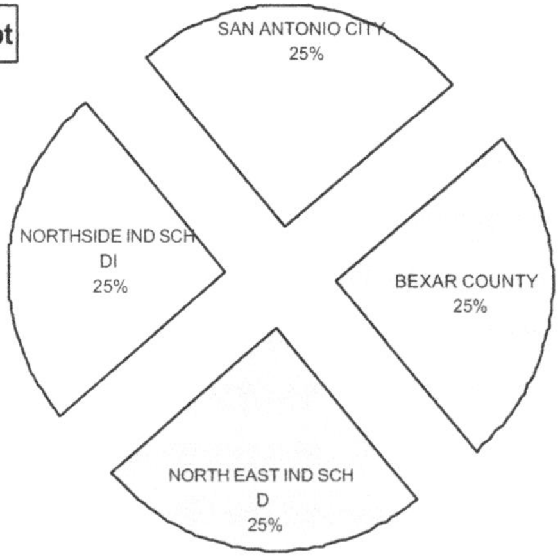

VERSUS

% of County Taxes

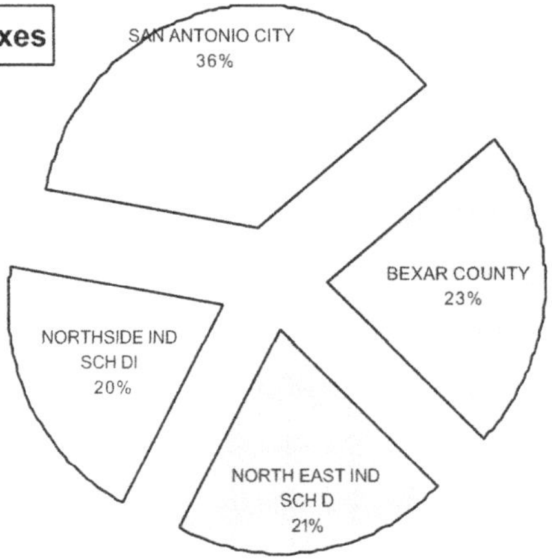

Are you getting your share of debt and taxes in your county?

S1

% of County Debt

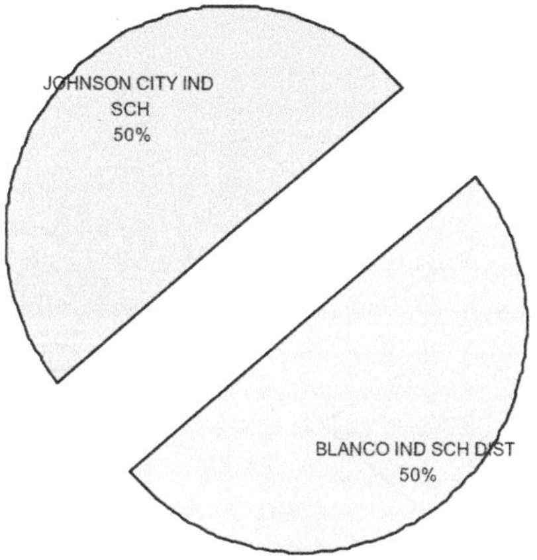

State/County

TX / BLANCO

VERSUS

% of County Taxes

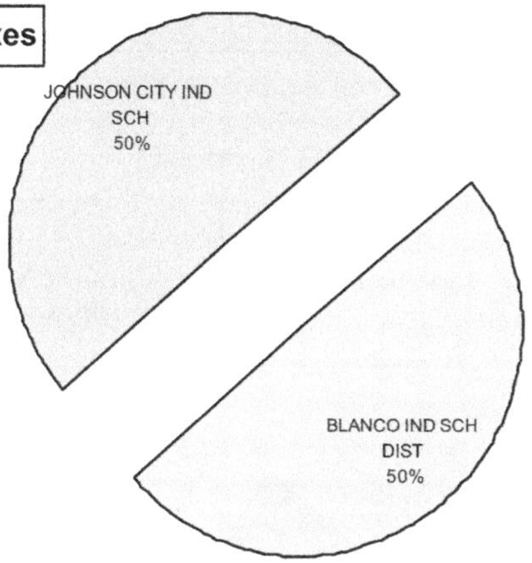

% of County Debt

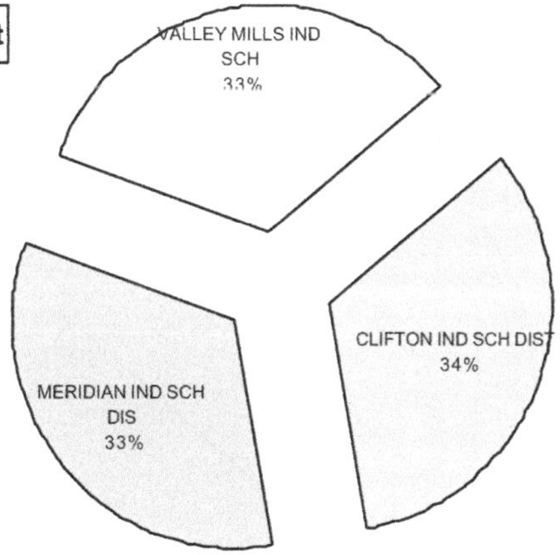

State/County

TX / BOSQUE

VERSUS

% of County Taxes

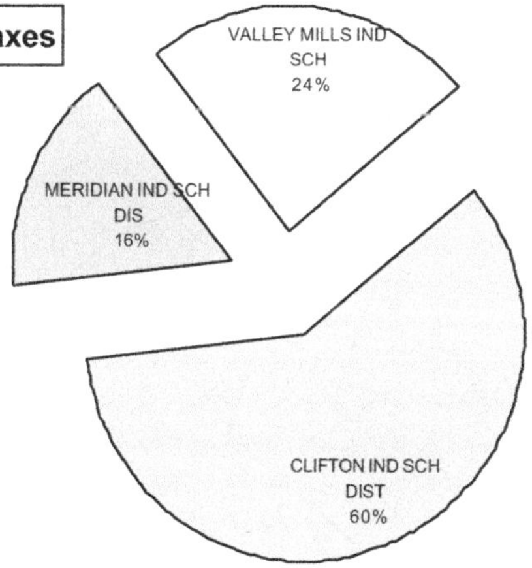

Are you getting your share of debt and taxes in your county? S1

State/County
TX / BOWIE

% of County Debt

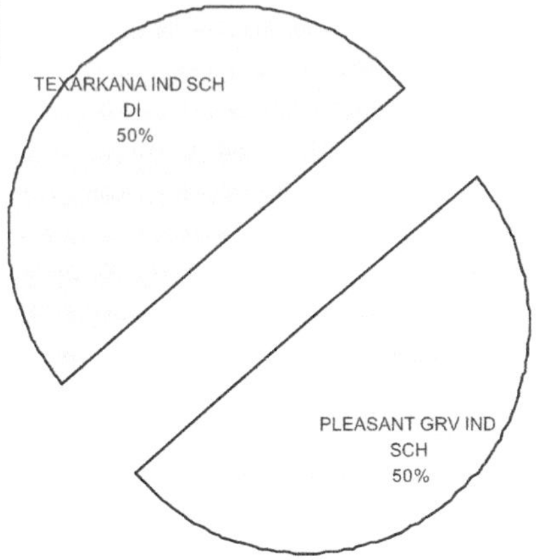

VERSUS

% of County Taxes

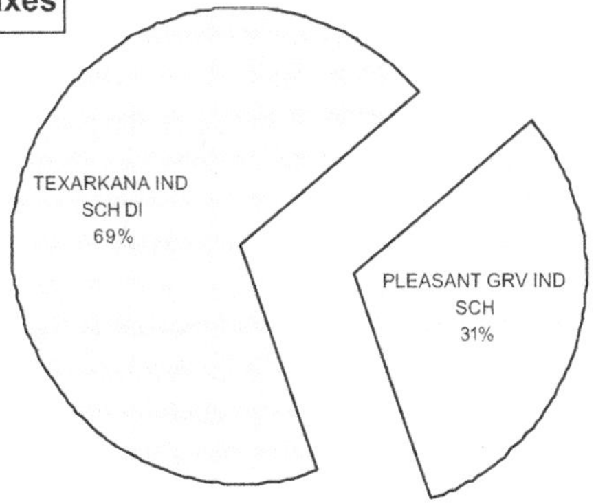

State/County
TX / BRAZORIA

% of County Debt

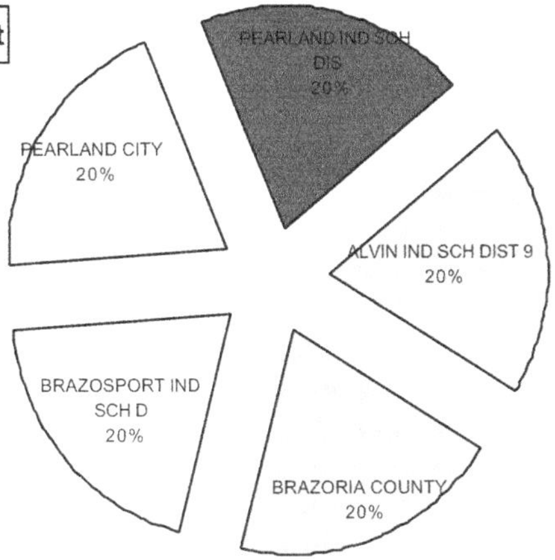

VERSUS

% of County Taxes

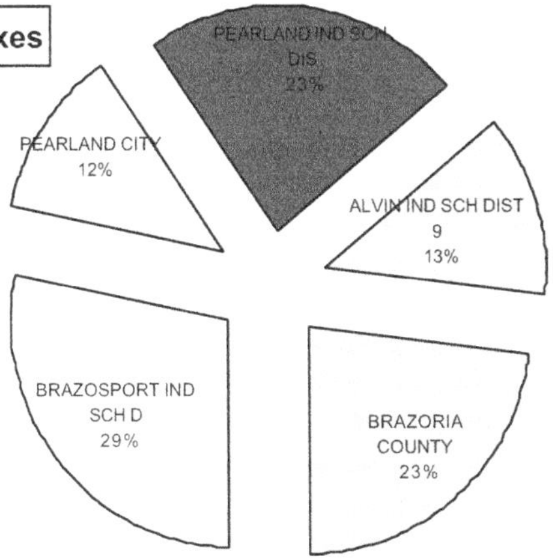

Are you getting your share of debt and taxes in your county?

S1

% of County Debt

State/County

TX / BRAZOS

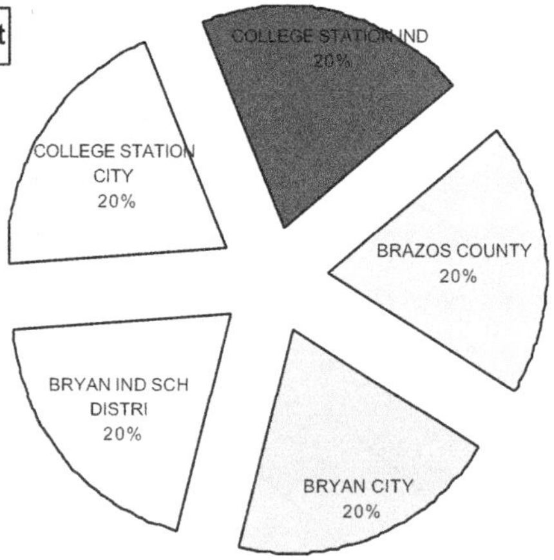

VERSUS

% of County Taxes

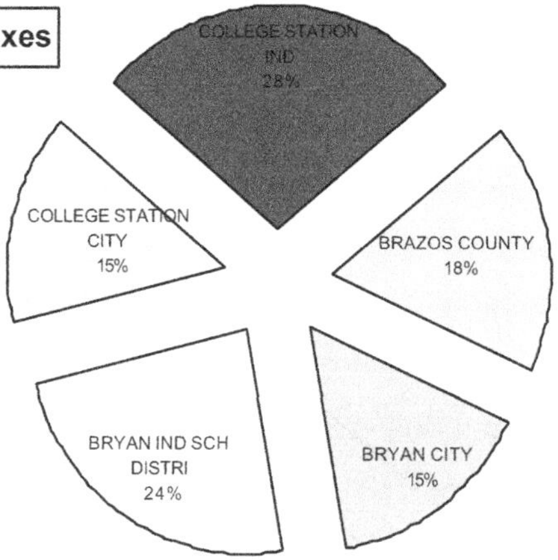

% of County Debt

State/County

TX / BREWSTER

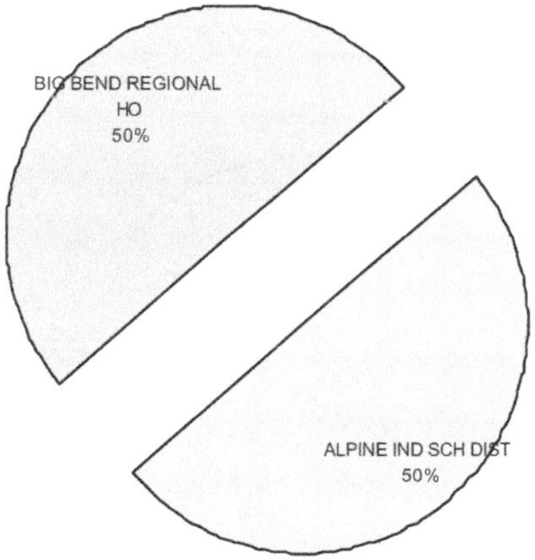

VERSUS

% of County Taxes

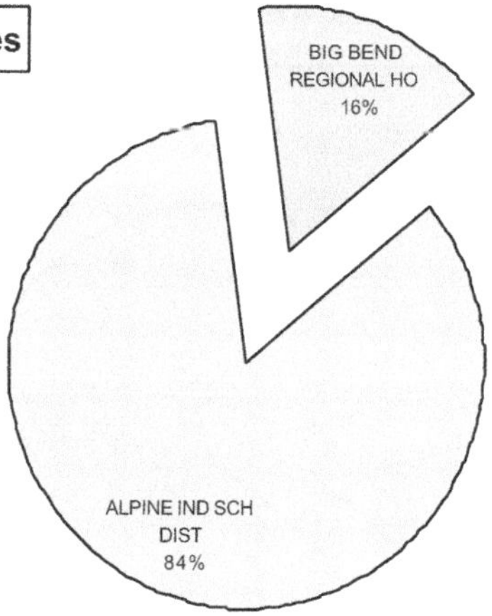

Are you getting your share of debt and taxes in your county? **S1**

% of County Debt

State/County
TX / BROWN

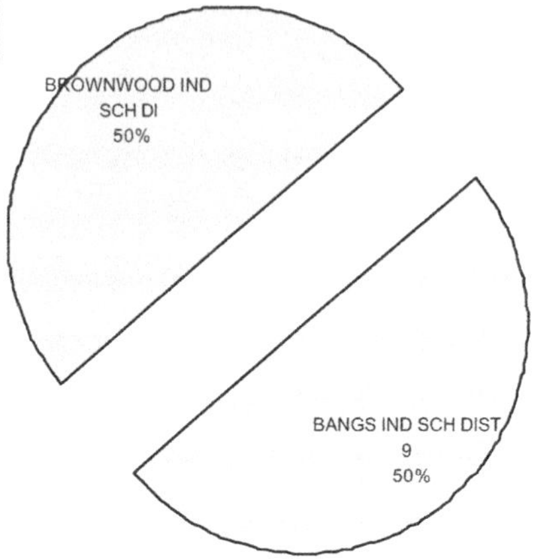

VERSUS

% of County Taxes

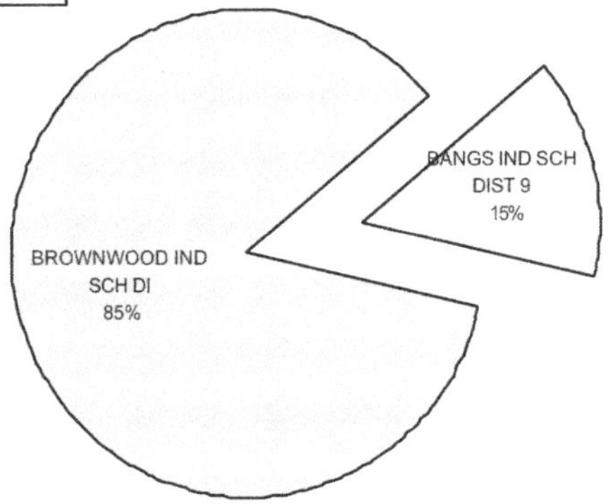

% of County Debt

State/County
TX / BURLESON

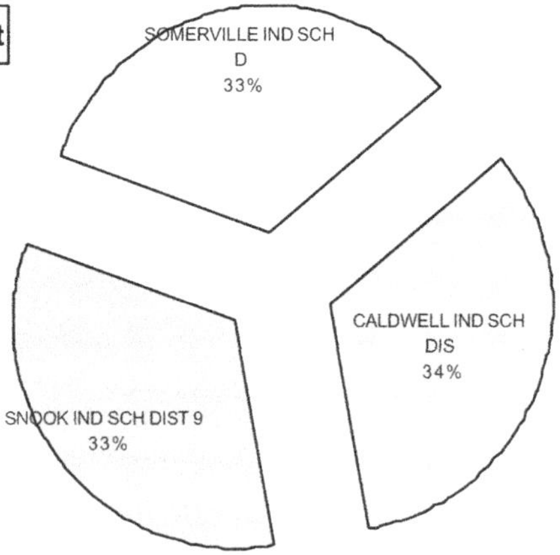

VERSUS

% of County Taxes

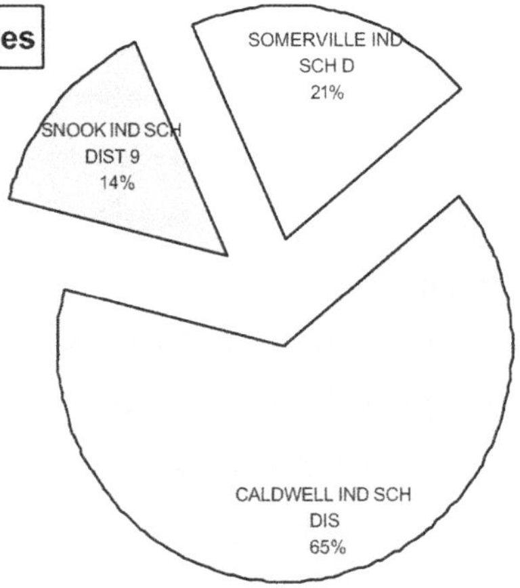

Are you getting your share of debt and taxes in your county?

S1

% of County Debt

State/County

TX / BURNET

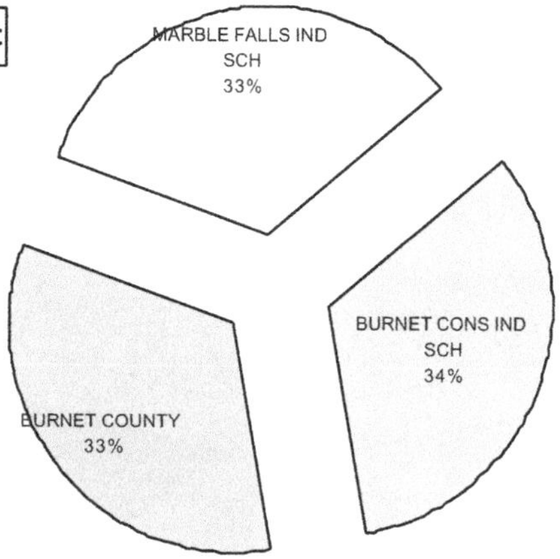

VERSUS

% of County Taxes

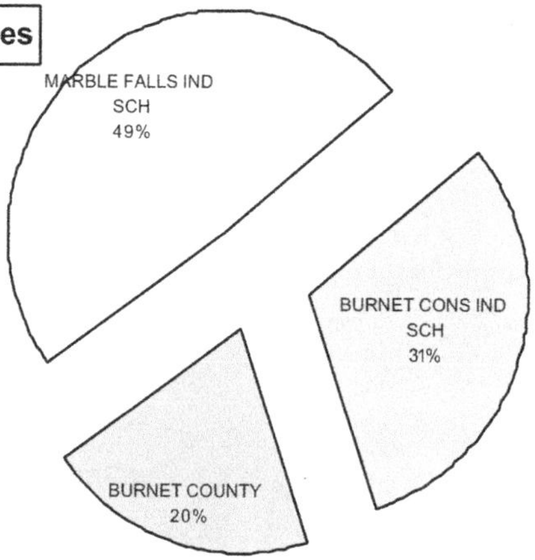

% of County Debt

State/County

TX / CALDWELL

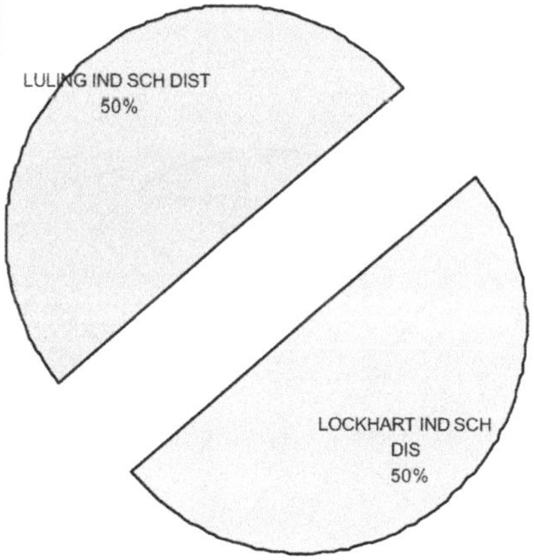

VERSUS

% of County Taxes

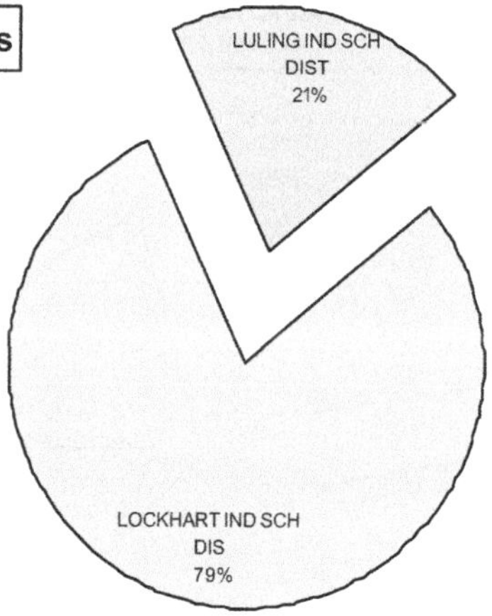

Are you getting your share of debt and taxes in your county? S1

State/County

TX / CALLAHAN

% of County Debt

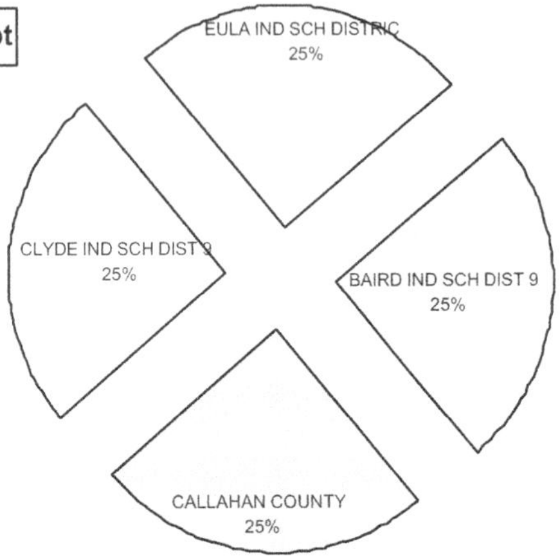

VERSUS

% of County Taxes

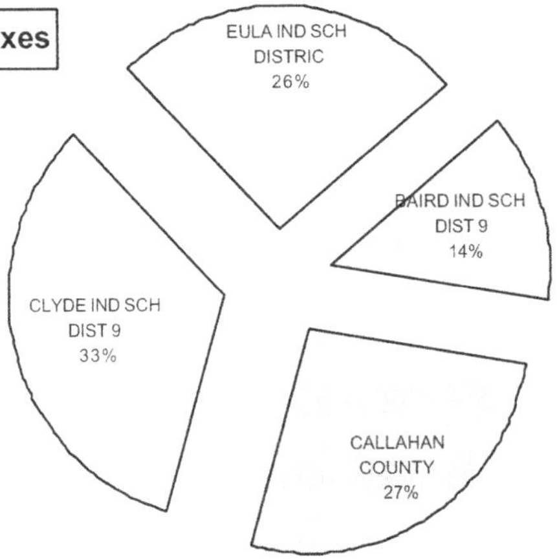

State/County

TX / CAMERON

% of County Debt

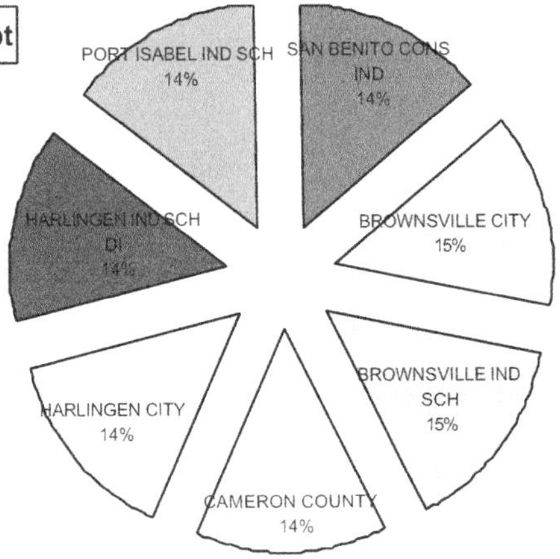

VERSUS

% of County Taxes

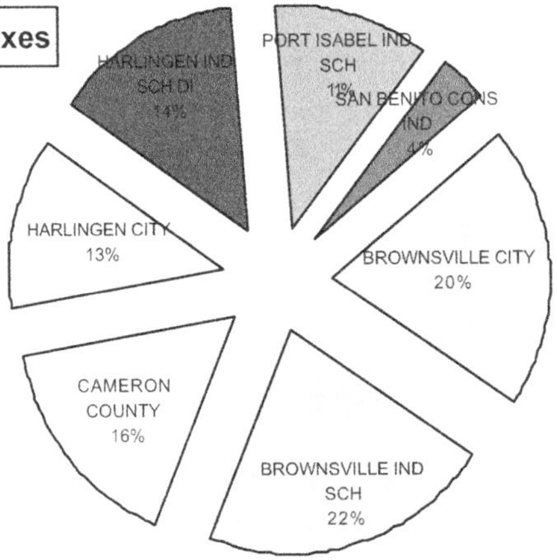

Are you getting your share of debt and taxes in your county?

S1

State/County

TX / CARSON

% of County Debt

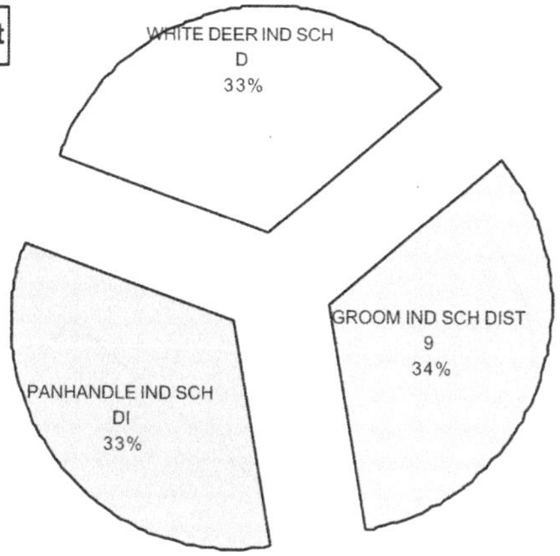

VERSUS

% of County Taxes

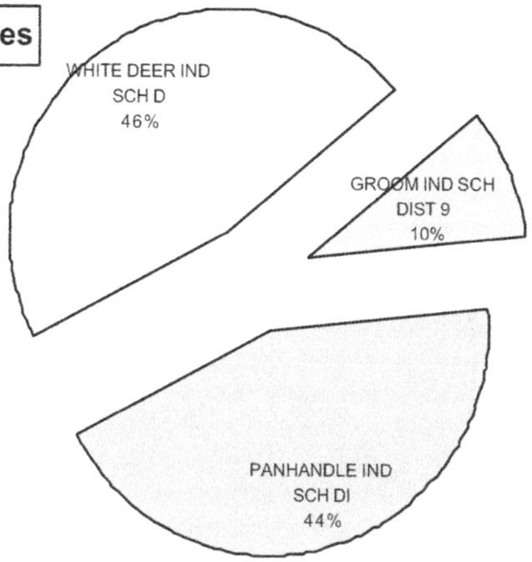

State/County

TX / CASS

% of County Debt

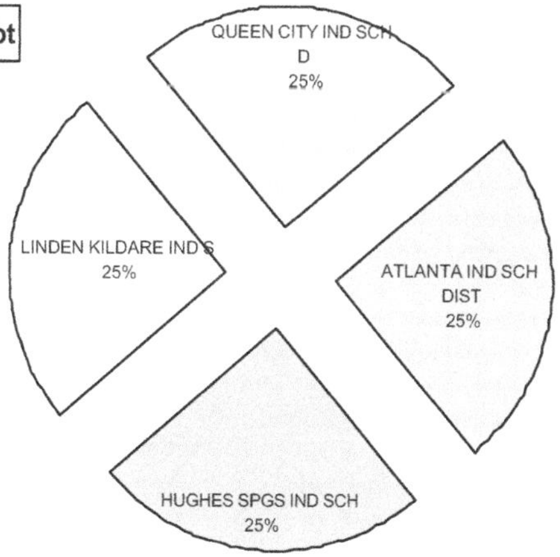

VERSUS

% of County Taxes

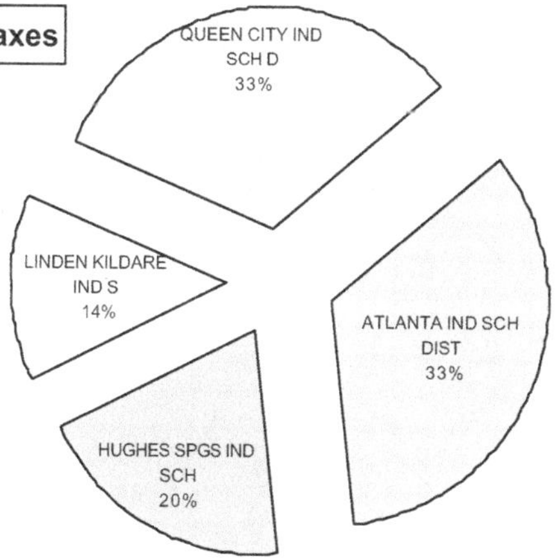

Are you getting your share of debt and taxes in your county? **S1**

% of County Debt

State/County
TX / CASTRO

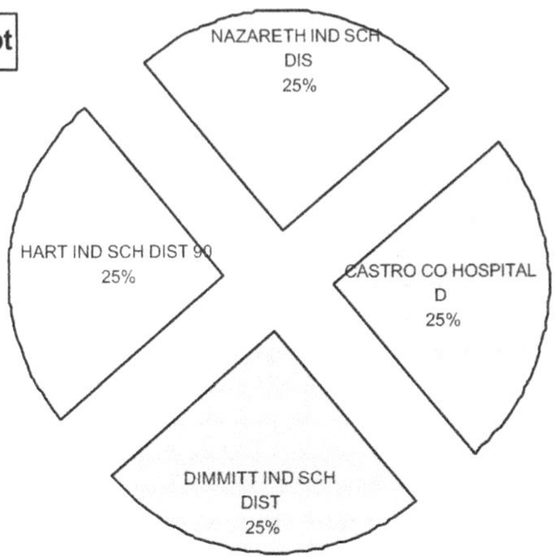

VERSUS

% of County Taxes

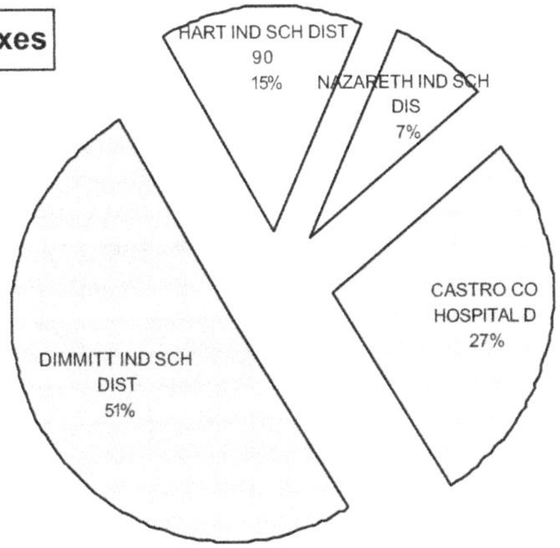

% of County Debt

State/County
TX / CHEROKEE

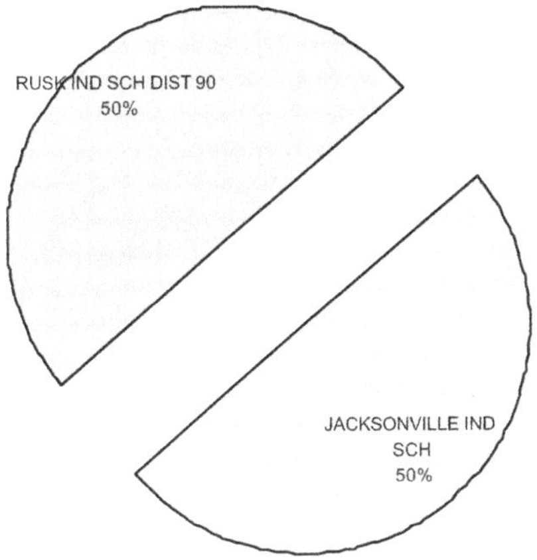

VERSUS

% of County Taxes

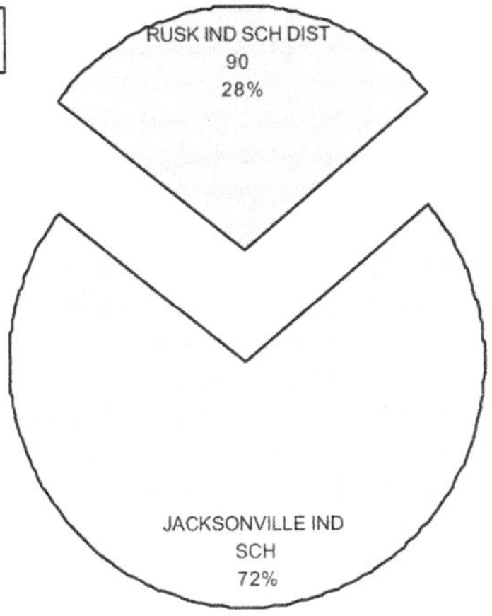

Are you getting your share of debt and taxes in your county? S1

% of County Debt

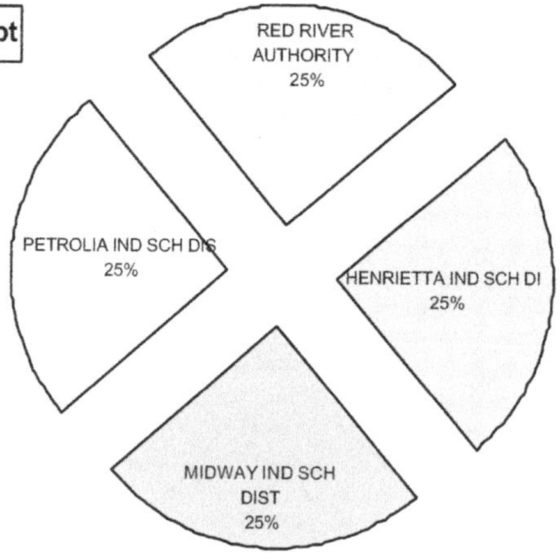

State/County

TX / CLAY

VERSUS

% of County Taxes

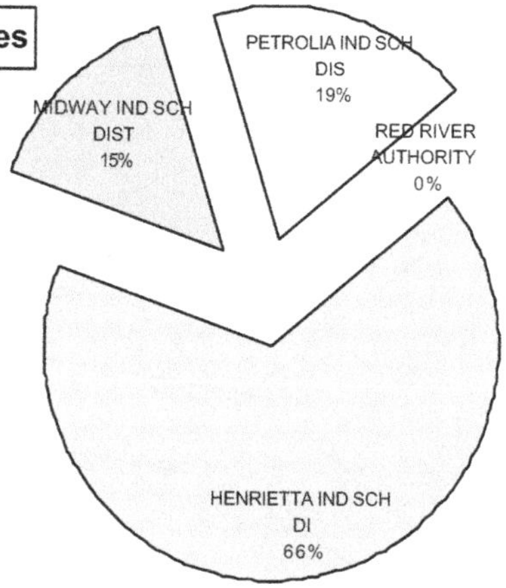

% of County Debt

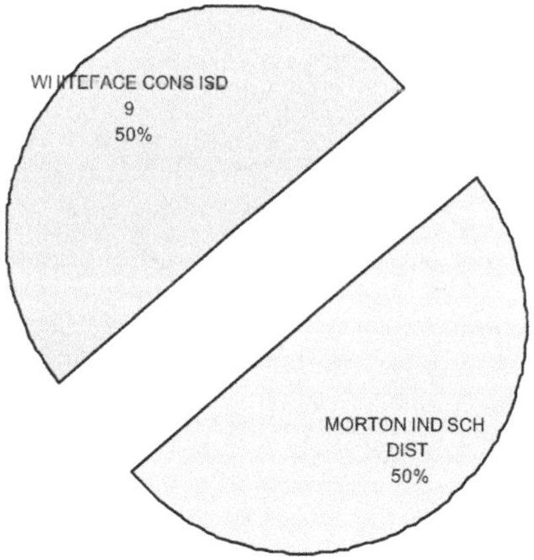

State/County

TX / COCHRAN

VERSUS

% of County Taxes

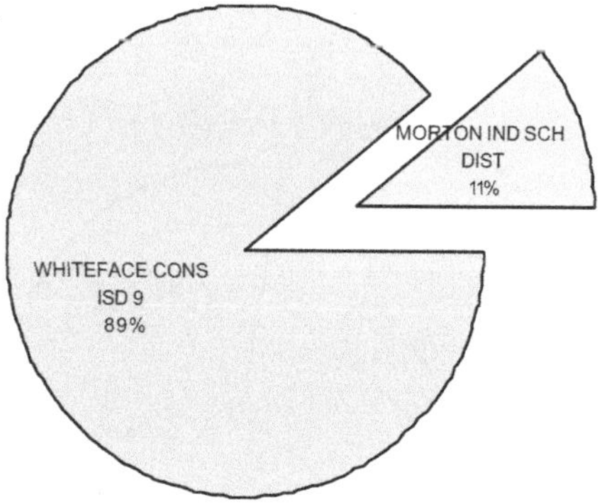

Are you getting your share of debt and taxes in your county? S1

State/County
TX / COKE

% of County Debt

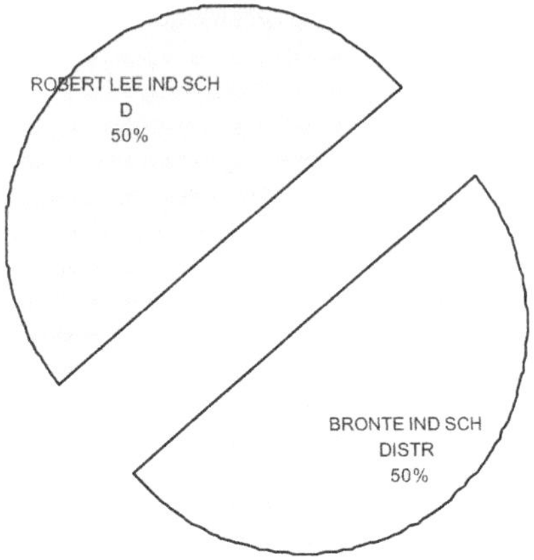

VERSUS

% of County Taxes

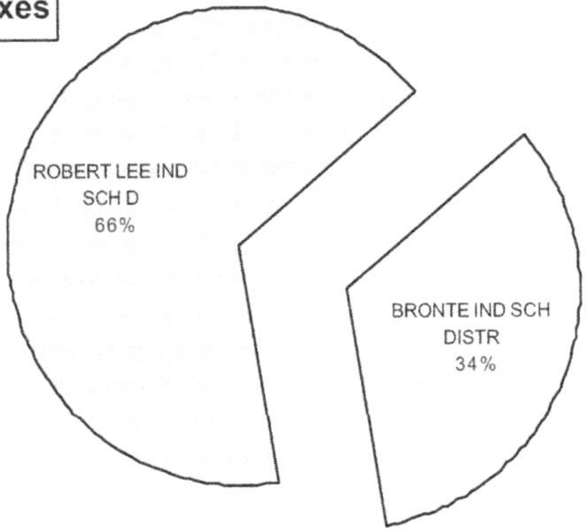

State/County
TX / COLEMAN

% of County Debt

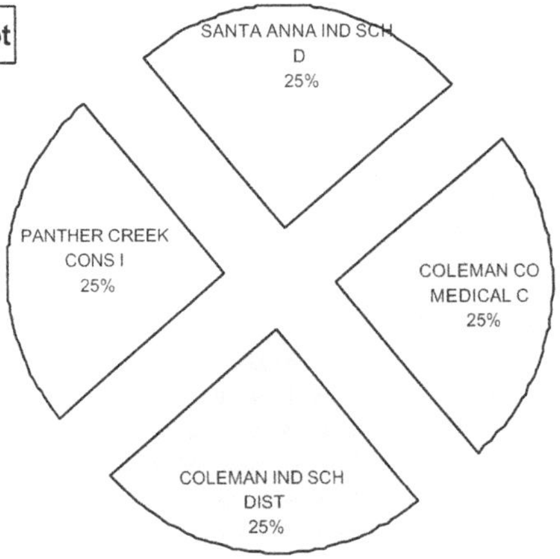

VERSUS

% of County Taxes

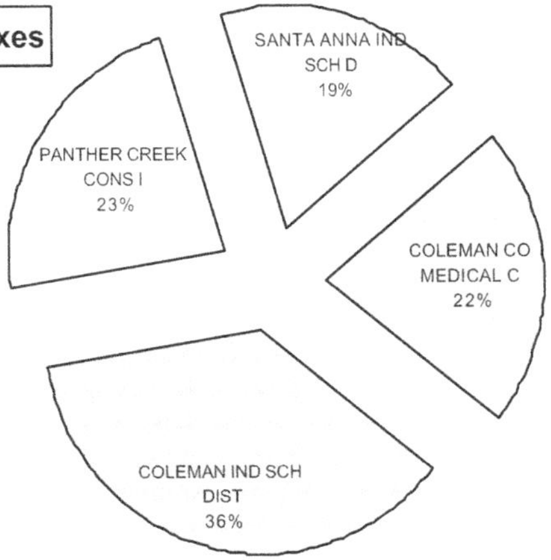

Are you getting your share of debt and taxes in your county?

S1

% of County Debt

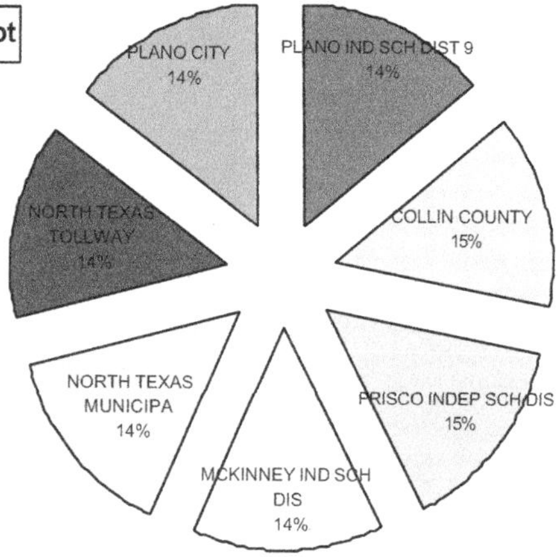

State/County

TX / COLLIN

VERSUS

% of County Taxes

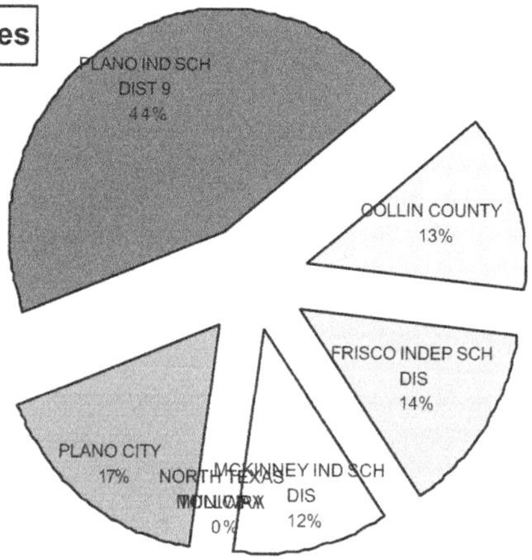

% of County Debt

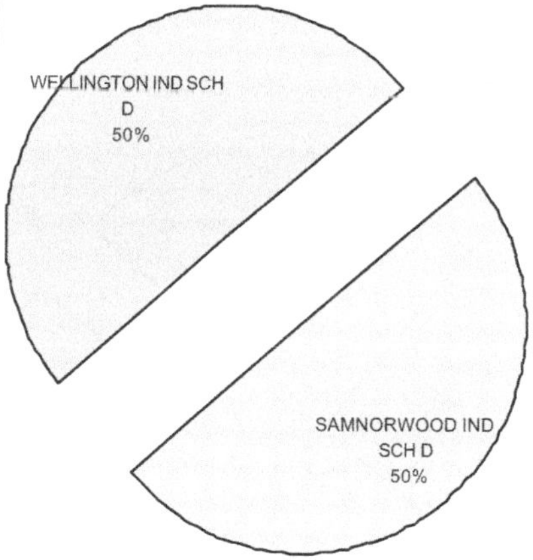

State/County

TX / COLLINGSWORTH

VERSUS

% of County Taxes

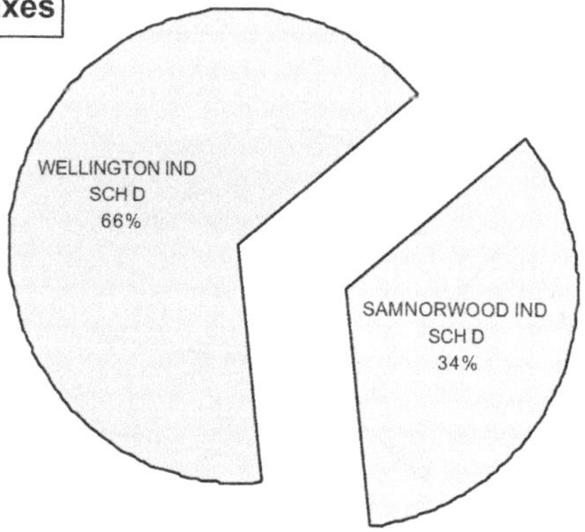

Are you getting your share of debt and taxes in your county? S1

State/County
TX / COLORADO

% of County Debt

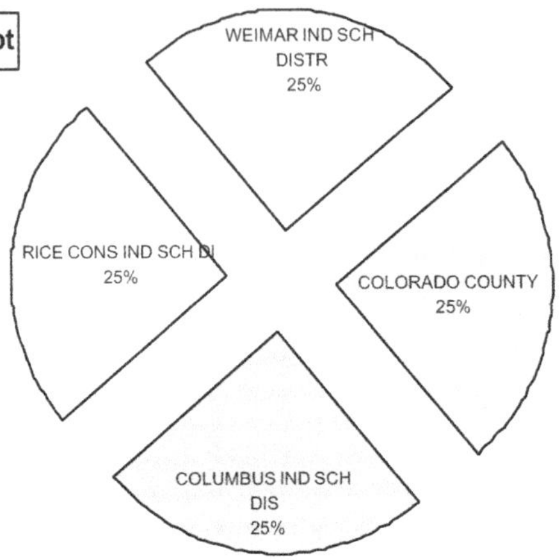

VERSUS

% of County Taxes

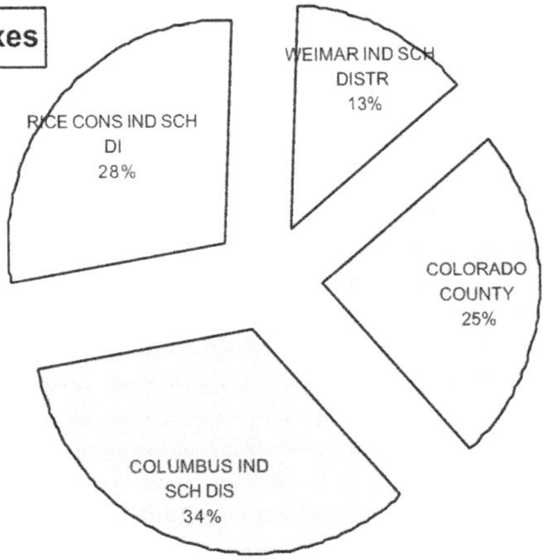

State/County
TX / COMAL

% of County Debt

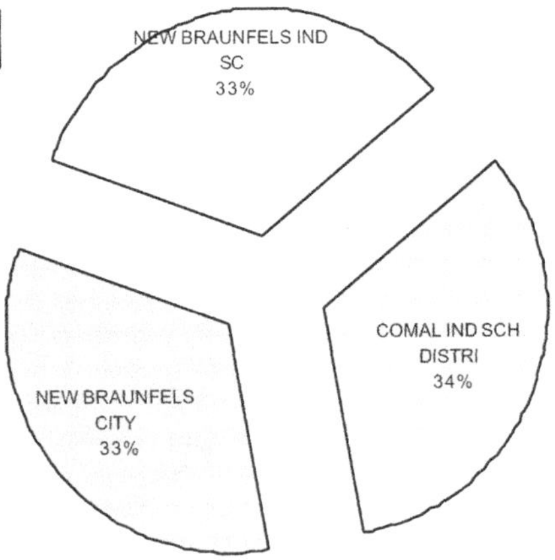

VERSUS

% of County Taxes

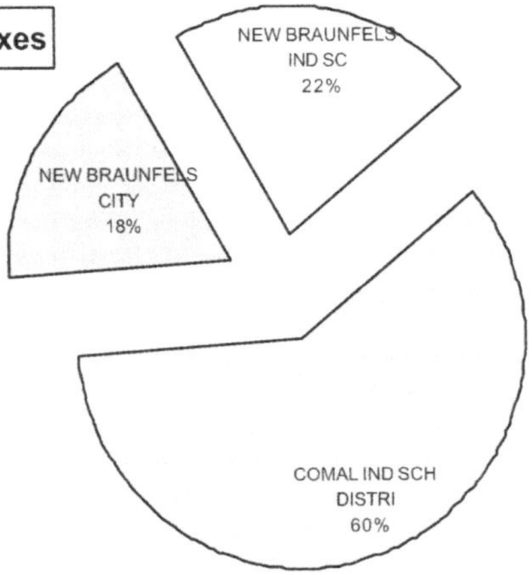

Are you getting your share of debt and taxes in your county?

S1

% of County Debt

State/County

TX / COMANCHE

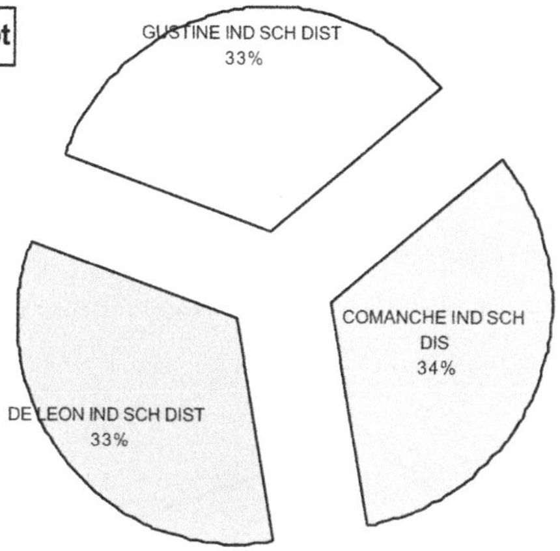

VERSUS

% of County Taxes

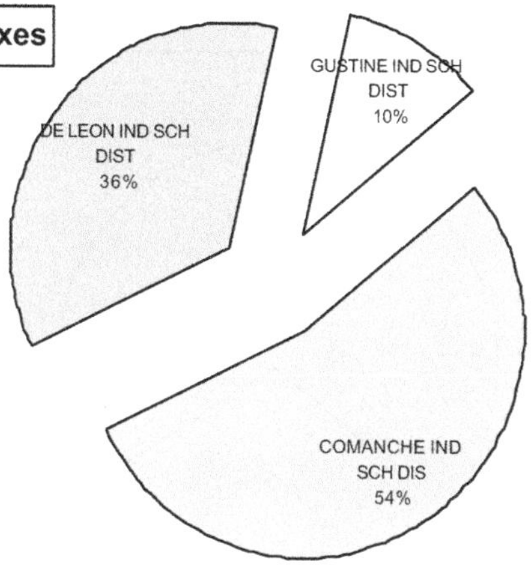

% of County Debt

State/County

TX / CONCHO

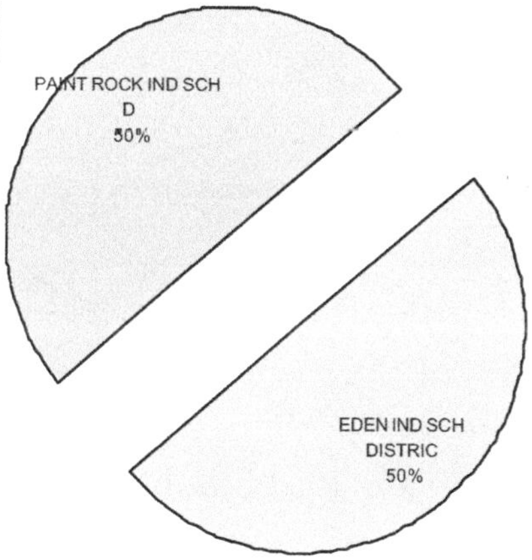

VERSUS

% of County Taxes

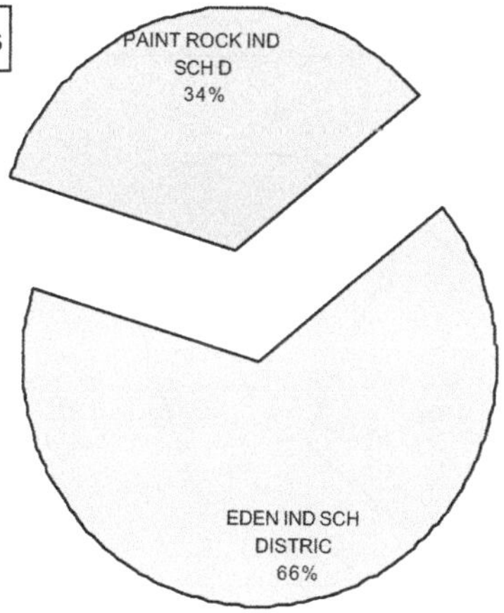

Are you getting your share of debt and taxes in your county? S1

State/County
TX / COOKE

% of County Debt

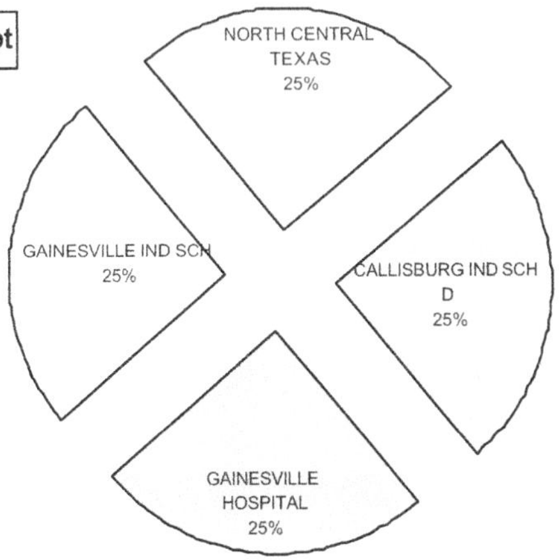

VERSUS

% of County Taxes

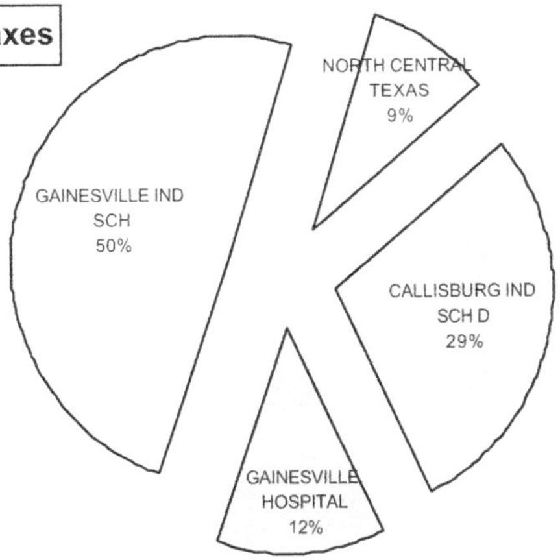

State/County
TX / CORYELL

% of County Debt

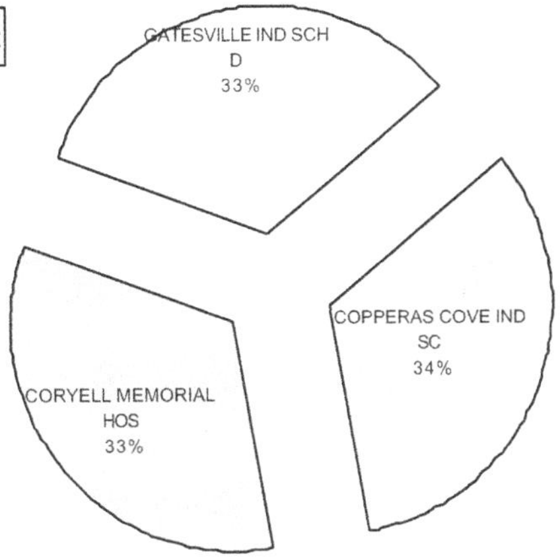

VERSUS

% of County Taxes

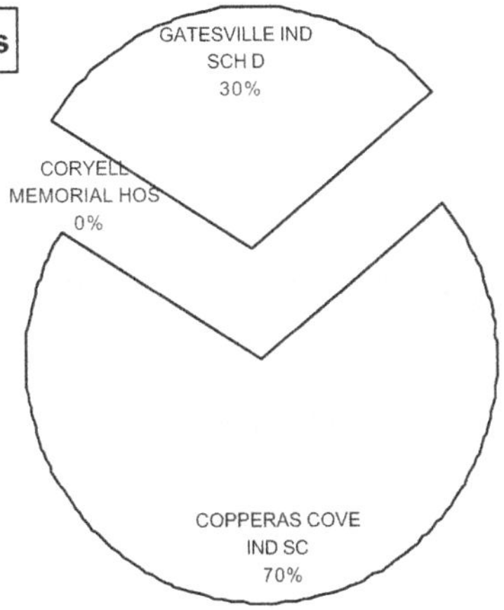

Are you getting your share of debt and taxes in your county? S1

% of County Debt

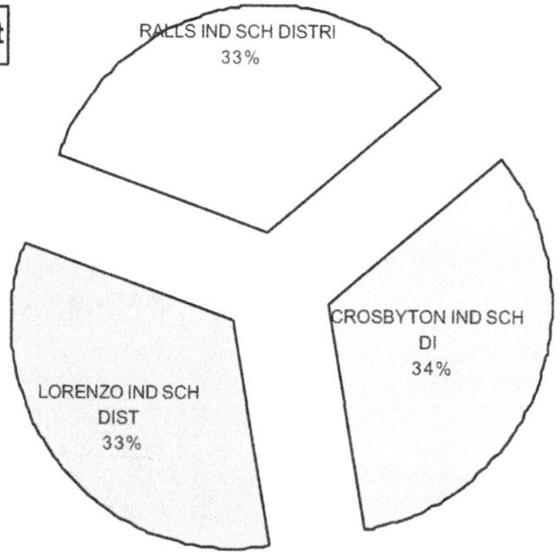

State/County

TX / CROSBY

VERSUS

% of County Taxes

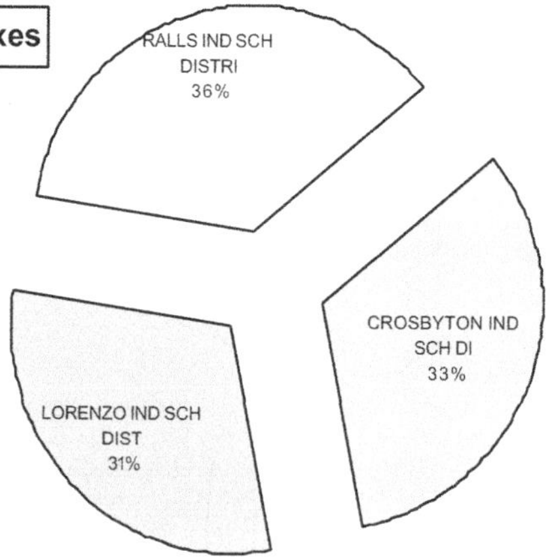

% of County Debt

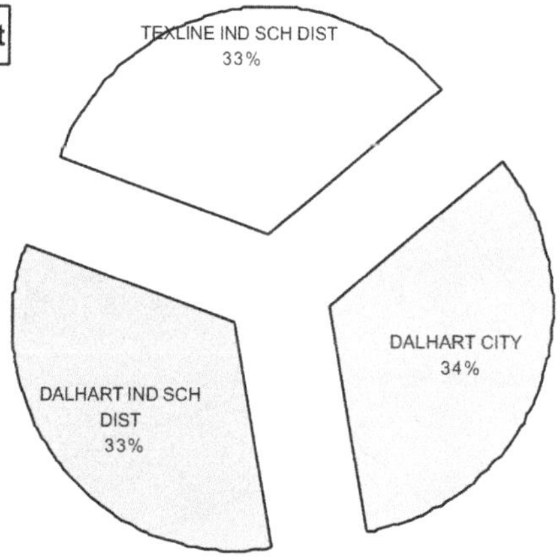

State/County

TX / DALLAM

VERSUS

% of County Taxes

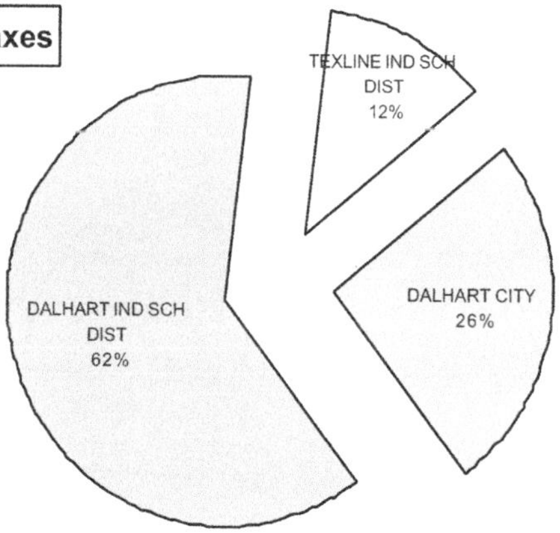

Are you getting your share of debt and taxes in your county? **S1**

State/County
TX / DALLAS

% of County Debt

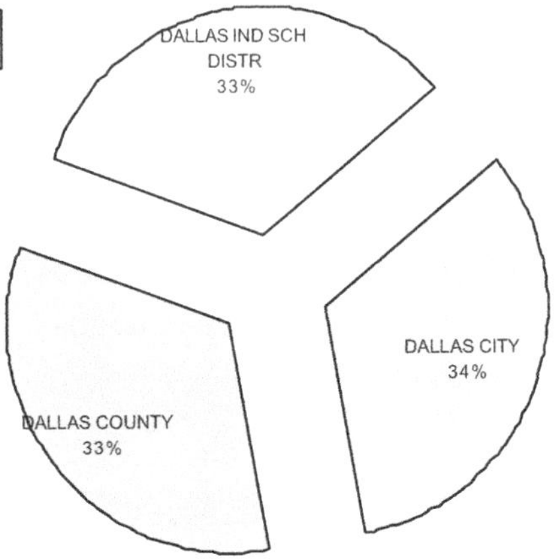

VERSUS

% of County Taxes

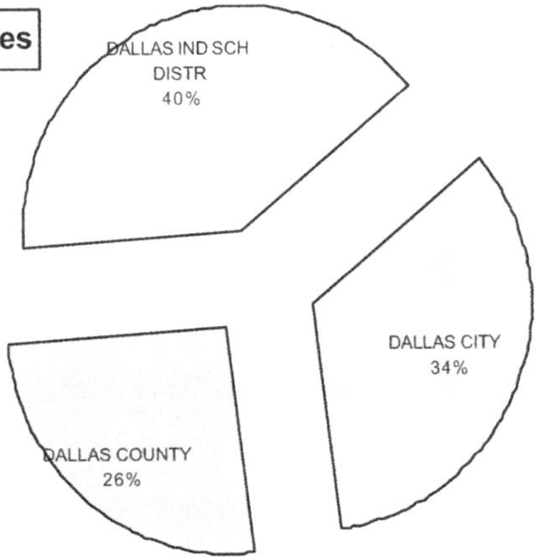

State/County
TX / DAWSON

% of County Debt

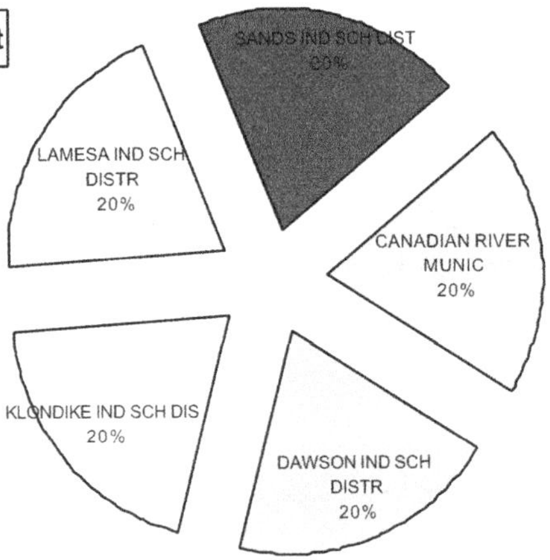

VERSUS

% of County Taxes

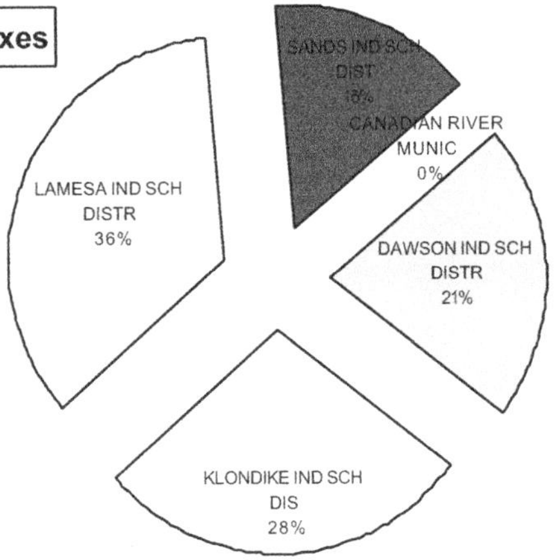

Are you getting your share of debt and taxes in your county? S1

State/County
TX / DE WITT

% of County Debt

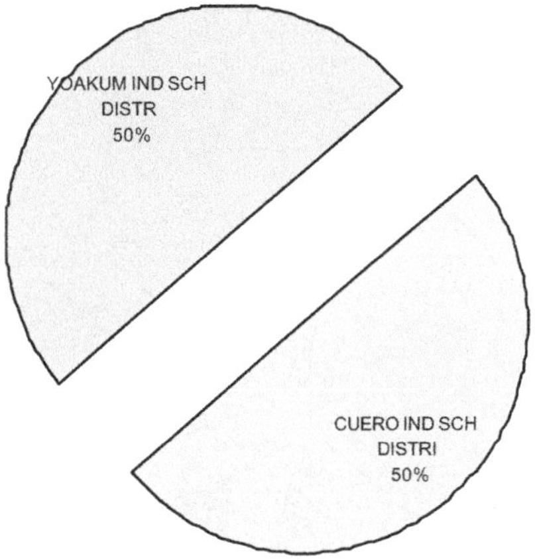

VERSUS

% of County Taxes

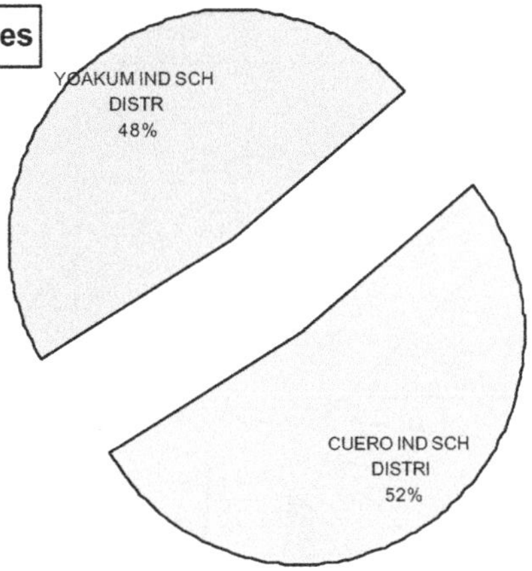

State/County
TX / DEAF SMITH

% of County Debt

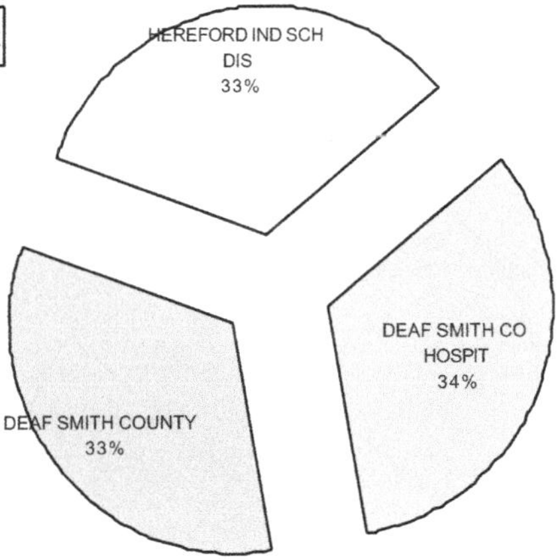

VERSUS

% of County Taxes

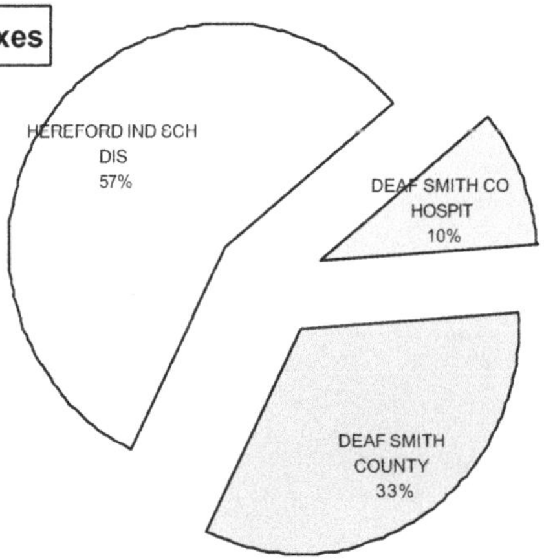

Are you getting your share of debt and taxes in your county? **S1**

State/County

TX / DELTA

% of County Debt

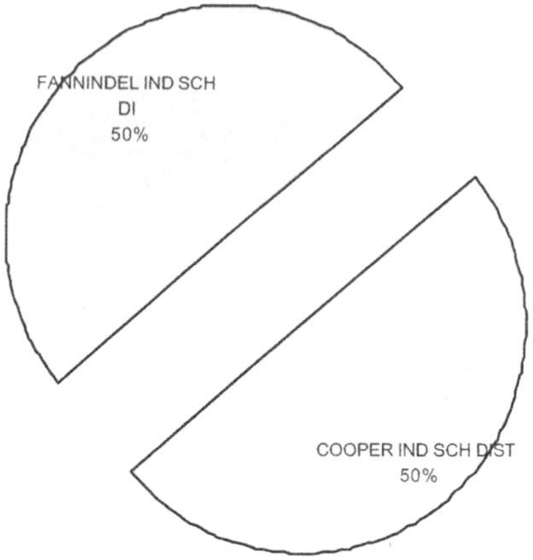

VERSUS

% of County Taxes

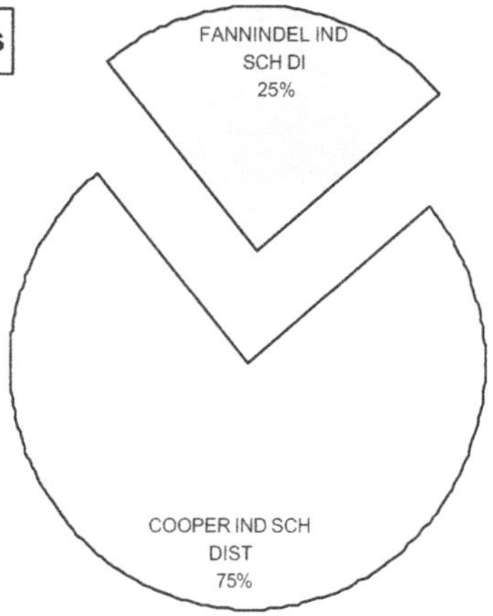

State/County

TX / DENTON

% of County Debt

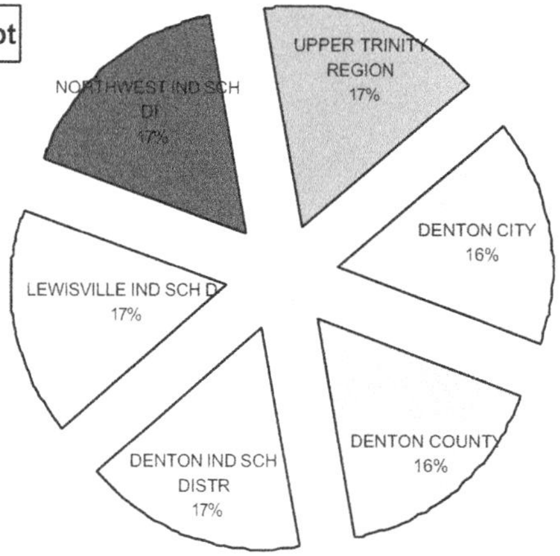

VERSUS

% of County Taxes

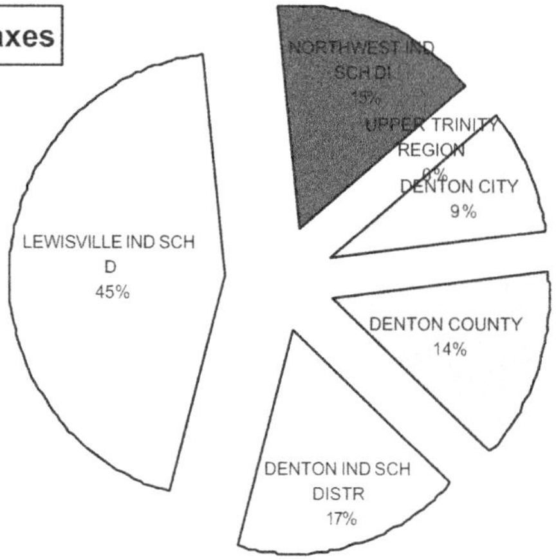

Are you getting your share of debt and taxes in your county?

S1

State/County

TX / DICKENS

% of County Debt

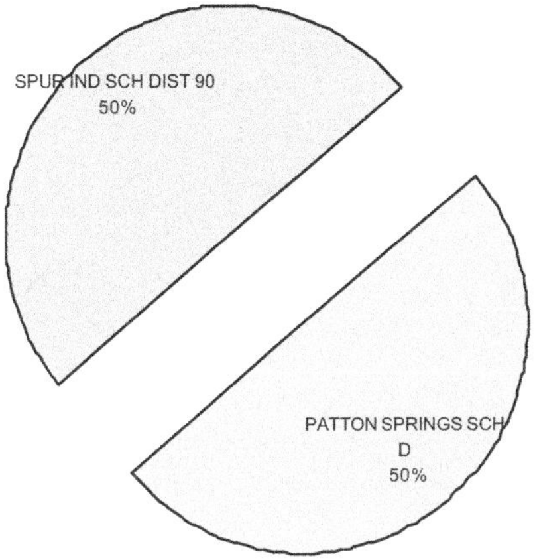

VERSUS

% of County Taxes

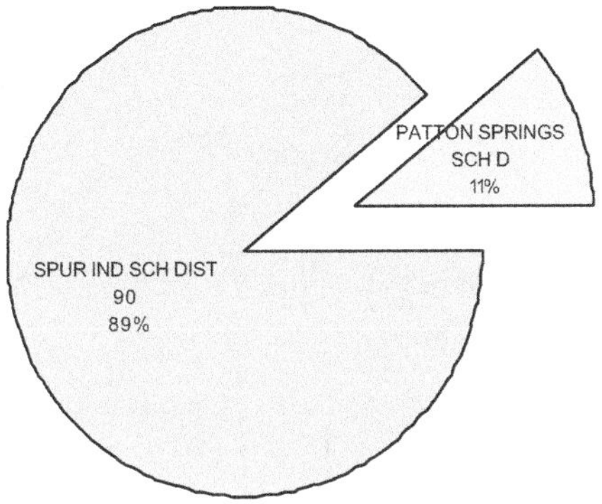

State/County

TX / DONLEY

% of County Debt

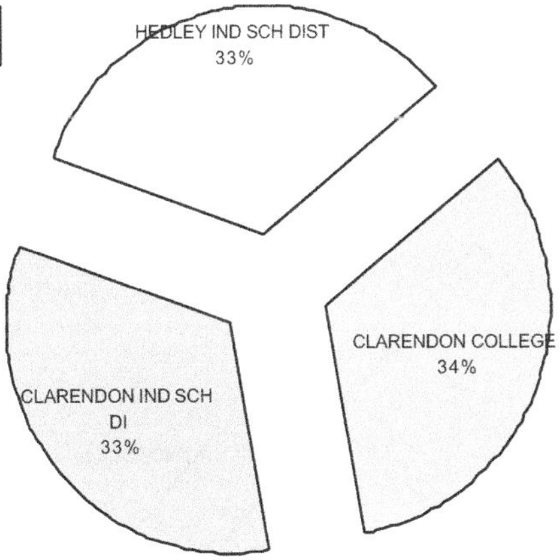

VERSUS

% of County Taxes

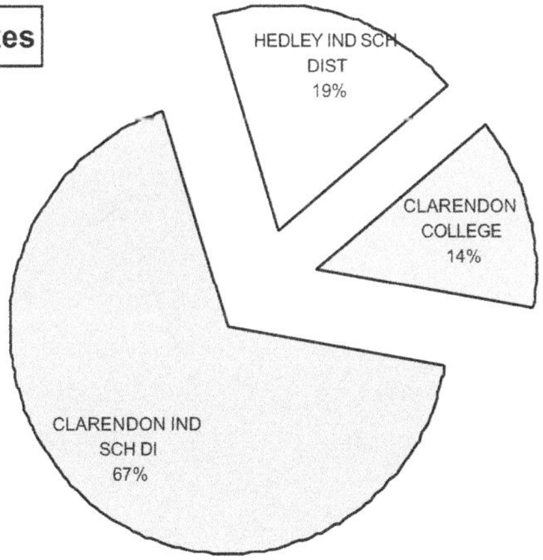

Are you getting your share of debt and taxes in your county?

State/County

TX / DUVAL

% of County Debt

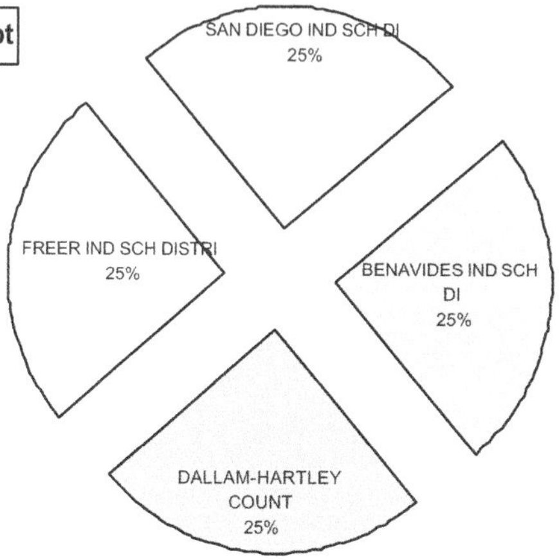

VERSUS

% of County Taxes

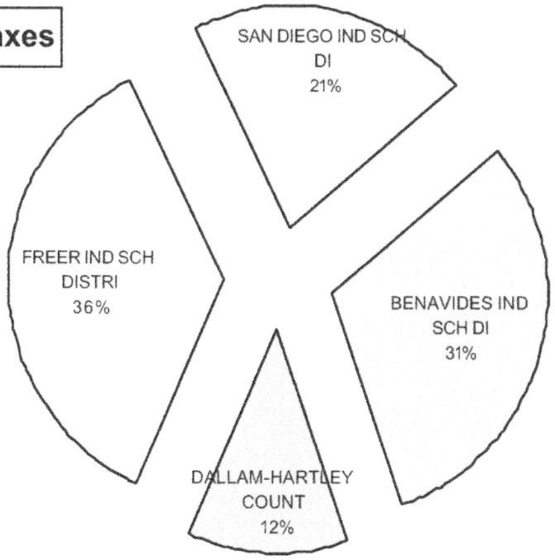

State/County

TX / EASTLAND

% of County Debt

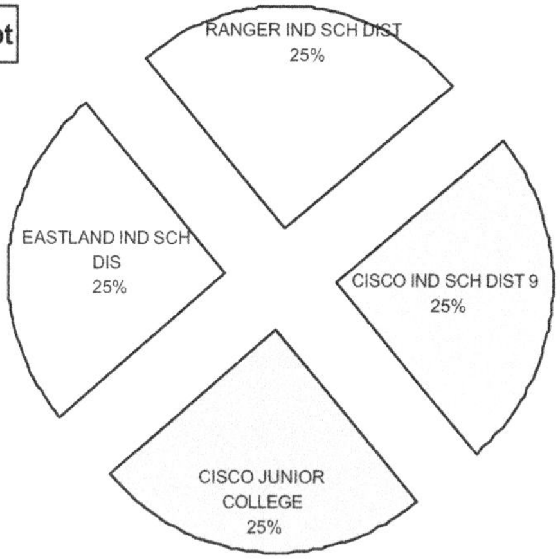

VERSUS

% of County Taxes

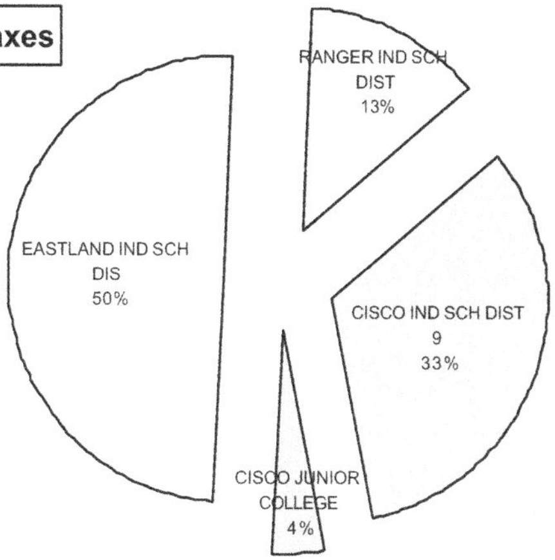

Are you getting your share of debt and taxes in your county?

S1

% of County Debt

State/County

TX / ECTOR

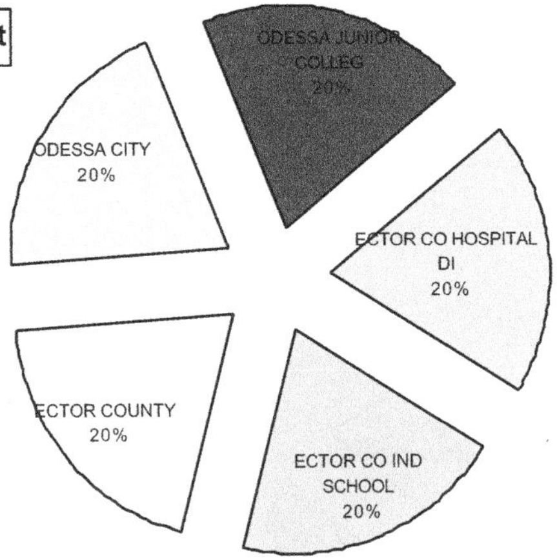

VERSUS

% of County Taxes

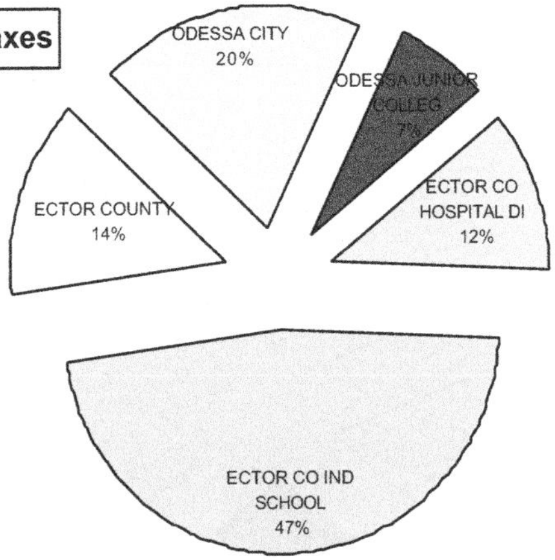

% of County Debt

State/County

TX / EDWARDS

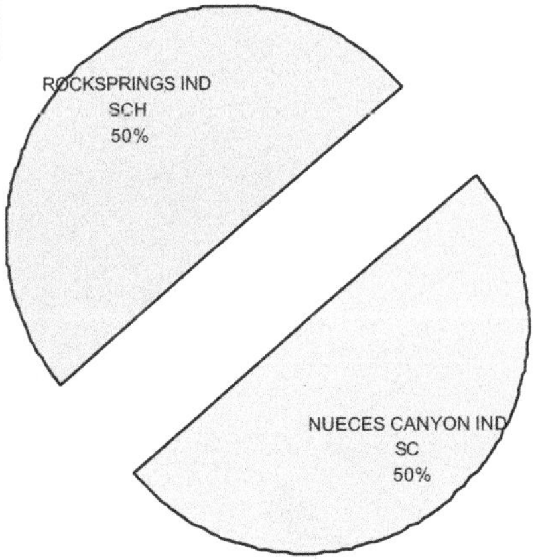

VERSUS

% of County Taxes

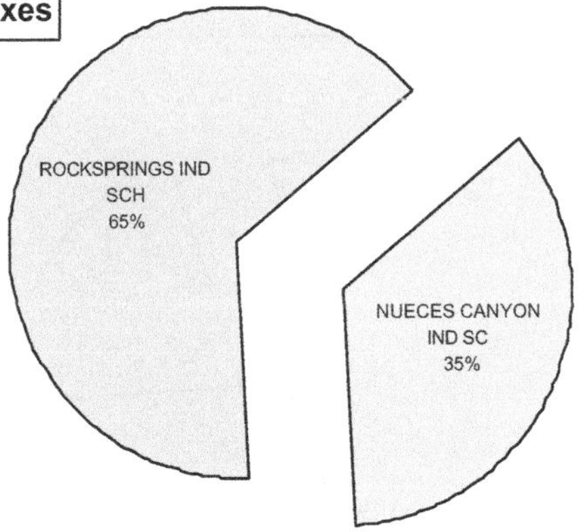

Are you getting your share of debt and taxes in your county? S1

State/County
TX / EL PASO

% of County Debt

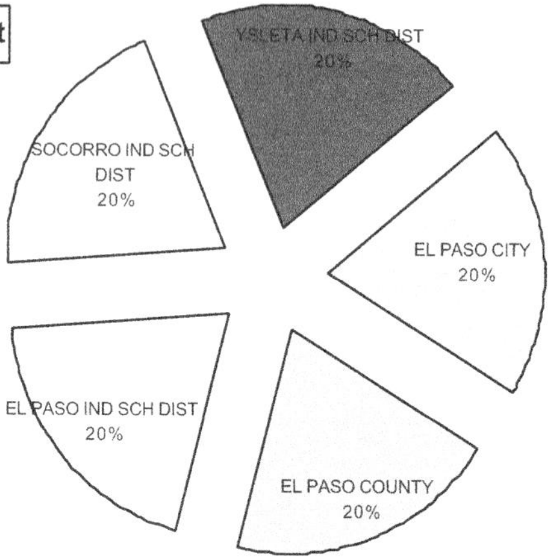

VERSUS

% of County Taxes

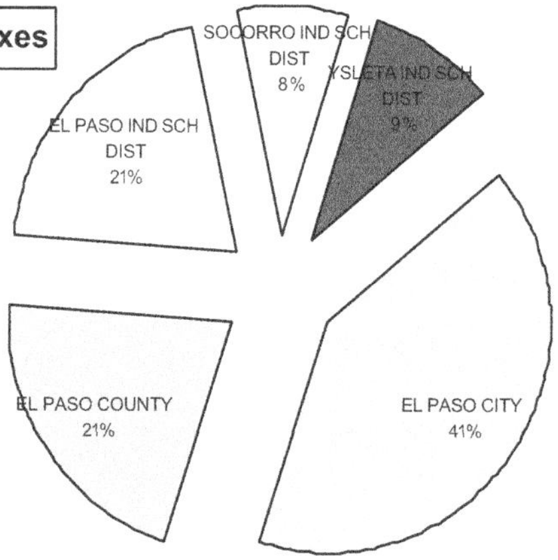

State/County
TX / ELLIS

% of County Debt

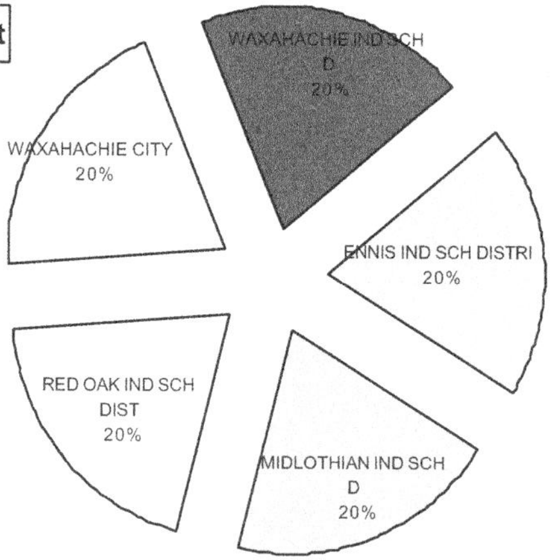

VERSUS

% of County Taxes

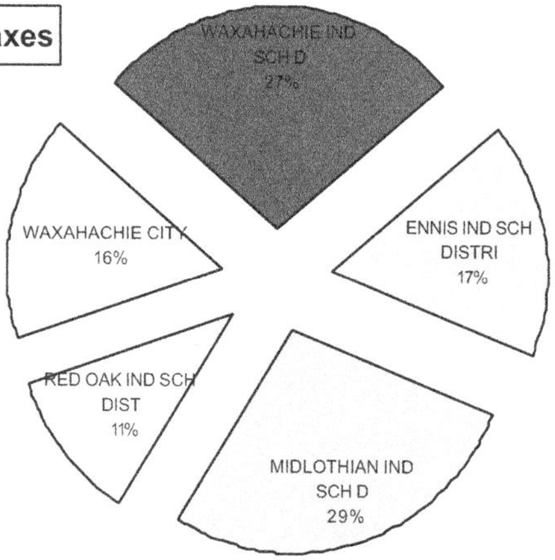

Are you getting your share of debt and taxes in your county?

S1

% of County Debt

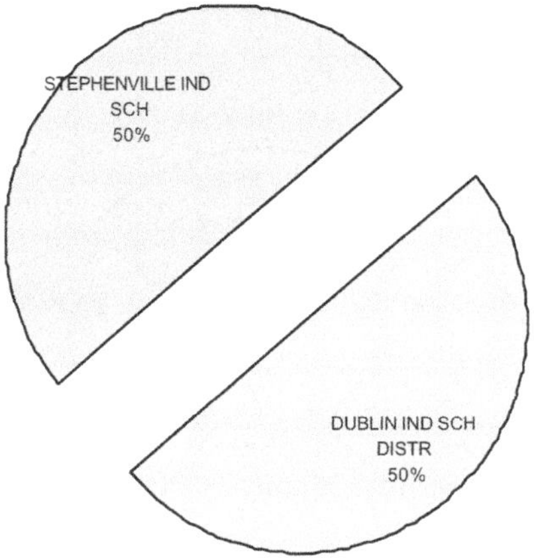

State/County

TX / ERATH

VERSUS

% of County Taxes

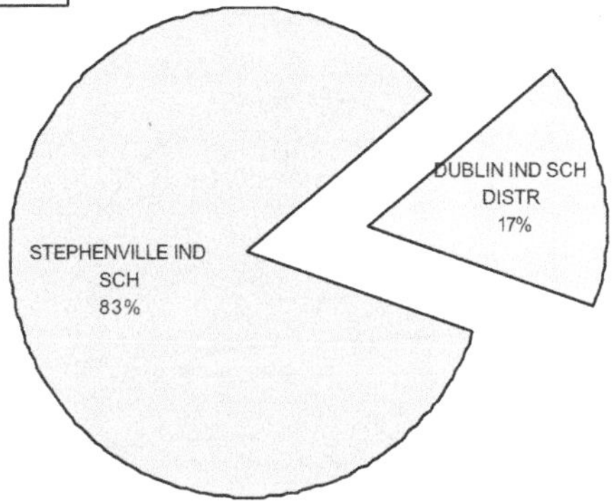

% of County Debt

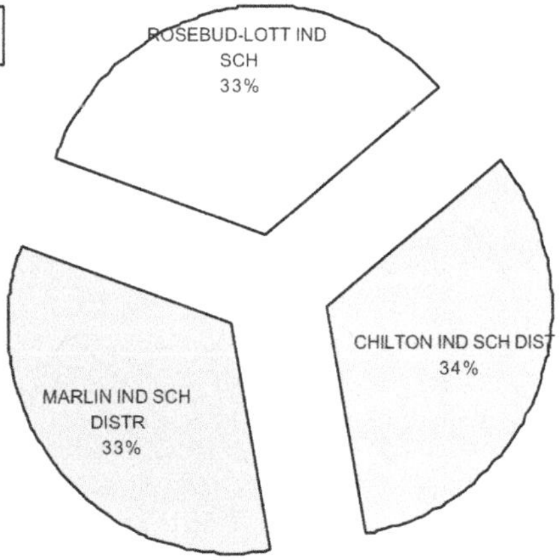

State/County

TX / FALLS

VERSUS

% of County Taxes

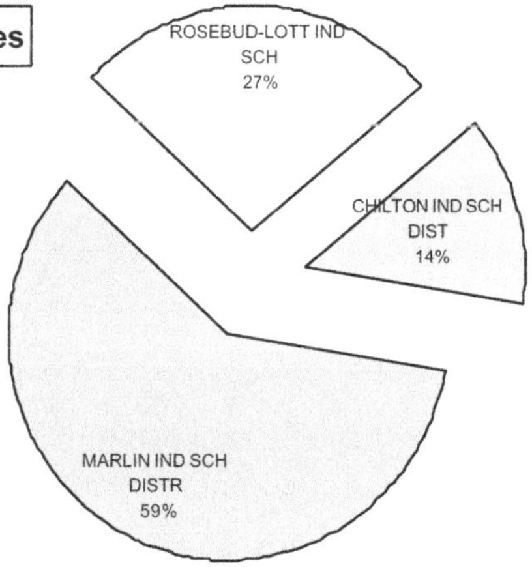

Are you getting your share of debt and taxes in your county? **S1**

State/County
TX / FANNIN

% of County Debt

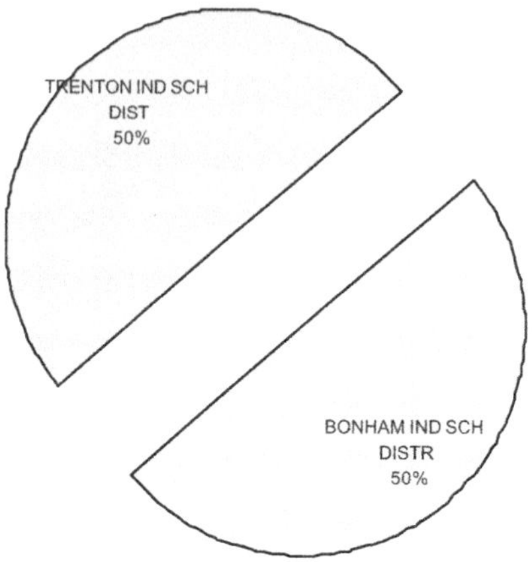

VERSUS

% of County Taxes

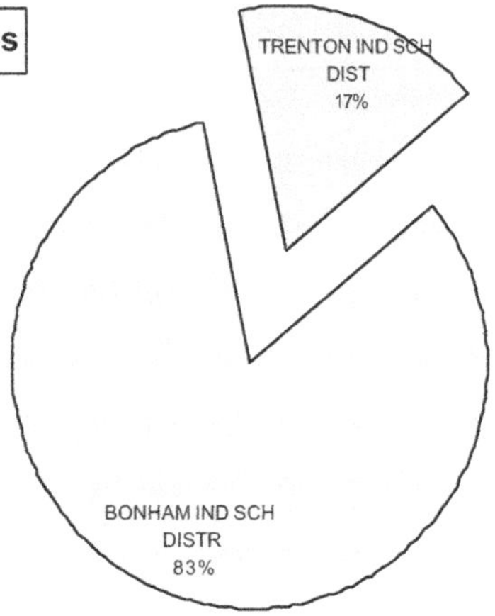

State/County
TX / FAYETTE

% of County Debt

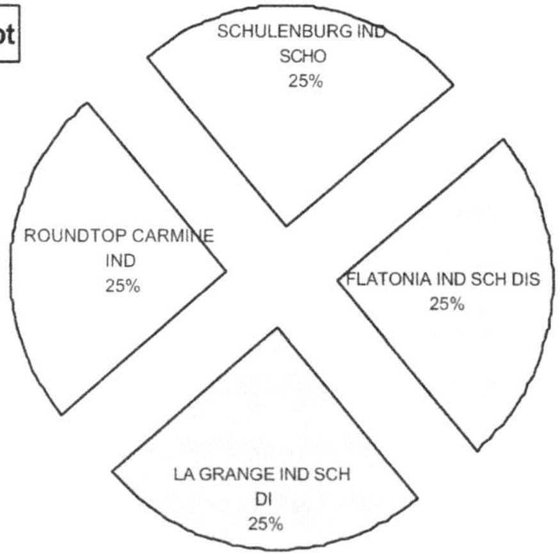

VERSUS

% of County Taxes

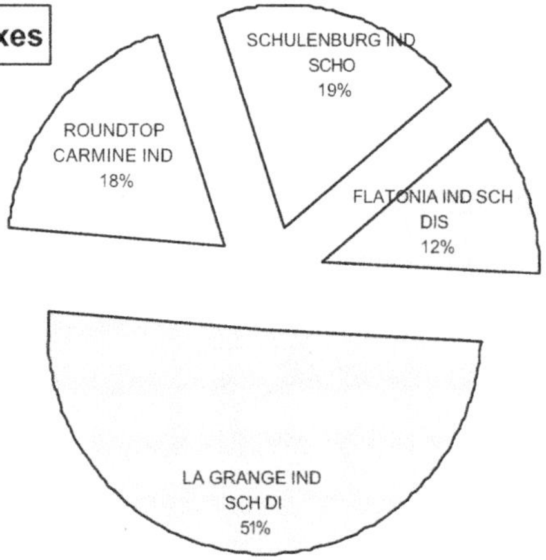

Are you getting your share of debt and taxes in your county?

% of County Debt

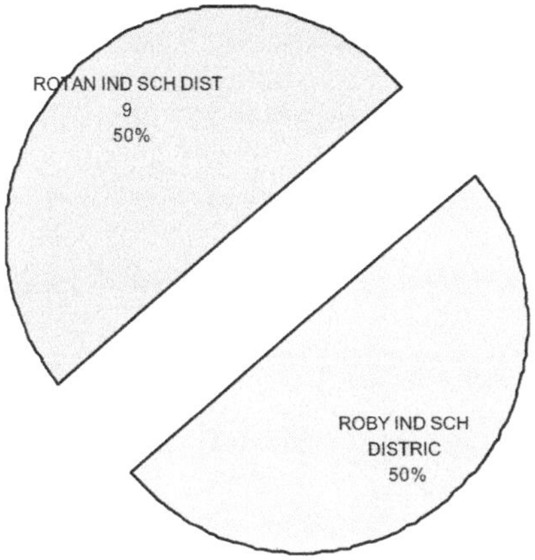

State/County

TX / FISHER

VERSUS

% of County Taxes

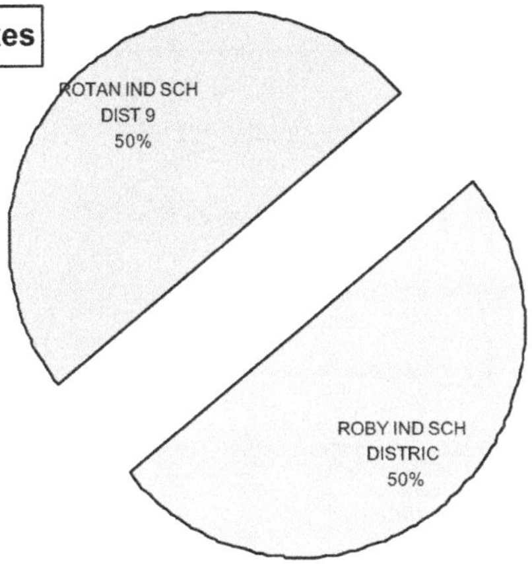

% of County Debt

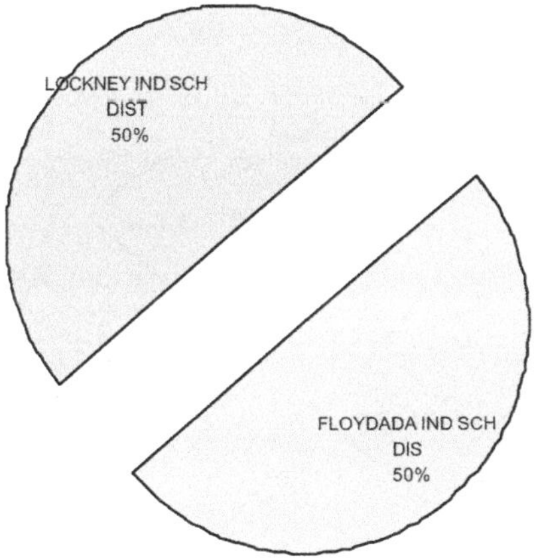

State/County

TX / FLOYD

VERSUS

% of County Taxes

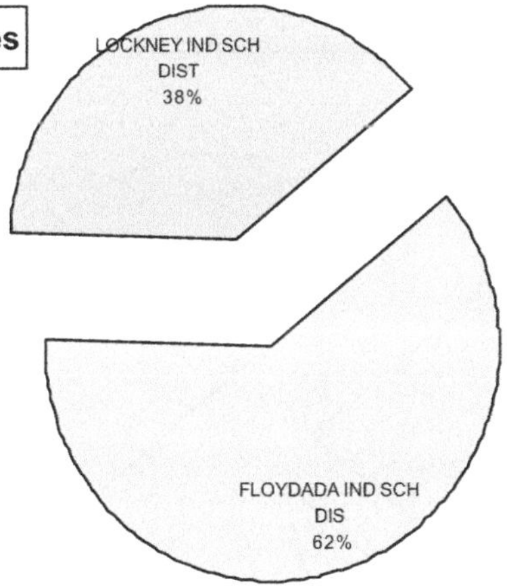

Are you getting your share of debt and taxes in your county? **S1**

State/County

TX / FORT BEND

% of County Debt

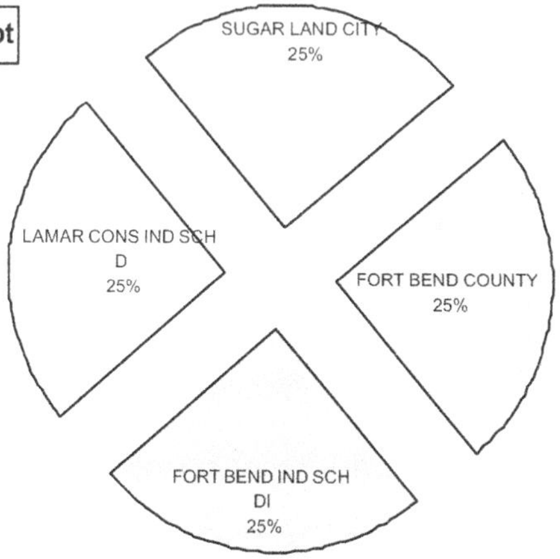

VERSUS

% of County Taxes

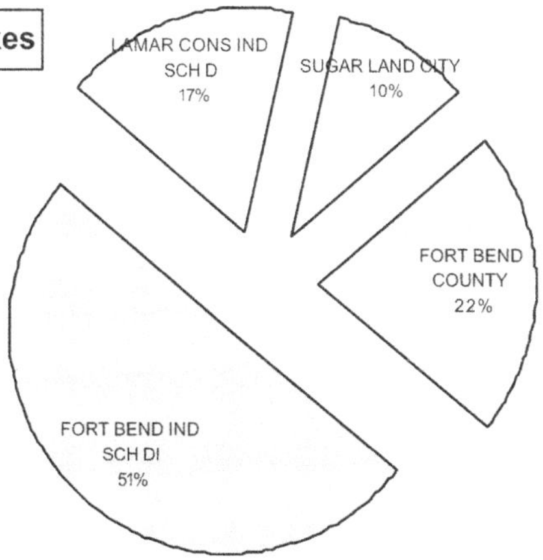

State/County

TX / FREESTONE

% of County Debt

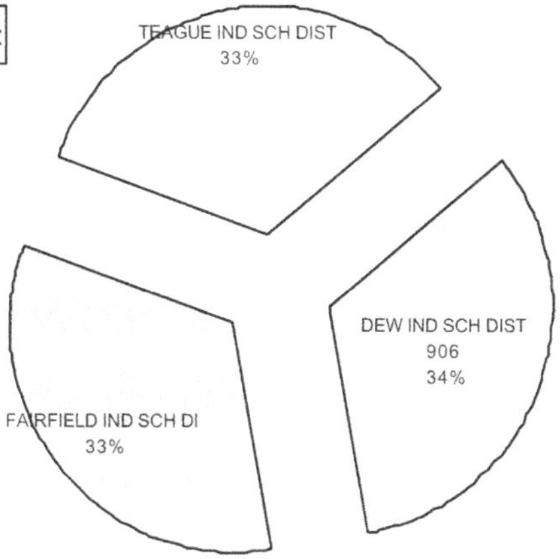

VERSUS

% of County Taxes

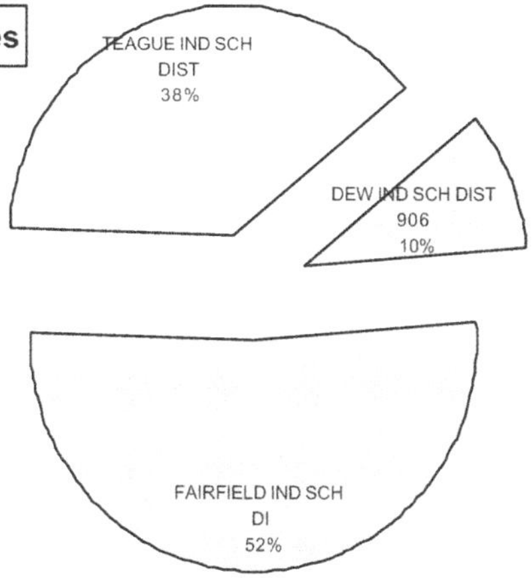

Are you getting your share of debt and taxes in your county?

S1

% of County Debt

State/County

TX / FRIO

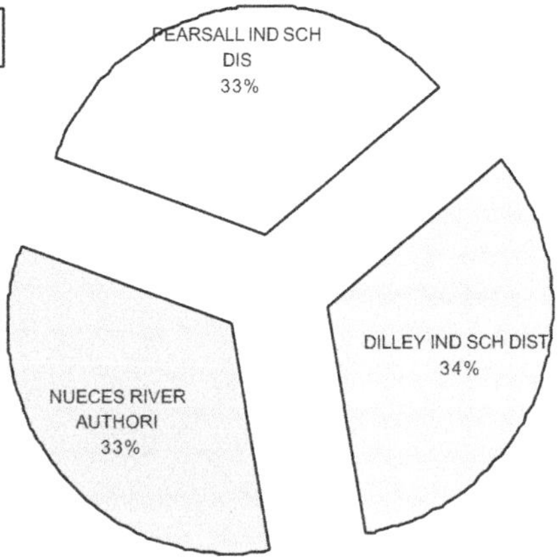

VERSUS

% of County Taxes

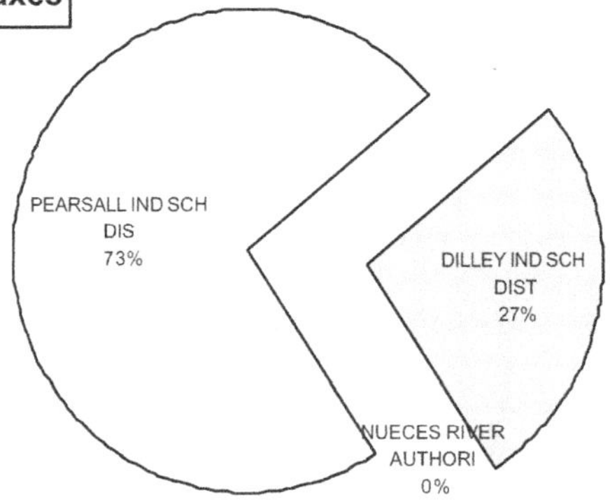

% of County Debt

State/County

TX / GAINES

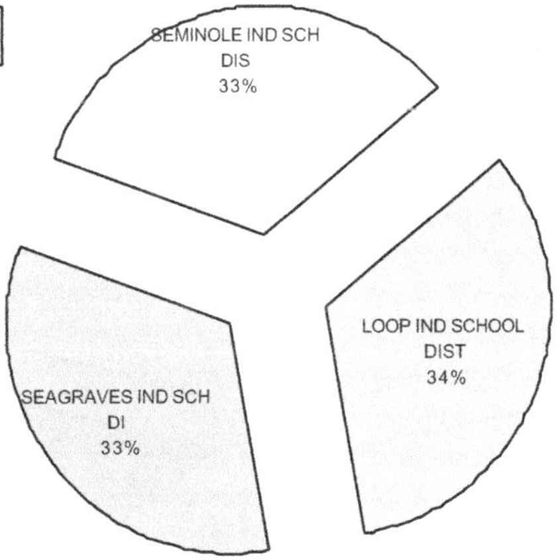

VERSUS

% of County Taxes

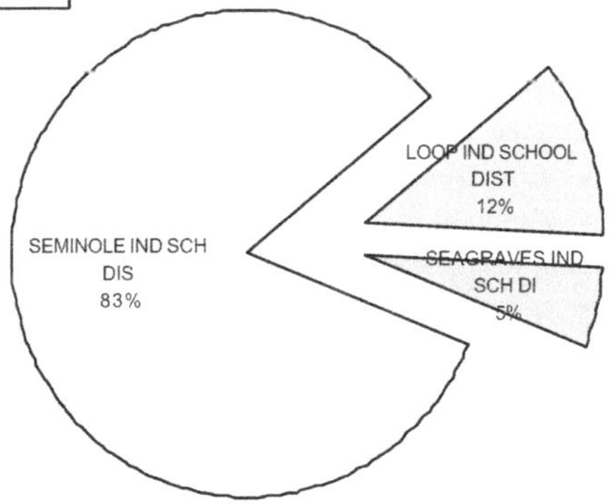

Are you getting your share of debt and taxes in your county?

S1

State/County
TX / GALVESTON

% of County Debt

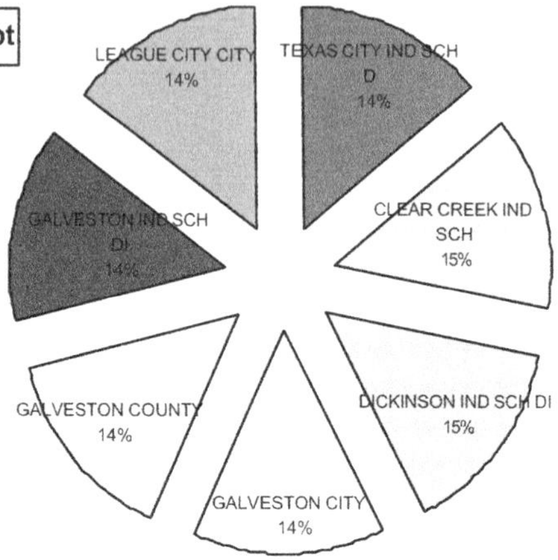

VERSUS

% of County Taxes

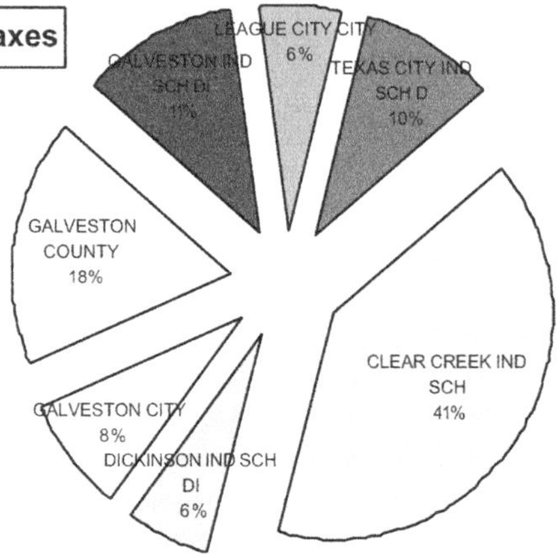

State/County
TX / GILLESPIE

% of County Debt

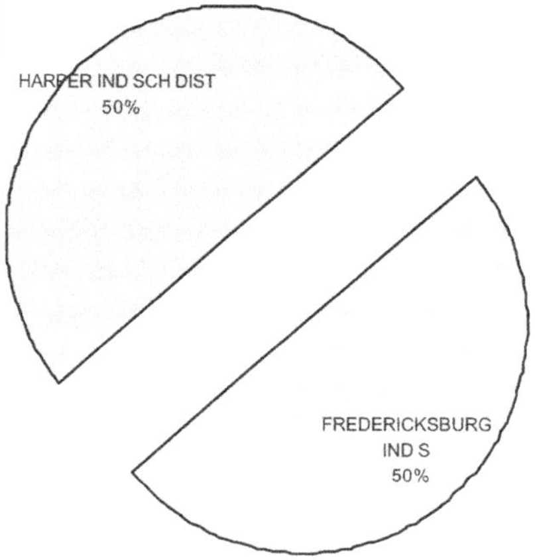

VERSUS

% of County Taxes

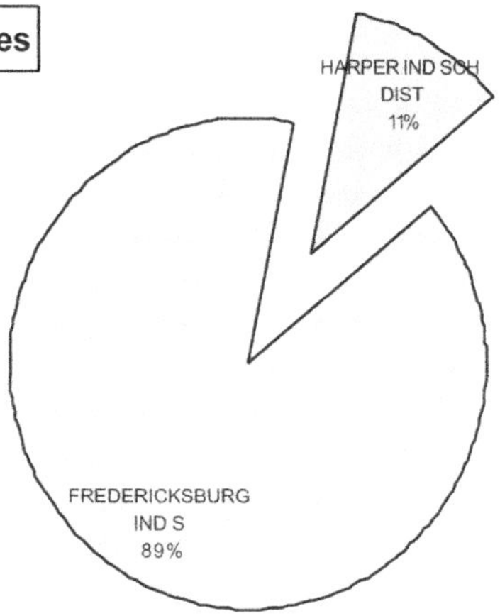

Are you getting your share of debt and taxes in your county? S1

% of County Debt

State/County

TX / GONZALES

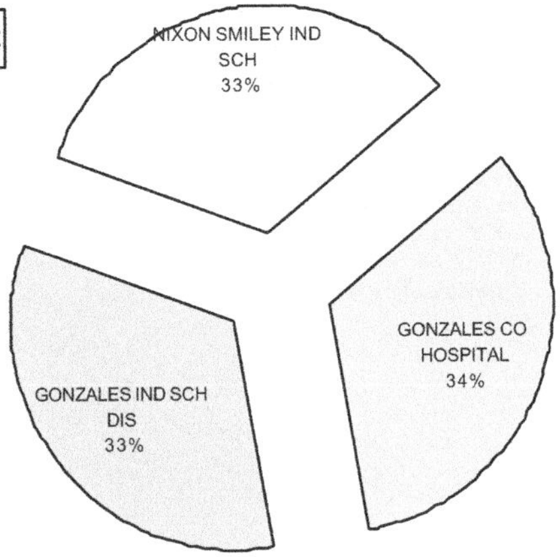

VERSUS

% of County Taxes

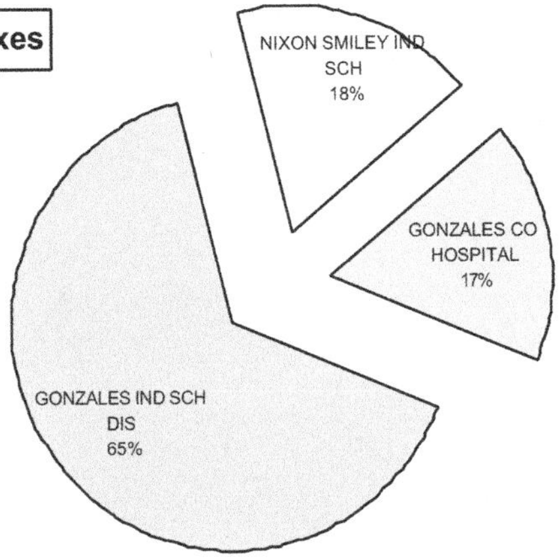

% of County Debt

State/County

TX / GRAYSON

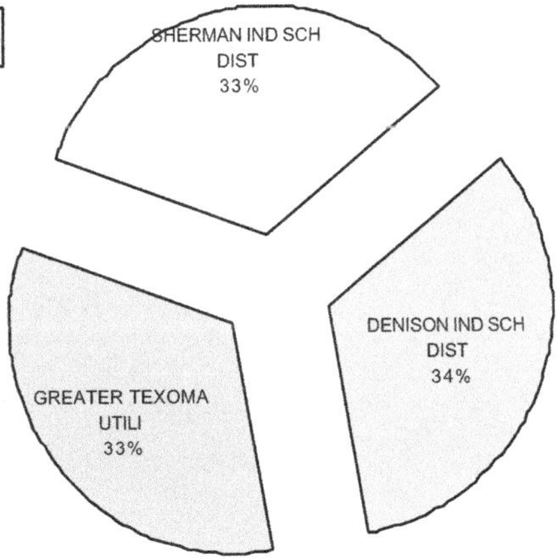

VERSUS

% of County Taxes

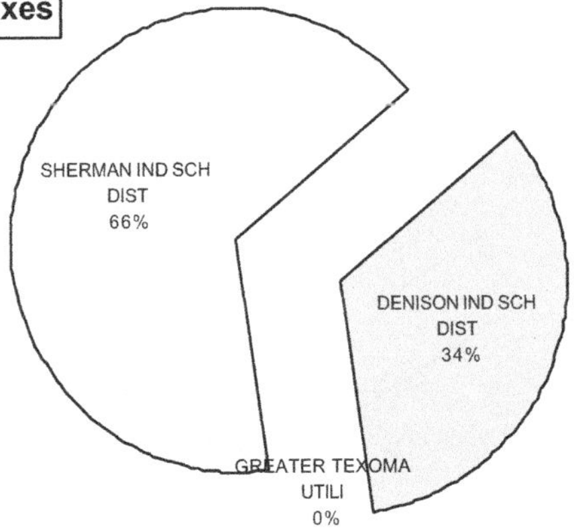

Are you getting your share of debt and taxes in your county?

S1

State/County
TX / GREGG

% of County Debt

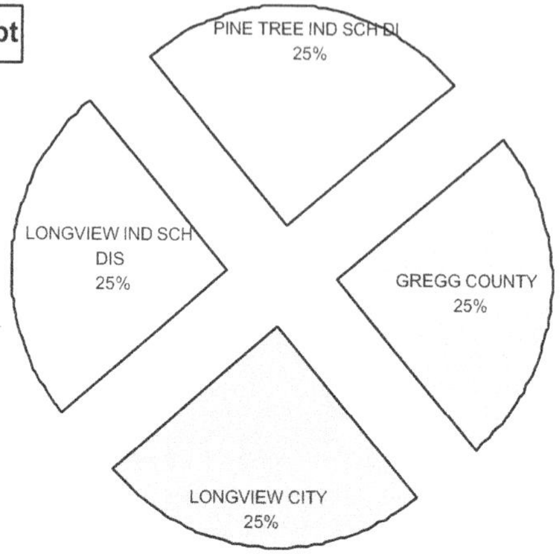

VERSUS

% of County Taxes

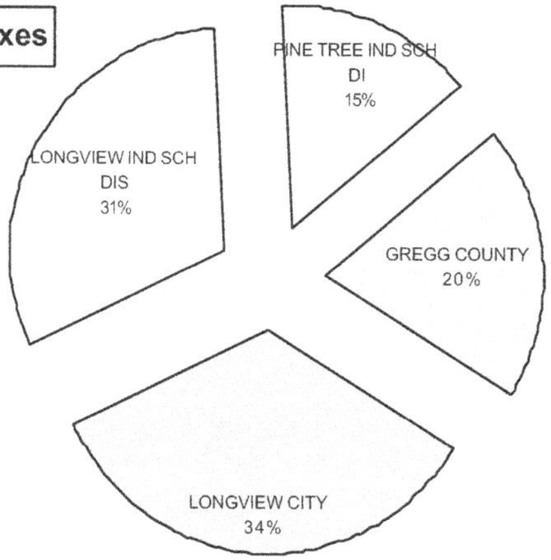

State/County
TX / GRIMES

% of County Debt

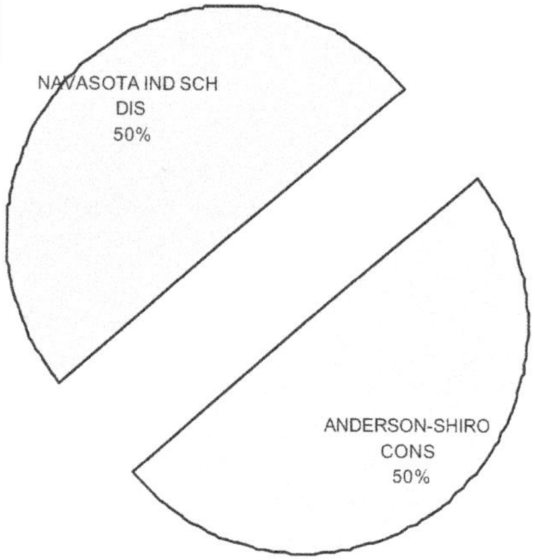

VERSUS

% of County Taxes

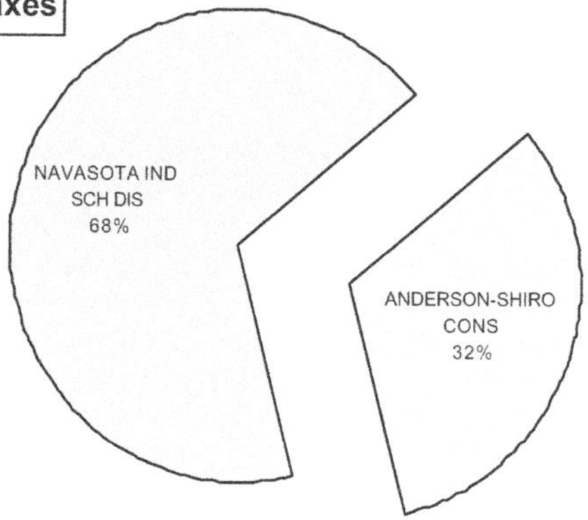

Are you getting your share of debt and taxes in your county? S1

% of County Debt

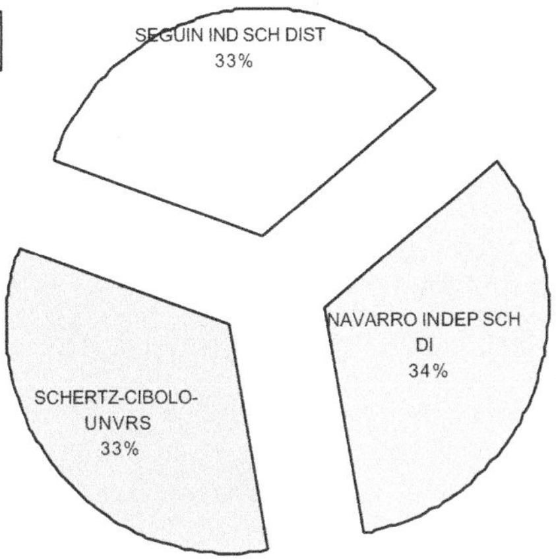

State/County

TX / GUADALUPE

VERSUS

% of County Taxes

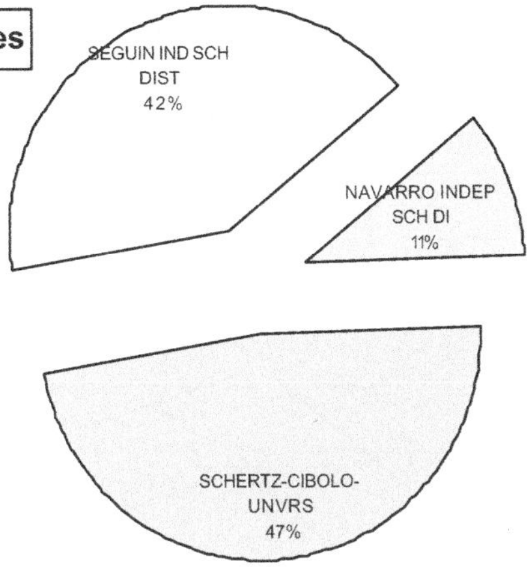

% of County Debt

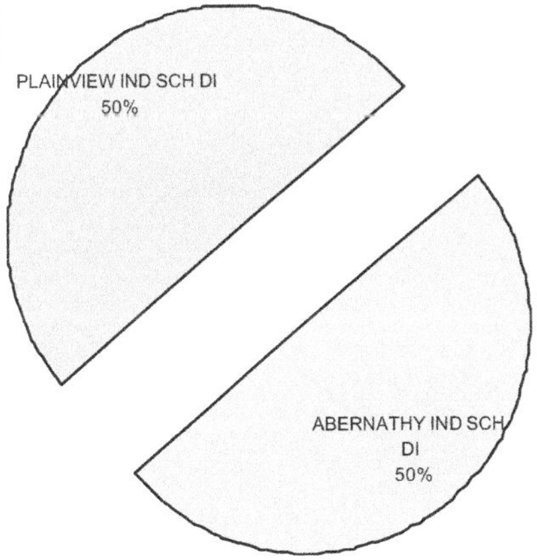

State/County

TX / HALE

VERSUS

% of County Taxes

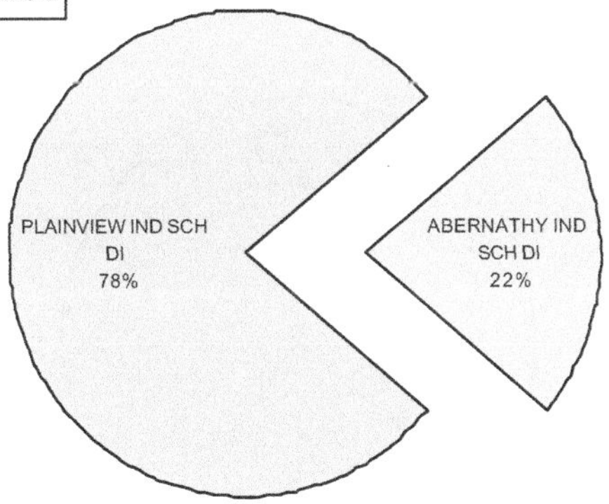

Are you getting your share of debt and taxes in your county? S1

% of County Debt

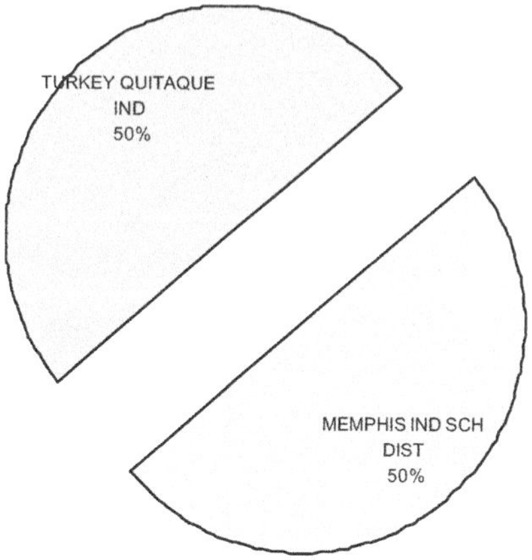

State/County
TX / HALL

VERSUS

% of County Taxes

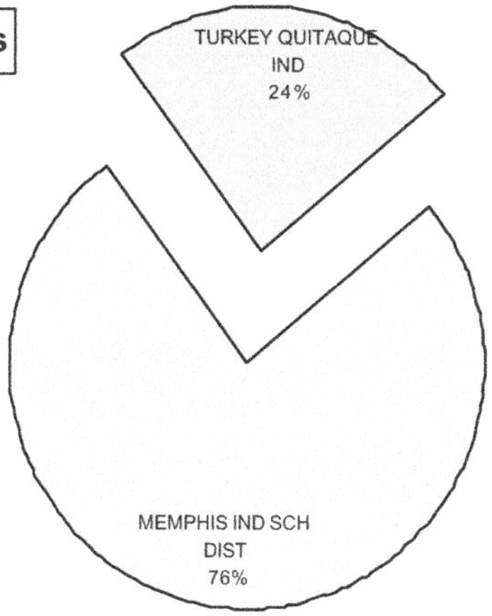

% of County Debt

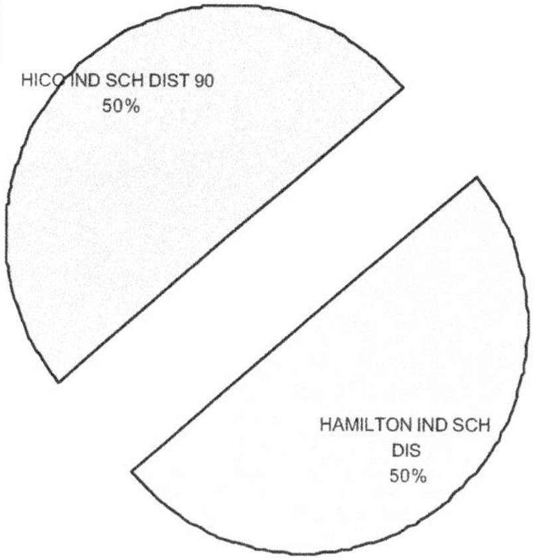

State/County
TX / HAMILTON

VERSUS

% of County Taxes

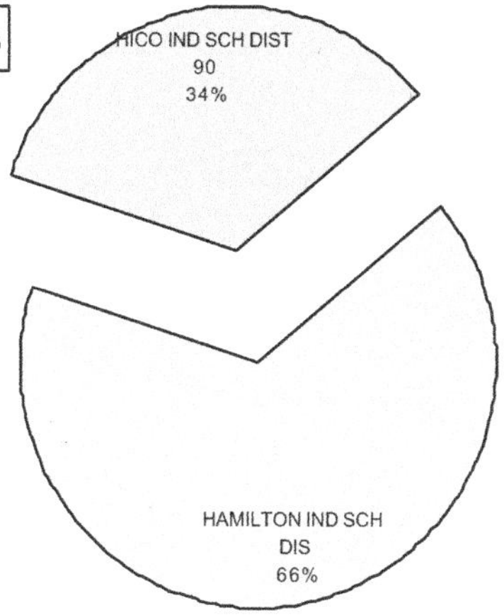

Are you getting your share of debt and taxes in your county?

S1

State/County

TX / HANSFORD

% of County Debt

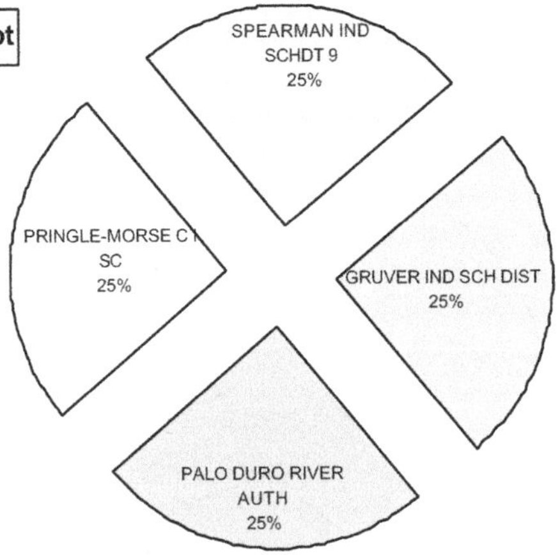

VERSUS

% of County Taxes

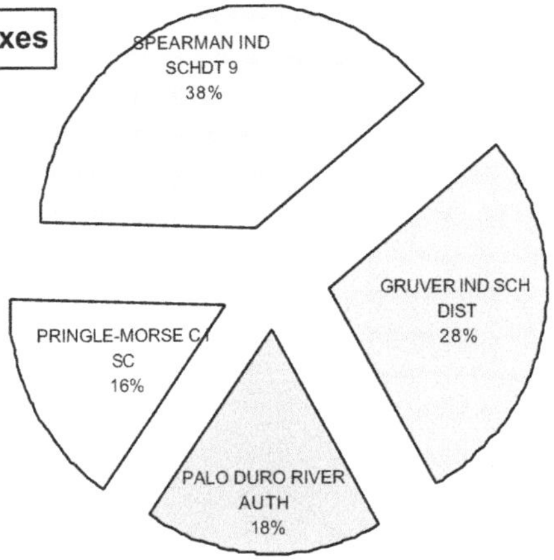

State/County

TX / HARDEMAN

% of County Debt

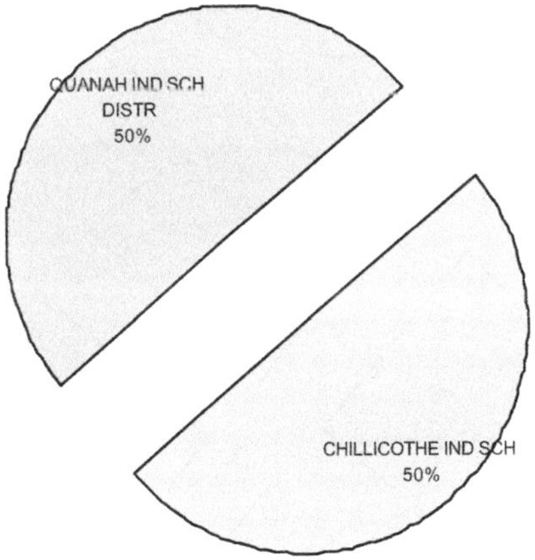

VERSUS

% of County Taxes

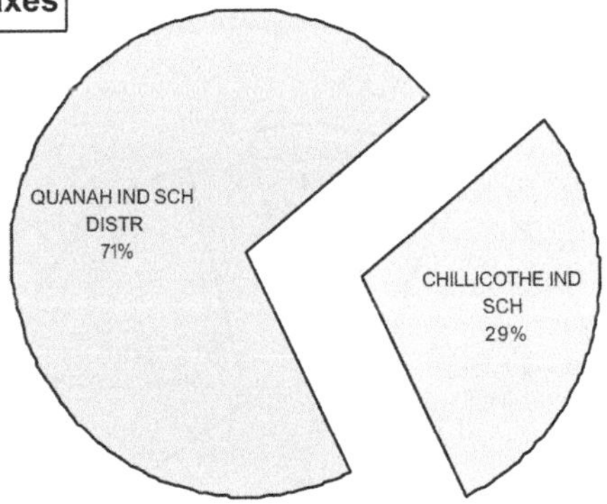

Are you getting your share of debt and taxes in your county?

S1

State/County
TX / HARDIN

% of County Debt

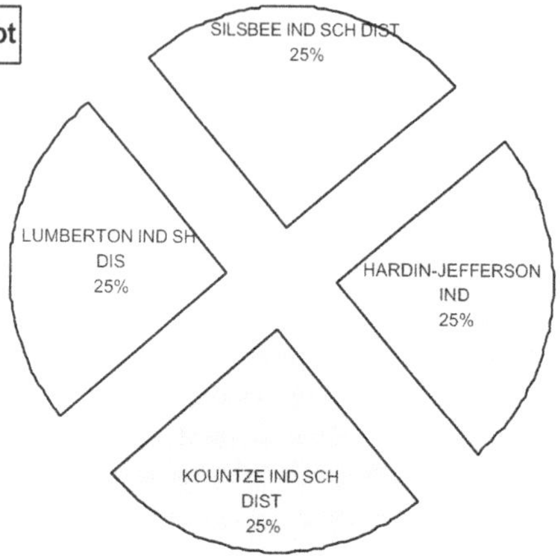

VERSUS

% of County Taxes

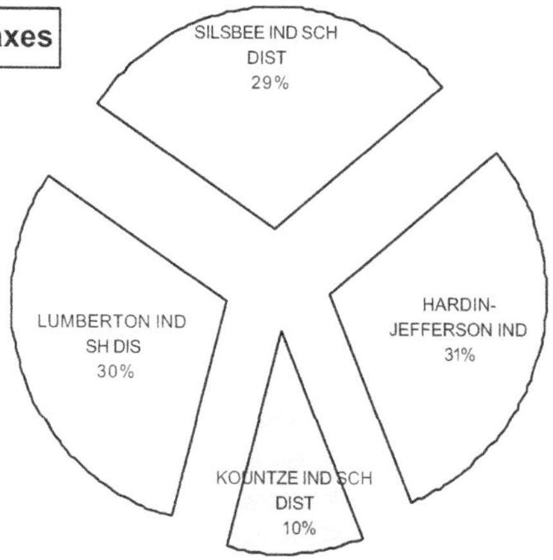

State/County
TX / HARRIS

% of County Debt

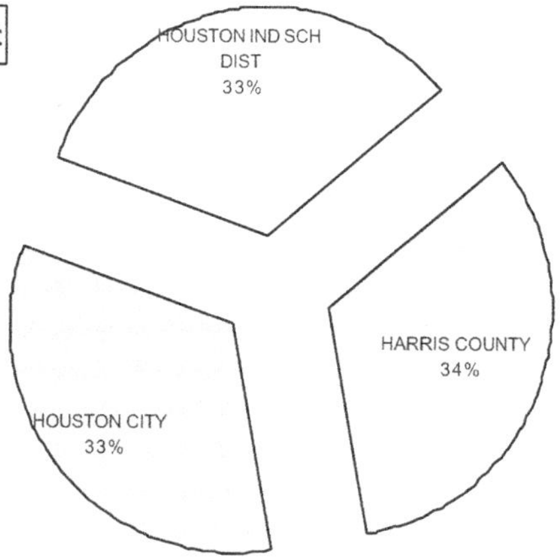

VERSUS

% of County Taxes

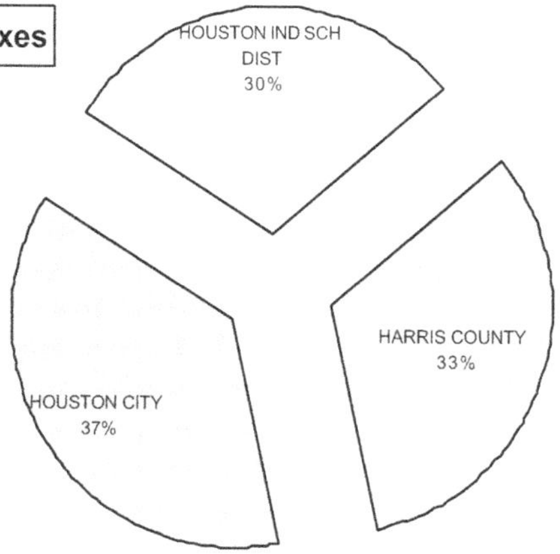

Are you getting your share of debt and taxes in your county?

S1

% of County Debt

State/County

TX / HARRISON

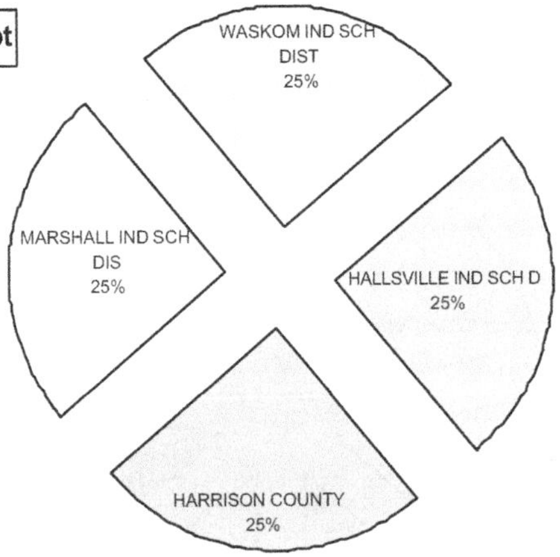

VERSUS

% of County Taxes

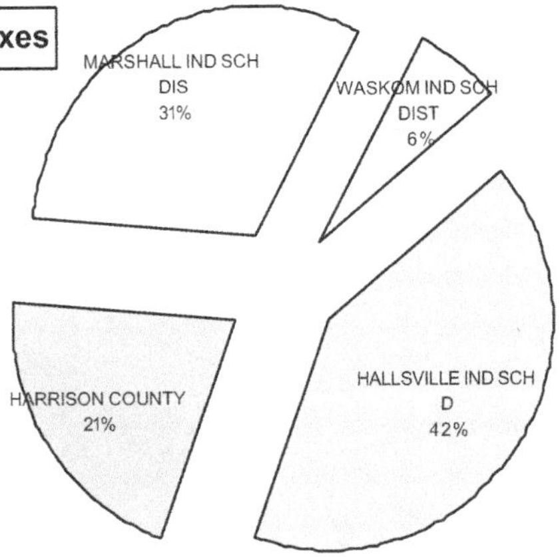

% of County Debt

State/County

TX / HARTLEY

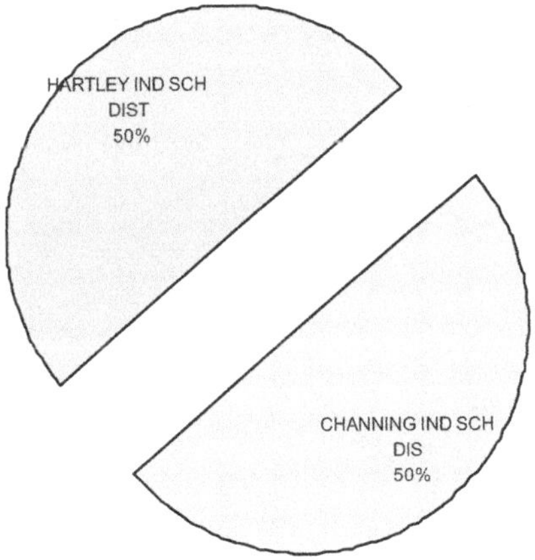

VERSUS

% of County Taxes

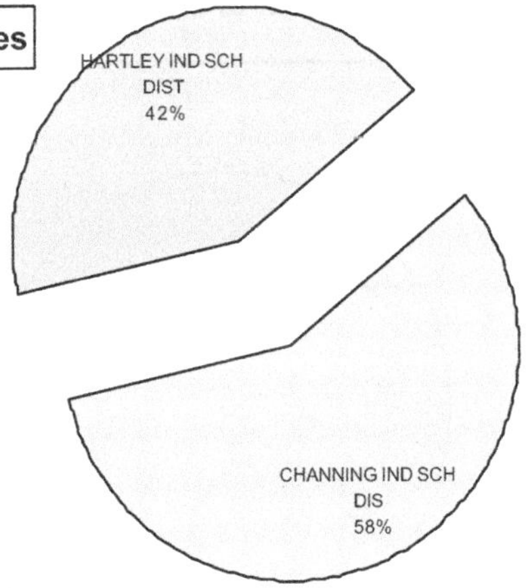

Are you getting your share of debt and taxes in your county? S1

State/County
TX / HASKELL

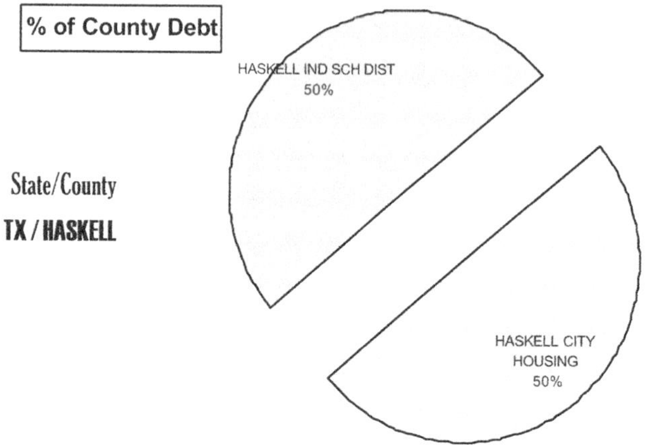

VERSUS

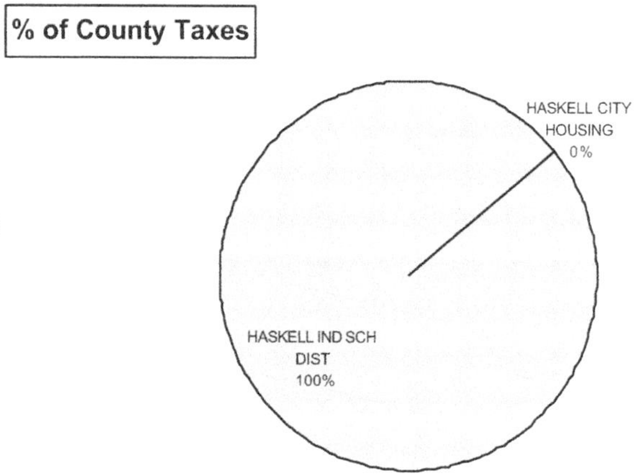

State/County
TX / HAYS

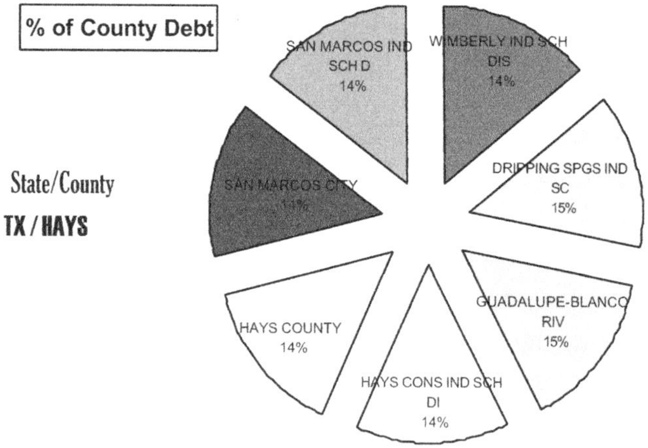

VERSUS

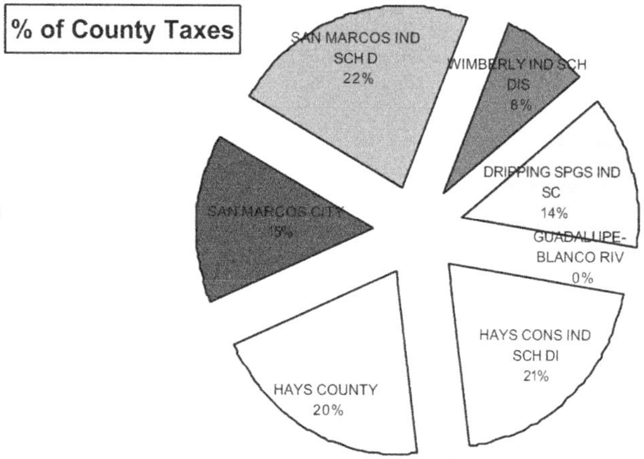

Are you getting your share of debt and taxes in your county?

S1

% of County Debt

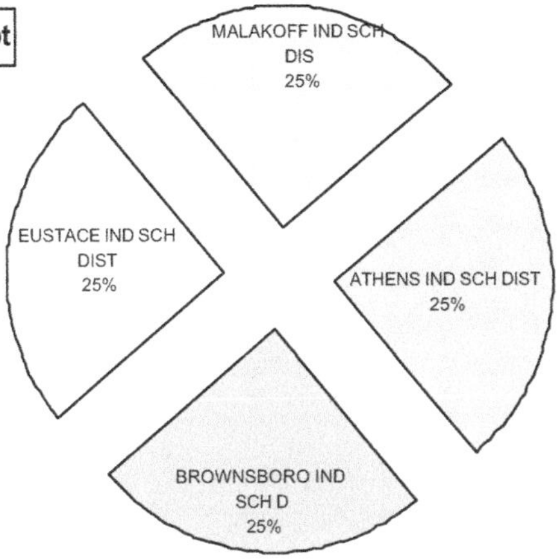

State/County

TX / HENDERSON

VERSUS

% of County Taxes

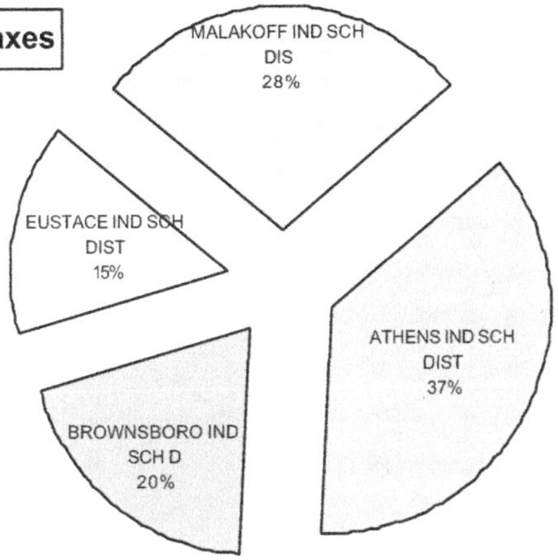

% of County Debt

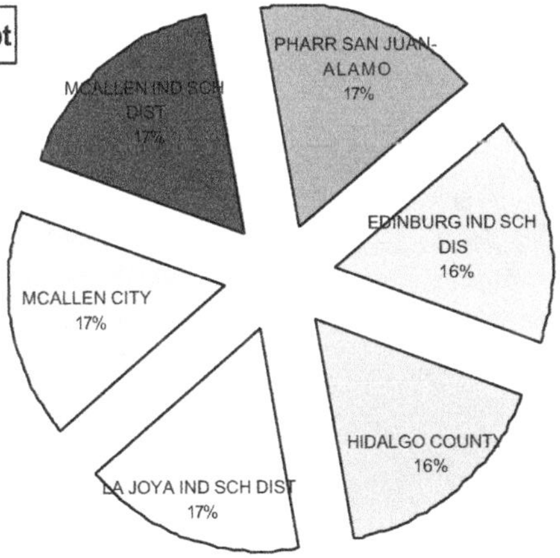

State/County

TX / HIDALGO

VERSUS

% of County Taxes

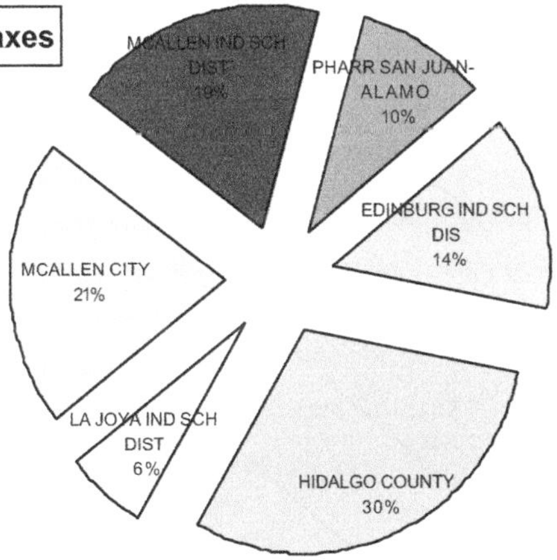

Are you getting your share of debt and taxes in your county?

S1

State/County

TX / HILL

% of County Debt

VERSUS

% of County Taxes

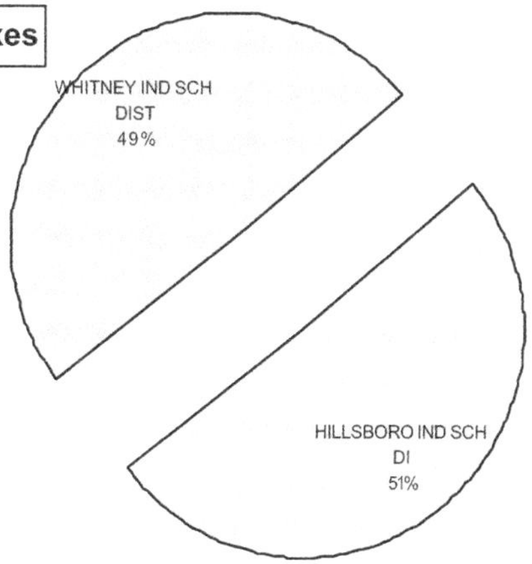

State/County

TX / HOCKLEY

% of County Debt

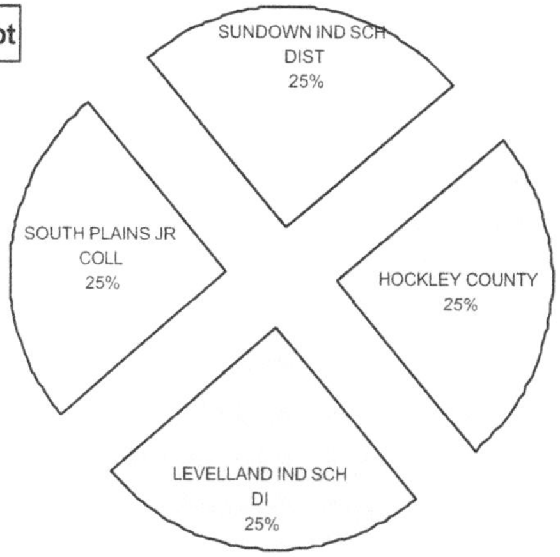

VERSUS

% of County Taxes

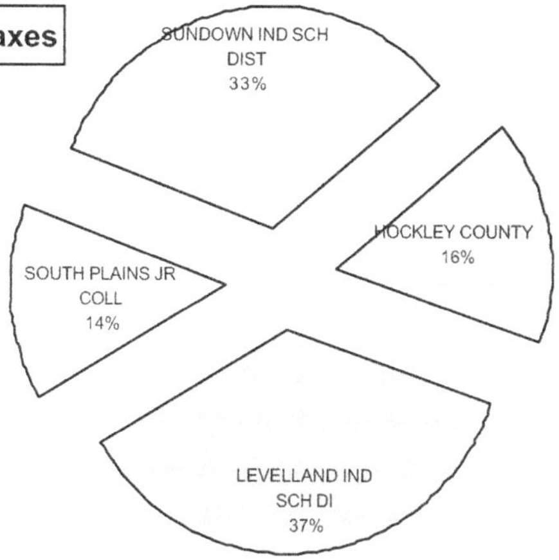

Are you getting your share of debt and taxes in your county? S1

% of County Debt

State/County

TX / HOOD

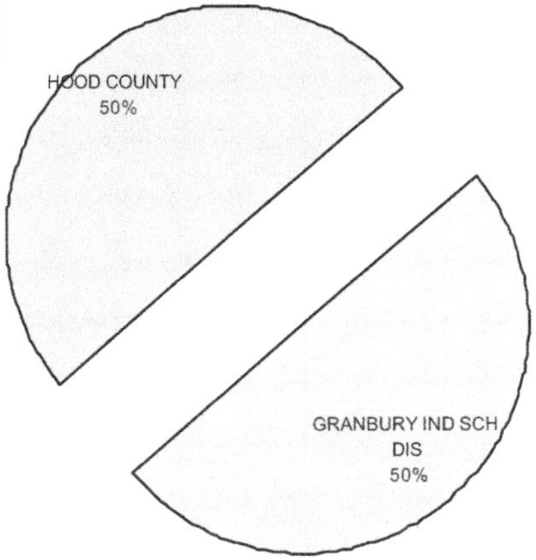

VERSUS

% of County Taxes

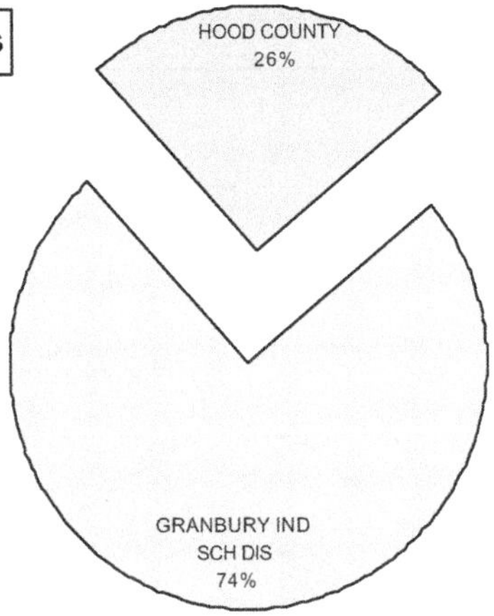

% of County Debt

State/County

TX / HOPKINS

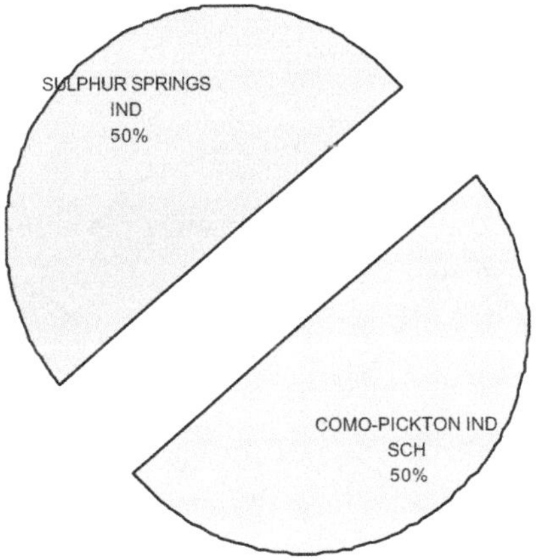

VERSUS

% of County Taxes

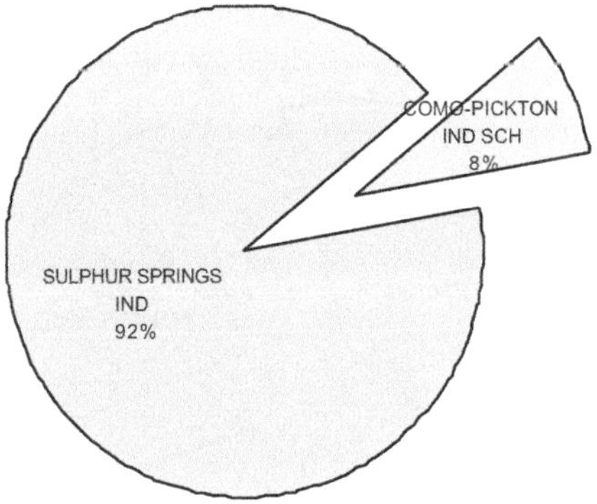

Are you getting your share of debt and taxes in your county?

S1

State/County

TX / HOUSTON

% of County Debt

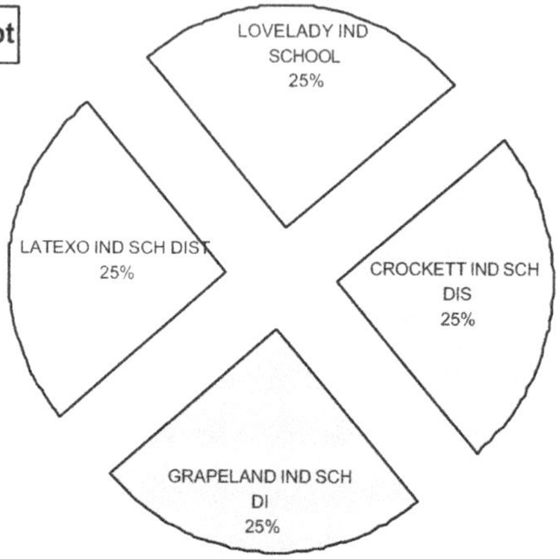

VERSUS

% of County Taxes

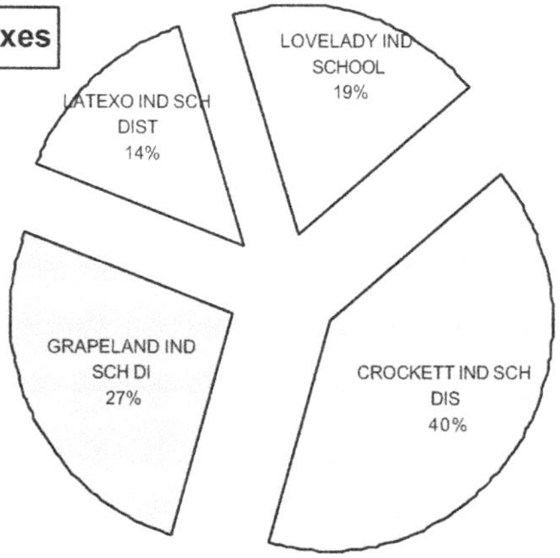

State/County

TX / HOWARD

% of County Debt

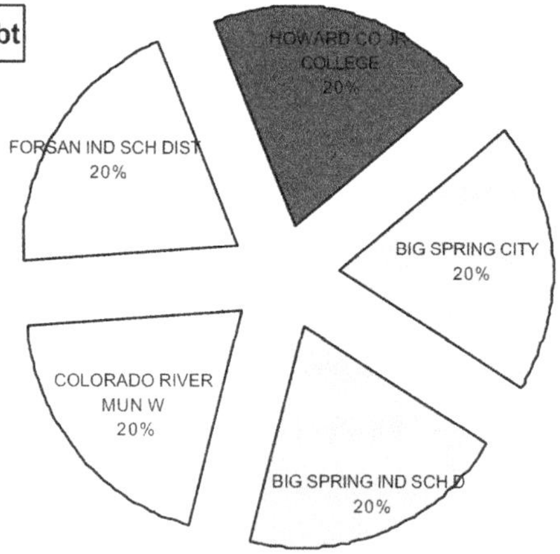

VERSUS

% of County Taxes

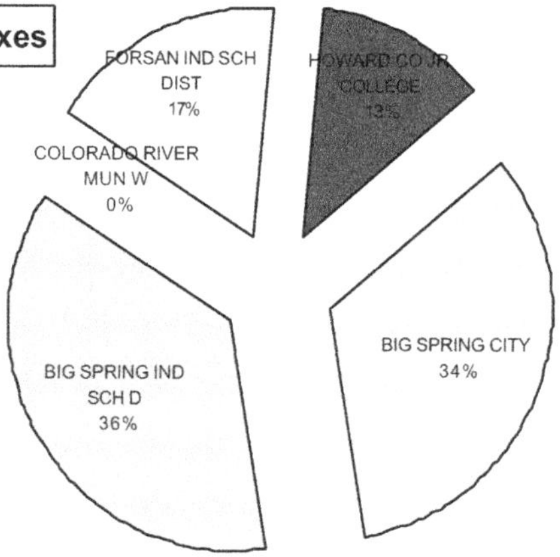

Are you getting your share of debt and taxes in your county?

S1

State/County

TX / HUDSPETH

% of County Debt

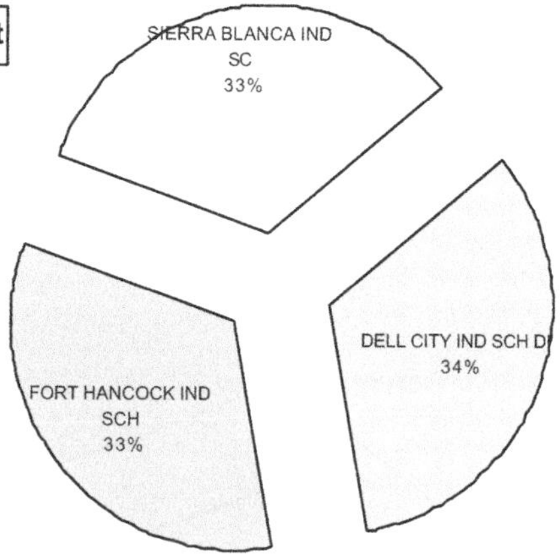

VERSUS

% of County Taxes

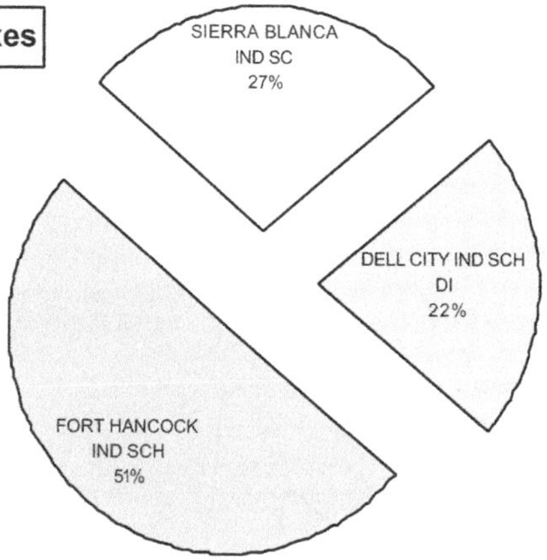

State/County

TX / HUNT

% of County Debt

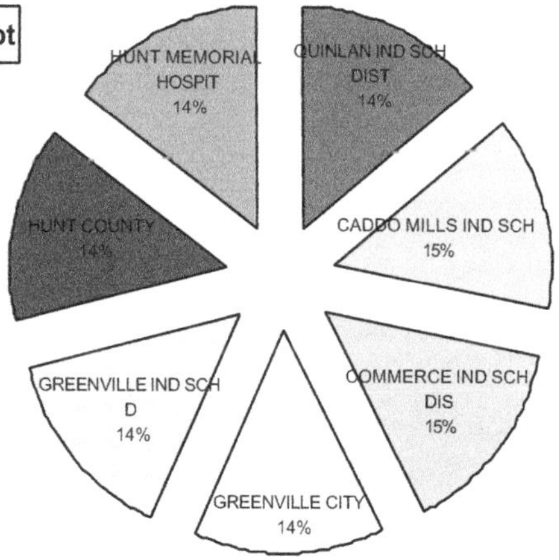

VERSUS

% of County Taxes

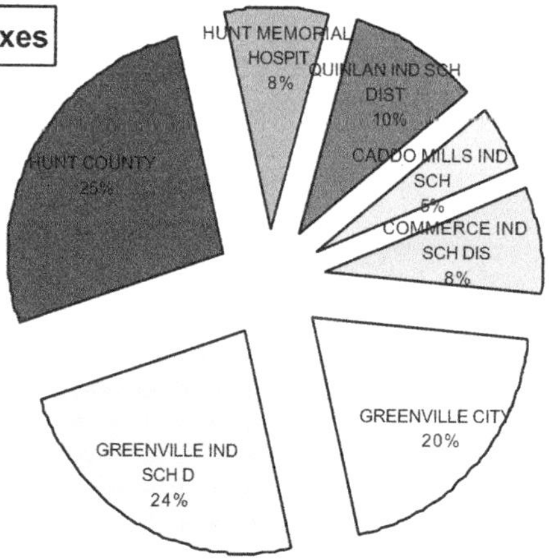

Are you getting your share of debt and taxes in your county?

S1

State/County

TX / HUTCHINSON

% of County Debt

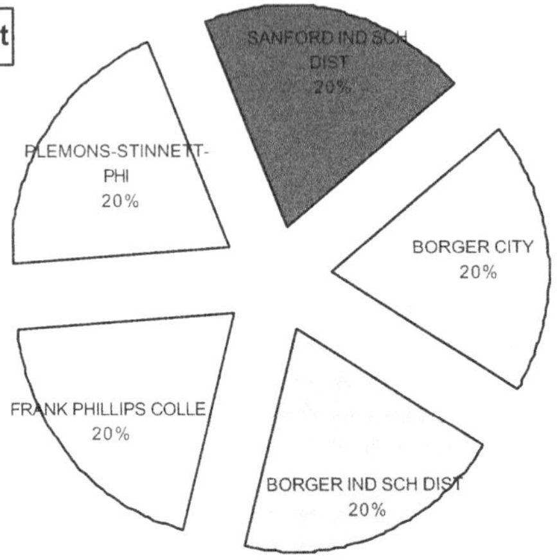

VERSUS

% of County Taxes

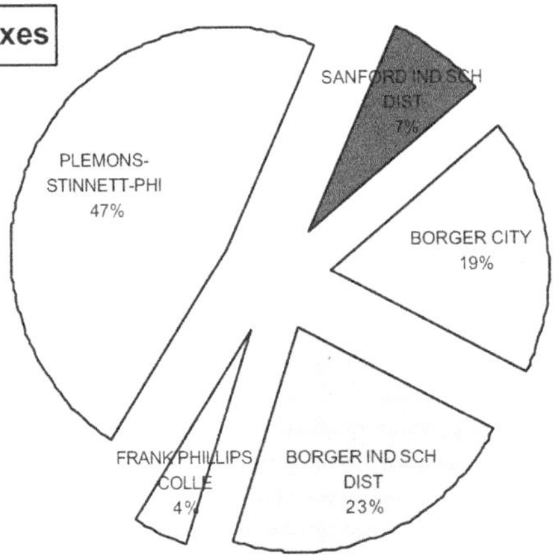

State/County

TX / JACK

% of County Debt

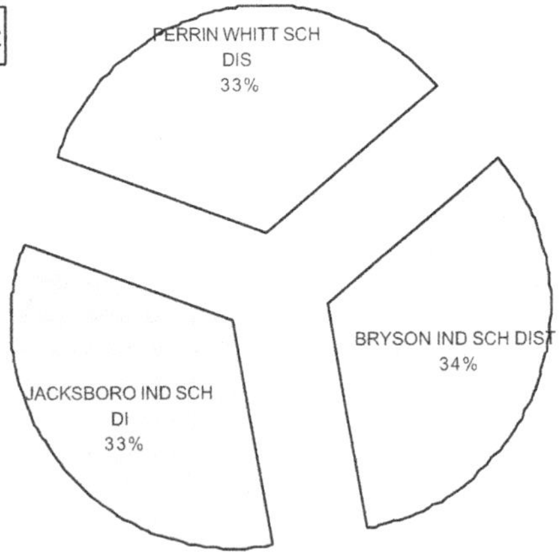

VERSUS

% of County Taxes

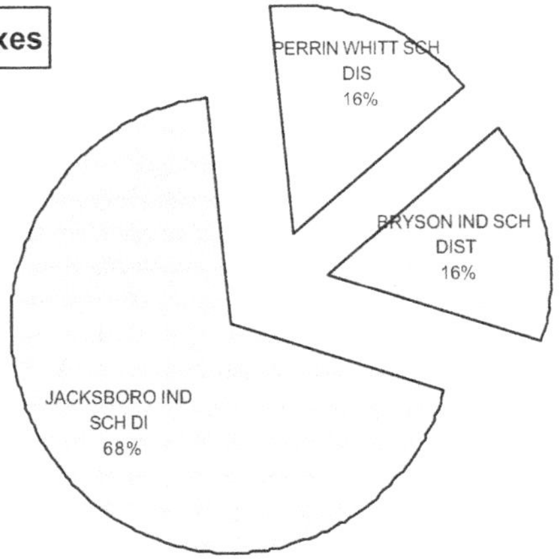

Are you getting your share of debt and taxes in your county?

S1

% of County Debt

State/County

TX / JACKSON

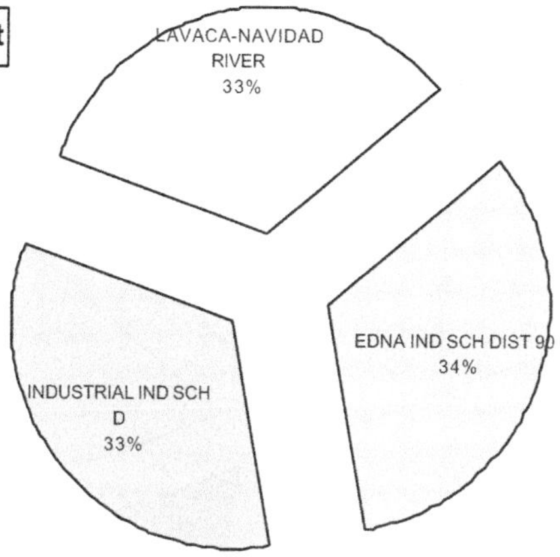

VERSUS

% of County Taxes

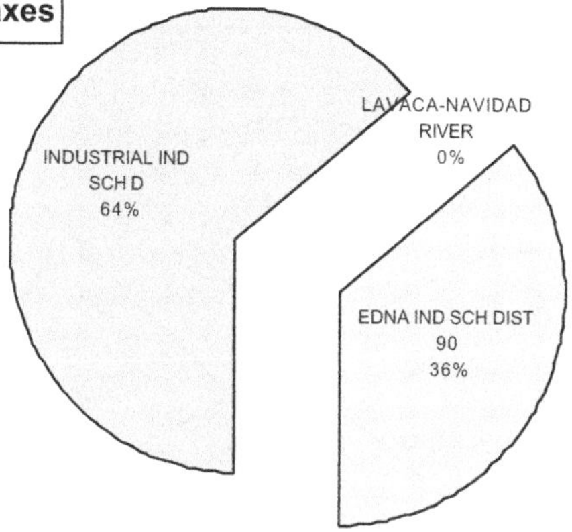

% of County Debt

State/County

TX / JASPER

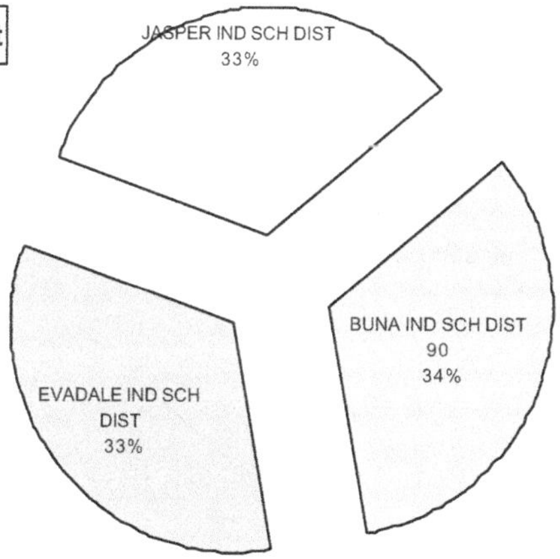

VERSUS

% of County Taxes

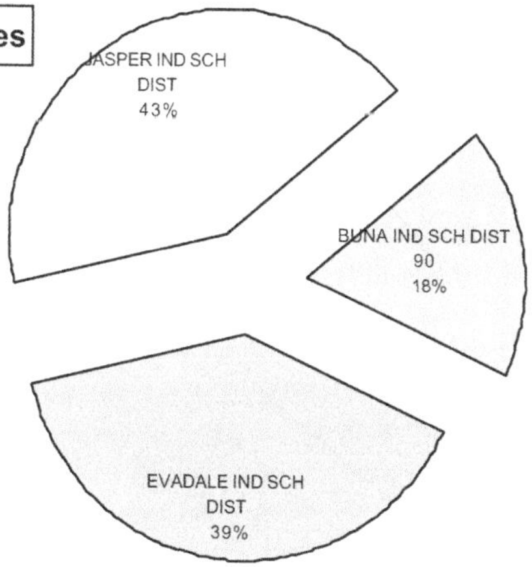

Are you getting your share of debt and taxes in your county? S1

State/County

TX / JEFF DAVIS

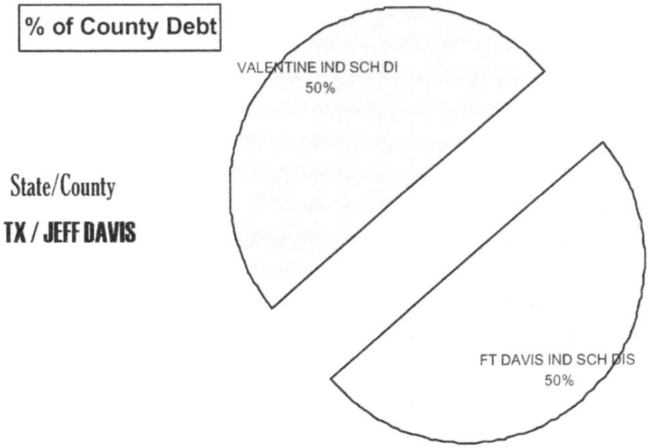

VERSUS

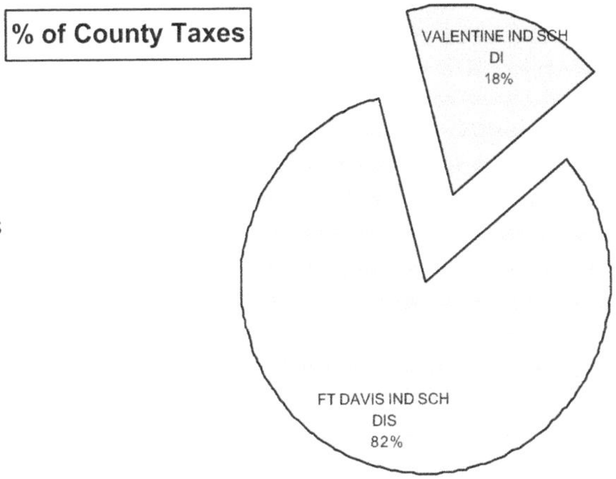

State/County

TX / JEFFERSON

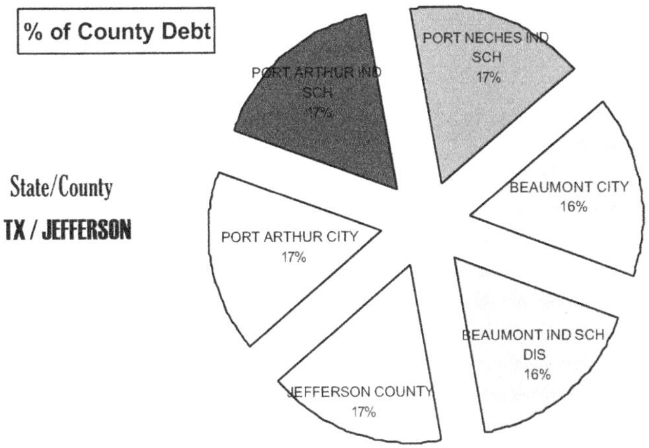

VERSUS

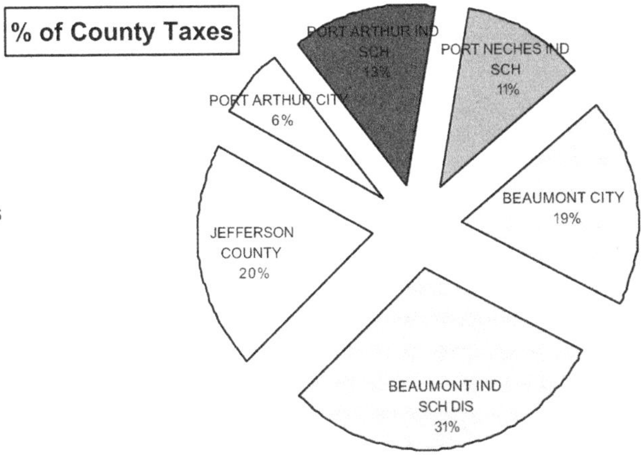

Are you getting your share of debt and taxes in your county?

S1

% of County Debt

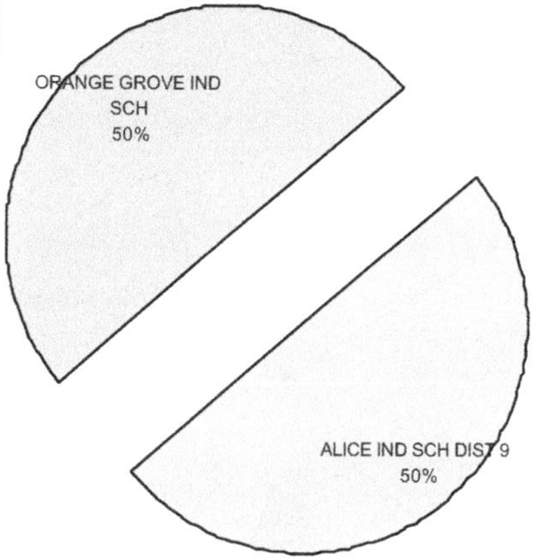

State/County

TX / JIM WELLS

VERSUS

% of County Taxes

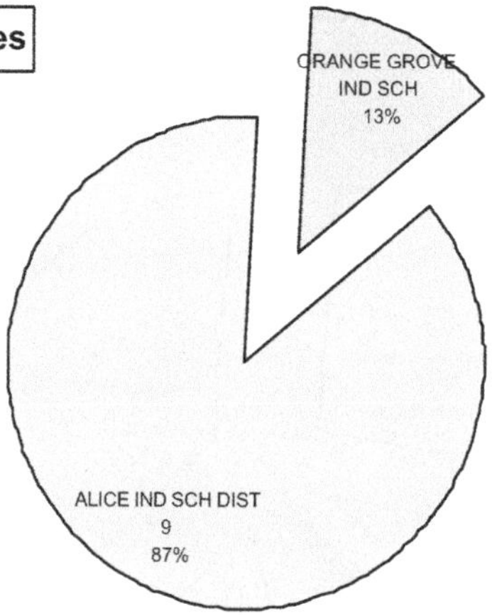

% of County Debt

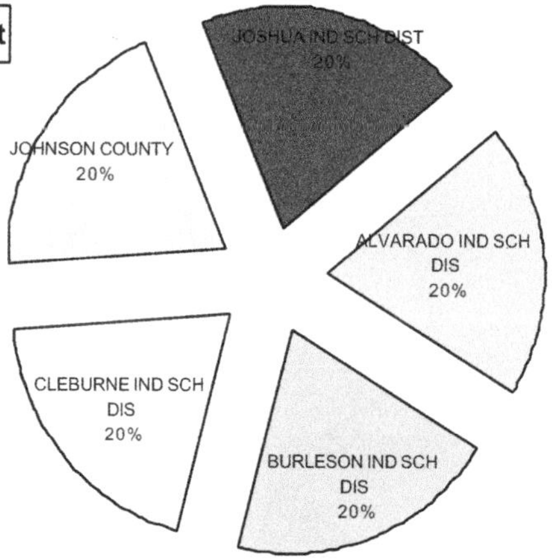

State/County

TX / JOHNSON

VERSUS

% of County Taxes

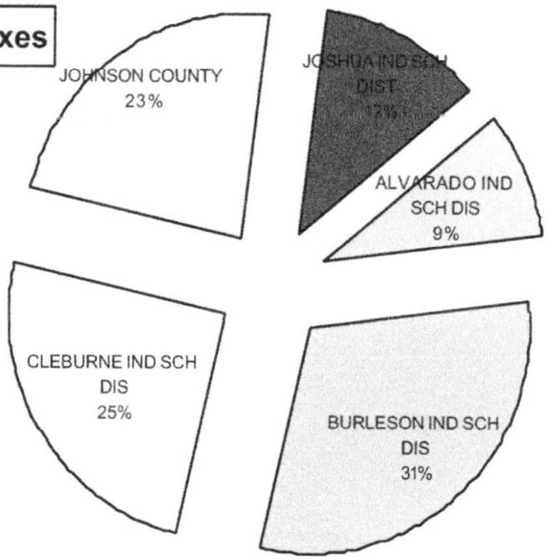

Are you getting your share of debt and taxes in your county? S1

State/County
TX / JONES

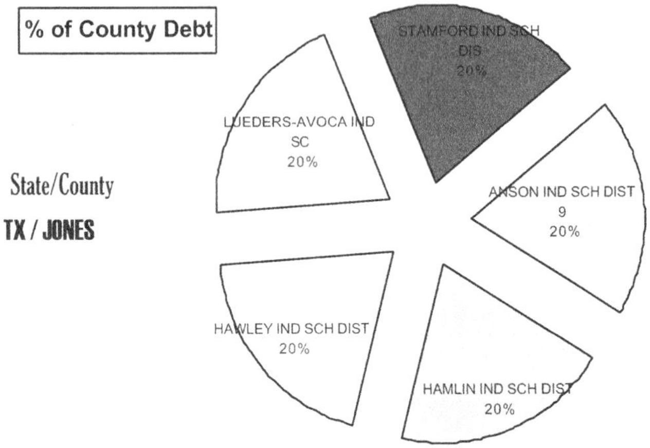

VERSUS

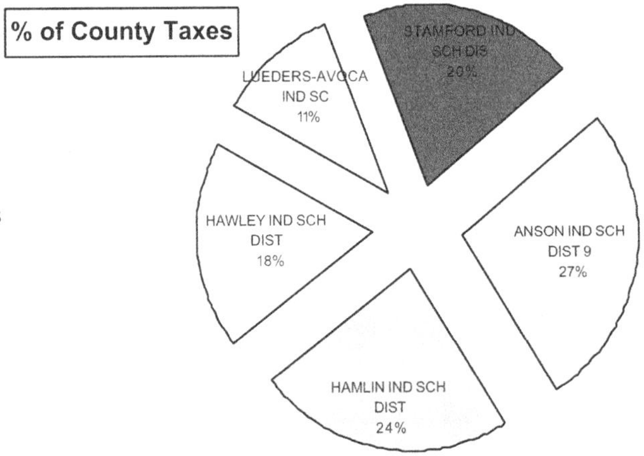

State/County
TX / KARNES

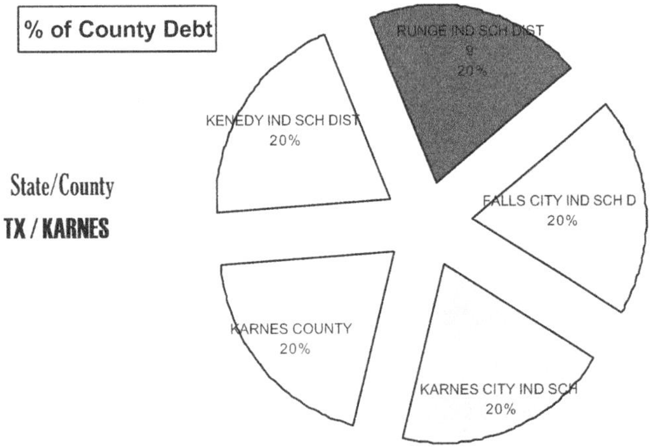

VERSUS

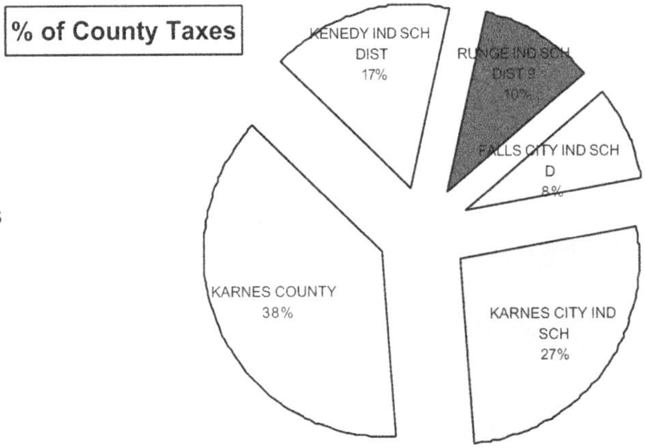

Are you getting your share of debt and taxes in your county? S1

% of County Debt

State/County

TX / KAUFMAN

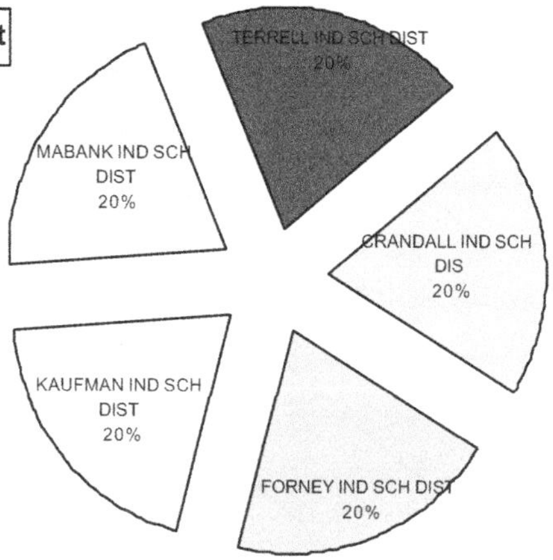

VERSUS

% of County Taxes

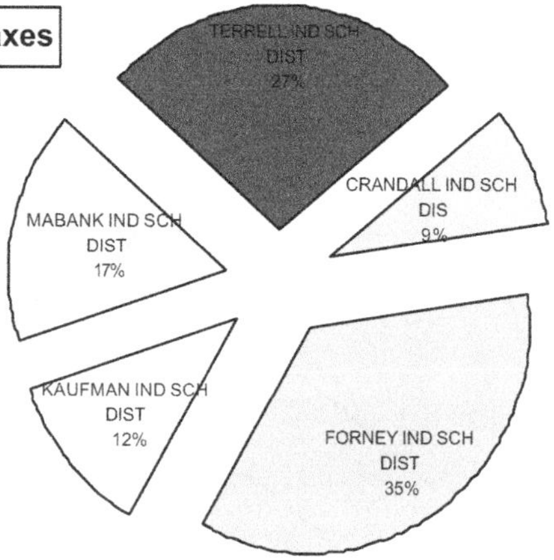

% of County Debt

State/County

TX / KENDALL

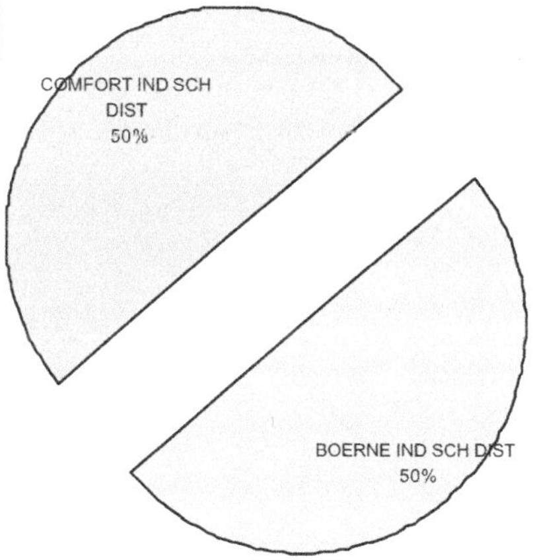

VERSUS

% of County Taxes

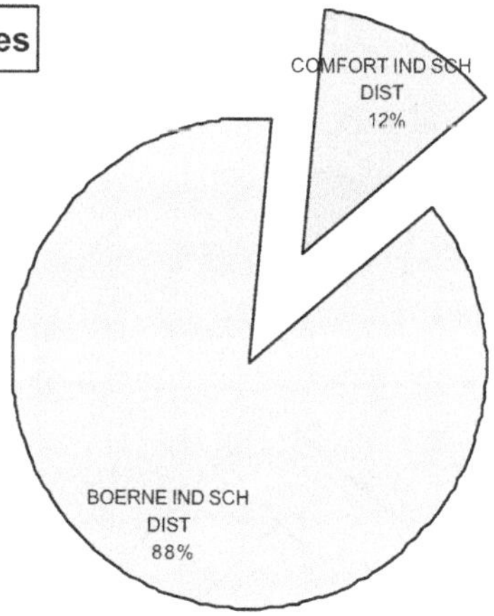

Are you getting your share of debt and taxes in your county?

State/County

TX / KLEBERG

% of County Debt

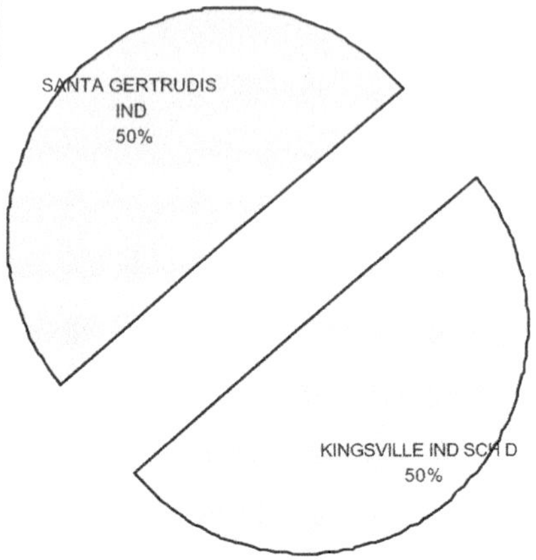

VERSUS

% of County Taxes

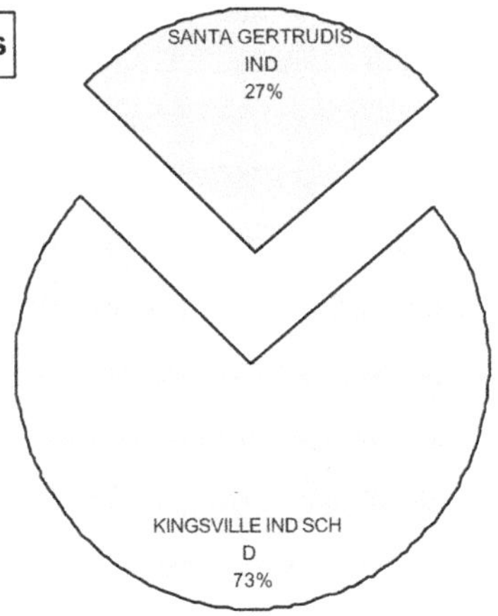

State/County

TX / KNOX

% of County Debt

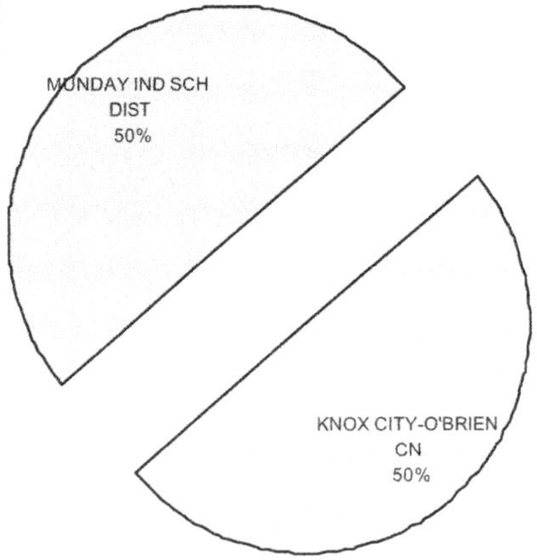

VERSUS

% of County Taxes

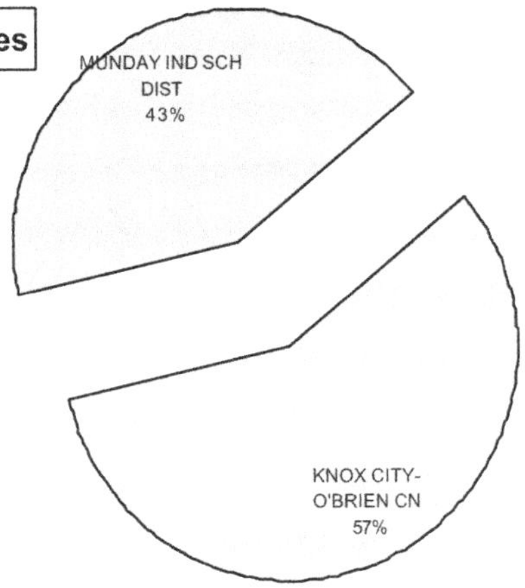

Are you getting your share of debt and taxes in your county?

S1

% of County Debt

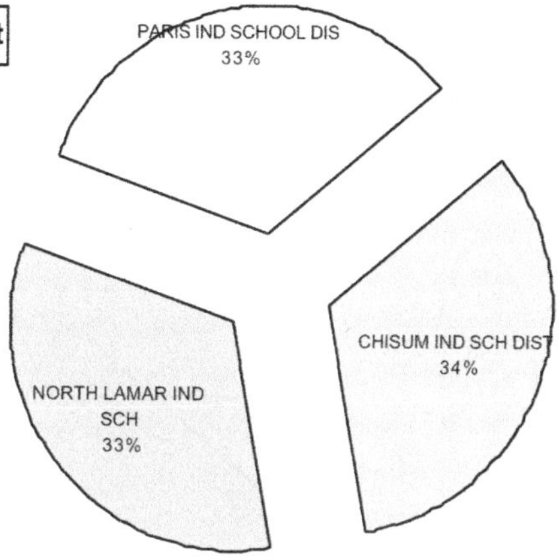

State/County
TX / LAMAR

VERSUS

% of County Taxes

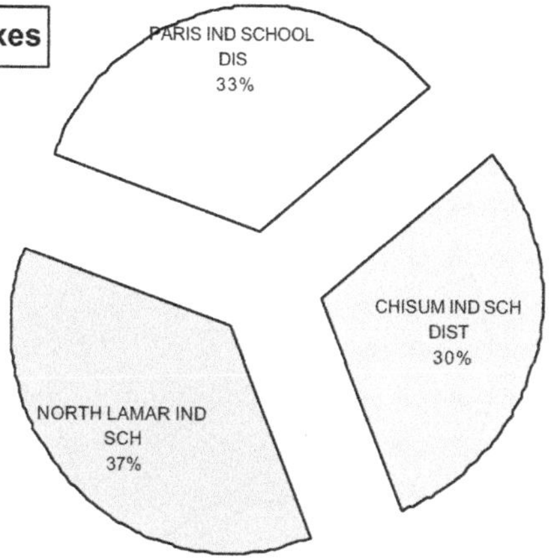

% of County Debt

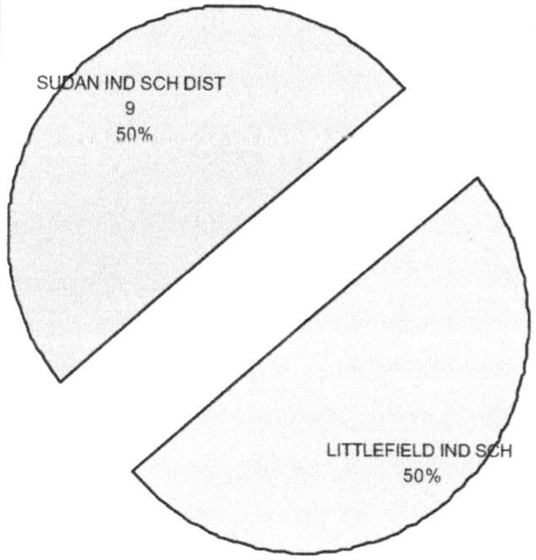

State/County
TX / LAMB

VERSUS

% of County Taxes

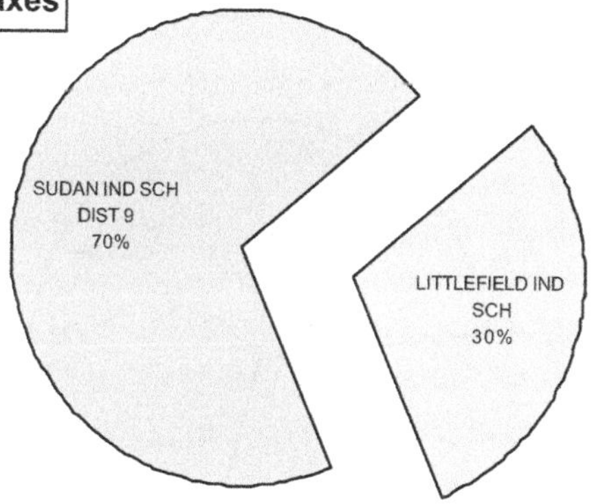

Are you getting your share of debt and taxes in your county? S1

State/County

TX / LAVACA

% of County Debt

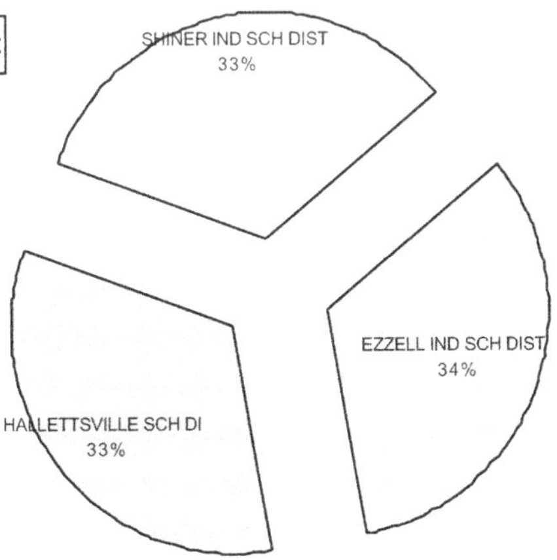

VERSUS

% of County Taxes

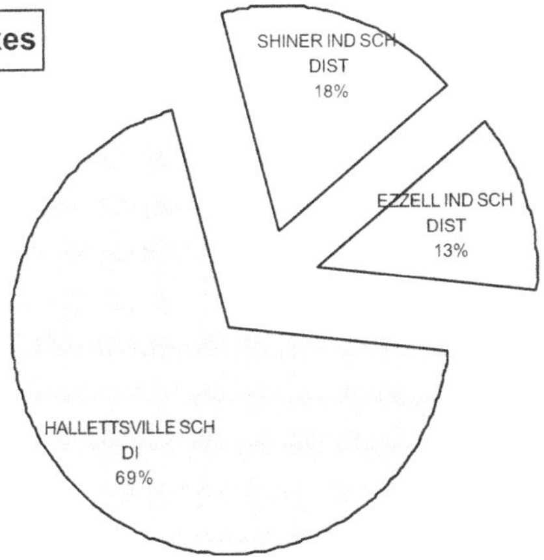

State/County

TX / LEE

% of County Debt

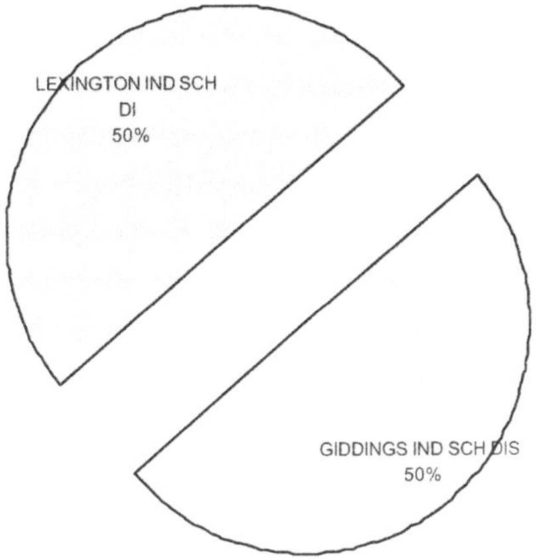

VERSUS

% of County Taxes

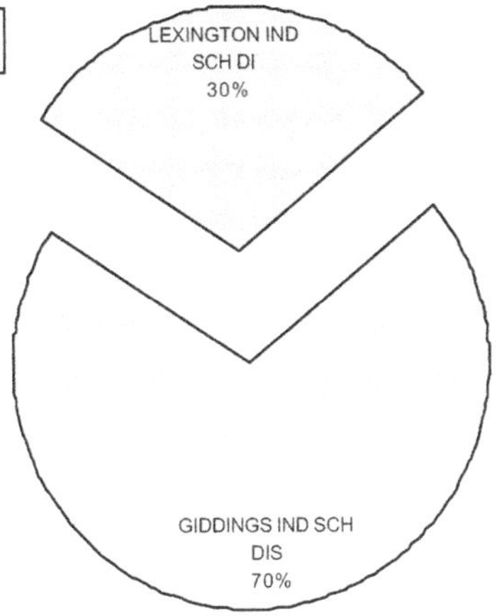

Are you getting your share of debt and taxes in your county?

S1

% of County Debt

State/County
TX / LEON

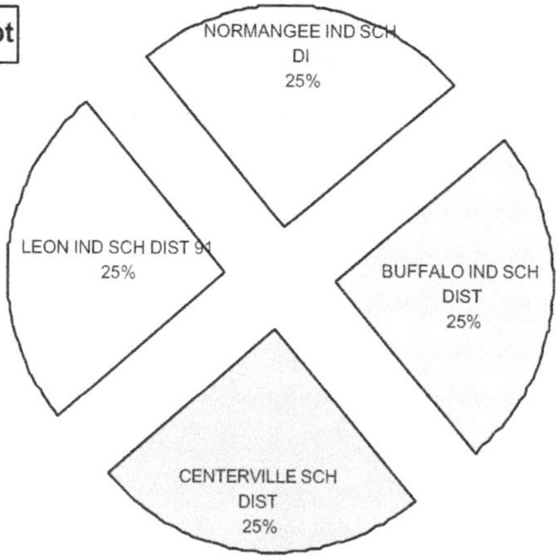

VERSUS

% of County Taxes

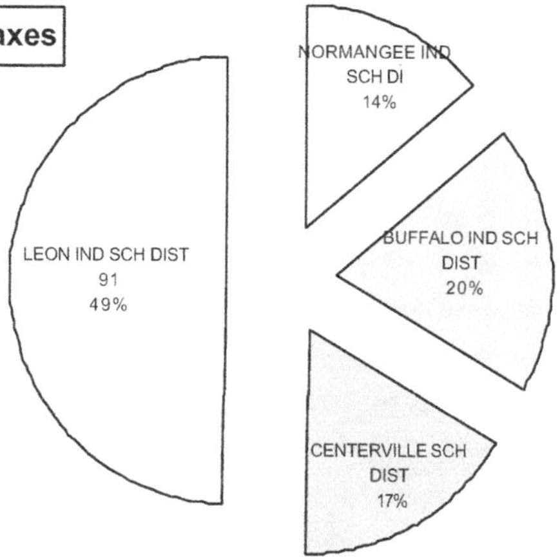

% of County Debt

State/County
TX / LIBERTY

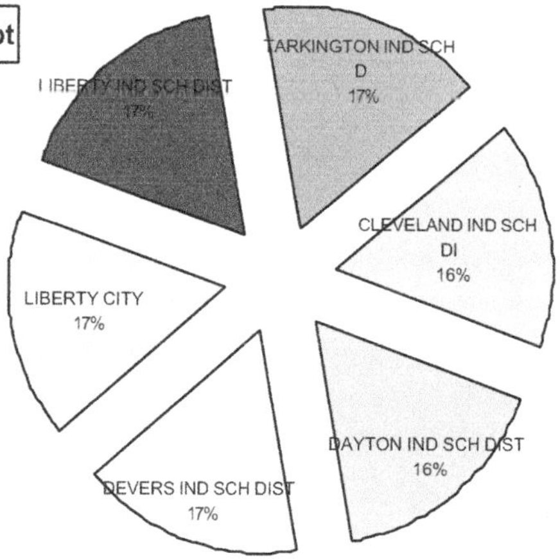

VERSUS

% of County Taxes

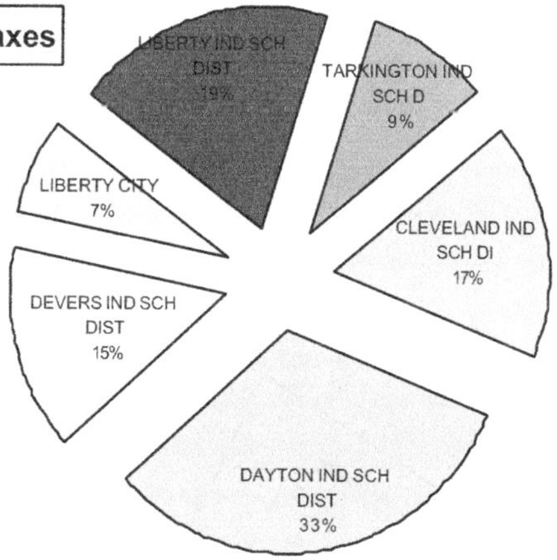

Are you getting your share of debt and taxes in your county?

S1

State/County

TX / LIMESTONE

% of County Debt

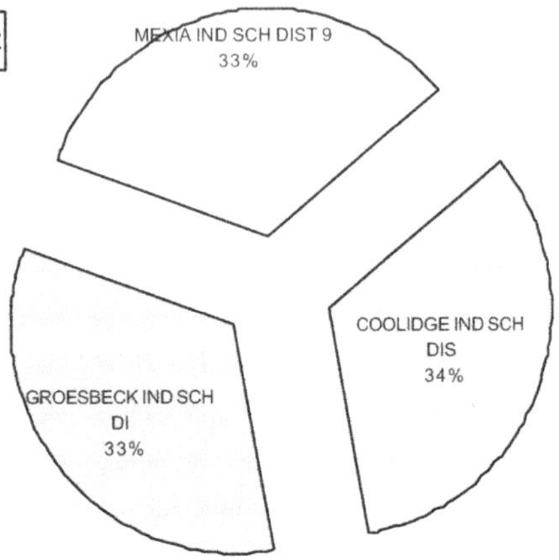

VERSUS

% of County Taxes

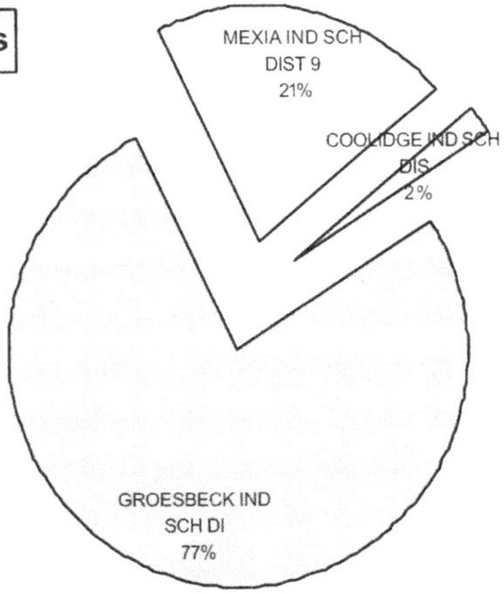

State/County

TX / LIPSCOMB

% of County Debt

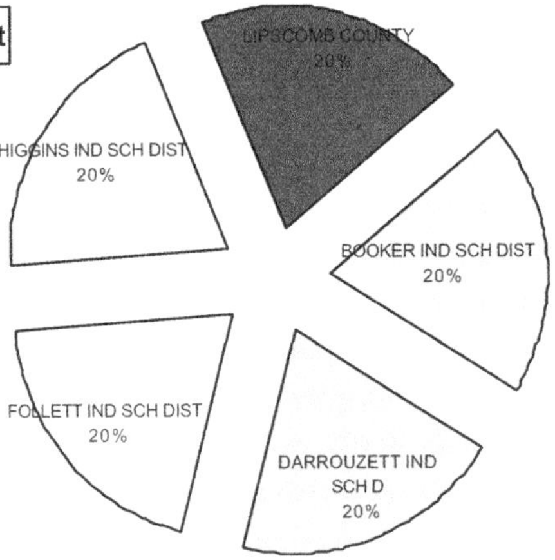

VERSUS

% of County Taxes

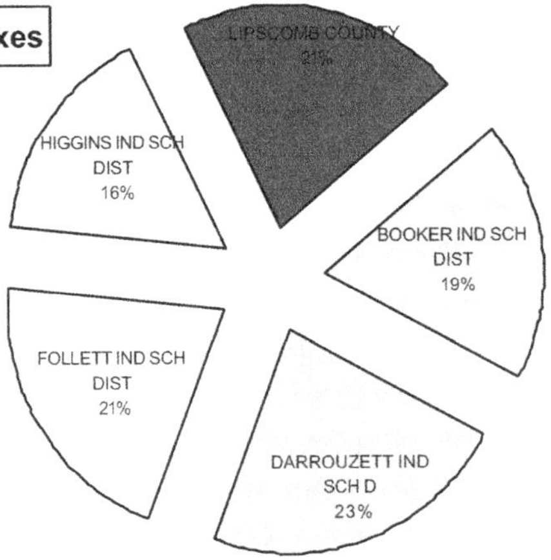

Are you getting your share of debt and taxes in your county?

S1

State/County

TX / LIVE OAK

% of County Debt

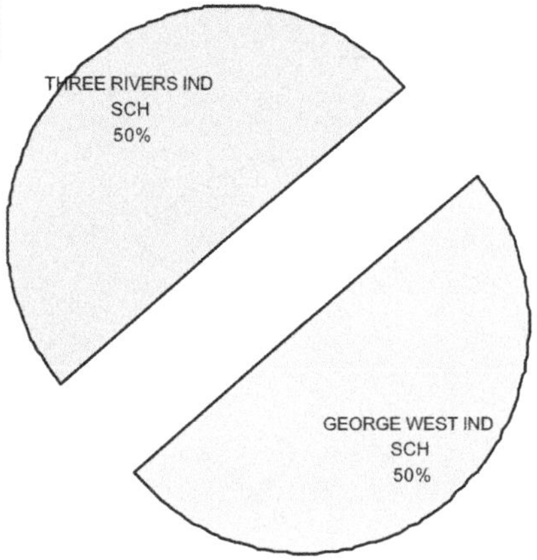

VERSUS

% of County Taxes

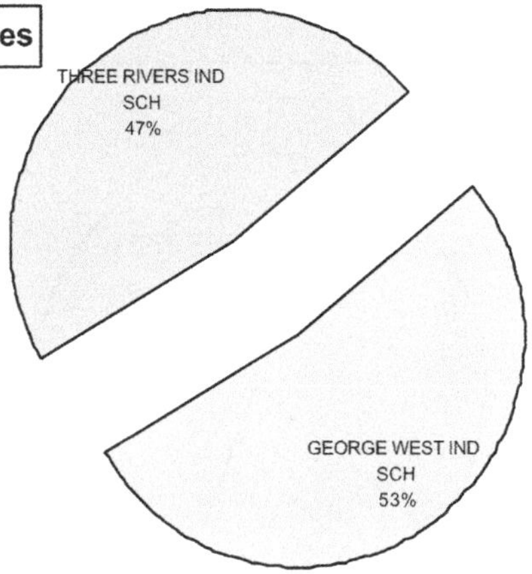

State/County

TX / LUBBOCK

% of County Debt

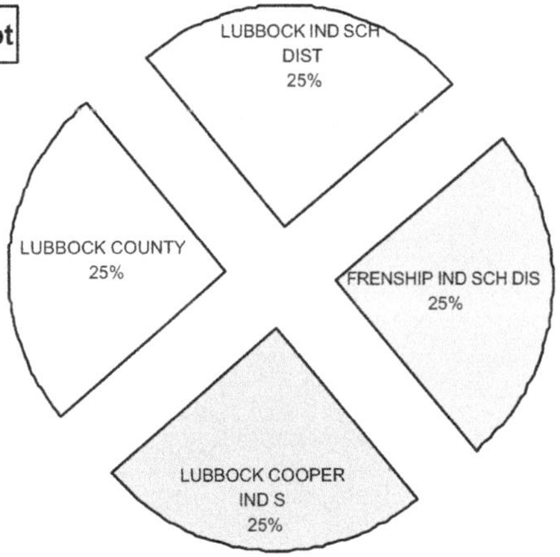

VERSUS

% of County Taxes

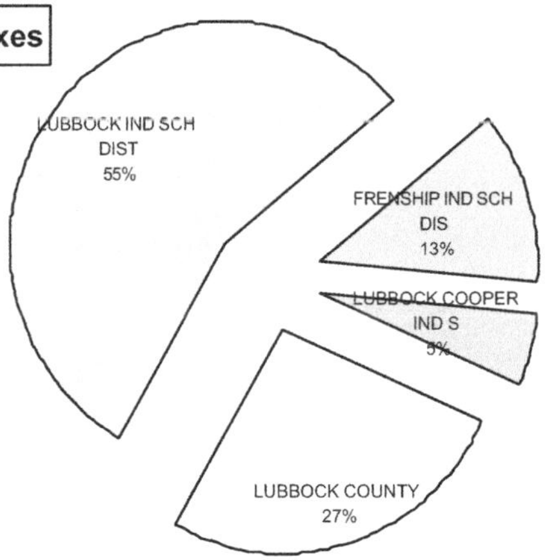

Are you getting your share of debt and taxes in your county? S1

State/County
TX / LYNN

% of County Debt

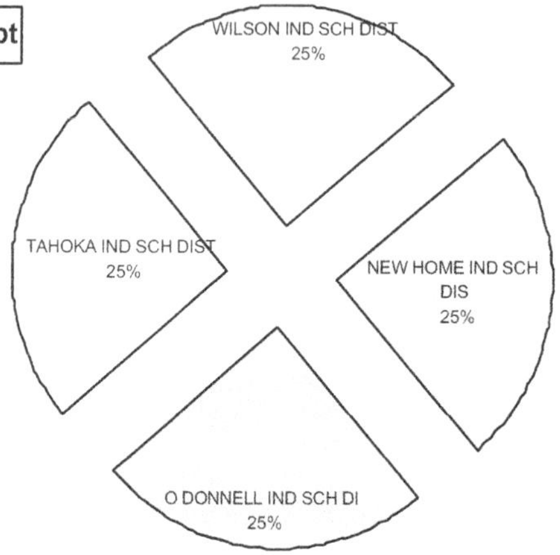

VERSUS

% of County Taxes

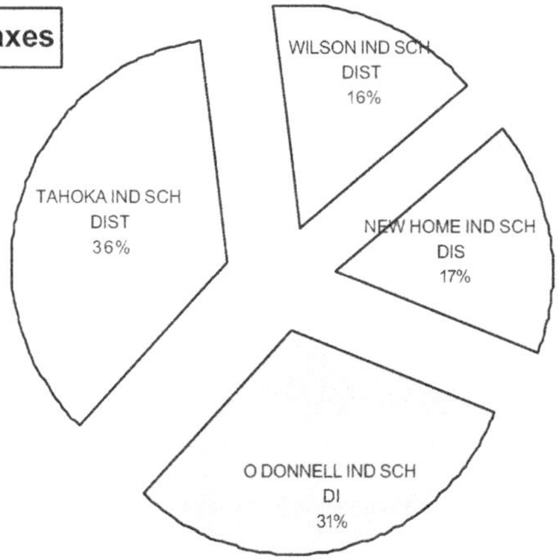

State/County
TX / MADISON

% of County Debt

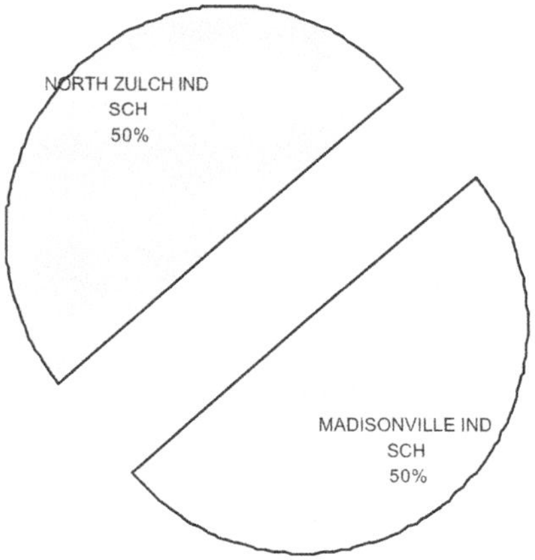

VERSUS

% of County Taxes

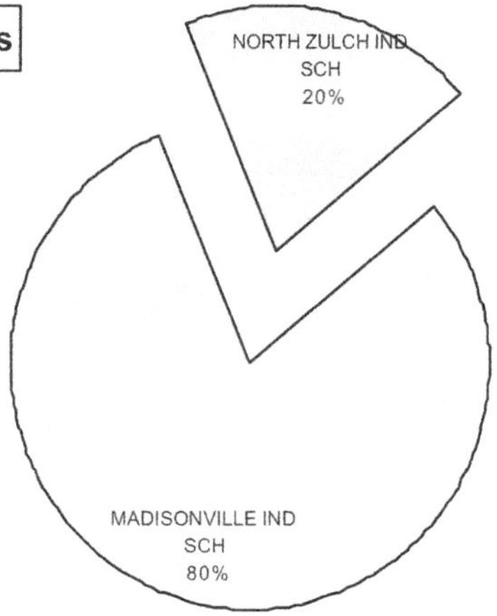

Are you getting your share of debt and taxes in your county? S1

% of County Debt

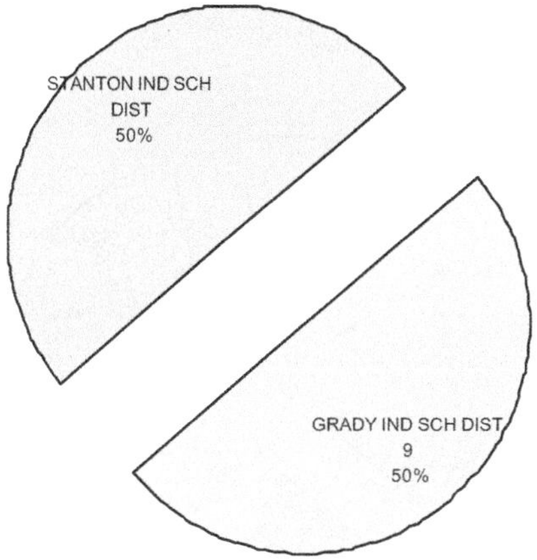

State/County

TX / MARTIN

VERSUS

% of County Taxes

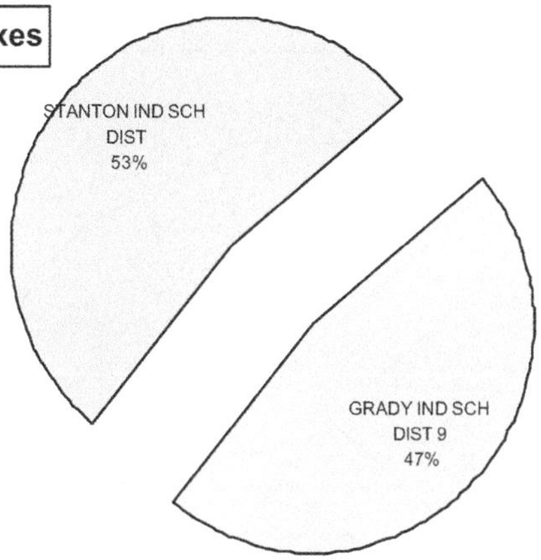

% of County Debt

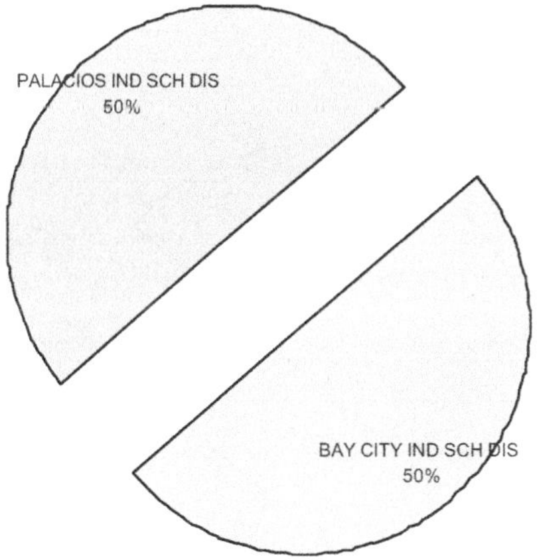

State/County

TX / MATAGORDA

VERSUS

% of County Taxes

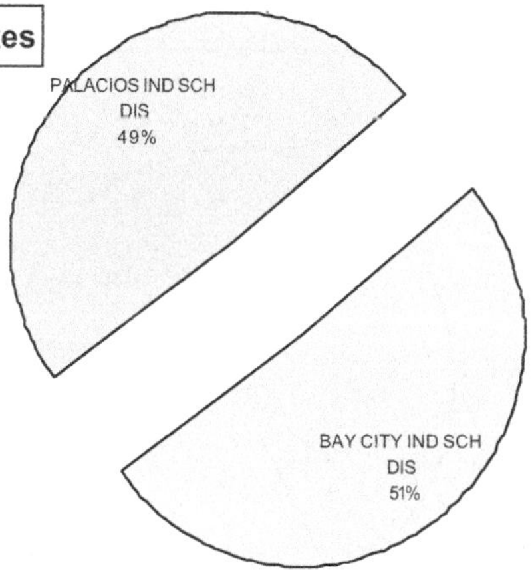

Are you getting your share of debt and taxes in your county? **S1**

% of County Debt

State/County
TX / MCCULLOCH

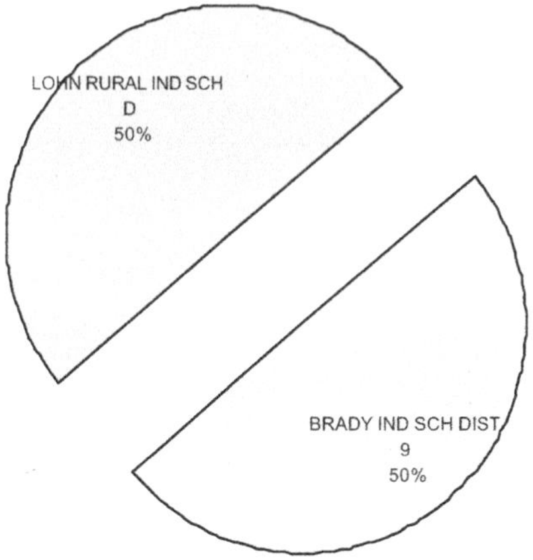

VERSUS

% of County Taxes

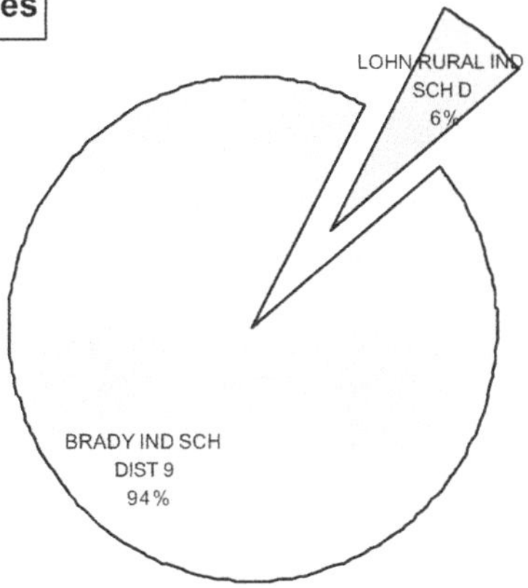

% of County Debt

State/County
TX / MCLENNAN

VERSUS

% of County Taxes

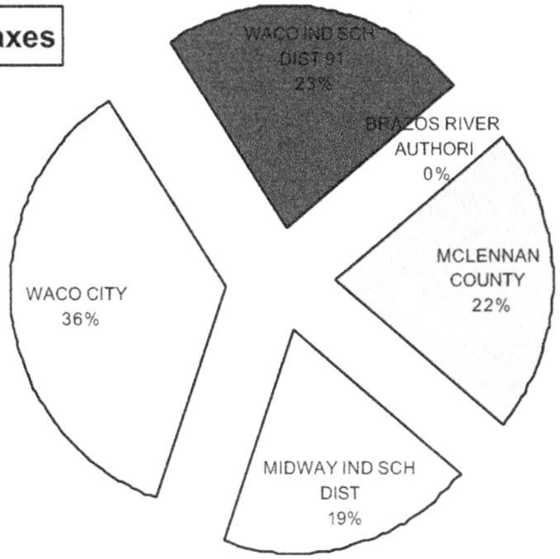

Are you getting your share of debt and taxes in your county? S1

State/County

TX / MEDINA

% of County Debt

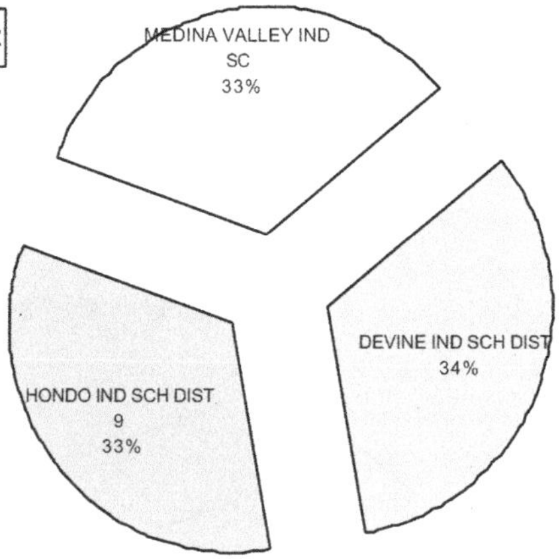

VERSUS

% of County Taxes

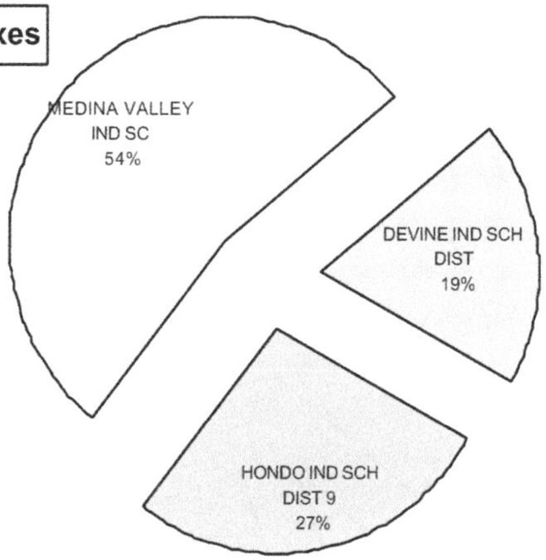

State/County

TX / MIDLAND

% of County Debt

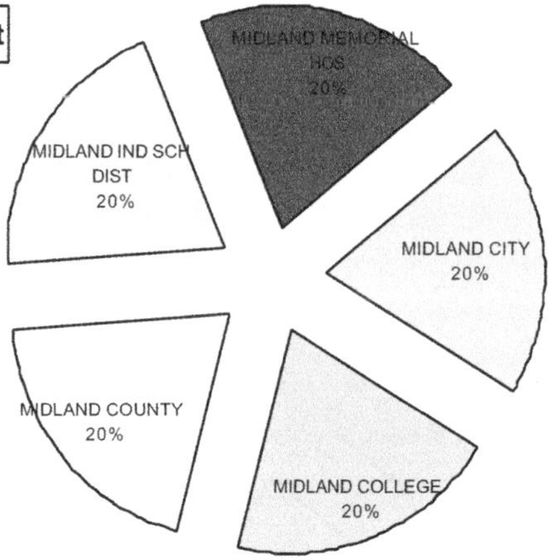

VERSUS

% of County Taxes

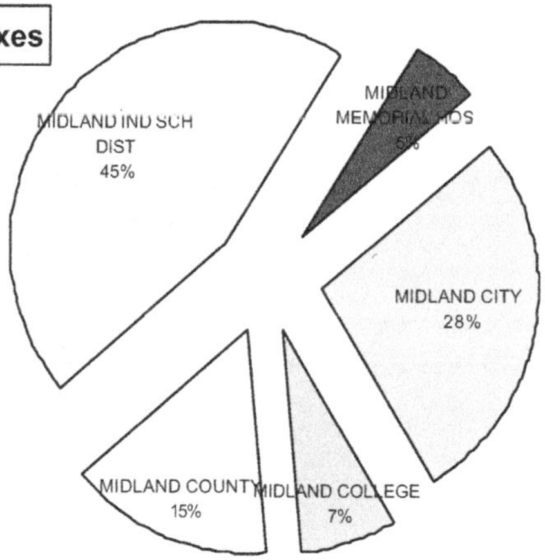

Are you getting your share of debt and taxes in your county? S1

State/County

TX / MILAM

% of County Debt

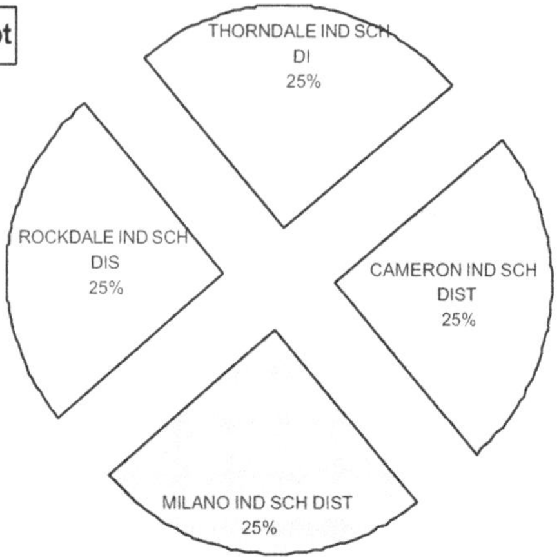

VERSUS

% of County Taxes

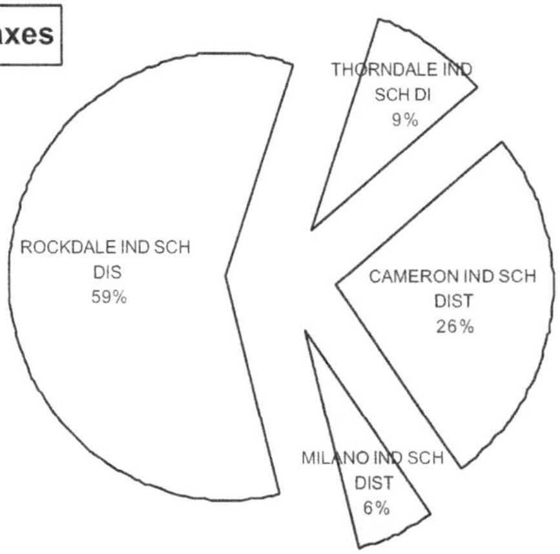

State/County

TX / MILLS

% of County Debt

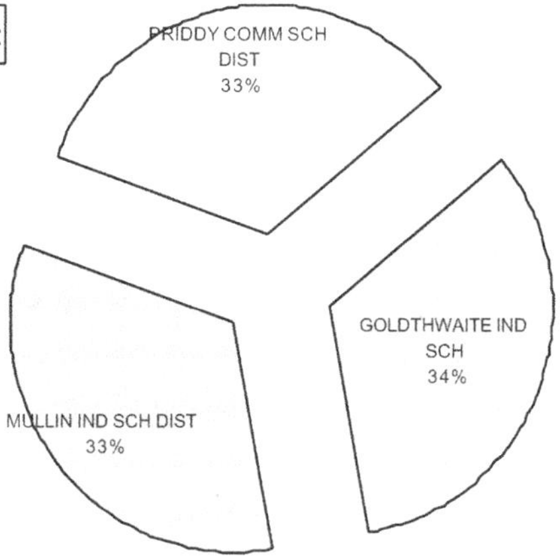

VERSUS

% of County Taxes

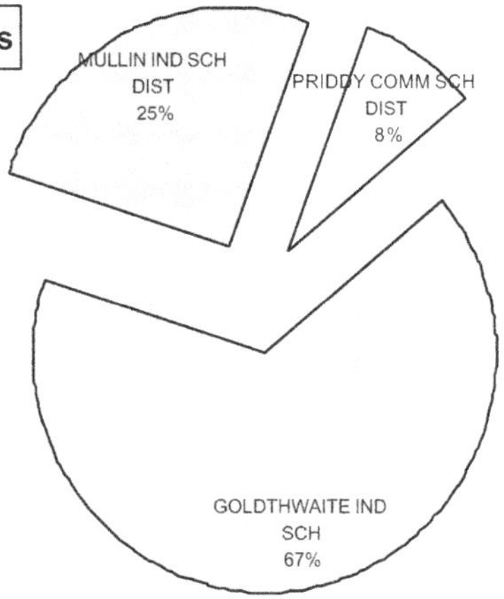

Are you getting your share of debt and taxes in your county?

S1

State/County

TX / MITCHELL

% of County Debt

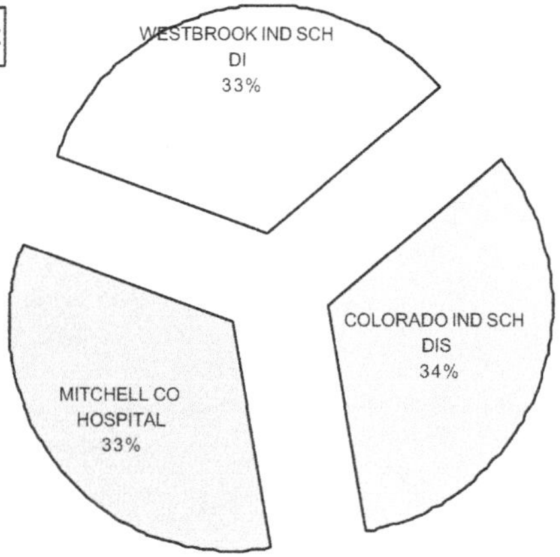

VERSUS

% of County Taxes

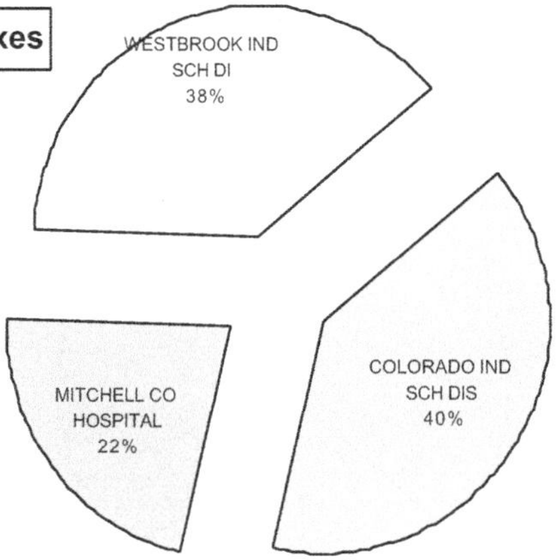

State/County

TX / MONTAGUE

% of County Debt

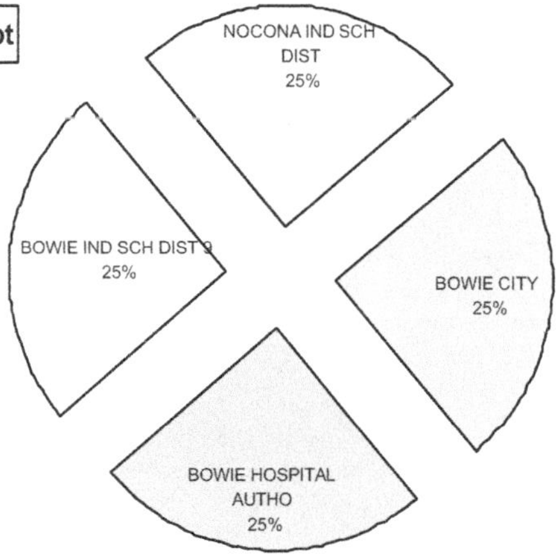

VERSUS

% of County Taxes

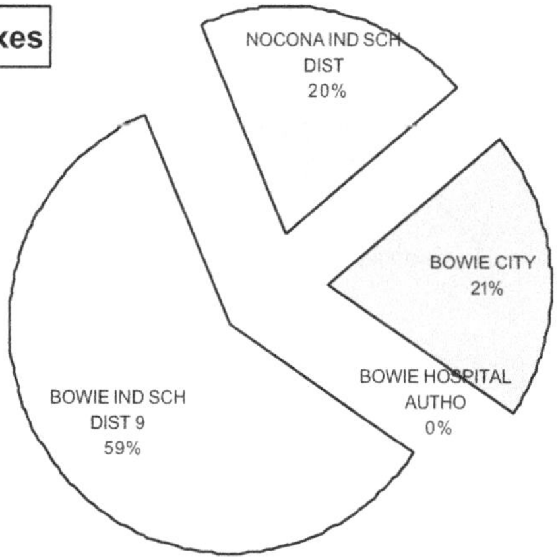

Are you getting your share of debt and taxes in your county?

State/County

TX / MONTGOMERY

% of County Debt

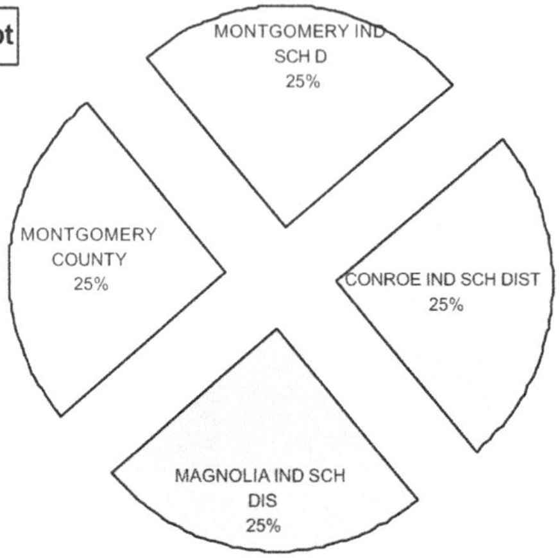

VERSUS

% of County Taxes

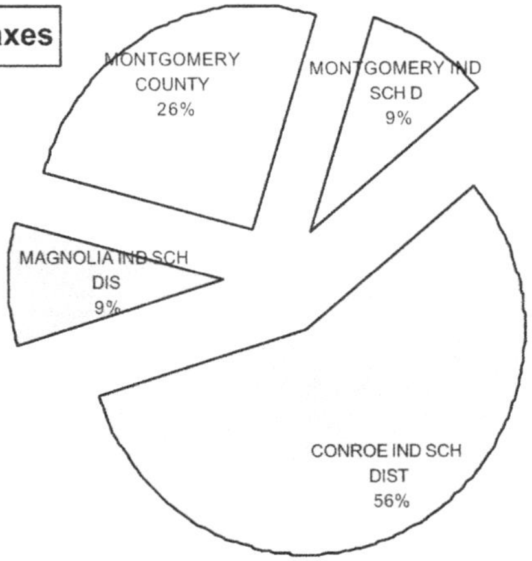

State/County

TX / MOORE

% of County Debt

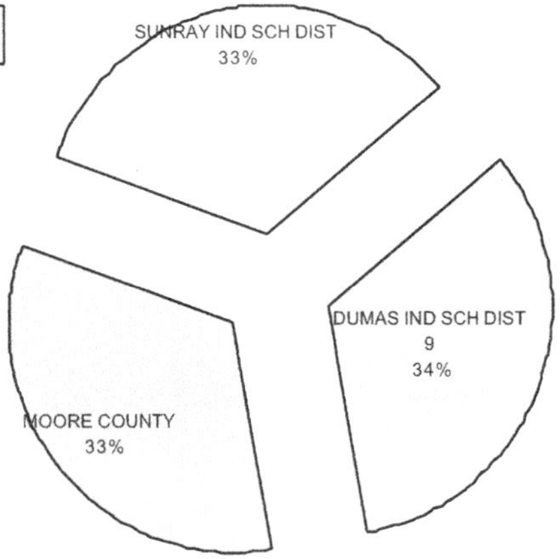

VERSUS

% of County Taxes

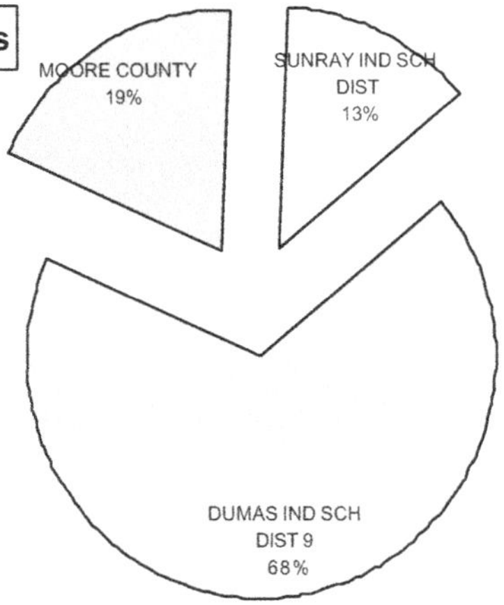

Are you getting your share of debt and taxes in your county? S1

% of County Debt

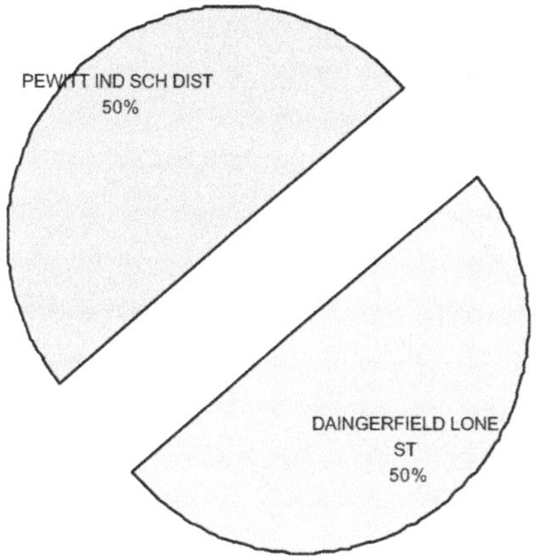

State/County

TX / MORRIS

VERSUS

% of County Taxes

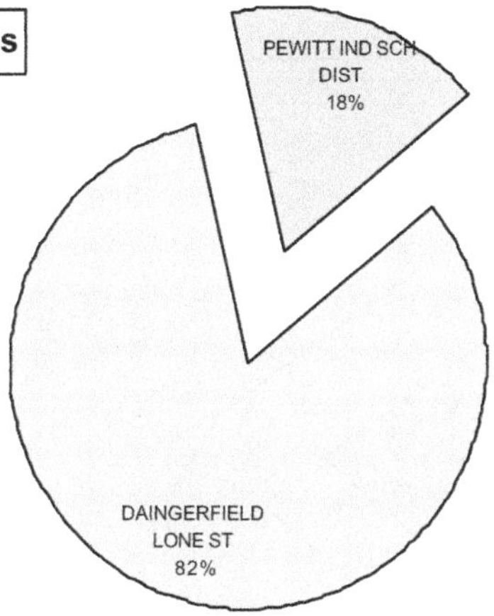

% of County Debt

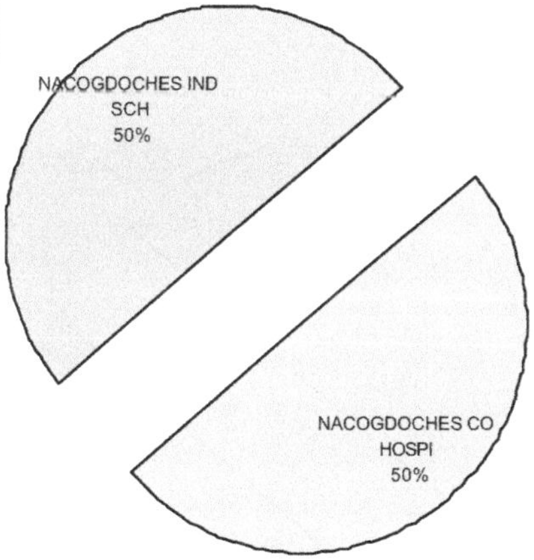

State/County

TX / NACOGDOCHES

VERSUS

% of County Taxes

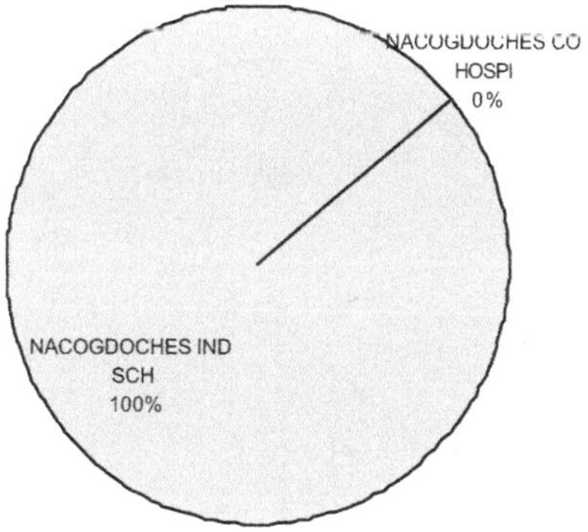

Are you getting your share of debt and taxes in your county? S1

State/County
TX / NAVARRO

% of County Debt

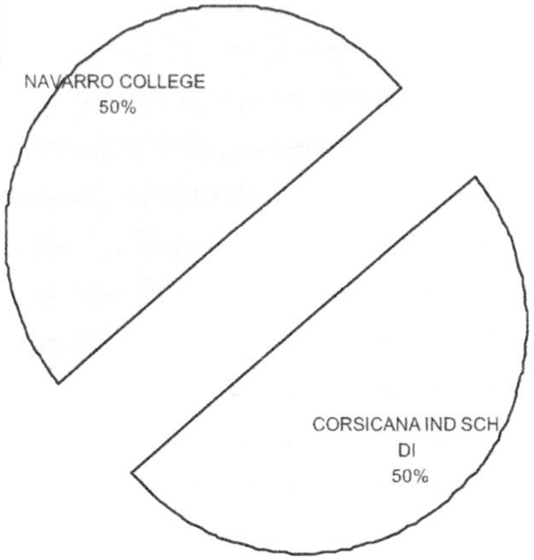

VERSUS

% of County Taxes

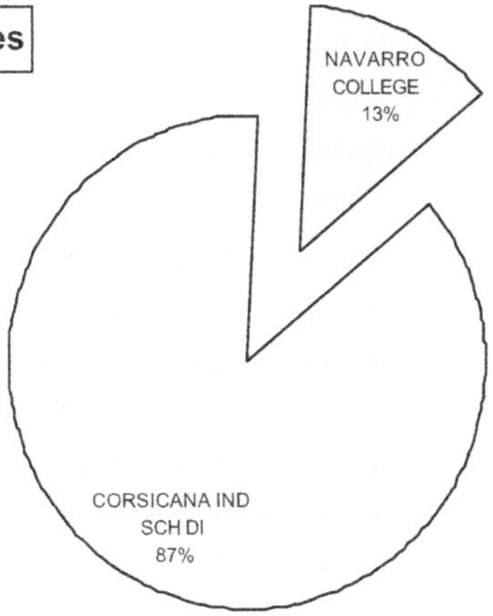

State/County
TX / NEWTON

% of County Debt

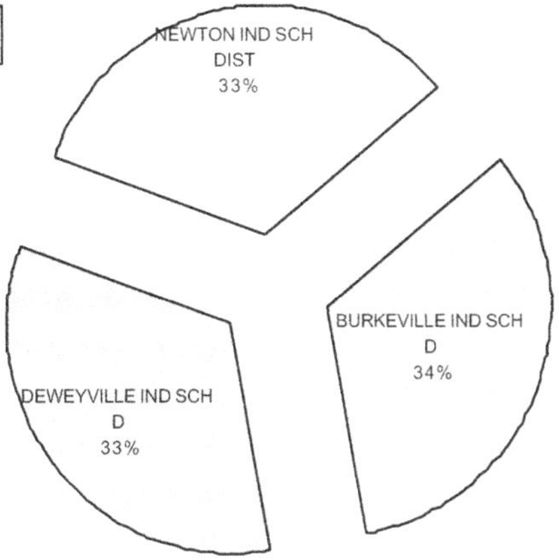

VERSUS

% of County Taxes

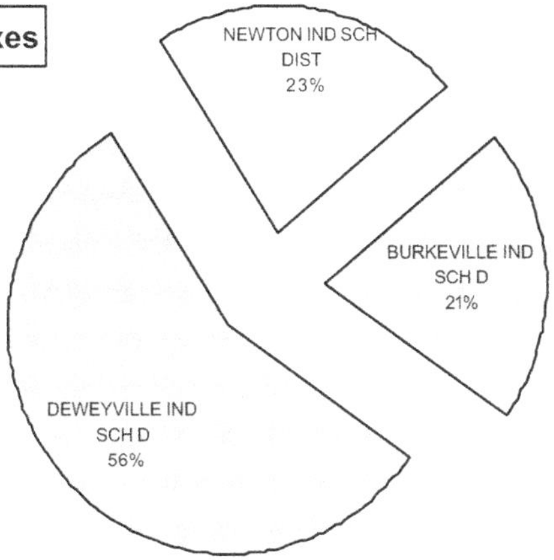

Are you getting your share of debt and taxes in your county? S1

% of County Debt

State/County

TX / NOLAN

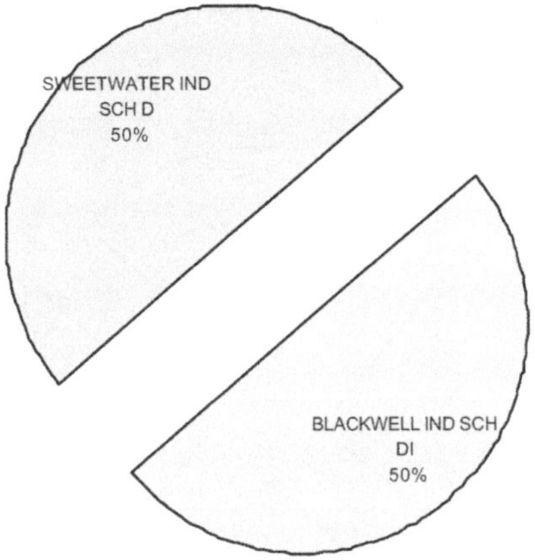

VERSUS

% of County Taxes

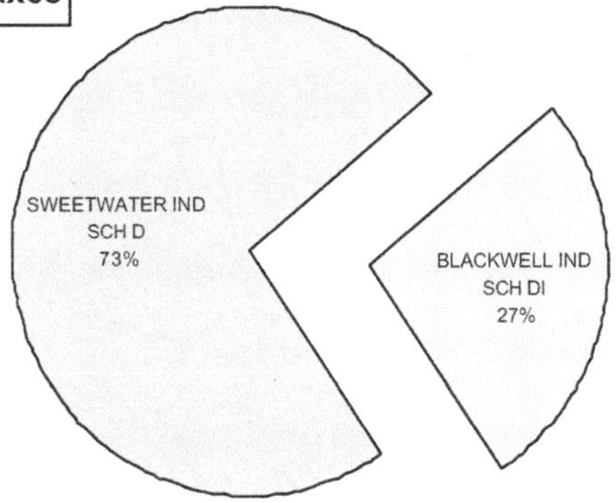

% of County Debt

State/County

TX / NUECES

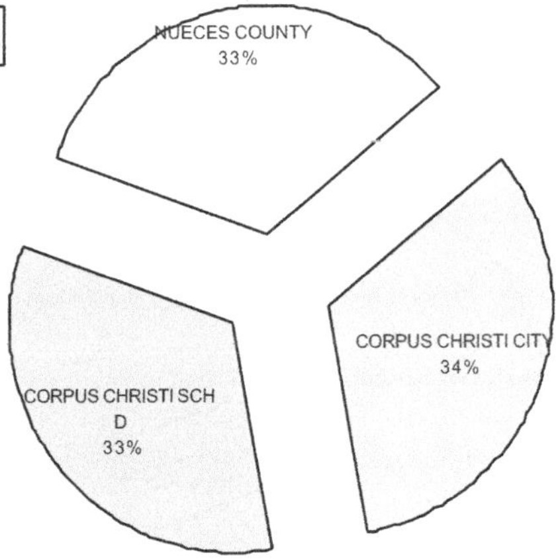

VERSUS

% of County Taxes

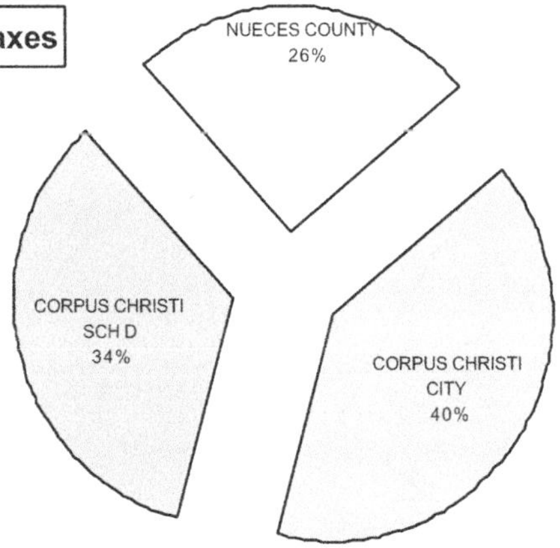

Are you getting your share of debt and taxes in your county? **S1**

State/County
TX / OLDHAM

% of County Debt

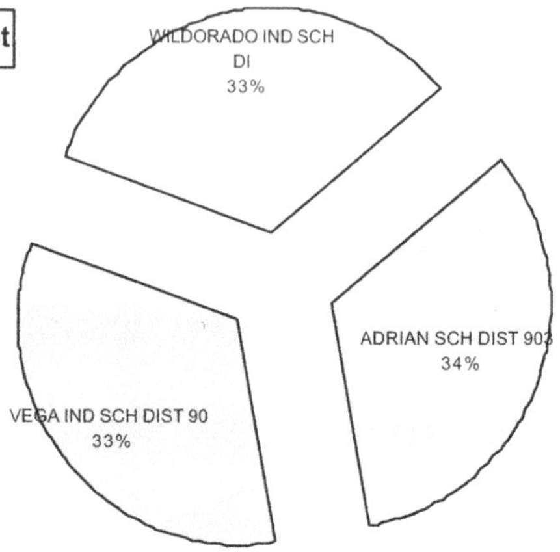

VERSUS

% of County Taxes

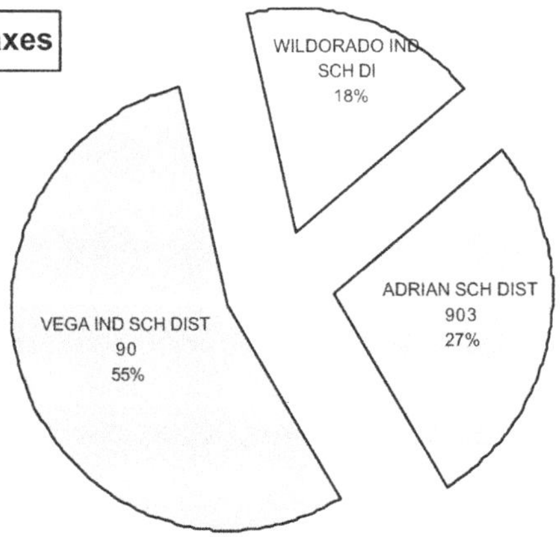

State/County
TX / ORANGE

% of County Debt

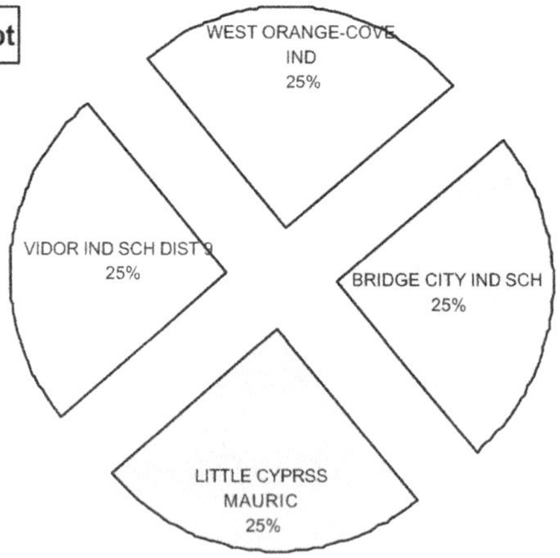

VERSUS

% of County Taxes

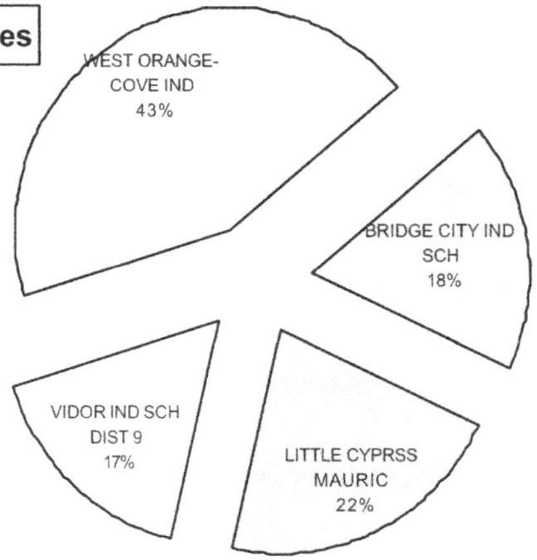

Are you getting your share of debt and taxes in your county? S1

% of County Debt

State/County

TX / PALO PINTO

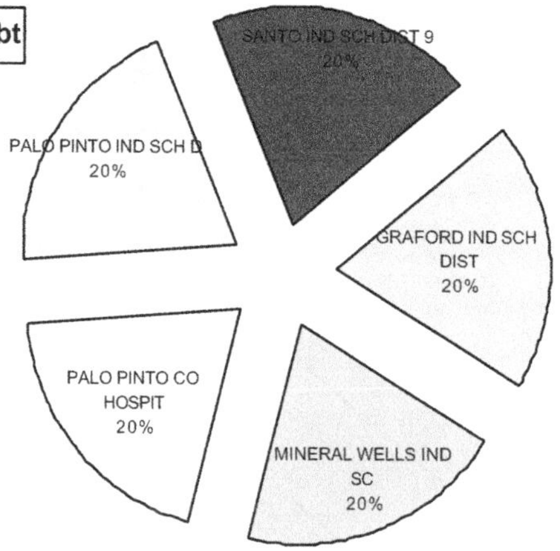

VERSUS

% of County Taxes

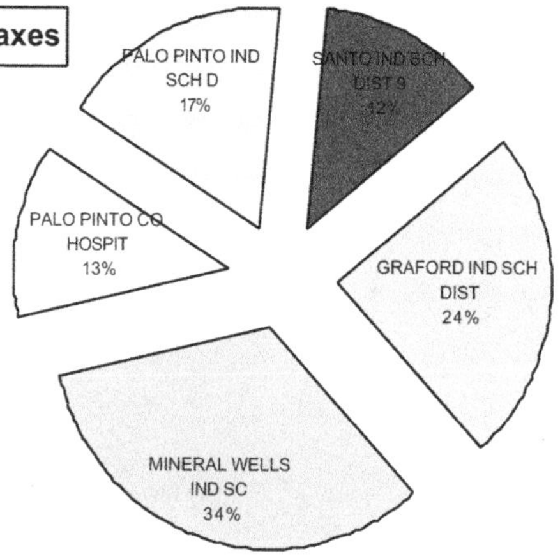

% of County Debt

State/County

TX / PANOLA

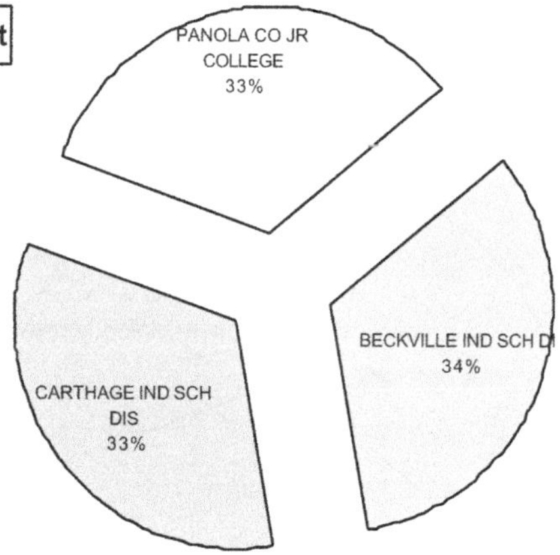

VERSUS

% of County Taxes

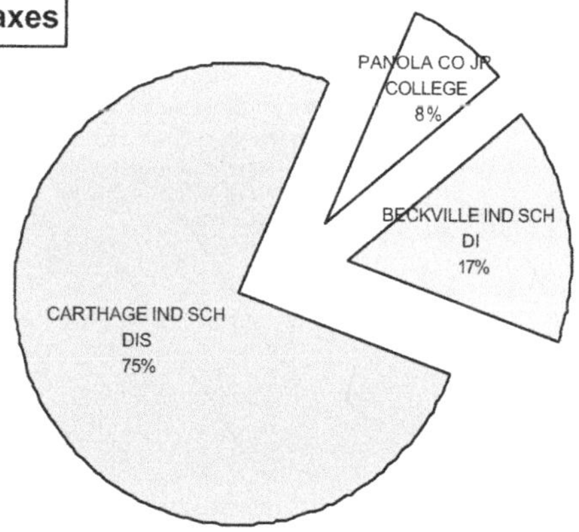

Are you getting your share of debt and taxes in your county? S1

State/County

TX / PARKER

% of County Debt

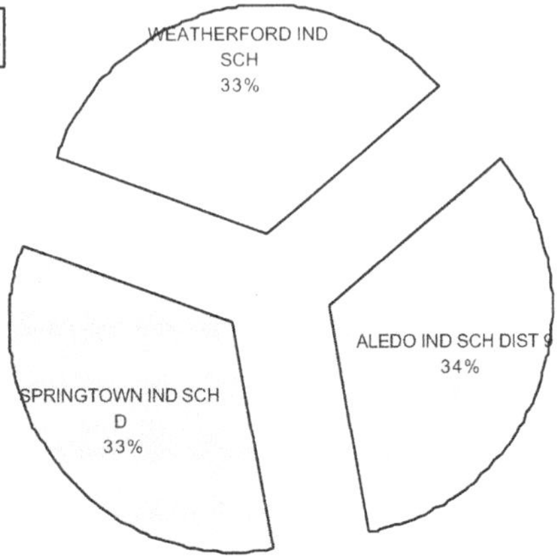

VERSUS

% of County Taxes

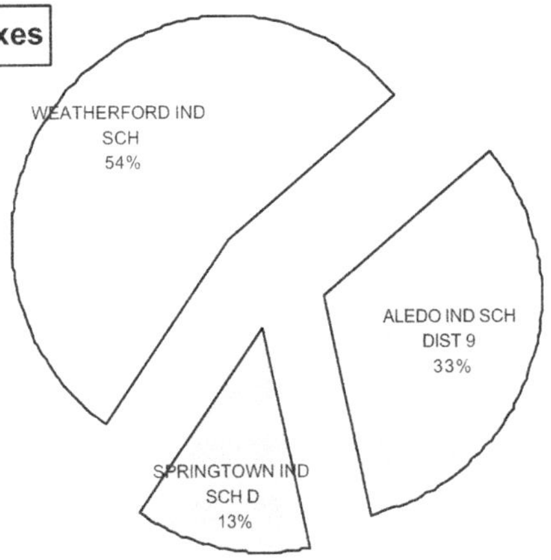

State/County

TX / PARMER

% of County Debt

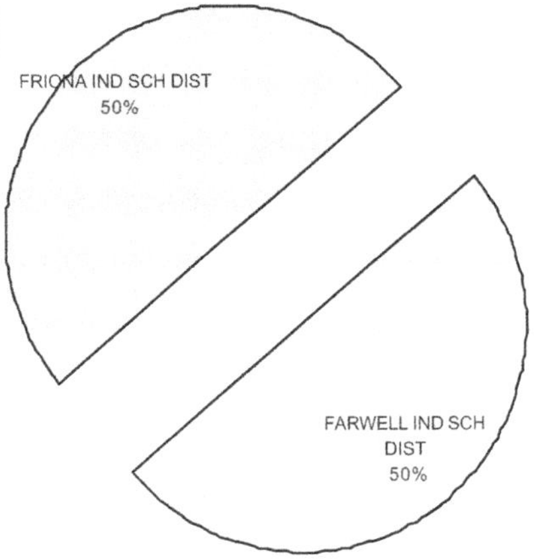

VERSUS

% of County Taxes

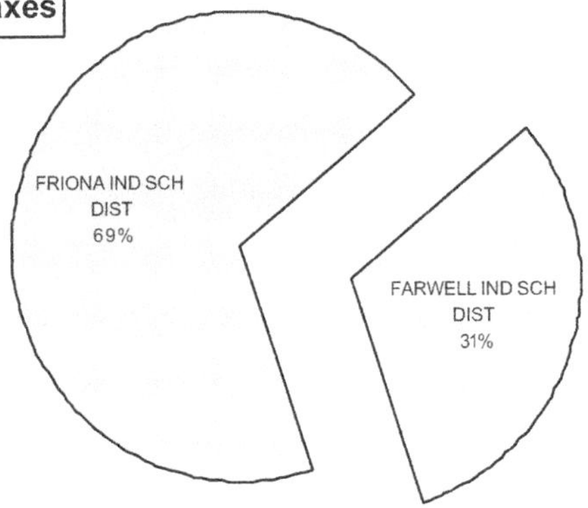

Are you getting your share of debt and taxes in your county?

S1

% of County Debt

State/County

TX / PECOS

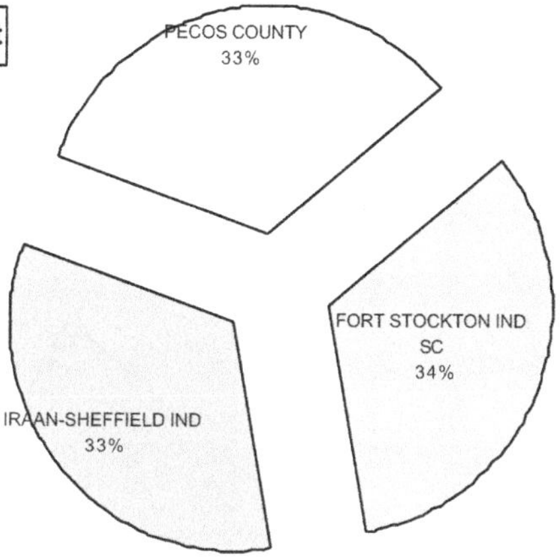

VERSUS

% of County Taxes

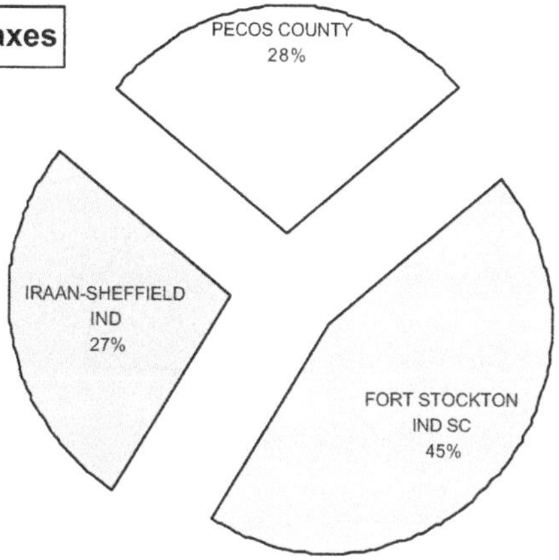

% of County Debt

State/County

TX / POLK

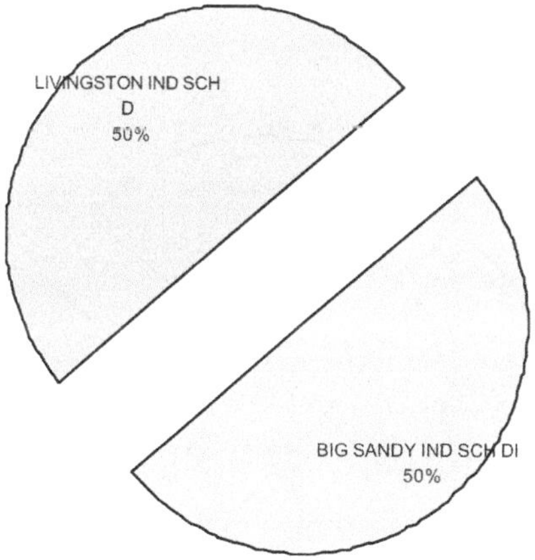

VERSUS

% of County Taxes

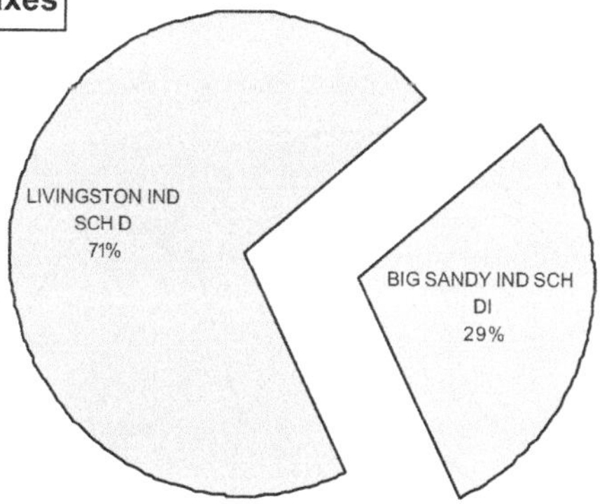

Are you getting your share of debt and taxes in your county? S1

State/County
TX / POTTER

% of County Debt

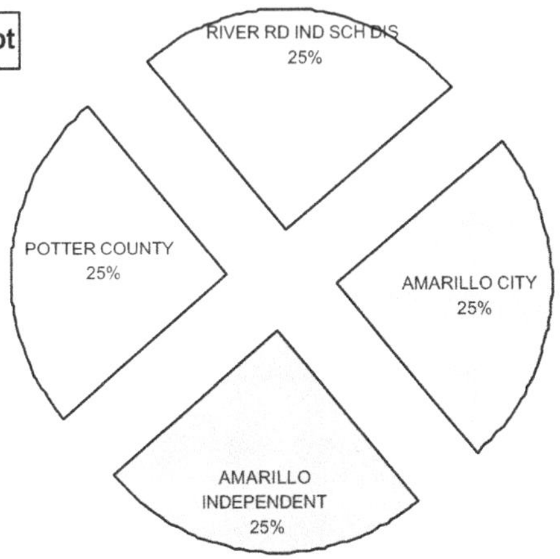

VERSUS

% of County Taxes

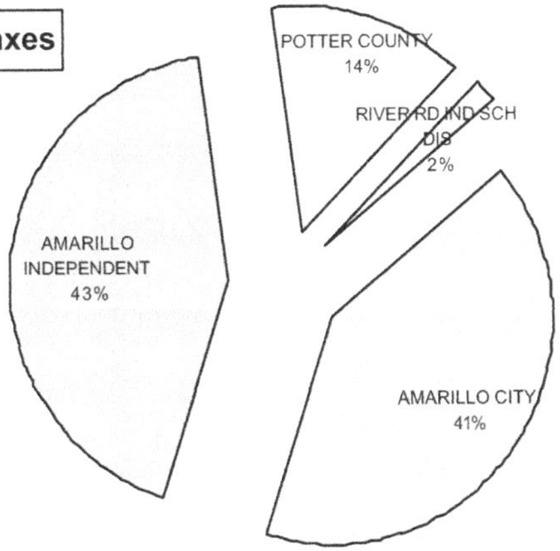

State/County
TX / PRESIDIO

% of County Debt

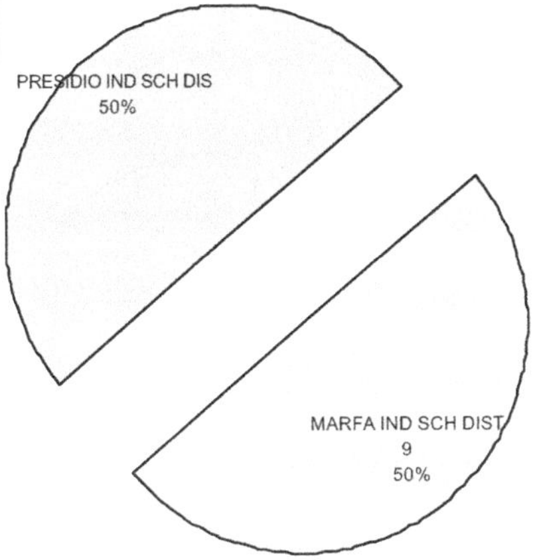

VERSUS

% of County Taxes

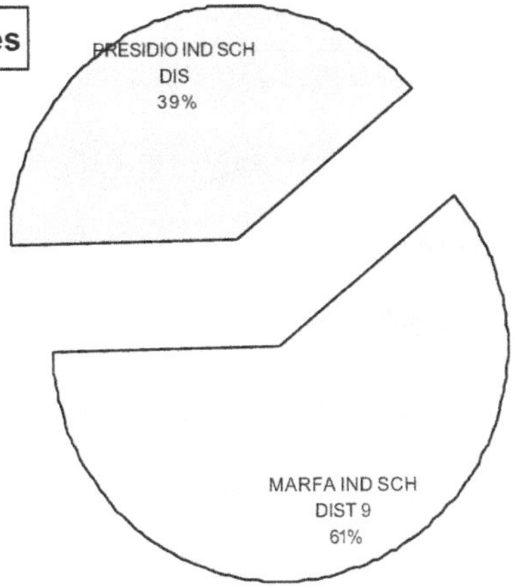

Are you getting your share of debt and taxes in your county? **S1**

% of County Debt

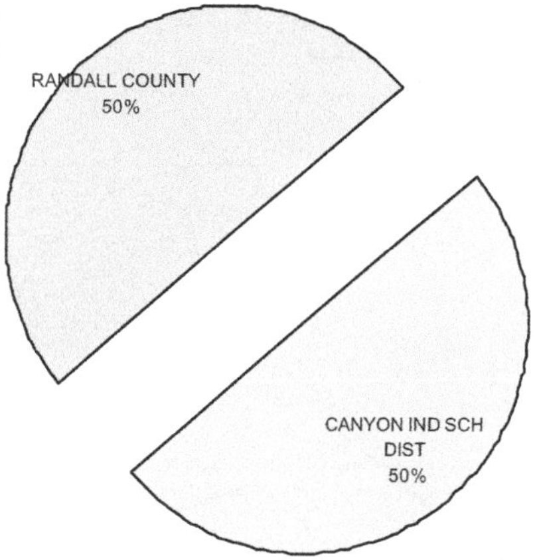

State/County

TX / RANDALL

VERSUS

% of County Taxes

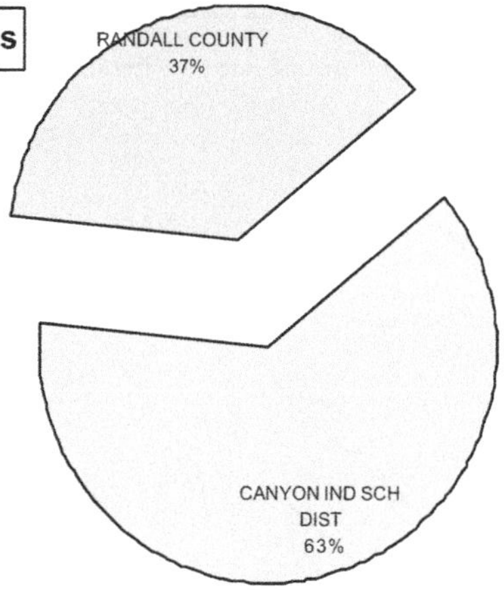

% of County Debt

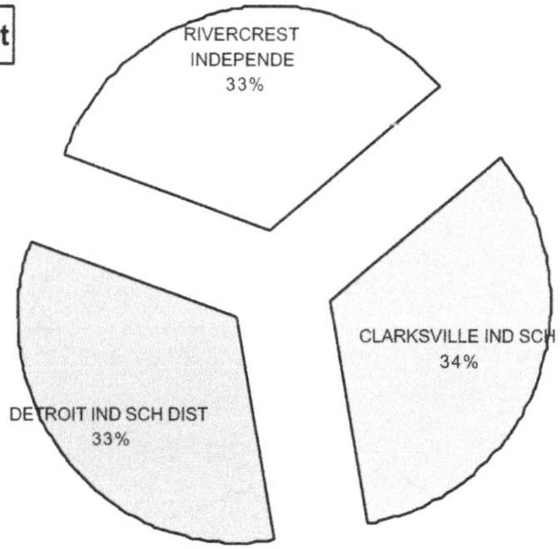

State/County

TX / RED RIVER

VERSUS

% of County Taxes

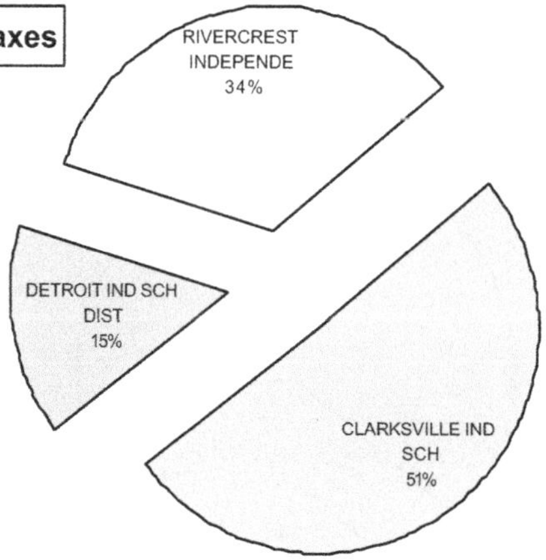

Are you getting your share of debt and taxes in your county?

S1

State/County

TX / REEVES

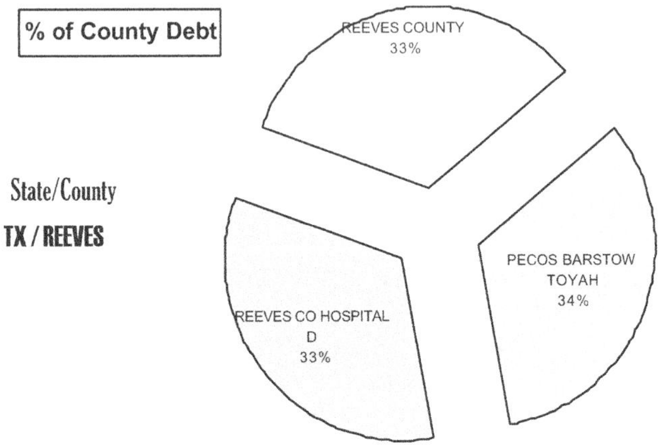

VERSUS

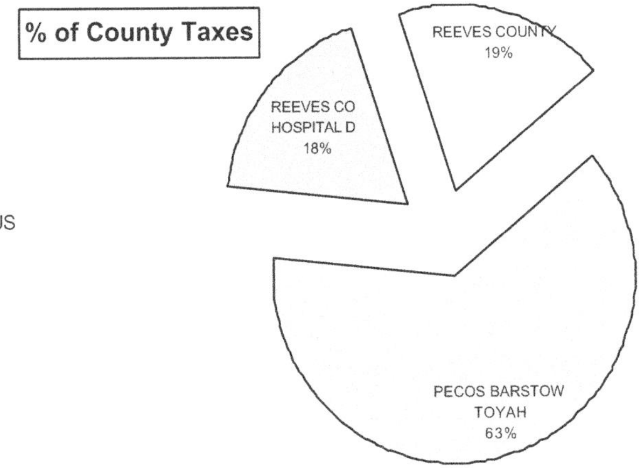

State/County

TX / REFUGIO

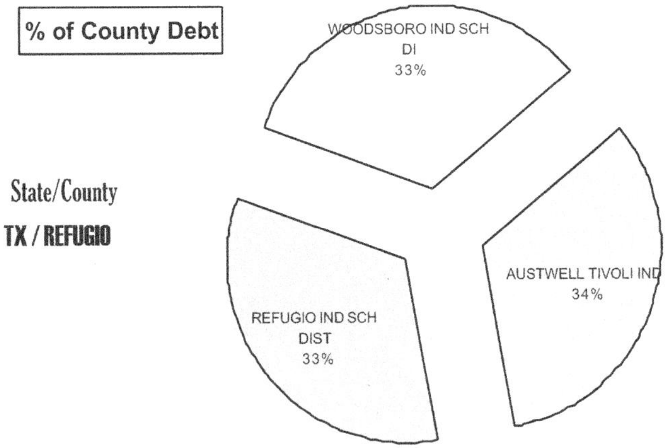

VERSUS

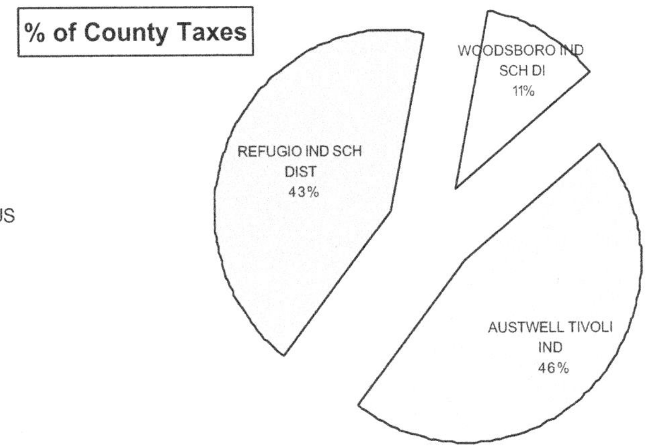

Are you getting your share of debt and taxes in your county?

% of County Debt

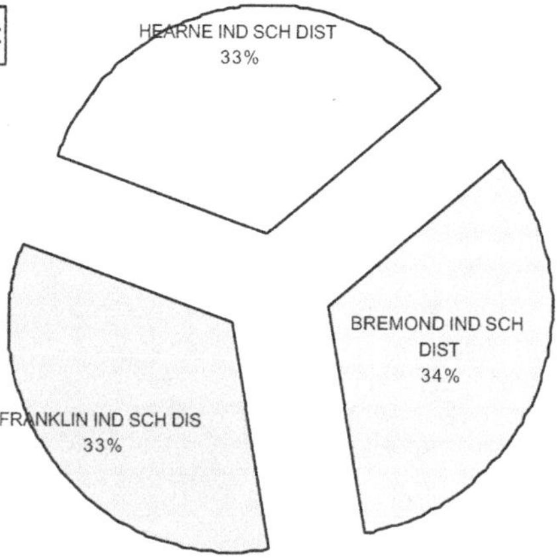

State/County

TX / ROBERTSON

VERSUS

% of County Taxes

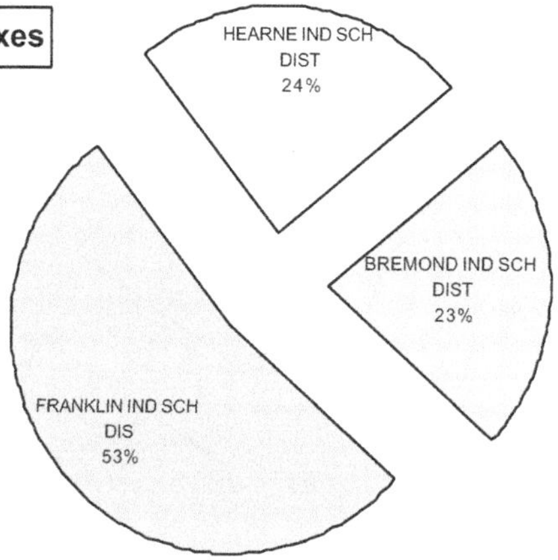

% of County Debt

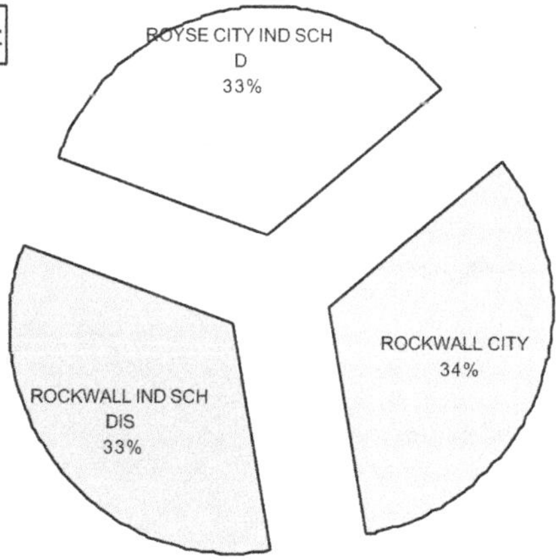

State/County

TX / ROCKWALL

VERSUS

% of County Taxes

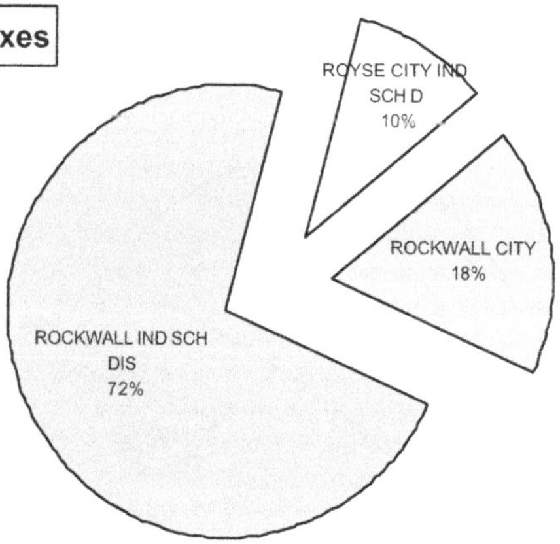

Are you getting your share of debt and taxes in your county? **S1**

State/County
TX / RUNNELS

% of County Debt

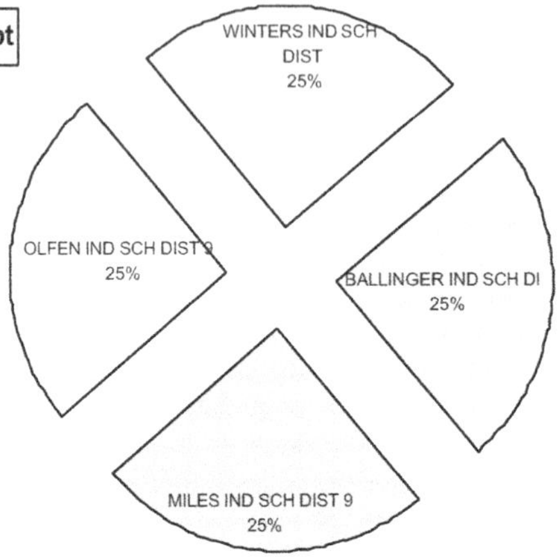

VERSUS

% of County Taxes

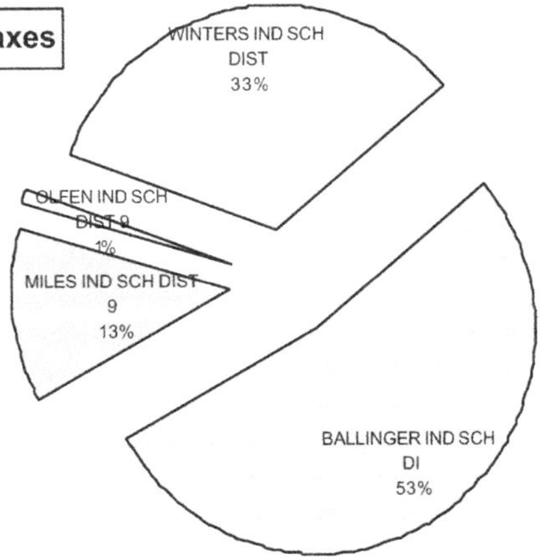

State/County
TX / RUSK

% of County Debt

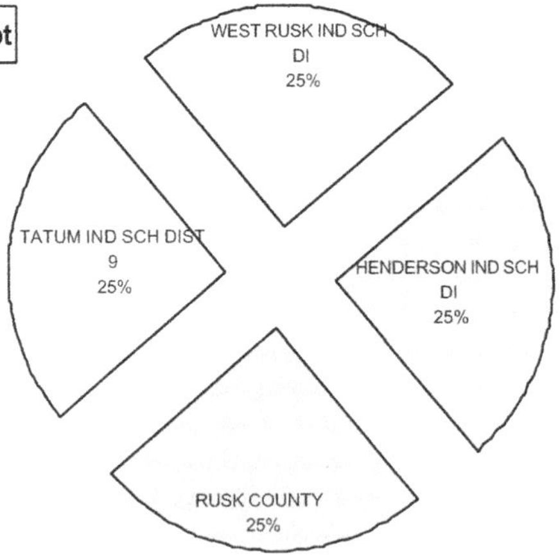

VERSUS

% of County Taxes

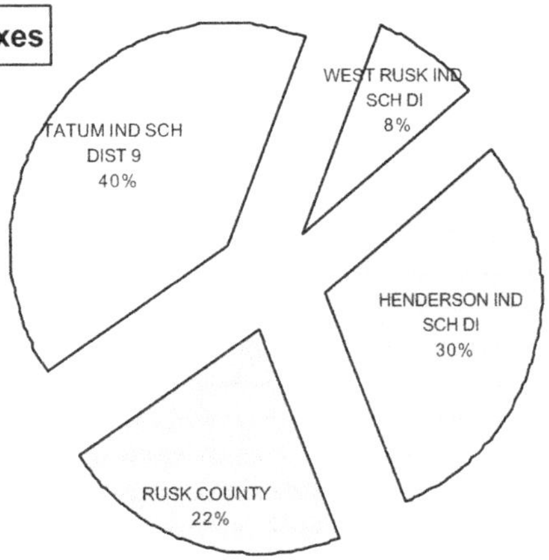

Are you getting your share of debt and taxes in your county? S1

% of County Debt

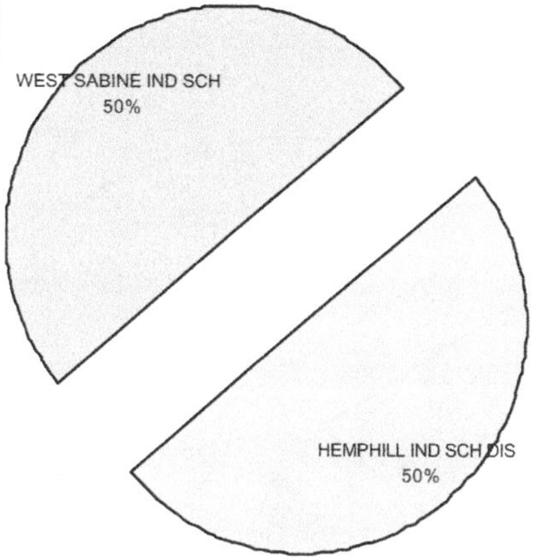

State/County

TX / SABINE

VERSUS

% of County Taxes

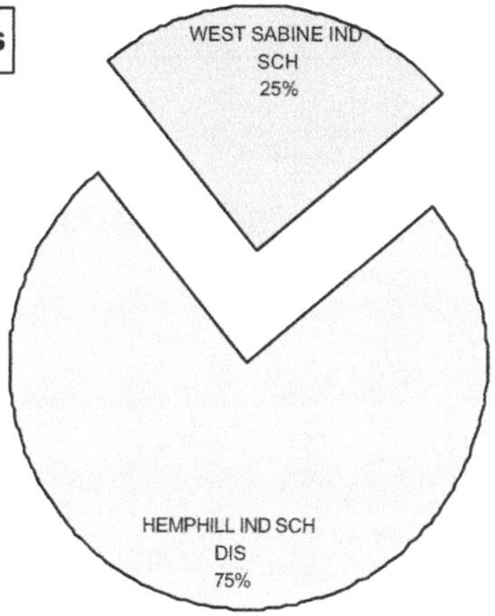

% of County Debt

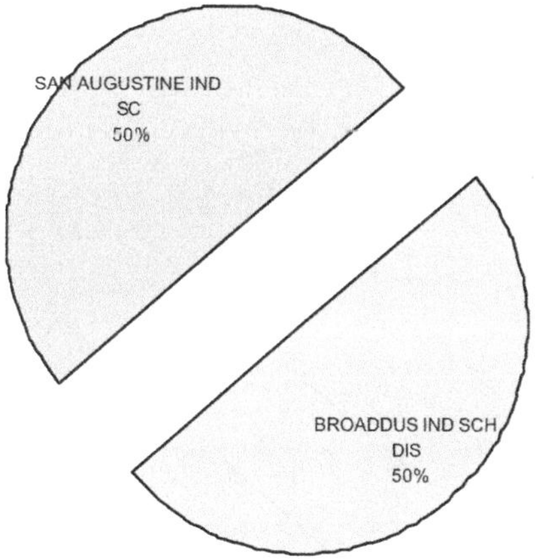

State/County

TX / SAN AUGUSTINE

VERSUS

% of County Taxes

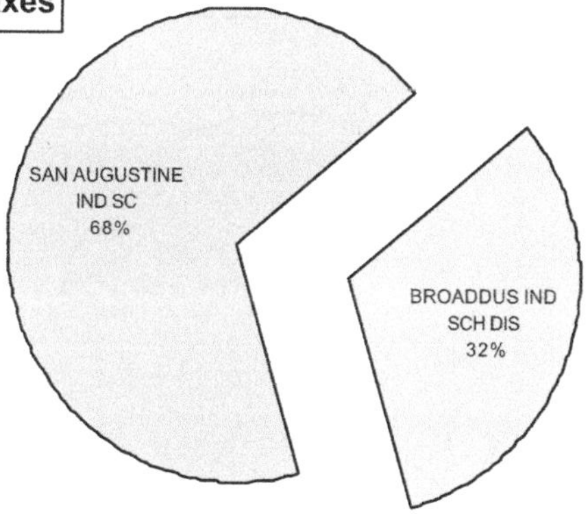

Are you getting your share of debt and taxes in your county? S1

State/County

TX / SAN JACINTO

% of County Debt

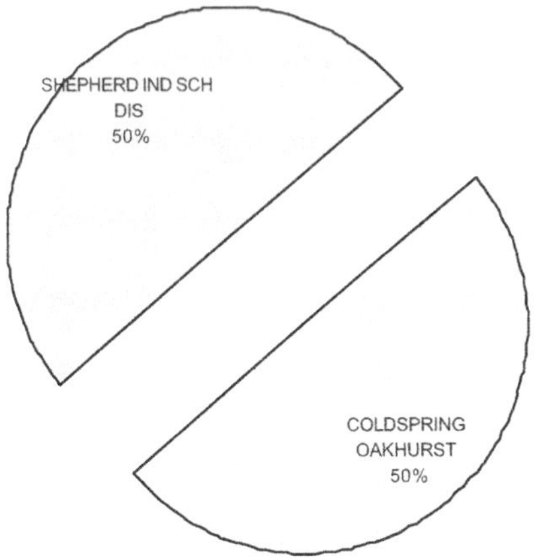

VERSUS

% of County Taxes

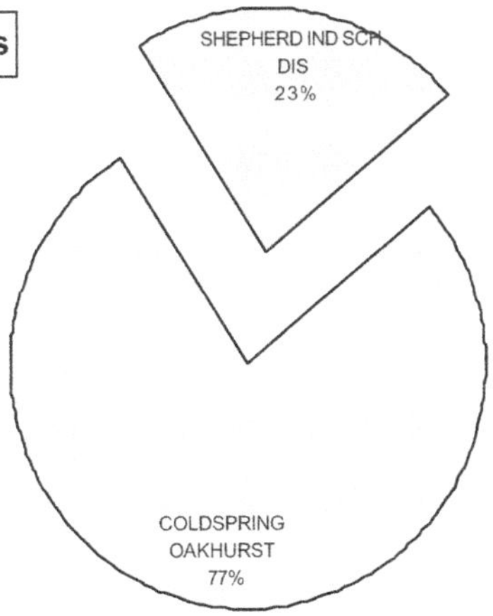

State/County

TX / SAN PATRICIO

% of County Debt

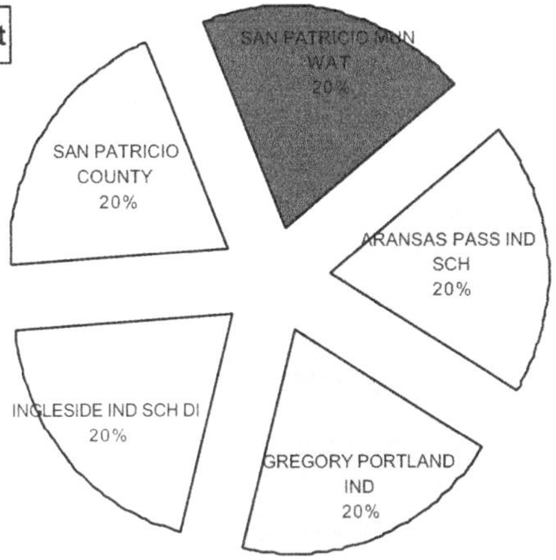

VERSUS

% of County Taxes

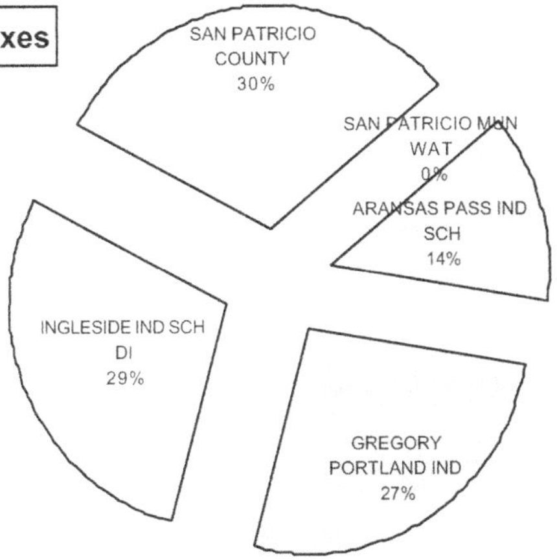

Are you getting your share of debt and taxes in your county?

S1

State/County

TX / SAN SABA

% of County Debt

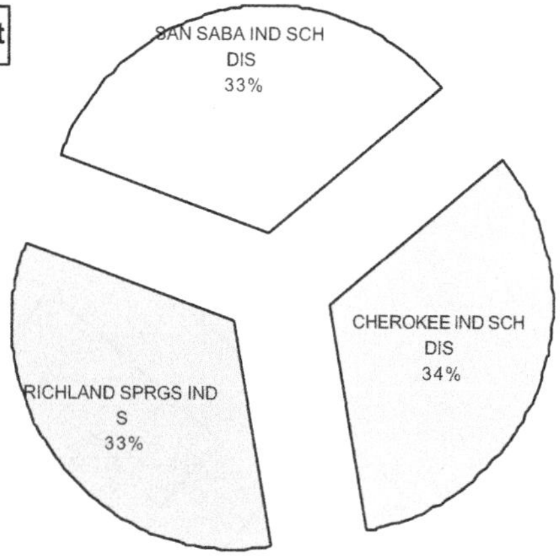

VERSUS

% of County Taxes

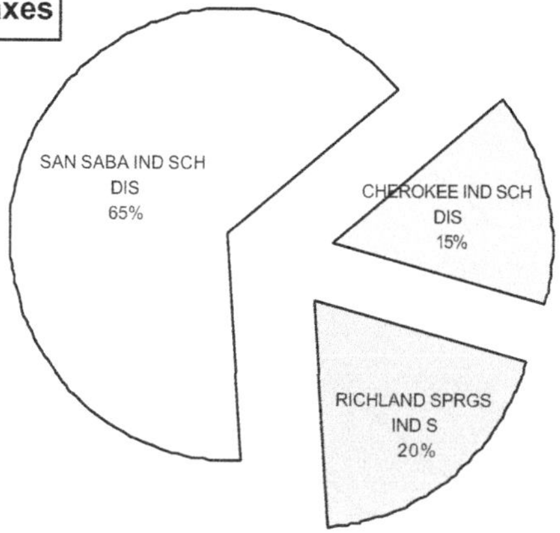

State/County

TX / SCURRY

% of County Debt

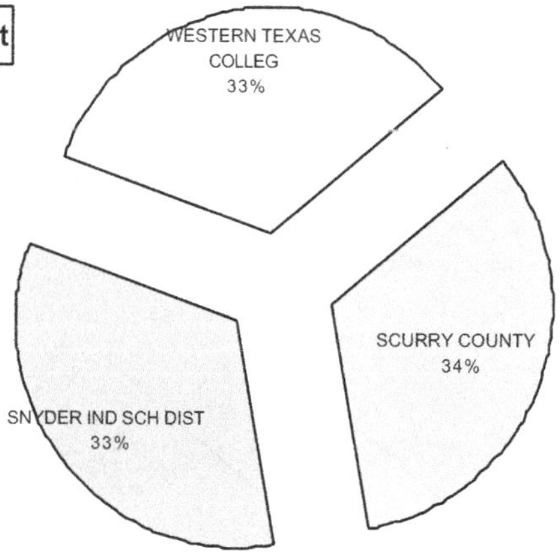

VERSUS

% of County Taxes

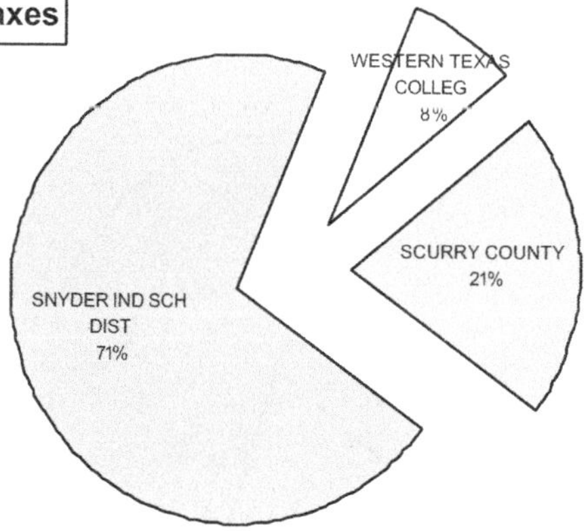

Are you getting your share of debt and taxes in your county? **S1**

State/County

TX / SHACKELFORD

% of County Debt

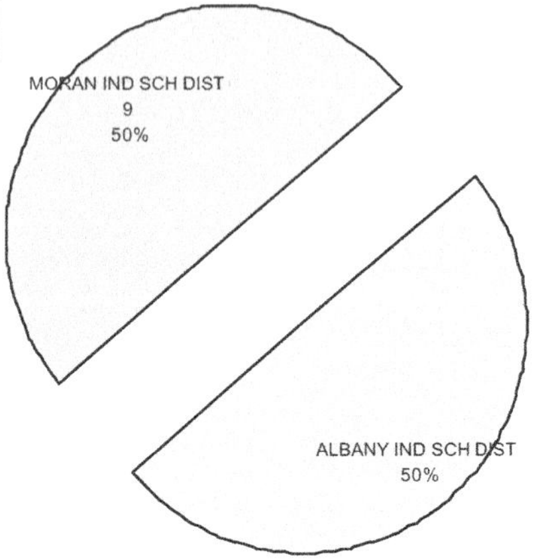

VERSUS

% of County Taxes

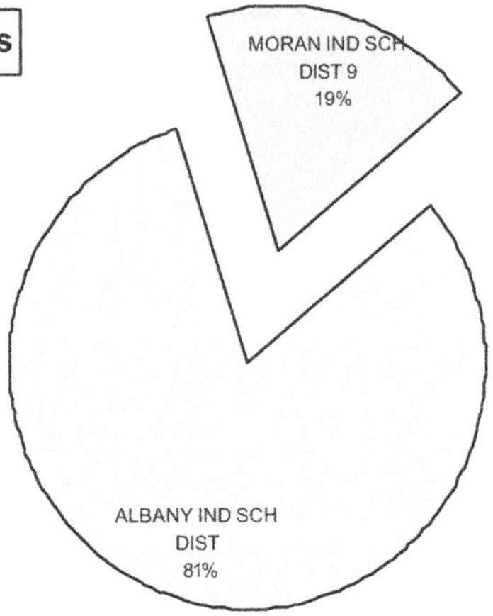

State/County

TX / SHELBY

% of County Debt

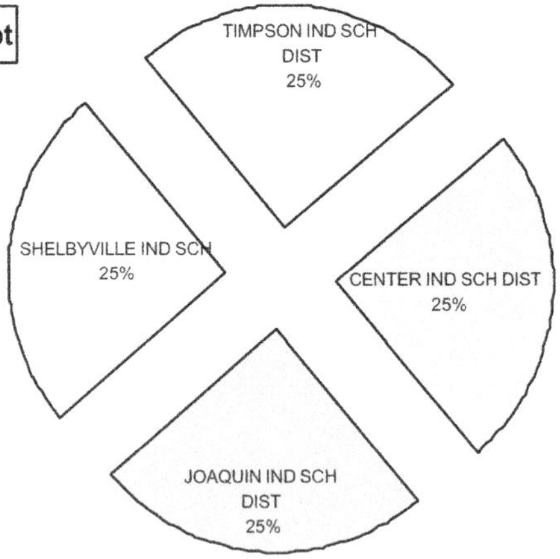

VERSUS

% of County Taxes

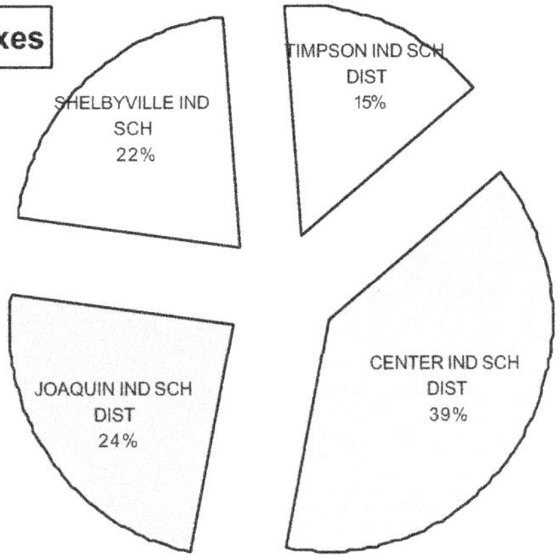

Are you getting your share of debt and taxes in your county?

S1

% of County Debt

State/County

TX / SHERMAN

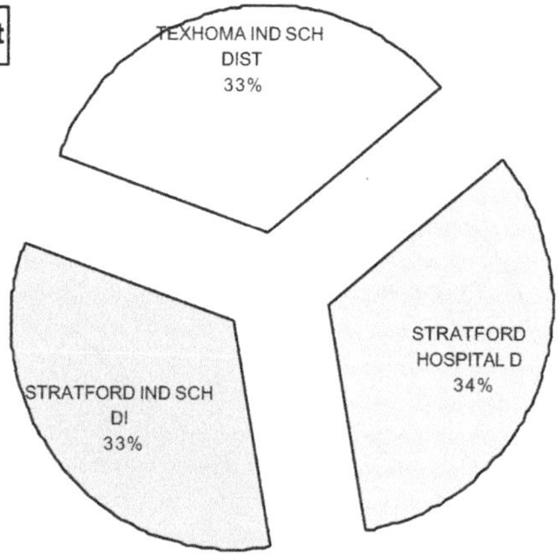

VERSUS

% of County Taxes

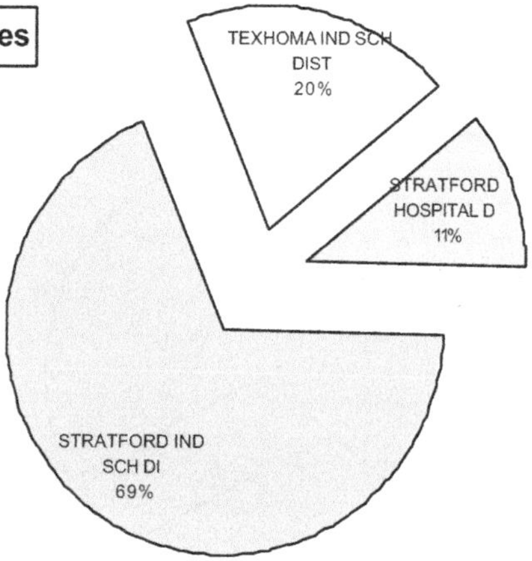

% of County Debt

State/County

TX / SMITH

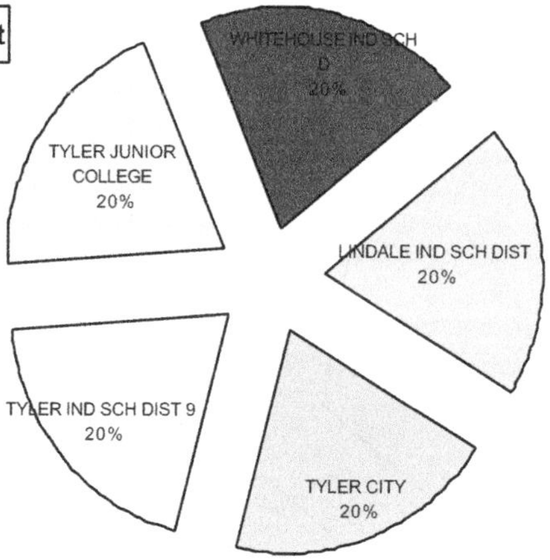

VERSUS

% of County Taxes

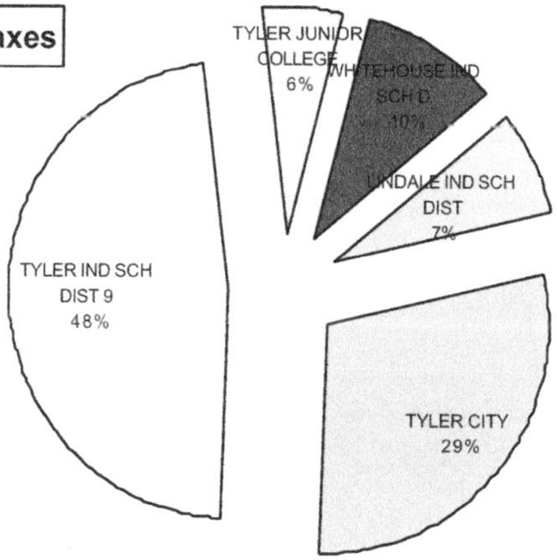

Are you getting your share of debt and taxes in your county? **S1**

% of County Debt

State/County
TX / STARR

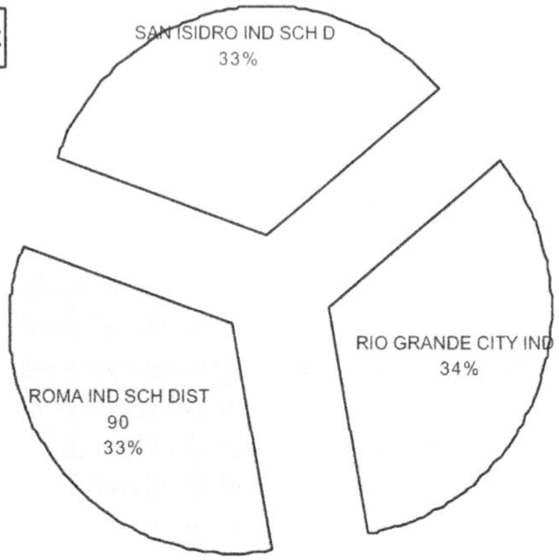

VERSUS

% of County Taxes

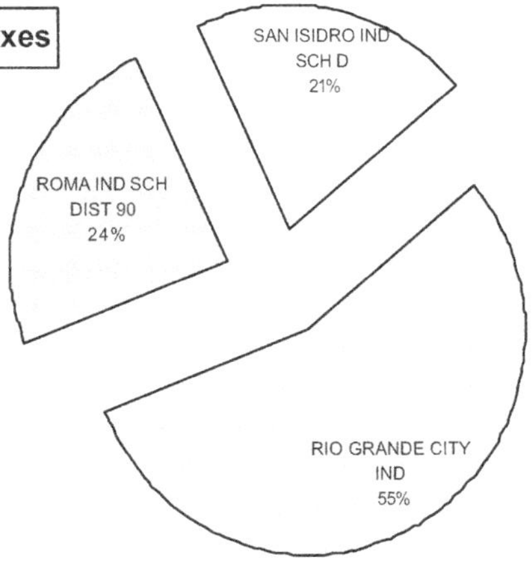

% of County Debt

State/County
TX / STEPHENS

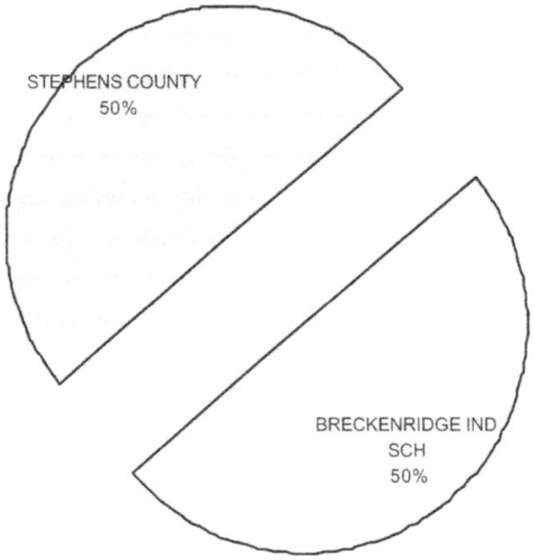

VERSUS

% of County Taxes

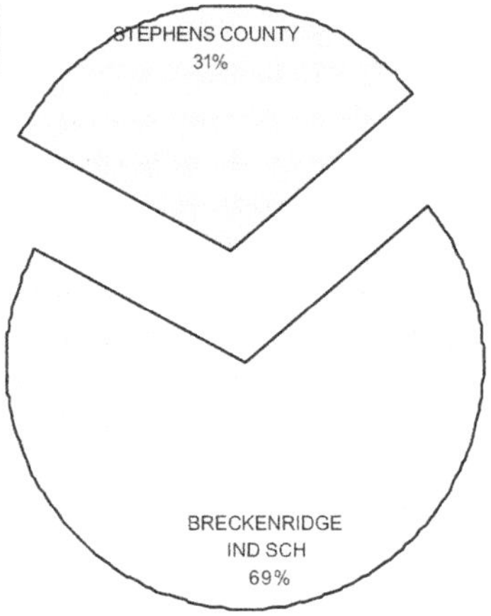

Are you getting your share of debt and taxes in your county?

S1

State/County

TX / SWISHER

% of County Debt

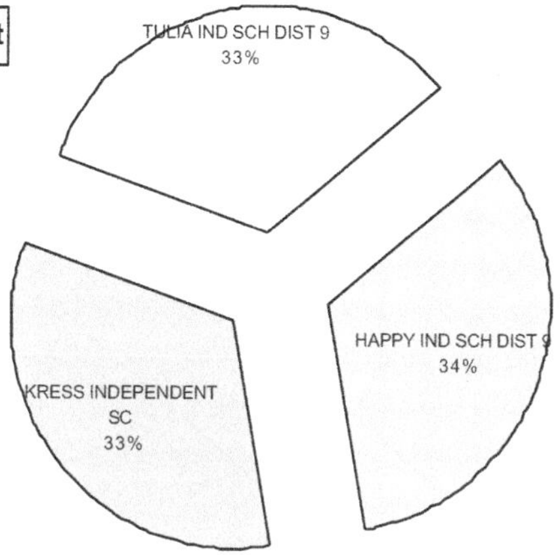

VERSUS

% of County Taxes

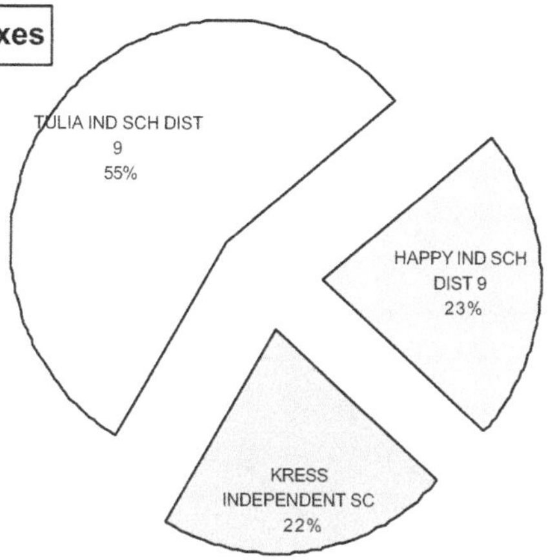

State/County

TX / TARRANT

% of County Debt

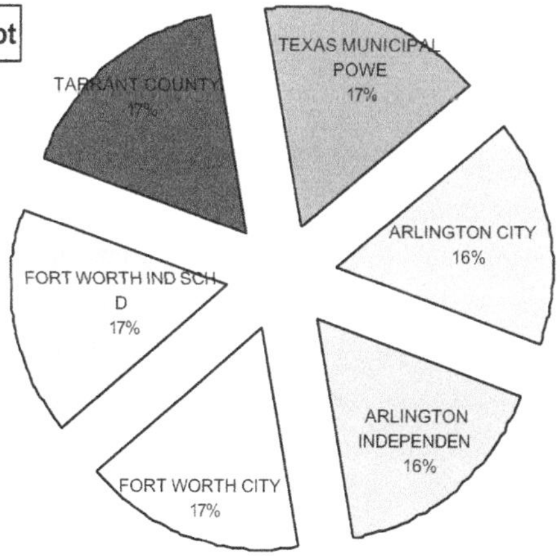

VERSUS

% of County Taxes

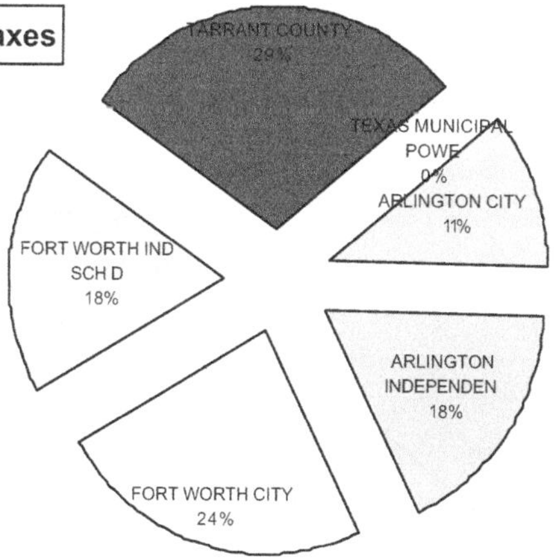

Are you getting your share of debt and taxes in your county? **S1**

State/County

TX / TAYLOR

% of County Debt

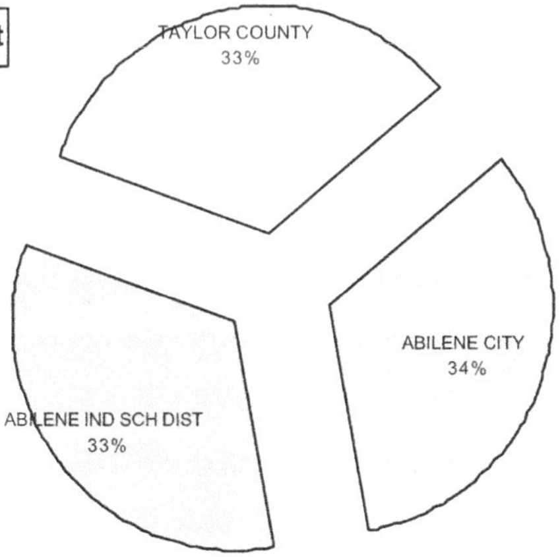

VERSUS

% of County Taxes

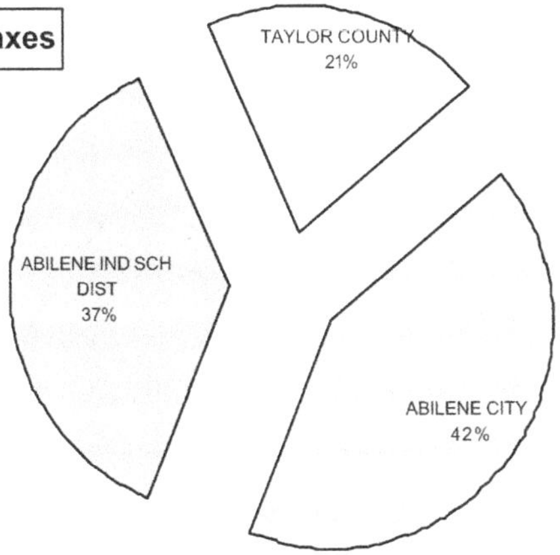

State/County

TX / TERRY

% of County Debt

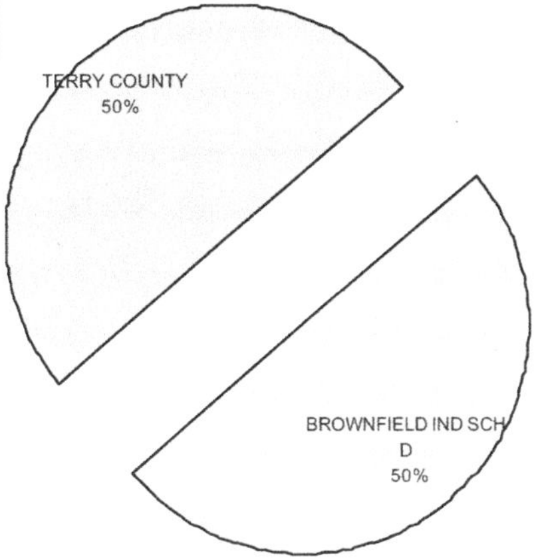

VERSUS

% of County Taxes

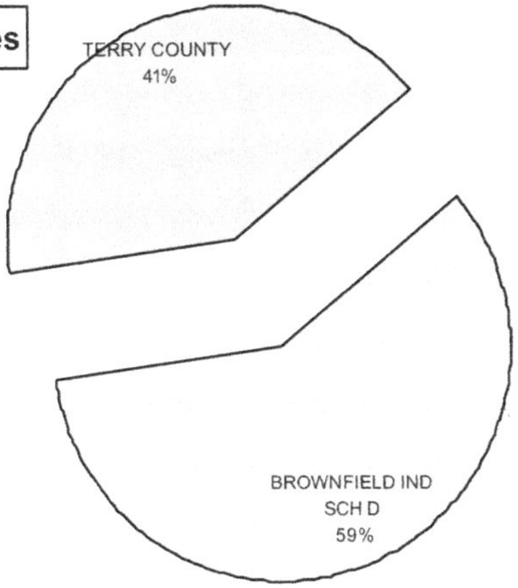

Are you getting your share of debt and taxes in your county?

S1

State/County

TX / THROCKMORTON

% of County Debt

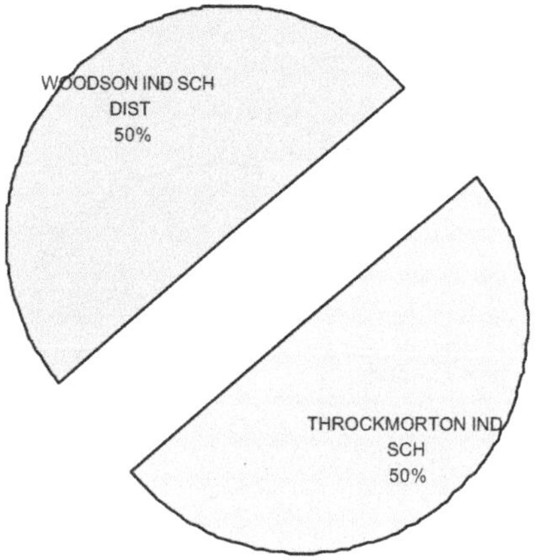

VERSUS

% of County Taxes

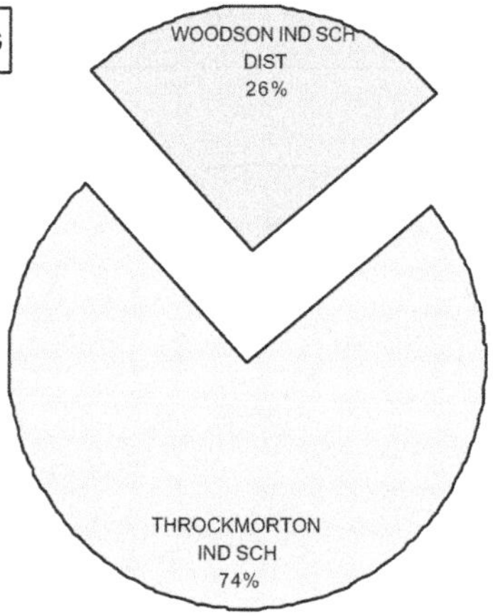

State/County

TX / TITUS

% of County Debt

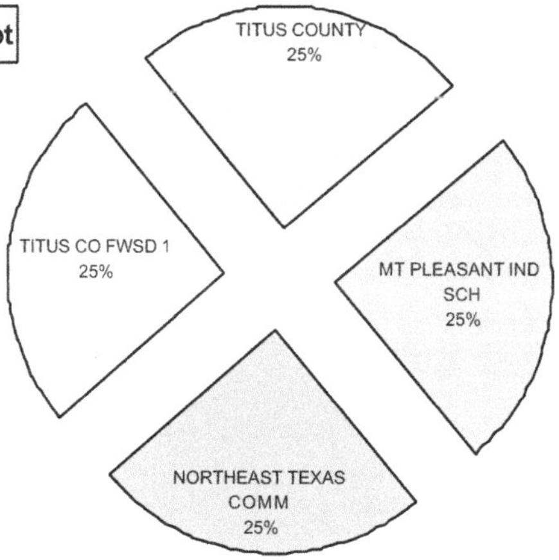

VERSUS

% of County Taxes

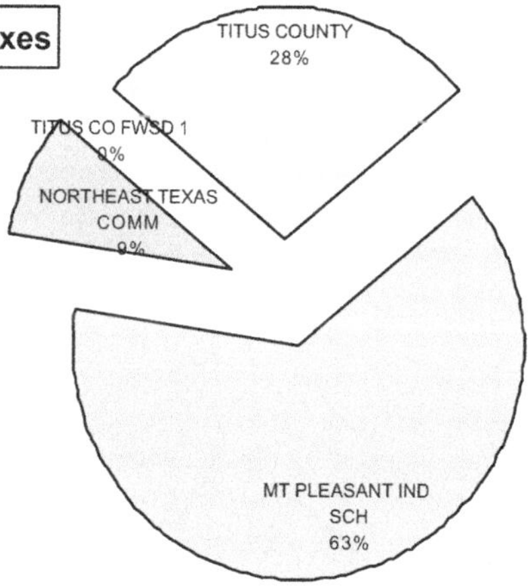

Are you getting your share of debt and taxes in your county? S1

State/County

TX / TOM GREEN

% of County Debt

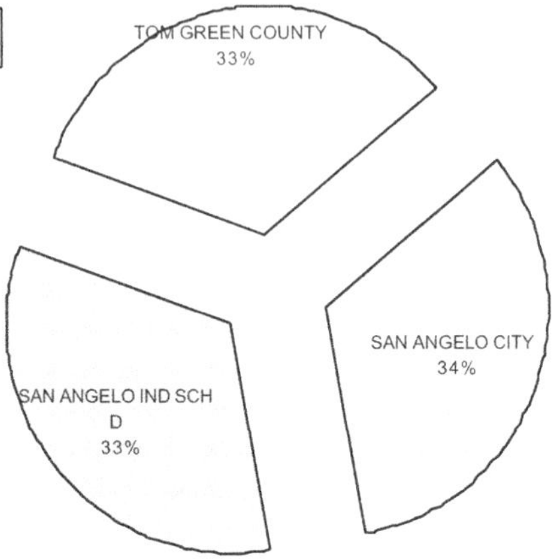

VERSUS

% of County Taxes

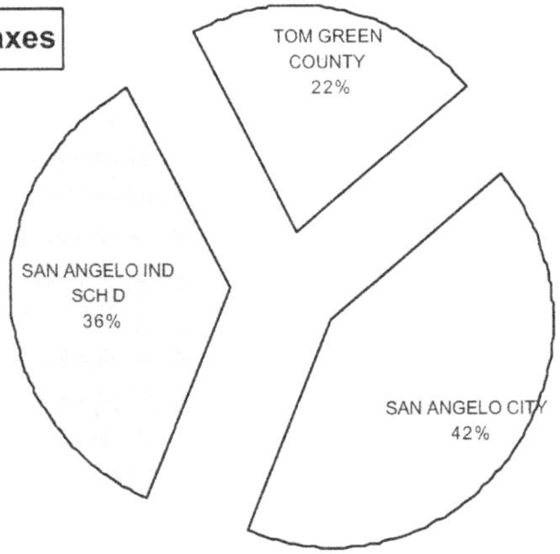

State/County

TX / TRAVIS

% of County Debt

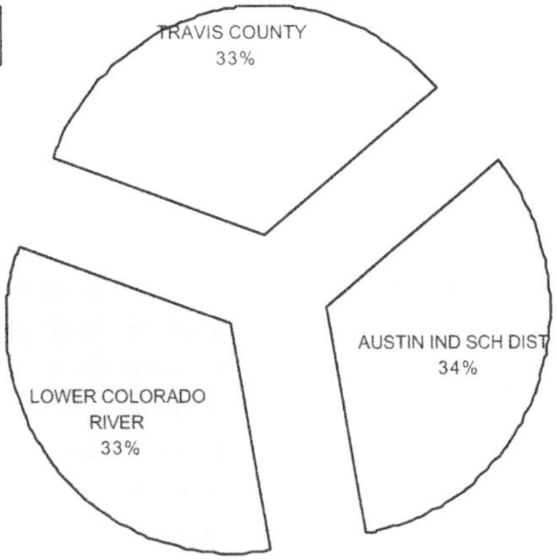

VERSUS

% of County Taxes

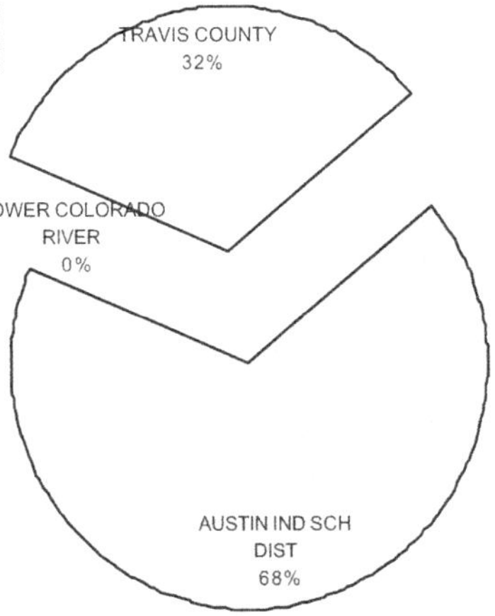

Are you getting your share of debt and taxes in your county?

S1

State/County

TX / TRINITY

% of County Debt

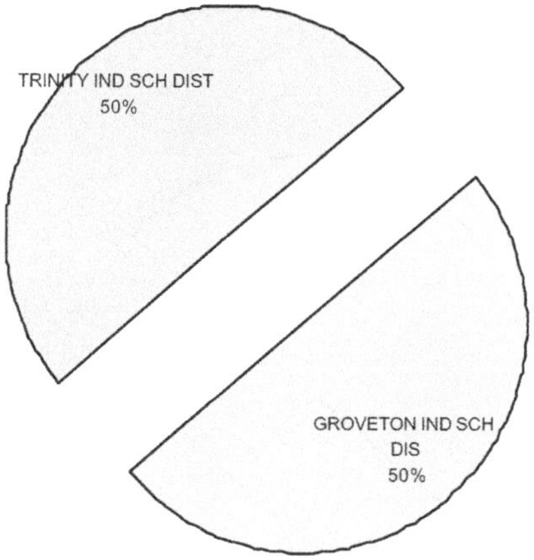

VERSUS

% of County Taxes

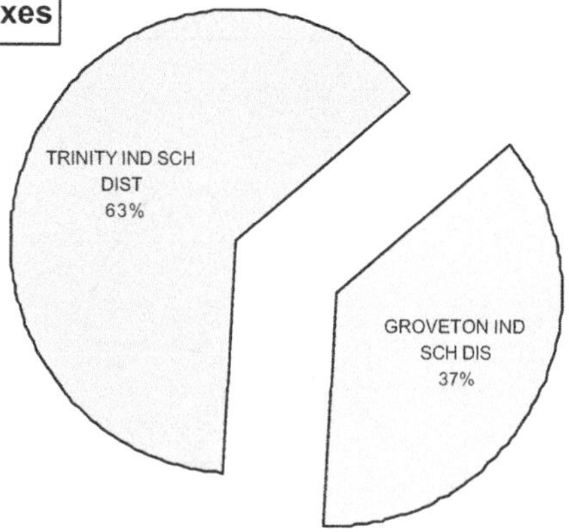

State/County

TX / TYLER

% of County Debt

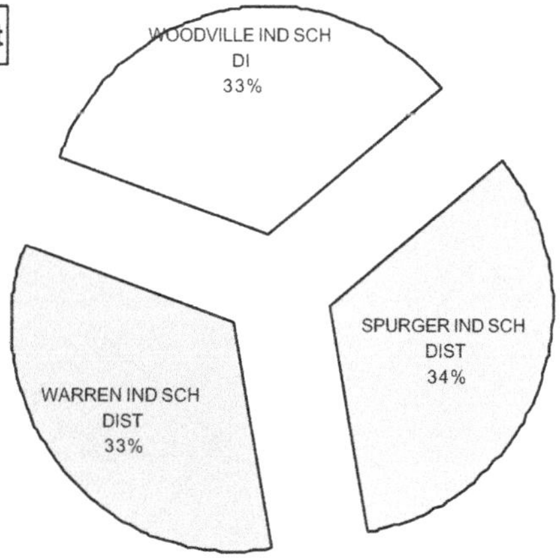

VERSUS

% of County Taxes

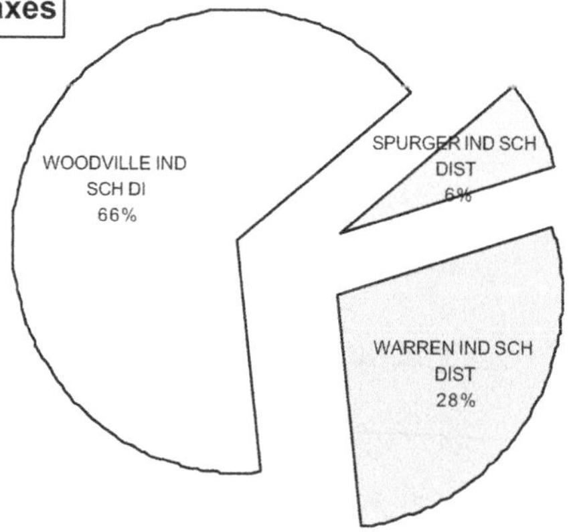

Are you getting your share of debt and taxes in your county?

S1

State/County

TX / UPSHUR

% of County Debt

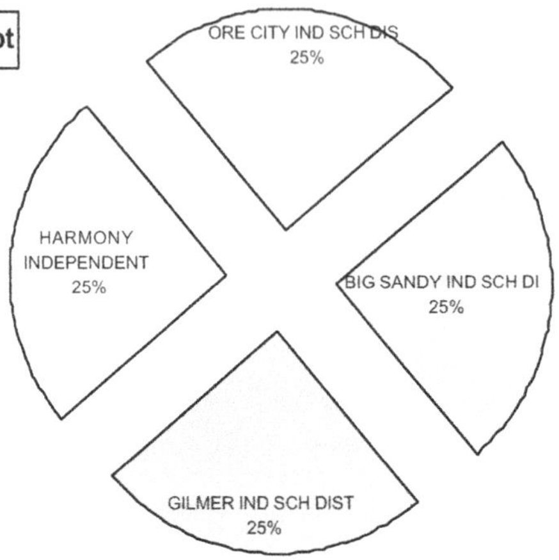

VERSUS

% of County Taxes

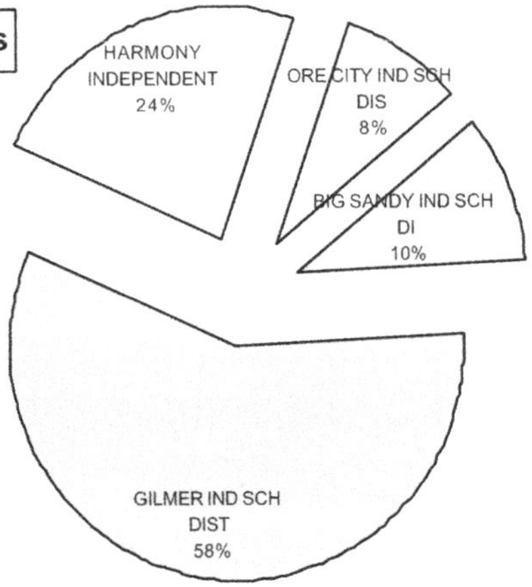

State/County

TX / UPTON

% of County Debt

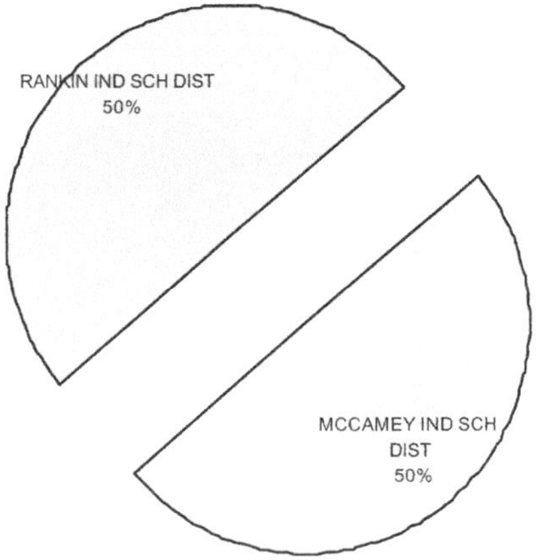

VERSUS

% of County Taxes

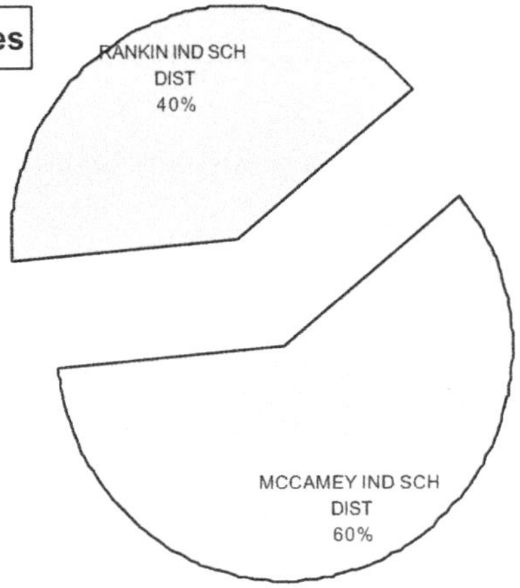

Are you getting your share of debt and taxes in your county?

S1

% of County Debt

State/County

TX / UVALDE

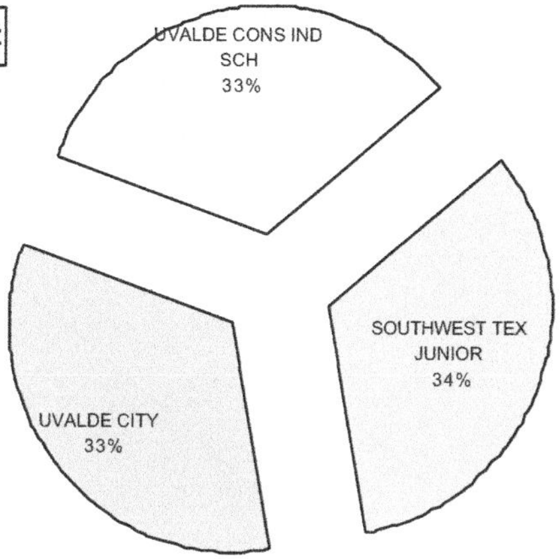

VERSUS

% of County Taxes

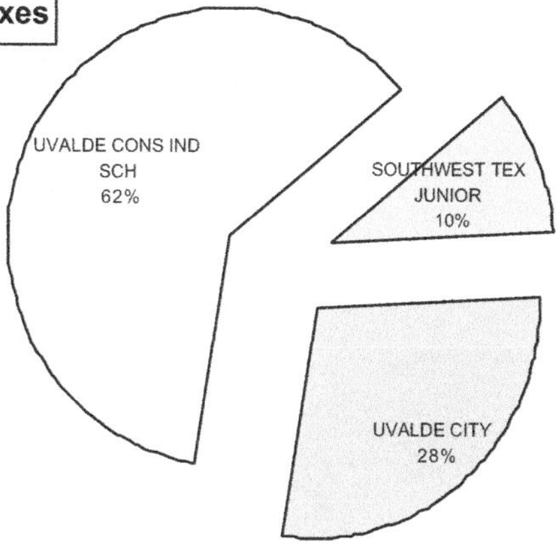

% of County Debt

State/County

TX / VAL VERDE

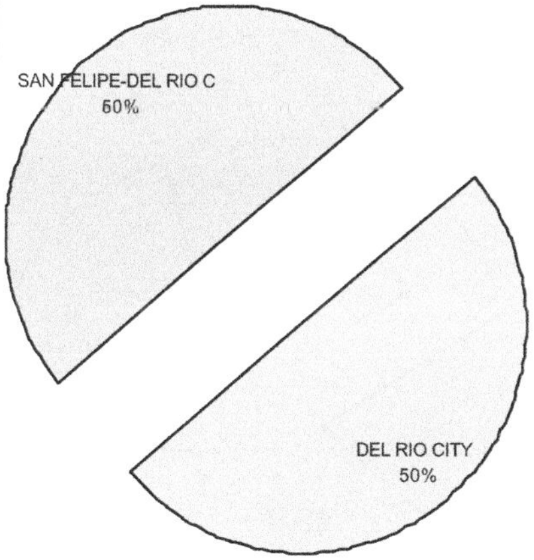

VERSUS

% of County Taxes

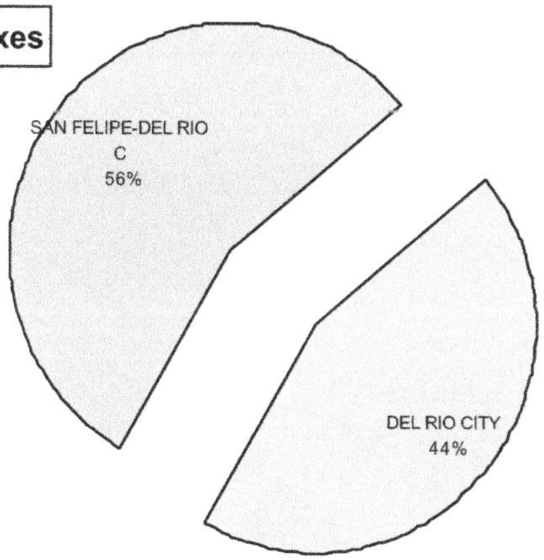

Are you getting your share of debt and taxes in your county? **S1**

State/County

TX / VAN ZANDT

% of County Debt

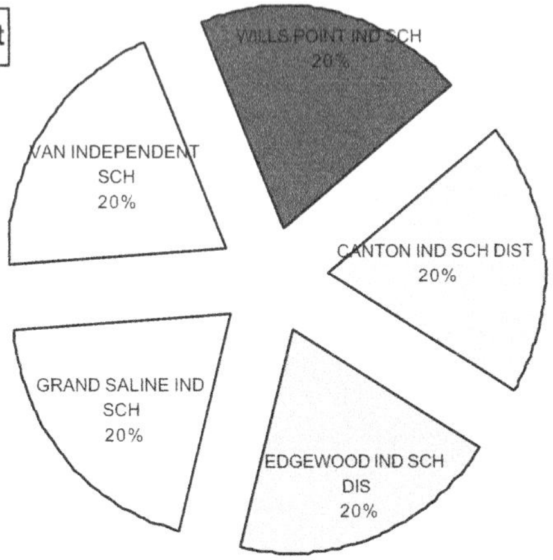

VERSUS

% of County Taxes

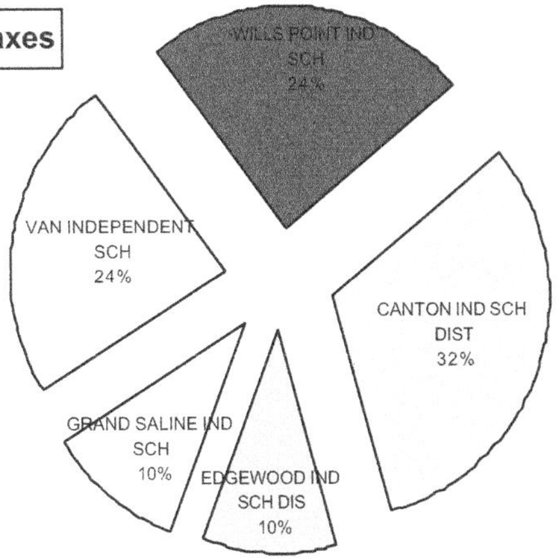

State/County

TX / VICTORIA

% of County Debt

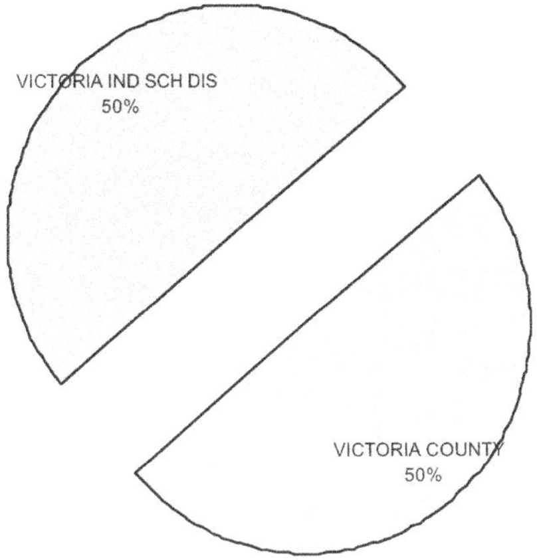

VERSUS

% of County Taxes

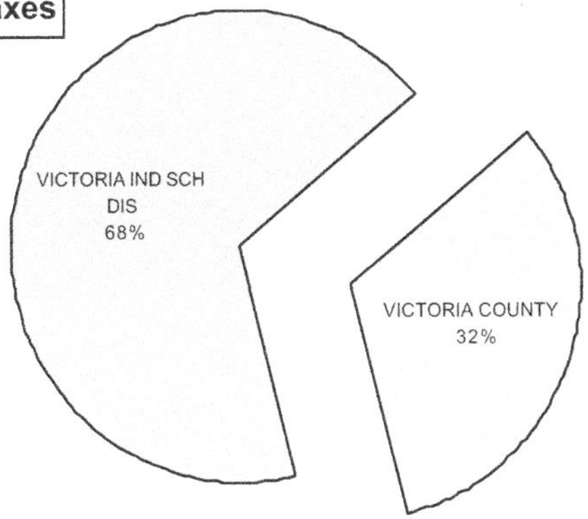

Are you getting your share of debt and taxes in your county? S1

% of County Debt

State/County
TX / WALKER

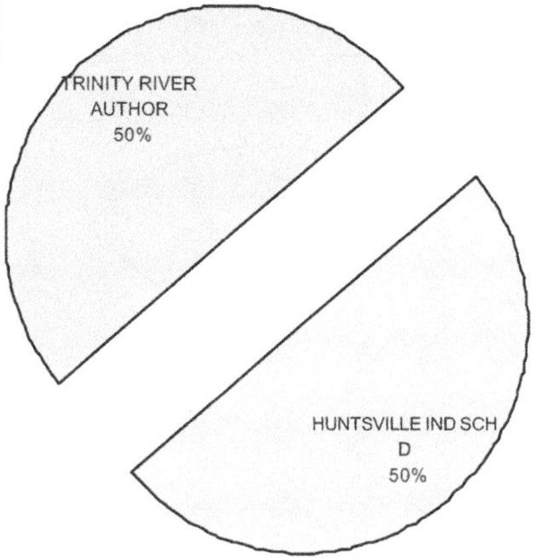

VERSUS

% of County Taxes

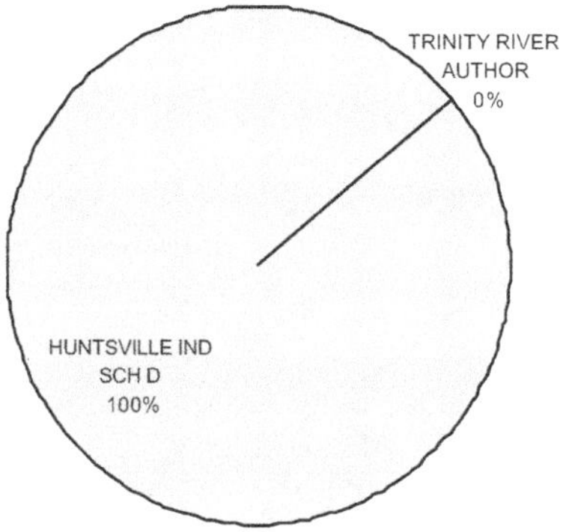

% of County Debt

State/County
TX / WALLER

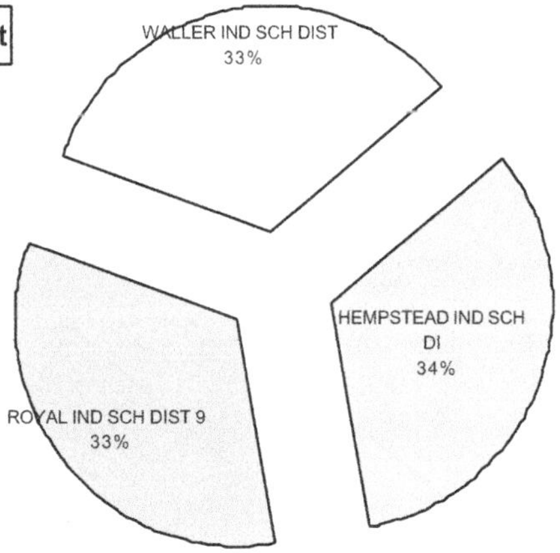

VERSUS

% of County Taxes

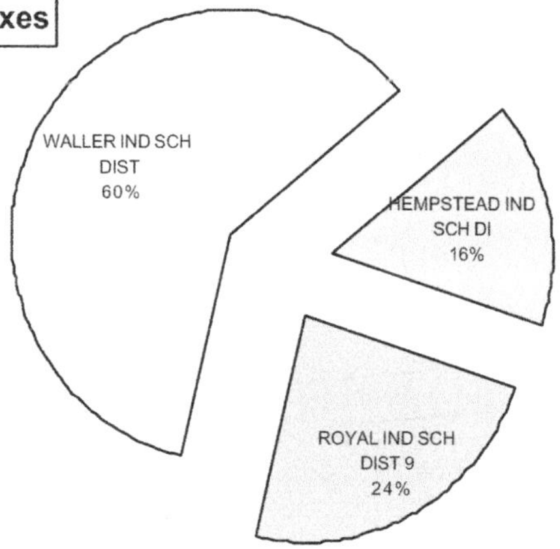

Are you getting your share of debt and taxes in your county?

S1

State/County
TX / WARD

% of County Debt

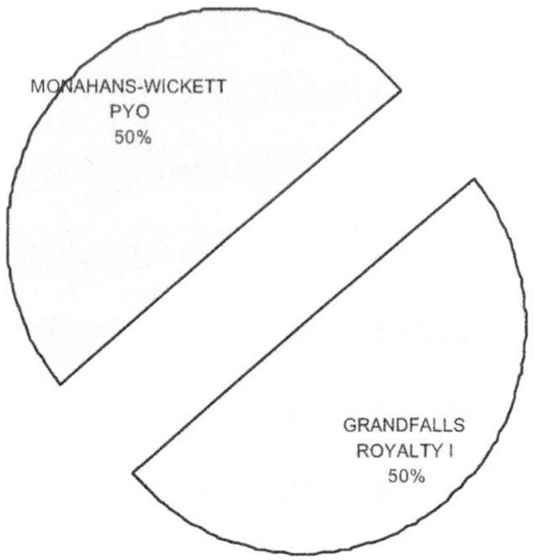

VERSUS

% of County Taxes

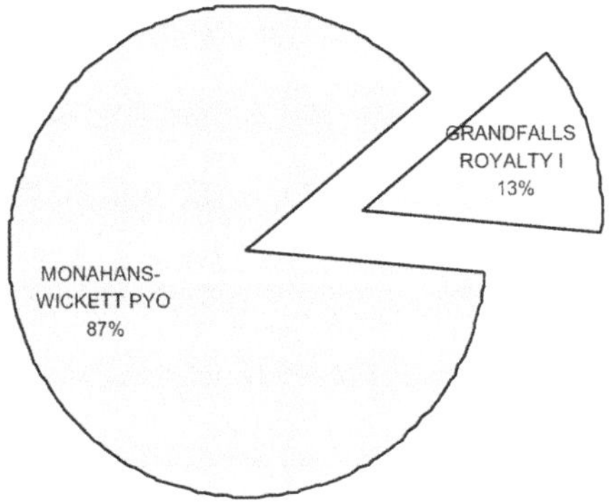

State/County
TX / WASHINGTON

% of County Debt

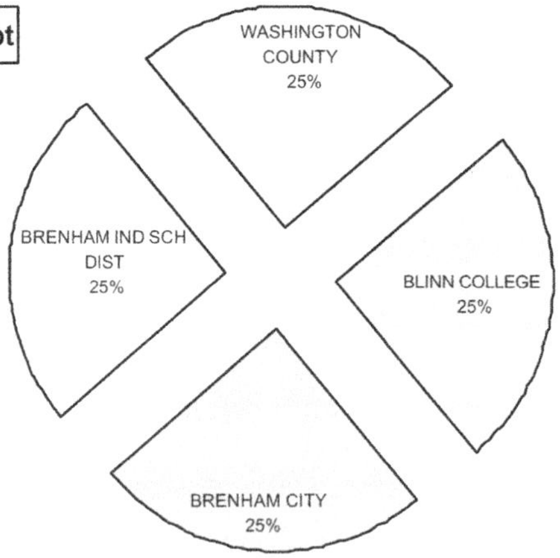

VERSUS

% of County Taxes

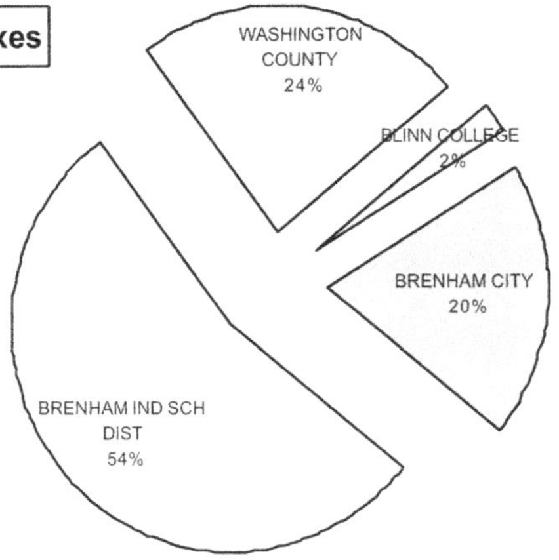

Are you getting your share of debt and taxes in your county?

S1

State/County

TX / WEBB

% of County Debt

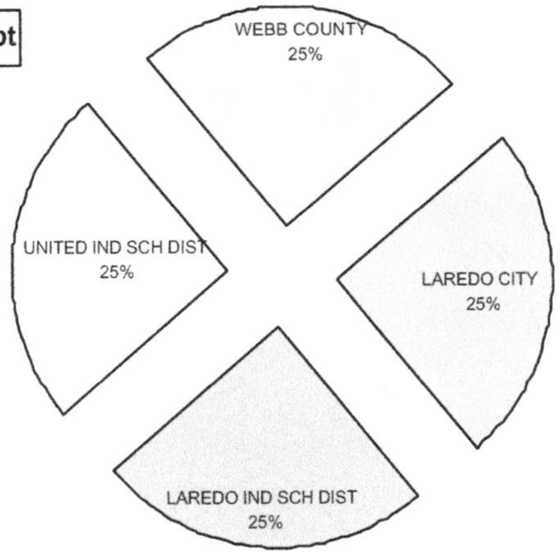

VERSUS

% of County Taxes

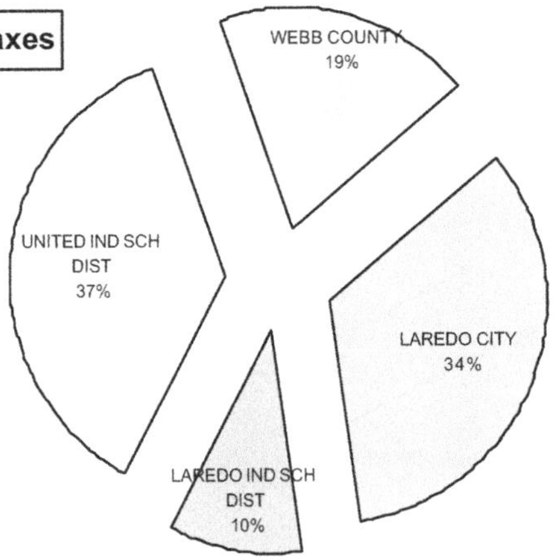

State/County

TX / WHARTON

% of County Debt

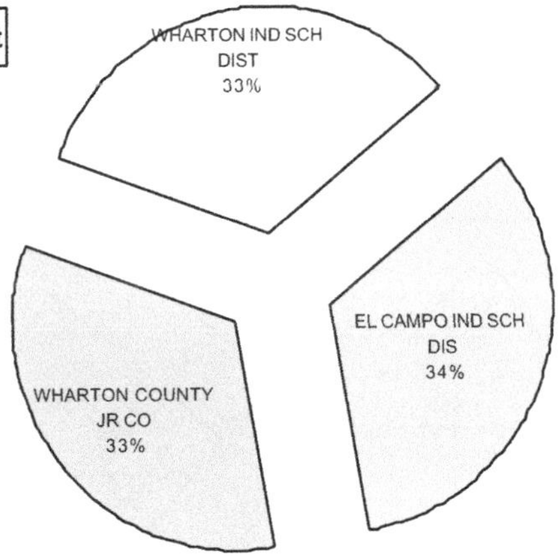

VERSUS

% of County Taxes

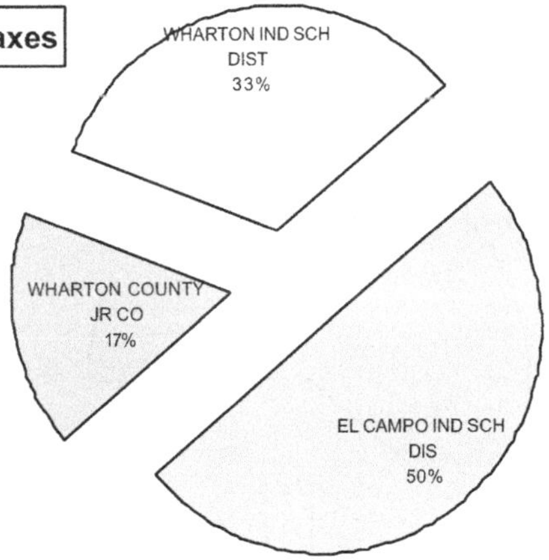

Are you getting your share of debt and taxes in your county? S1

State/County

TX / WHEELER

% of County Debt

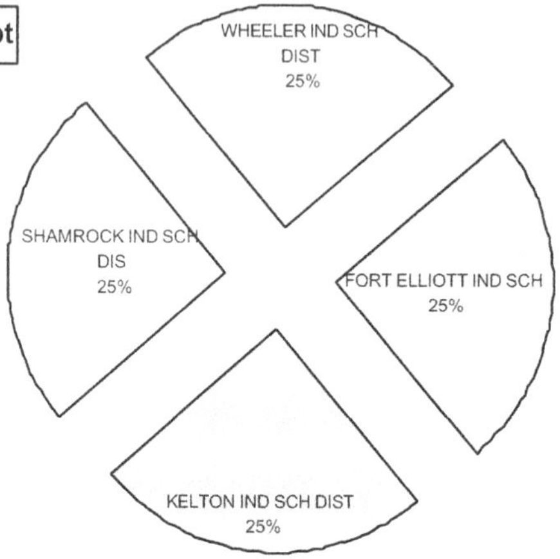

VERSUS

% of County Taxes

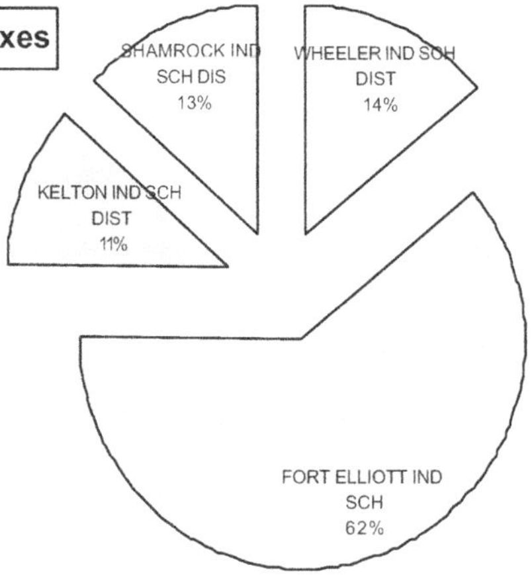

State/County

TX / WICHITA

% of County Debt

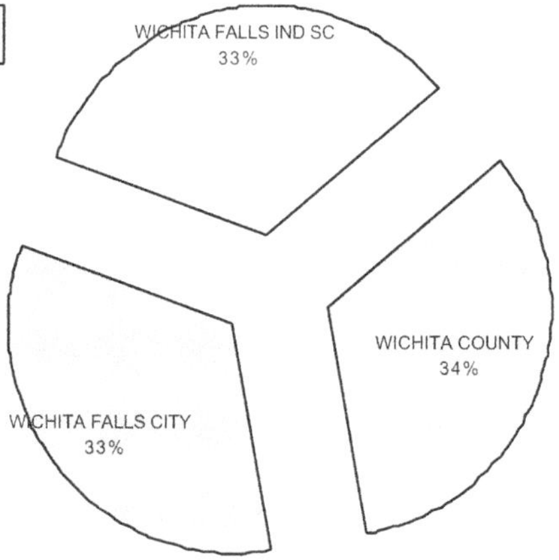

VERSUS

% of County Taxes

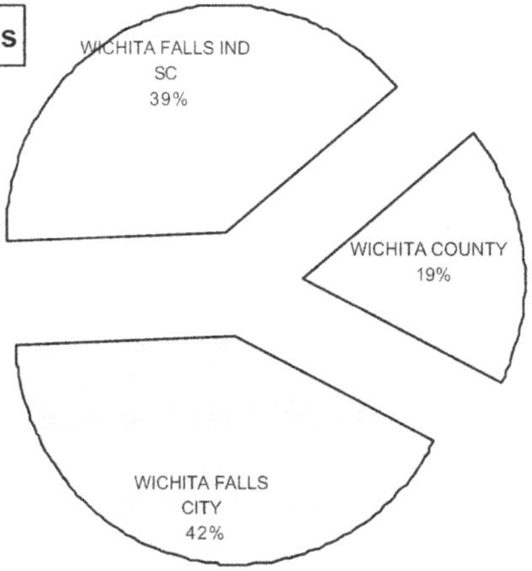

Are you getting your share of debt and taxes in your county? **S1**

State/County

TX / WILBARGER

% of County Debt

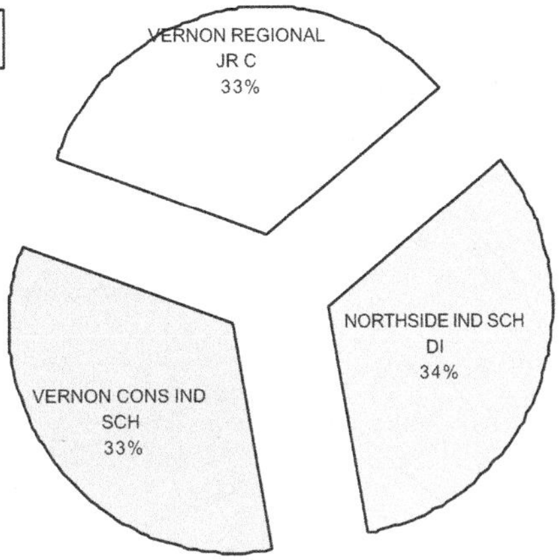

VERSUS

% of County Taxes

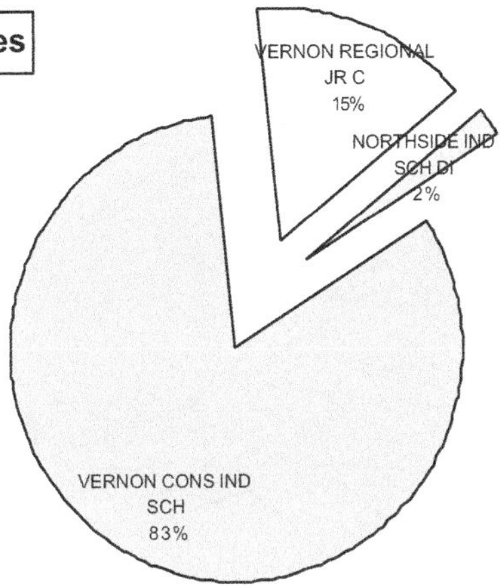

State/County

TX / WILLACY

% of County Debt

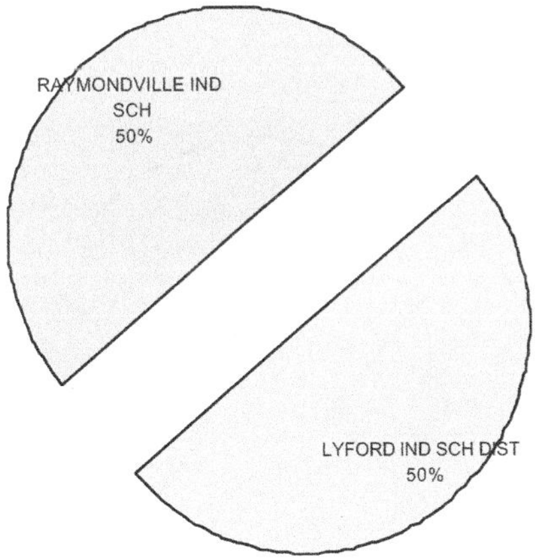

VERSUS

% of County Taxes

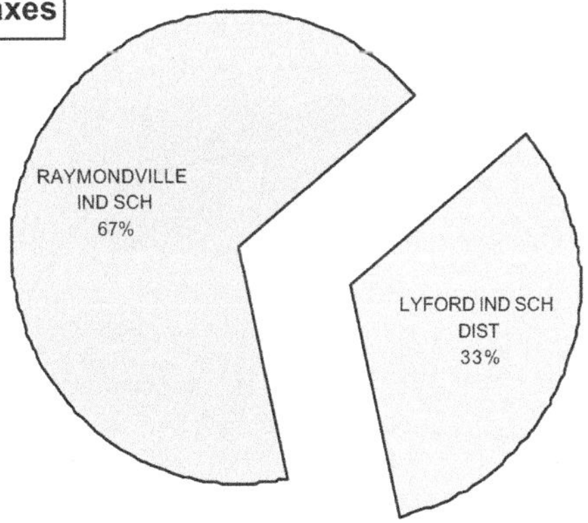

Are you getting your share of debt and taxes in your county? S1

State/County
TX / WILLIAMSON

% of County Debt

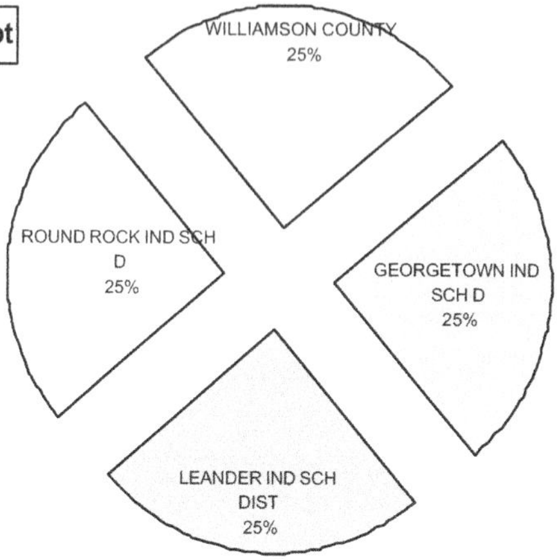

VERSUS

% of County Taxes

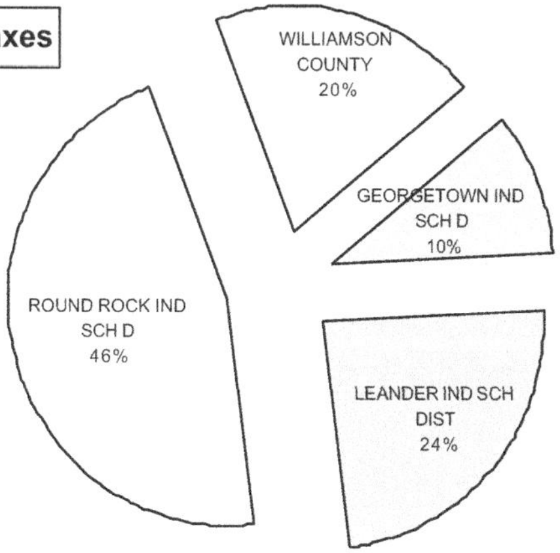

State/County
TX / WILSON

% of County Debt

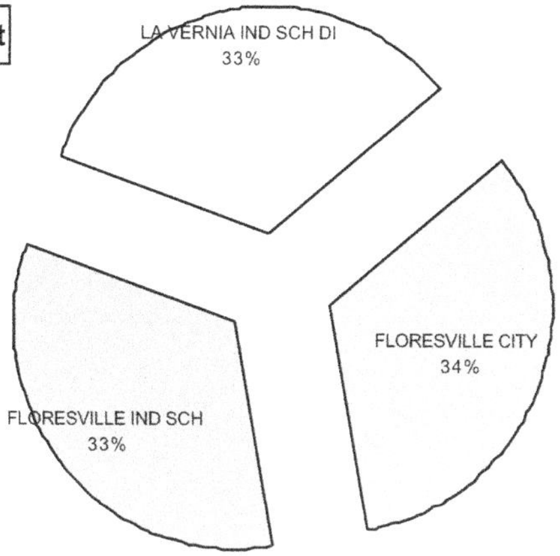

VERSUS

% of County Taxes

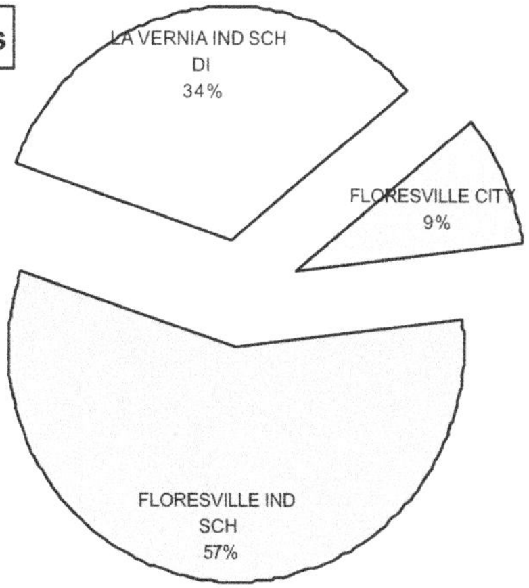

Are you getting your share of debt and taxes in your county?

S1

% of County Debt

State/County

TX / WINKLER

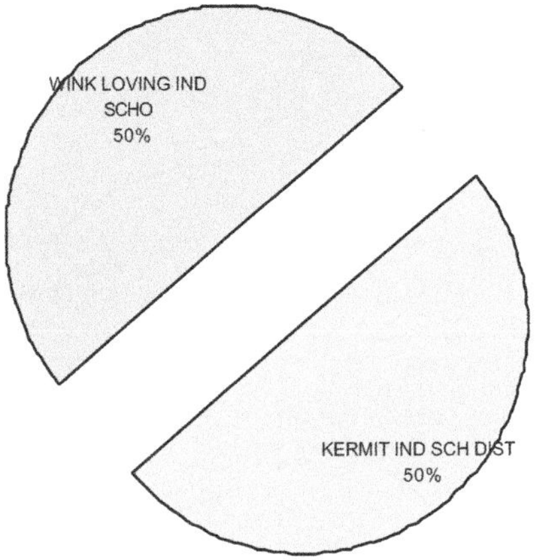

VERSUS

% of County Taxes

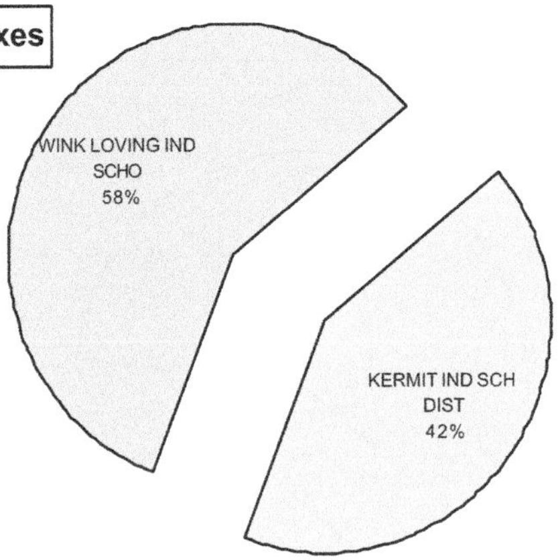

% of County Debt

State/County

TX / WISE

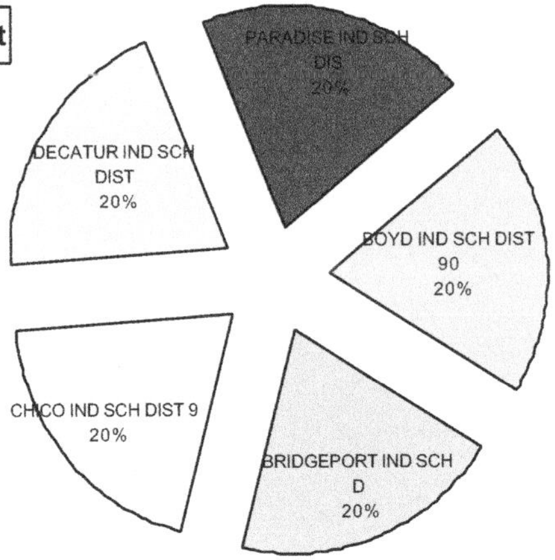

VERSUS

% of County Taxes

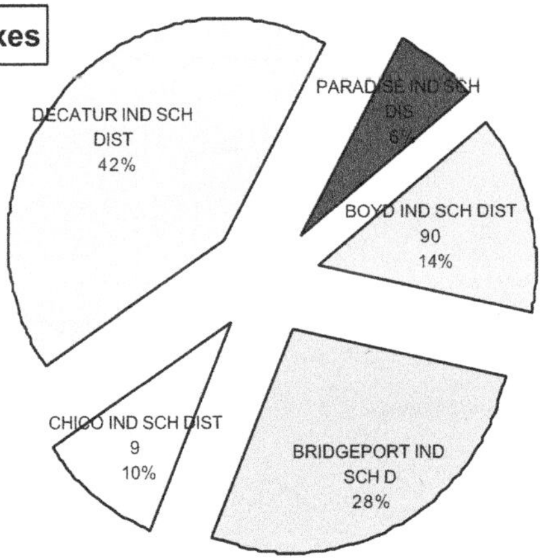

Are you getting your share of debt and taxes in your county? **S1**

State/County
TX / WOOD

% of County Debt

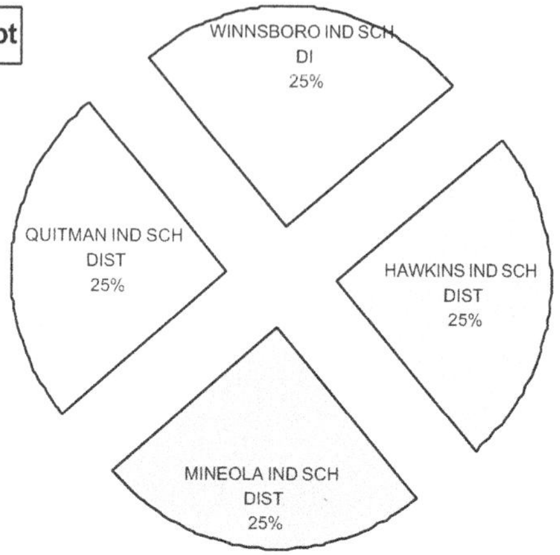

VERSUS

% of County Taxes

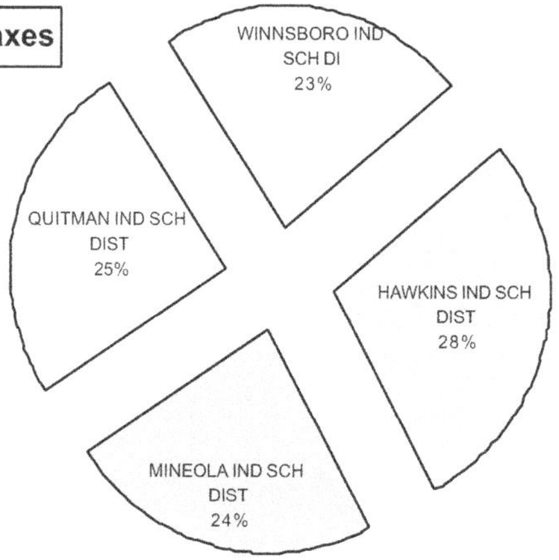

State/County
TX / YOAKUM

% of County Debt

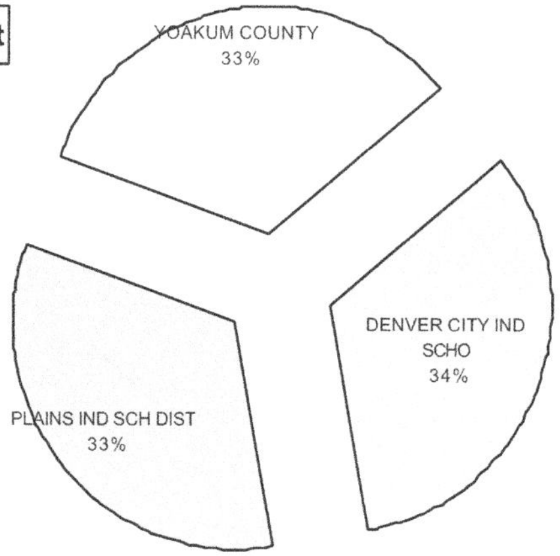

VERSUS

% of County Taxes

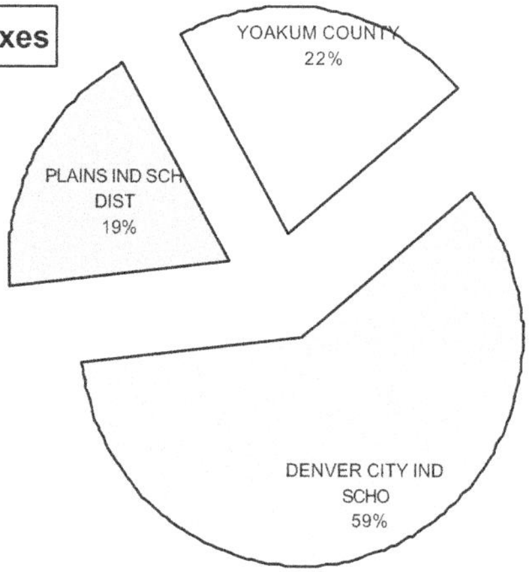

Are you getting your share of debt and taxes in your county? S1

State/County

TX / YOUNG

% of County Debt

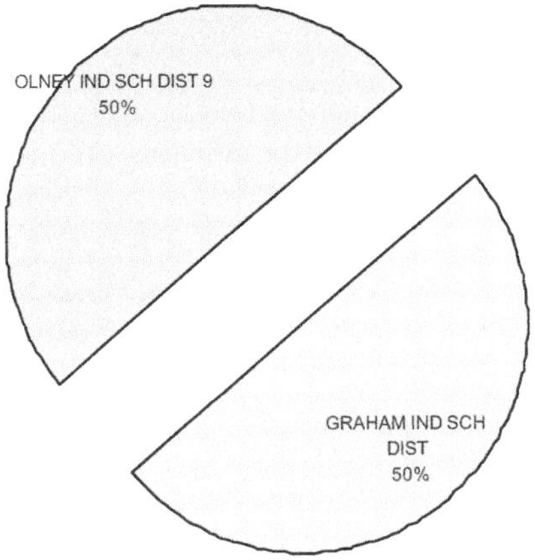

VERSUS

% of County Taxes

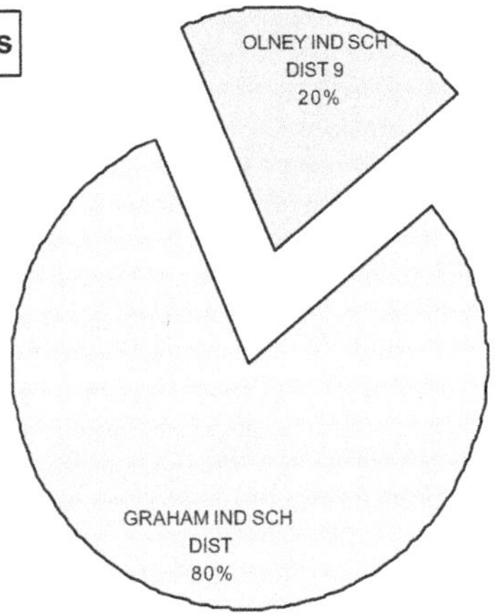

State/County

TX / ZAVALA

% of County Debt

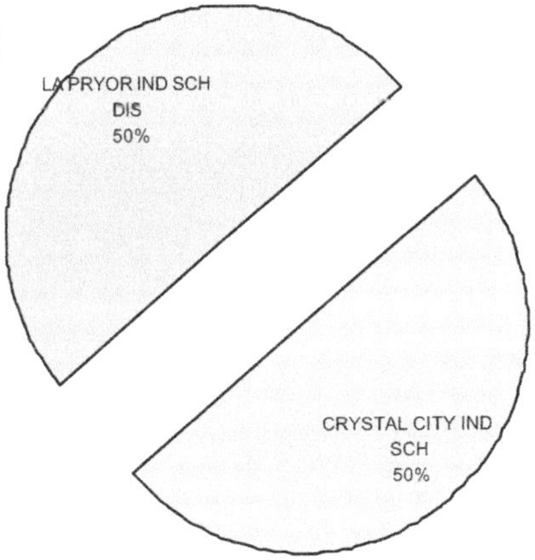

VERSUS

% of County Taxes

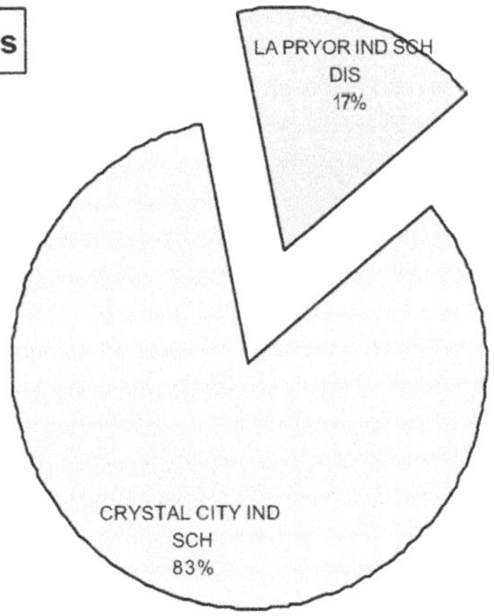

Made in the USA
Middletown, DE
04 November 2026

36537968R00117